The George Grant Reader
Edited by William Christian and Sheila Grant

Called the most forceful voice of philosophic radicalism that Canada has so far produced, George Grant was a prolific writer, engaged by subjects ranging from Canadian politics to ancient philosophy. *The George Grant Reader* is the first book to bring together in one volume a comprehensive selection of his work, allowing readers to sample the whole range of his interests.

The reader includes selections from all phases of Grant's career, beginning with *The Empire: Yes or No?* (1945) and ending with an article on Heidegger, left unfinished at the time of his death in 1988. Forty-six essays, grouped into six sections, encompass his views on politics, morality, philosophy, education, technology, faith, and love. Also featured are Grant's writings on those who most influenced his thought, ranging from St Augustine to Karl Marx and Simone Weil. A number of his more disturbing essays are also included, such as his controversial writings on abortion. The editors' substantial introduction places the articles in the wider context of Grant's life and thought.

This long-overdue collection contains classic works, little-known masterpieces, and previously unpublished material. The volume is an ideal starting point for those who have never read Grant as well as an indispensable reference for Grant specialists.

WILLIAM CHRISTIAN is Professor of Political Studies at the University of Guelph. He is author of *George Grant: A Biography* and editor of *George Grant: Selected Letters.*

SHEILA GRANT was married to George Grant for forty-one years and is a graduate in English language and literature from Oxford University.

The
George Grant
Reader

Edited by

WILLIAM CHRISTIAN

and

SHEILA GRANT

UNIVERSITY OF TORONTO PRESS
Toronto London Buffalo

© University of Toronto Press Incorporated 1998
Toronto Buffalo London

Printed in Canada

ISBN 0-8020-0973-5 (cloth)
ISBN 0-8020-7934-2 (paper)

Printed on acid-free paper

Canadian Cataloguing in Publication Data

Grant, George, 1918–1988
The George Grant reader

ISBN 0-8020-0973-5 (bound)   ISBN 0-8020-7934-2 (pbk.)
1. Philosophy.   2. Political science.   3. Canada – Politics
and government. I. Christian, William, 1945–   .
II. Grant, Sheila, 1920–   .

B995.G74A4 1998   191   C97-931550-6

University of Toronto Press acknowledges the financial assistance
to its publishing program of the Canada Council for the Arts and the
Ontario Arts Council.

Contents

Acknowledgments

It has been pleasant to work with generous and cooperative people while preparing this reader. Dr Ron Schoeffel, editor-in-chief of the University of Toronto Press, actively supported the idea from the very beginning. Mark Haslett of the University of Waterloo helped with some hard-to-find material. Kim Groenendyk brought her scholarly training and typing skills to the formidable task of inputting the text into the word processor. Matthew Christian of Toronto prepared the Index. Jay Newman and Jim Geary of the philosophy department of the University of Guelph were kind enough to read the introduction and to give us their thoughts, as was Nita Graham of Halifax. Louis Greenspan, a long-time friend and colleague of Grant at McMaster, gave us his advice on the whole text and his suggestions made it stronger. An anonymous University of Toronto Press reviewer provided us with reams of detailed corrections and improvements. We are grateful to his keen eye and thankful for his generosity. We also thank the following for permission to reprint material: University of Toronto Press for selections from *Time as History* and *Philosophy in the Mass Age*; House of Anansi and Stoddart for selections from *Technology and Empire, English-Speaking Justice,* and *Technology and Justice*; Carleton University Press for *Lament for a Nation*; the Privy Council Office, Government of Canada, for 'Philosophy;' the *Queen's Quarterly* for 'Céline – Art and Politics'; and the *Dalhousie Review* for the review of *The Philosophy of Francis Bacon* and 'Pursuit of an Illusion.'

THE GEORGE GRANT READER

Introduction

Life

George Parkin Grant was born in Toronto on 13 November 1918, two days after the armistice. His father, William Grant, was principal of Upper Canada College, a private boys' school. He had previously taught history at Oxford and at Queen's University in Kingston, Ontario, before enlisting as an officer in the First World War and serving overseas. In his thirties, William Grant had courted and, in 1911, married Maude Parkin, whom Eugene Forsey described as someone who 'could have run the whole British Empire at the height of its power single-handed.'[1] Maude was a woman of great strength and surpassing charm. George's three elder sisters – Margaret, Charity, and Alison – were each powerful personalities, and it was always rather hard for George to understand why women had ever been called the weaker sex.

In later life, Grant regretted that he had attended a school where his father was principal, since he thought that the other boys saw him as a sort of spy, but his undergraduate studies in history at Queen's were happier. Even there, however, he felt that he was known as his mother's son or the grandson of the legendary George Monro Grant, Queen's most famous principal. Still more oppressive was the influence of his other grandfather, George Parkin, the founding secretary of the Rhodes Scholarship trust. Maude Grant idolized her father and the younger George felt under tremendous pressure to be a worldly success in the mould of his grandfathers.

In 1939 Grant won a Rhodes scholarship and set out for Oxford to study law at the start of the Second World War. He completed his first year of study but felt increasingly guilty in the aloof comfort of Oxford. Though a pacifist, he decided to remain in England and, in the summer of 1940, joined an ambulance unit. When the Battle of Britain started, he became an air raid precautions warden in Bermondsey in the east end of London, one of the most heavily bombed parts of the capital. It is an understatement to say that it was during this period that he grew up. His life of privilege was over.

The gruelling experience of violence and death broke him forever from the comfortable liberalism in which he had been raised. It also destroyed his health. The nightly bombing stopped when the Germans invaded Russia. Under enormous pressure from his family and friends to do his duty to king and country, he attempted to join the merchant marine, although this compromised his pacifist principles. He was turned down because the medical examination revealed signs of tuberculosis. Not waiting for a formal discharge, he ran away and worked on a farm, saying later that it was a way to be left alone and also to get food (since he was without a ration book). It was at this point, in December 1941, while bicycling to work one morning, that he experienced a sudden total conviction that beyond the chaos of the world there was eternal order, that God existed, and that we are not our own. This certainty lasted all his life.

After being nursed back to health in Toronto, he spent two years working for the Canadian Association for Adult Education. This job involved much travelling across Canada, writing, and speaking. The experience proved a useful preparation for his later career as a university teacher, and he probably owed to it much of his ease in writing and speaking to the public, and perhaps also something of his powerful radio personality. (The selection with which this reader begins, a radio talk on philosophy, exemplifies his skill at clarifying complicated issues for a mass audience.)

After the war, he returned to Oxford, but he had decided not to pursue a legal career. He wanted instead to explore the implications of his religious experience and to find out more about Christianity. The master of Balliol College, A.D. Lindsay, suggested that he write a DPhil thesis on the philosophy of a Scottish Presbyterian theologian, John Oman. Grant had never heard of Oman and his lack of enthusiasm for his subject probably accounts for the small progress he made on his thesis. However, he threw himself into reading Plato, St Augustine, and other philosophers. After two years in Oxford, he married Sheila Allen, a student of English literature and a fellow pacifist, who had also resumed her university education after spending the war as a nurse. Together they set out for Dalhousie University in Halifax, Nova Scotia, where Grant had been hired to teach philosophy.

His years in Halifax (1947–60) transformed him. As he explained to a former student, he was learning to be a philosopher at the same time as he was teaching philosophy:

> Not being a person who would naturally (whatever that means) have turned to speculation – that is having been driven to it – I am simply flabbergasted at where philosophy has taken me. Just not at all the sort of course I expected. It is like setting out on what one expected to be a jaunt across the Arm[2] – finding oneself shipwrecked time after time and yet knowing one has no alternative but to go on – moods of dereliction – moods of amusement and moments of joy – but above all sheer unadulterated amazement. I just could have expected anything of life, but not this. Above all the dereliction is when philosophy is in direct conflict with ambition. For a variety of reasons my adolescence was taken up by the idea of fame as the *summum bonum*[3] and it is really shattering to me to have to face it for what it is.[4]

During this time at Dalhousie, he and Sheila had six children, three girls and three boys, and Grant made many lasting friendships. As well as his formal teaching, Grant continued to be active in adult education. He gave numerous speeches to teachers, delivered papers at all kinds of gatherings, and spoke on many radio programs (which had the added advantage of helping to supplement his meager academic salary.) After their third child was born, the Grants acquired a second-hand car and life became a little easier. Grant found Nova Scotian students wonderfully open to thought. They had not been 'wised up' at high school, and so they did not have to unlearn a lot of progressive modern dogma.

By 1958 Canada's economy was booming and Grant was still weighing the character of the progressive society that was forming. James Doull, a learned friend and colleague, had taught him how to understand Plato and was leading him through the maze of Hegel's thought. The good students he encountered also gave him reason to hope for a better future. This optimism was apparent in *Philosophy in the Mass Age*, originally presented as a series of radio lectures for the CBC's first *University of the Air*, the predecessor of the program *Ideas*. *Philosophy in the Mass Age* was an immediate and immense success.

By the end of the 1950s Grant was eager for a change. He accepted an offer to head the philosophy department at the newly founded York University in Toronto, but he resigned before having taught a class. (See his letter to Murray Ross in Part 2.) After fearing for over a year that he might have to move to the United States to find a teaching job, he was finally offered a promising position in the new department of religion at McMaster University in Hamilton. The next twenty years there were rewarding ones. By the mid-1960s his thought had become more coherent and more confident. He had explicitly rejected Hegel's philosophy and was avidly reading the German-American political philosopher Leo Strauss, and he was also planning to write a book on the French mystic and philosopher Simone Weil. Philip Sherrard's *The Greek East and the Latin West* helped to clarify his misgivings about Western Christianity. Living in southern Ontario was itself an educational experience. The booming technological world was all around him and he worked at a university that had its own nuclear reactor. In 1966 he read Jacques Ellul's *The Technological Society,* and he felt as if a new planet had swum into his ken. It further clarified the meaning of the political events with which he had dealt in his best-selling book *Lament for a Nation.* In 1969, with the help of poet and editor Dennis Lee, he put together a collection of essays on mainly political themes, *Technology and Empire.*

It might appear that in this great flurry of activity in the mid-1960s Grant had changed some of his views dramatically. The admiration for Hegel seen in *Philosophy in the Mass Age* and renounced in 1966 would seem to be an example of this. But in fact the change had been gradual and his view of Hegel had been ambivalent, as is clear from a 1956 notebook. Grant did not have a cut-and-dried system and did not seek to create one. 'One thing about life: how is one to suppose that one's position at the moment is final, when one already knows so much from life and has learnt it on the way? Presumably one is going to learn more.'[5] Grant had indeed learnt more since the 1950s, but his profound adherence to Christianity and to Plato never wavered. His understanding of both was enriched by his continuing study of Simone Weil, who could herself be described as a Platonist within Christianity. Grant's next book, *Time as History* (1970), was a study of Nietzsche's thought and its influence on modernity. It was originally delivered as the 1969 Massey lectures on CBC. In the middle of revising it for publication, Grant and his wife were nearly killed in an automobile accident. His injuries required a long convalescence and he never quite regained his old zest for life.

The question that haunted him during the early 1970s was how one could think about the Good (or God) when technology had destroyed the very language by which such thought could be expressed. He started to use the word 'justice' rather than 'good,' since he thought that justice was a word that still had resonance. He struggled with this dilemma in two unfinished manuscripts, 'Good and Technique' and 'Technique and the Good.' They contained some of the ideas that appeared much later in *Technology and Justice* (1986). In 1977 he completed the revision of the Wood lectures he had delivered at Mount Allison University in 1974. *English-Speaking Justice* was a devastating critique of modern liberalism and its deterioration under the corrosive influence of the very technology it had made possible.

Towards the end of the 1970s Grant became increasingly frustrated by the direction the department of religion at McMaster was taking. It had once centred on the great religious traditions of East and West. Its teachers explored these from within the traditions themselves and raised with students the universal questions inherent in them. Now, Grant thought, the department had come to concentrate on historical scholarship at the expense of raising philosophical questions (see 'The Battle between Teaching and Research' in Part 2). In 1980 Grant left McMaster and returned to Dalhousie, where he taught classes in political science and classics until his retirement in 1984. He still had close friends at Dalhousie, though he found the university itself changed for the worse.

Many honours came to him during this period: the Chauvais Medal from the Royal Society, several honorary degrees, and an appointment to the Order of Canada. These honours were curious, since most influential Canadians did not share his views, particularly his critique of technology, and his Christianity was not fashionable in the secular atmosphere of the modern university. As his former student and colleague Louis Greenspan expressed it: 'As one who loved his country, he welcomed this recognition, but not without the dismay that Tertullian or Justin Martyr or any other early Christian might have felt had their indictments of the Roman gods as demons been greeted with thunderous ovations from the Roman Senate.'[6]

During the early 1980s Grant's main philosophical experience was reflecting on Jean-Jacques Rousseau's *Discourse on the Origins of Inequality among Men*. Grant had come to believe that Rousseau's importance as a maker of modernity had not been fully understood. To explore this theme, he started writing a work on history and justice. His other great experience was a literary one: he read and re-read the three last novels of Louis-Ferdinand Céline, about which he made voluminous notes towards a possible book. His last book, *Technology and Justice* (1986), was a collection of essays which he revised for publication.

Poor health and frequent visits to the hospital took up a great deal of his time and energy after he retired. However, he became more and more interested in the writings of the German philosopher Martin Heidegger and began work on what he hoped would be his magnum opus, a defence of Christianity and Platonism against Heidegger's attack. In August 1988 he began the preliminary chapter, but on 6 September he learned he had pancreatic cancer. He died on 27 September 1988.

Politics and Morality

Why is the first section of this reader titled 'Politics and Morality?' George Grant was usually described as a political philosopher, and he accepted that description. Why then 'morality?' In his last book, *Technology and Justice*, he portrayed himself as one who in political philosophy was above all 'a lover of Plato within Christianity.' This position is implicit in his writings from beginning to end. He would not, and perhaps could not, separate political philosophy from the central question of how it is good for human beings to live together. His thought about political subjects was necessarily part of his thought about the whole. If political thought is concerned with judgments about goodness, it must depend on what one believes human beings to be.

For the ancients (particularly Plato and Aristotle), wisdom and the virtue that led to it and flowed from it was the highest achievement of human beings and constituted their excellence. In the modern world, especially since Machiavelli, freedom and equality have replaced wisdom and virtue as the highest goods for men and women. Grant had no doubt that the conceptions held by the ancients were more profound than those of the moderns. He always questioned the position that freedom defined the essence of human beings. Are we free to make our own values? If so, whose values are to determine how we should be governed? Is there an eternal order which defines and limits us, as Plato believed, or is it our destiny to make ourselves and our world? Is there any truth that it is incumbent upon us to know, or is truth simply a means of dominating the world as an extension of our limitless freedom?

Although the samples of Grant's writings on politics and morality presented in this section might seem a curious mixture, they represent the way he engaged not only his fellow academics but the general public as well. Here are the speeches describing the kind of society developing in Canada; the value of the British Empire; words of encouragement and warning to the young students of the New Left who were protesting against the Vietnam War; articles about prime ministers and political writers; a chapter written to help define the direction the New Democratic Party might take; a polemic against abortion on demand; and praise for Canadian authors who wrote against the free-trade agreement with the United States. The two most important excerpts are those from Grant's *Lament for a Nation* and *English-Speaking Justice.*

Grant had doubted that he would find a publisher for his lament, since it so directly challenged the orthodoxy of the continentalist Canadian elite. However, McClelland and Stewart quickly agreed to publish it and it became an immediate best-seller. The central subject was an account of Conservative Prime Minister John Diefenbaker's actions, particularly in 1962–3 when he revealed the tragic flaws in his own conservatism and, more seriously, in the conservatism that stood as Canada's foundation. Diefenbaker's government was defeated in 1963 on the issue of whether Canada should accept or reject nuclear weapons for its armed forces. Diefenbaker saw the American pressure to accept these weapons as an intolerable affront to Canadian independence, though Liberal leader Lester Pearson regarded it as an aspect of a friendly and dutiful relationship with an important ally. (Trudeau's metaphor of the mouse going to bed with the elephant comes to mind.) What Grant was lamenting was not the downfall of an imperfect, though brave, politician, but the fact that it had become impossible for Canada to retain any real independence as a nation. The surprising effect of this bleak conclusion was that it stirred a generation of young Canadians to an unprecedented outpouring of Canadian nationalism.

Lament for a Nation was not only an account of a few years of Canadian politics and a description of the decay of conservatism. It was a deep philosophical analysis, but what really moved its readers was its character as a prose poem about the love of one's own, about the hopes that had inspired the founders of Canada, about loyalty that is unseduced and unterrified, about the deeper issues of necessity and goodness, the limits of freedom, and the terrible practical consequences of believing that providence could be understood in terms of historical progress. As Jim Laxer, then a prominent student leader, recollected: '*Lament for a Nation* is the most important book I ever read in my life. Here was a crazy old philosopher of religion at McMaster and he woke up half our generation. He was saying Canada was dead, and, by saying it, he was creating the country.'[7] Even thirty years after the publication of *Lament*, it does not ring false. Conservative insider Hugh Segal, when asked to name a single book that could convey to a foreigner the character of Canada, unhesitatingly chose *Lament for a Nation:* '[It] had an indelible effect on me, encapsulating the difference between the Tory vision for Canada and the continentalist, mechanistic, commercialist view.'[8]

In *English-Speaking Justice* Grant analysed the nature of modern contractarian liberalism. He made clear that he was not attacking the original principles on which our political and legal institutions were founded, based on the conception of a justice that required liberty and equality. It would be insane, he declared, to deny that political liberty is a central human good. But contemporary contractual liberalism had darkened the very conception of justice. To illustrate that insight, Grant analysed the American Supreme Court decision on abortion, *Roe v. Wade.*

The survival of our traditional liberty, Grant thought, is also threatened by the concentration of our technology on mastery, including now the mastery of human beings. 'The practical question is whether a society in which technology must be oriented to cybernetics can maintain the institutions of free politics and the protection by law of the rights of the individual.' *English-Speaking Justice* is probably Grant's most powerfully sustained writing in political philosophy.

Philosophy and Education

In this section, we meet a Grant who is as passionately concerned about the centrality of philosophy to education as he is about the significance of morality for politics. In the world of politics, the good for men and women is either supported or neglected through action. In the context of learning, knowledge must be related to its proper place in the whole. Without adequate foundations, both action and knowledge become shallow or perverse. In both cases, our well-being as something more than comfortable animals is involved.

Grant's first occasion to reflect seriously about philosophy came to him soon after he had received his DPhil from Oxford in 1950. He was invited to contribute a research essay on the state of philosophy in English-speaking Canada to the Massey royal commission on arts and letters (See his article 'Philosophy') At this time Grant was inexperienced in academic politics. His essay offended many influential Canadian philosophers, not least because he wrote about the teaching of philosophy in Canada with supreme confidence in the justice of his disapproval of the prevailing approaches. We can see in it a brilliant statement of a conviction that the next forty years would in no way invalidate. Nor was this emphasis on the fundamental role of philosophy reserved only for his professional colleagues. In 'What Is Philosophy,' a radio talk which serves as a prologue to this book, the style is much less academic and, although the talk ends rather as the earlier report had begun, the approach is gentler. In the former essay, the word God is thrown down like a challenge in the first sentence. Here it comes as a climax, defining an experience open to us all if we choose to meditate on the mystery and meaning of human life.

Through the 1950s Grant spoke frequently about the unrecognized dignity of the teacher's vocation. 'I learned early that there is no more honourable or skilled profession, nor any more open to temptation in a society such as ours.' He never refused when schoolteachers invited him to speak, mainly because of his almost unlimited hope as to what might be achieved through genuine education. In 'The Paradox of Democratic Education,' written in 1955, he was able to say about the activity of thinking: 'It will teach you what is real, it will give you the vision of God.' He used the words 'real' and 'God' as if they were synonymous. And to him they were. What could either word mean if separated? It was to be many years before Grant learned to be more cautious about the word 'God' and to find alternatives that had more resonance for his audience. It was already quite acceptable to hear God called 'the supreme value'; that could mean anything or nothing at all. But to identify God with reality is quite another matter.

When Grant moved to Ontario in 1960 he realized gradually that he had much to learn about society's view of education. He had not been able fully to experience the technological world in the Maritimes; he hoped to be able to do so in Ontario. His own early hope for progress had been hard to give up, and his sense that Hegel might be right had reinforced the confidence with which he had faced the teaching profession in those years. It is interesting to note that, when in 1969 he republished an article on religion in the state school system that had originally appeared six years earlier in the *Queen's Quarterly*, he added a scathing introduction about how stupid the initial piece had been. 'The folly of this writing is that it did not grasp what the technological society really is ... I had hoped for years that our ecclesiastical organizations (being guardians of the beauty of the gospel) might continue to be able to permeate this society with something nobler than the barrenness of technical dynamism ... I could not believe that the only interpretation of Christianity that the technological liberalism would allow to survive publicly would be that part of it (eg the thought of Teilhard) which played the role of flatterer to modernity.'[9] This was not a change in Grant's view of education, but a recognition that he had overestimated the possible influence of the churches.

While teaching in Ontario during the 1960s, Grant wrote 'The University Curriculum,' a complex analysis of how the aims of the technological society were reflected in Ontario universities and how much modern ideology determined what subjects were to be central in the curriculum. At first glance the subjects appeared to be an eclectic mixture, lacking an overall unity. Grant believed this to be false. Under continental capitalism, the dominant classes had the money and therefore the power to dictate to the universities, and they knew exactly what they wanted. Whatever subjects would help to push the world in their preferred direction were the ones that they supported. Subjects would be taught as techniques, unrelated to any conception of the whole other than that of serving technological progress. Advances in technology would themselves be identified with advances in human excellence. The openness of mind required by philosophy towards modern assumptions would be a waste of time and money.

When considering the curriculum of Ontario universities, Grant was struck by the unspoken application of the fact/value distinction. Since Max Weber invented this expression for use in social science, it has trickled down from the academic to the popular level and has gradually been accepted as part of modern wisdom. Most of us now take for granted that 'facts' and 'values' are completely separate. 'Facts' are objective, and they give us knowledge, but only knowledge that is quantifiable by the scientific method. Questions of good and bad are not factual, and can be relegated to our value systems, which are private preferences, without rational content, and have no basis in the nature of things; so judgments as to good and bad can be attributed mainly to our emotional make-up. The distinction has been very useful in achieving mastery over human as well as non-human nature. It determines what those in power decide is important to teach at universities: the studies that deal with facts – like engineering, commerce, chemistry, and medicine. This kind of research, which is praised because it is value free, leads to unchecked technological progress. The high prestige of these areas of study spill over into the humanities and social sciences, which are in their turn expected also to be value free.

In his early essay for the Massey royal commission, Grant had defined philosophy as having some relation to our intuitions of the perfection of God. However, Grant was not a proselytizer. It should be understood that neither then nor later did he try to turn his students into Christians, although they might be aware of his own faith. Nor did he expect all of them to spend their lives in the systematic study of philosophy. What he hoped to foster in them were minds open to the whole and the ability to give their attention to careful thought. Given these qualities, the important questions are likely to arise. They will be questions such as: What is my eternal destiny? What for? – whither? – and what then? What is the nature of love, of beauty, of goodness? 'These questions are real questions, tough and intractable intellectual questions and, above all, they are questions for which education is required if a clear and cogent answer is to be given. Therefore they cannot be excluded from the university.'[10] Grant's students would sometimes complain that when they asked him a question his answer would be another question. They came gradually to understand the reason behind his teaching style. It was implicit in his frequently quoted passage from Luther: 'A man must do his own believing as he does his own dying.'

After twenty years at McMaster, Grant decided to return to Dalhousie for his last four years before retirement. He had become dissatisfied with the department of religion because of its concentration on research to the exclusion of other methods of intellectual enquiry. As he explained in 'The Battle between Teaching and Research,' the most important questions cannot be answered by research conducted along the lines of the scientific method. They require the method of dialectic – sustained and disciplined conversation between teacher and student, or student and student. If one writes an essay for a teacher, one is engaged in a kind of conversation. This short article summarizes not only the kind of teaching that opens others to philosophic thinking, but also reflects Grant's increasing despair over the direction of Canadian universities since the 1960s.

Thinking Their Thoughts

Readers of Grant's work will not find systematic and comprehensive expositions of the philosophers named in this section. They were simply the thinkers from whom he learnt most about what primarily concerned him as being philosophy's most urgent need; such questions as the nature of modernity here and now, its potentiality for good or ill, and its relation to and difference from the traditions of the ancients. He did not aspire to be 'creative' but rather to attempt to be 'open to the whole,' which he thought should be the aim of philosophy. He hoped to go a little way towards understanding and clarifying some ultimate questions about human existence. From the genius of certain other thinkers he found insights that greatly illuminated his own intuitions as to what was happening in modernity, and why the obscurity that surrounded us was so dark.

Grant thought that the Gospels stood at the centre of any attempt to understand the world and the human predicament. He believed that Christianity was truth, and that true philosophy would never contradict the Gospels. But he needed philosophy to help him understand them. He did not seek one philosophic mentor, or even one area of expertise to make his own and in which to produce systematic expositions, valuable as these might be. Especially in the modern world, when the tradition had been so shattered, he could never have become the follower of an exclusive school. He liked to quote Jonathan Swift's description of modern thinkers as spiders, spinning their thoughts out of themselves. Grant thought himself more like one of the ancients, whom Swift pictured as bees, taking their nourishment from several flowers.

The philosophers included here are those Grant thought could teach us the most about modernity, its great accomplishments, its puzzling character, and its tragic limitations. He studied Plato, St Augustine, and Kant while at Oxford in the 1940s, and he continued to find new insights in their writings for the rest of his life. During the 1950s he was also much preoccupied with Marx, whom he understood as a great moral, even religious, thinker. Although he first encountered Simone Weil's writings in 1951, he was initially so disturbed by her moral and ascetic intensity that it was not until near the end of the 1950s that he understood her greatness as a philosopher. In the late 1950s he had discovered the writings of the German-American political philosopher Leo Strauss, and through him the French thinker Alexandre Kojève. He studied Martin Heidegger's 1927 existentialist classic

Sein und Zeit in the 1950s and taught Heidegger's writings in the 1960s; but it was not until the 1970s that he realized how brightly Heidegger's understanding of technology illuminated the modern condition. His understanding of Heidegger had been aided by his acceptance of the genius of Heidegger's master, Nietzsche, whose greatness as a philosopher of the modern fell on Grant like a revelation. Only in the 1980s did he seriously come to terms with the early writings of Jean-Jacques Rousseau, who clarified for him the historical character of being human in the contemporary world.

Grant was not without personal ambition (though he considered self-assertion a vice he had to fight); yet what he really sought was always in some sense outside himself, and outside even the greatest of his teachers. It was a wonderful joy to learn what Plato believed about the Beautiful Itself; but, as he said to his students, the final reason for studying Plato is the question of whether or not the Beautiful Itself exists. Reflection on the thought of Kant was a fascinating intellectual experience, but what mattered most was that Kant, for all his contradictions, clarified certain aspects of reality in a way no other thinker did.

Since Grant never published traditional scholarly expositions of Augustine, Plato, or Kant (though he lectured about them in great detail), it is difficult in this volume to make their importance to his thought sufficiently explicit. Many highly original lectures exist, but most are not in publishable form.

Grant's interest in St Augustine is shown here in a radio talk about a distinguished classics professor, Charles Cochrane. In 1941 Cochrane published a book, *Christianity and Classical Culture*, which showed how Augustine had unified Christianity with the truths of classical philosophy and in so doing had founded the Western Christian church and the civilization that flowed from it. Grant's reading of Cochrane taught him how to approach the complex relationship between philosophy and revealed religion. St Augustine's *City of God* and *De Trinitate* were fruitful texts in teaching, because they raised the most fundamental and perennial questions, such as the relation of time and history, of necessity and the good, and freedom and will. Grant found that the students responded passionately, for example, to Augustine's paradox that to be able not to sin is a great freedom, but not to be able to sin is the greatest freedom.

Although he later became convinced, partly by his study of Philip Sherrard's *The Greek East and the Latin West*, that Augustine had been the source of a fatal misunderstanding that has permeated Western

Christianity, Grant never doubted Augustine's central position in the development of the church, whether for good or for ill.

Grant first read and loved Plato's *Republic* while he was studying at Oxford after the war, but it was not until his years at Dalhousie in the 1950s that Plato became his greatest philosophic eros. He credited his friend and colleague James Doull with showing him the central truths of Plato's teaching, and it became Plato even more than St Augustine who helped him to see how his Christian faith could be thought. As he explained in a letter: 'Sureness is not necessarily dogmatism ... I know God exists. Plato shows to those who listen that one cannot avoid that conclusion ... Life has been too long for me and I had to learn at too great a price not to be frank about what one believes. At the personal and practical level I am always unsure and confused but at this level I know I am right, not because of the "I" but because the arguments are irrefutable. And nothing could be more important than this because in the next years the future of the world is tied up with those who have rational love of God ... one cannot speak wrongly when one has Plato and Augustine and Kant behind one. The issue is not really God but whether philosophy is a practical study which can help me to live.'[11]

Plato's thought was present in all Grant's work from the 1950s, sometimes explicit, though more often implicit. We find it most clearly in his essay 'Justice and Technology,' and also in 'Faith and the Multiversity.' It is implied in all his writings on politics and education. In the darkness of 'A Platitude' Plato shines in the last sentence like a great light. His understanding of Plato continued to evolve and deepen. The direction of his thought on Plato was first influenced by the pagan writer Plotinus, but he later found a sure and certain guide in the more clearly Christian perspective of Simone Weil.

Grant first read Kant while at Oxford and often attended lectures given in London by his close friend Peter Self. Grant was immediately attracted by Kant: '[I] was intoxicated by Kant's account of morality. It freed me from all the vulgar liberal pragmatism'[12] While he was teaching at Dalhousie, Grant would regularly have senior students over to his house for evening seminars. When these did not deal with St Augustine, they would be about Kant, usually the *Critique of Pure Reason*. This text certainly required students to develop the faculty of attention. The *Critique of Practical Reason* he left for his ordinary classes. He continued to teach Kant from time to time for the rest of his academic life and became increasingly fascinated by the complex position

Kant holds in the history of philosophy: an innovator of modernity, while at the same time the great delayer of its worst excesses. In later years, Grant mainly taught the *Critique of Practical Reason*, because, as Kant said, it is in the practical life, rather than in the theoretical, that we face the ultimate.

Grant's thought was powerfully attracted by the way society was developing and the moral problems that individuals would face as a consequence of these developments. He therefore turned to see what the great political philosophers could teach him about impending problems. The first of these thinkers was Karl Marx, who was much in Grant's mind during the 1950s. A humanism of universal salvation with no theological framework would have held little attraction for him in itself. Yet he admired the passion with which Marx hated the oppression of human beings, and the fervour with which he tried to understand the means of its overcoming. Such admiration was quite lacking in his attitude to Marx's great teacher, Hegel. While Hegel's massive system claimed a total comprehensiveness, Grant found nothing there of what he admired in Marx: a sense of the importance of individual men and women, and the pain they suffered. Although Grant continued to take great interest in Marx as a founder of the modern, in the 1980s, as was noted earlier, he turned increasingly to Rousseau and began to sketch out his thoughts on the role Rousseau, Marx, and Darwin had played in forming the modern idea of history.

If someone had asked him which thinker had the deepest understanding of the goodness of being, he might have hesitated between Plato and Simone Weil. Weil was a French philosopher, born nine years before Grant, who died tragically early. She wrote with genius about Christ and Plato and showed how they illuminated one another. Like Augustine, Weil believed that Plato knew all the truth of Christianity, except that the Word had been made flesh. Grant firmly believed that Weil was a saint as well as a philosopher of genius; her sanctity gave an added authority to the power of her thought. Nevertheless, he had two reservations about her. First, he believed that a public religion was necessary for the state, and he did not see how Weil's austere faith could provide this. Secondly, although she said clearly that one must never seek affliction for oneself, some of her writings seemed to imply the contrary, as did some of her actions. Other reservations were of a more personal nature concerning what Grant saw as his own limitations and failings. He was very much aware that he could not even desire a life like hers, with so much suffering. (This is not an uncommon reaction among readers of Weil.) Yet he was convinced that at the centre of her thought she was nearer the truth about the Divine than anyone else he had ever encountered.

Grant chanced upon Weil's writing when the CBC sent him her posthumous book, *Waiting on God*, to review over the radio. By the 1960s he hoped to write a biographical introduction to her thought. For this purpose he went to Paris in 1963 to consult her manuscripts and to meet her mother, her brother, and her friend and later biographer, Simone Pétrement. Although this book was never written, he continued to read and learn and teach about her, but, as he said, he wanted others to read what she herself had written rather than to learn about her thoughts second-hand through him.

In the later 1950s the University of Toronto philosopher Émile Fackenheim had suggested that Grant read the work of one of Heidegger's students, Leo Strauss. Starting with *What Is Political Philosophy?* Grant greedily devoured everything he could find of Strauss's. In these writings, he discovered a defence of Plato and Aristotle in terms of virtue and morality, and an analysis of the modern philosophers from Machiavelli to Nietzsche that showed the steady decline of the classical vision of human excellence. Grant was deeply moved by Strauss's *Thoughts on Machiavelli*, with its forthright condemnation of that thinker as a 'teacher of evil.' (Few political scientists still thought in terms of evil, since they were mostly converts to Max Weber's concept of a value-free social science.)

Grant learned much from Strauss and gratefully acknowledged his influence. However, throughout the 1960s, Grant came to understand that they differed on many important matters, primarily Strauss's understanding of Plato's dialogues. Strauss, Grant concluded, denied the presence in Plato of the transcendent, which Grant saw as inseparable from the heart of Plato's greatest writings. He also complained that Strauss seemed strangely reticent about his own belief concerning the relation between reason and revelation. Although most of Strauss's followers did not consider him in any way a religious thinker, Grant disagreed. He often mentioned the beautiful but ambiguous passage from the end of the essay 'What is Political Philosophy?': 'Modern thought reaches its culmination, its highest self-consciousness, in the most radical historicism, ie, in explicitly condemning to oblivion the notion of eternity. For oblivion of eternity, or in other words, estrangement from man's deepest desire and therewith from the primary issues, is the price which modern man had to pay, from the very beginning, for attempting to be absolutely sovereign, to become master and owner of nature, to conquer chance.'[13]

In the late 1960s Grant and Strauss had an affable correspondence but they had never met personally. When a mutual friend heard that Strauss was seriously ill, he arranged a meeting between Grant and Strauss, and Grant's admiration and affection for the man himself was confirmed. But by the late 1970s, Grant realized more and more that Strauss's interpretation of Plato was an indirect attack on Christianity. Strauss and Grant agreed on the importance of Platonism for Christianity, but Strauss thought that each had been harmed by the encounter. Strauss tried to counteract what he considered to be distortion in Christianized Platonism and sought a hermeneutic to recover Plato's authentic meaning. Strauss believed that Christianity led to an overextension of soul, and Grant always considered this criticism worthy of close attention. He continued to return to Strauss with enjoyment, especially when he felt intellectually and spiritually drained by his immersion in Simone Weil's thought. 'Simone Weil has a much greater authority for me than Strauss. Strauss has just enabled me to see what is involved in modern political philosophy and the means of rejecting it. S.W. seems to me at the highest level of illumination. Yet it leads to a life I am just not capable of living.'[14]

Grant was never one of the Straussians, but he was liked by them and admitted to their friendship. He received the unpublished notes from Strauss's graduate seminars and had a riotous relationship with Allan Bloom, then at the University of Toronto. Grant loved his outrageousness, though he disagreed with many of Bloom's opinions. Grant was invited quite often to gatherings at the Toronto flat of his Straussian friend, Howard Brotz, and was even allowed to bring his wife.

In the essay 'Tyranny and Wisdom' we can see Grant's entire agreement with Strauss about the nature of the universal and homogeneous state whose coming-to-be the Hegelian Alexandre Kojève confidently predicted. Grant thought that this could only be a terrible tyranny. The essay has great relevance for us today, now that such a state is often held up as an ideal, for example in Frances Fukuyama's *The End of History and the Last Man* (1992). We should also note that Grant learned much from Kojève, not least a darker view of Hegel that was evidenced in his praise of the universal and homogeneous state. Grant had not seen that ruthless side of Hegel in his conversations with his friend James Doull, still less in his reading of the English Hegelian writers. In this regard, Kojève, too, can be accounted a major influence on Grant.

Martin Heidegger's thought is notoriously obscure. Grant would normally introduce him to students by means of the essay 'The Question Concerning Technology,' or sometimes by the more accessible 'Memorial Address' in the book *Discourse on Thinking*. However, it is an oversimplification to suggest that he accepted Heidegger's analysis of technology and rejected the rest of the teaching. Grant was extremely anxious to understand modernity and he had no doubt that Heidegger was incomparably the greatest philosopher of the modern. Already, in the 1950s, before much of Heidegger was available in English, Grant recognized in the politically discredited philosopher a new and exciting voice. He would constantly quote Heidegger's dictum 'Let it lie before you, and take it to heart – the Being of beings.' He took seriously Heidegger's criticism of Plato's use of the concept of 'truth.' (Grant's refutation of this view can be found in the essay 'Justice and Technology'.)

Grant lectured on Heidegger in the 1970s, always with a deep respect and a certain agnosticism. He knew that there were some things in Heidegger's thought he did not yet understand, and he knew that he needed to do so. He did not want to go back to Plato like visiting a museum, ignoring all that had happened in philosophy since antiquity. Rather Grant strove to think Plato's certainties in the world as it has now become – the world of technology, modern science, and radical freedom. That was Grant's approach to all the thinkers with whose thought he wrestled and it is why we call this section 'Thinking Their Thoughts.'

For many years Grant hoped to write a book confronting Heidegger's dismissal of Plato's thought. Leo Strauss, when they met, advised him to approach what he wanted to do through Heidegger's writings on Nietzsche. After Grant retired in 1984, he concentrated on this task, reading and re-reading the four volumes of Heidegger's writings on Nietzsche, beautifully edited by David Krell. Grant found reading these an overwhelming experience – Heidegger at his best. The possible points of attack gradually became clearer. In attempting to defend Plato against Heidegger's profound criticisms, Grant knew that he would also (and more importantly) be defending Christianity against Heidegger's contempt. As already noted, Grant could only write a preliminary chapter (itself incomplete) before the onset of his final illness. He had intended it for inclusion in a volume honouring his friend James Doull.

One reason why Grant found Heidegger's *Nietzsche* so fascinating was that he had himself in his youth come to the conclusion that Nietzsche was unjustly underrated or ignored by English-speaking philosophers. He devoted his Massey lectures of 1969, *Time as History*, to an exposition of Nietzsche's role as the great philosopher of a new vision of existence. Here he clearly expresses a principle that regulated all his teaching and writing: it is not useful to reject a philosopher until one has first attempted to think his thought as clearly and consistently as possible. Even when expounding a thinker whom one considers a teacher of evil, it is both wrong and ineffective to try to innoculate students by presenting them at the outset with one's own negative conclusions. To do so is to deny that the students are free and rational, and also to deny the dialectic method, which lay at the heart of Grant's pedagogy.

Nietzsche so embodies the modern conception of the world that it is necessary, contrary to Strauss's view, to teach him in careful detail. At the end of 'Time as History' Grant explains this necessity. Many people who have never heard of Nietzsche may yet be thinking his thoughts. 'If one listens carefully to the revolt of the noblest young against bourgeois America, one hears deeper notes in it than were ever sounded by Marx, and those are above all the notes of Nietzsche.'[15] It is important that these notes be known for what they are. The love of one's fate for which he calls is not a passive acceptance but a dynamic willing. According to Nietzsche, the ability to will for the sake of willing is the very height for human beings. If we can overcome our *ressentiment* and our desire for revenge, and claim the earth as our true home, we may be able to love our fate and to know that we live beyond good and evil.

In *Time as History* Grant defends his decision to teach Nietzsche to the young. And in 'Nietzsche and the Ancients' he defends his own final rejection of Nietzsche. There, he goes so far as to say that this denial expresses his rejection of the whole modern project. Could it be that such a rejection on his part necessarily involves a failure to be open to the whole, a disposition that Grant held to be essential to a philosopher? He answers this question by asserting what he calls in *Philosophy and the Mass Age* 'the test of the limitless.' Nietzsche's failure is that he recognizes no limits beyond which we may not go. No other modern or ancient philosopher explicitly taught that there are human beings to whom nothing at all is due. In his constant denial of equality, Nietzsche does just that. Grant reminds us that Nietzsche's terrifying definition of what he calls 'justice' should be a warning to us as to what might be done to some other human beings if we go beyond good and evil.

Grant's discovery in his final years at Dalhousie was Jean-Jacques Rousseau's *Discourse on the Origins of Inequality*, a work he came to see as a revolutionary statement that human beings are fundamentally historical beings, rather than creatures of a transcendent Divinity: 'It is only this year that I discovered that Rousseau was a greater former of the modern than even Nietzsche. The result is that at the moment I am writing a long piece called "History and Justice" which is an attempt to understand the atheism of the left better than previously. Rousseau takes my breath away with how clever he is in destroying the old tradition by saying that reason is acquired by human beings in a way that can be explained without teleology. To try to demolish Rousseau (and, therefore, marxism) seems to me essential these days to free people from that which can hold them from ever thinking that Christianity might be true.'[16]

Reviews and Essays

The first item in this section, a short review of a study of Francis Bacon, is interesting for two reasons. Grant wrote it soon after taking his first teaching appointment at Dalhousie in 1947. It shows how early in his career he became interested in the questions that would later come to dominate his thought: the rise of modern science and its impact on society. However, the review is interesting for another, more personal, reason. Fulton Anderson, the author of the book, was head of the philosophy department at the University of Toronto and one of the most powerful academic philosophers in Canada. Anderson was furious when he read the criticism by a novice philosopher in faraway Halifax and telephoned Dalhousie's president to demand an apology. Later, when Grant wrote his article on philosophy for the Massey commission, he added to the offence he had given in his review, and from that time on Anderson was implacably hostile.

Grant learned from this experience and began to write more cautiously, or indirectly as he called it. His article on Bertrand Russell was, as he explained to his mother in a letter, a firm but oblique reply to Anderson's criticisms of him: 'The real substance of my disagreement with Anderson and Co. is that philosophy is not really a theoretical subject to be held in the confines of a university but a way of life that all men must strive for.'[17] 'Anderson's words were written too much in anger to answer them. I will answer them in the long years of writing philosophy. Controversy generally gets beclouded and I have a feeling that it would be a waste of time to argue with Anderson.'[18] His essay on Bertrand Russell was meant to serve as a reply to Anderson's position, since he considered that both philosophers shared a common confusion.

Readers will no doubt be struck by the hostile tone of most of the essays and reviews in this section. The reason for his critical stance is that Grant was already convinced, as *Philosophy in the Mass Age* shows, that the problems with modern society were deep and fundamental. In order to understand how this society had come about, Grant explored the writings of some of its exemplars and founders, such as Russell, Max Weber, Sigmund Freud, and C.G. Jung. His criticisms of these writers were trenchantly expressed because he felt so deeply about the kind of world they had created. He later addressed the inadequacies of some of his fellow Canadian thinkers, such as Harold Innis and Northrop Frye, whom he had earlier praised in his 'Philosophy' article. Although he thought that Innis was admirable, at least as a social scientist, Innis's critique of contemporary society was not radical enough for he failed to advance beyond the question of how modernity had developed.

Some of Grant's readers become frustrated with his writings. He is a brilliant critic, they complain. He articulates in telling detail what is wrong, but he never says what we should do about it. They will perhaps be surprised to learn that Grant felt the same way about some of his own writings. As he wrote in the mid-1970s to Dennis Lee, with whom he was discussing a proposed new collection of essays: 'On re-reading them they seem to be negative and austere. I intend to write an introduction in which the purpose of the negations is made plain – namely that they exist to clear away the junk of the modern era and to say how difficult it is to make positive affirmations. I hope the introduction will make clear that these essays are really attempts in the old manner of negative theology.'[19]

As a respite, he turned to music and literature. Mozart was his greatest love and a day rarely passed when he did not listen to one of the master's piano concertos. In the late 1970s he had discovered the wartime trilogy of the controversial French writer Louis-Ferdinand Céline. Although Céline had written vicious anti-Semitic pamphlets before the war, Grant was enraptured by his final writing, an account of his flight through war-ravaged Europe with his wife, Lili, and his cat, Bébert, during the collapse of the Nazi regime. He found in Céline the prodigality of imagination that he had previously encountered only in

Shakespeare and Tolstoy. He wrote of this in an article for the *Queen's Quarterly*, 'Céline – Art and Politics.' 'I have put aside "Technology and Justice" till I have written the Céline, largely because I was sick of negativity and criticism and was so enraptured by Céline.'[20] Dennis Lee had helped Grant enormously by his brilliant editing of *Technology and Empire* and by his constant prodding and encouragement. In a collection celebrating Dennis Lee at mid-career, Grant contributed an essay, 'Dennis Lee – Poetry and Philosophy.' Grant did not easily enjoy modern poetry, but his friendship with Lee made him more open to his work. Indeed, Lee was perhaps the only living poet with whose work Grant felt at ease.

Technology and Modernity

This section could almost be called 'Modernity as Technology.' In the 1950s Grant tried to come to terms with what was happening in North American society in a number of different ways. He analysed it as the expanding economy, the atomic age, the mass society. None was satisfactory because each sought to understand modernity as something 'out there.' Grant intuitively sensed that modernity was something more fundamental, that it was not merely a set of things that could be controlled. Technology was slowly and insidiously shaping not just external nature but human beings as well.

After the mid-1960s and for the rest of his life, Grant was deeply engrossed in the effort to understand technology: what it did to our world, what it portended for the future, and how it almost totally limited our ability to see anything outside itself. At the end of the 1950s he had even considered moving with his family to California so that he could experience the full force of the dynamic society that was developing in North America. The writings of Alexandre Kojève had pointed out that the world was moving remorselessly towards a universal and homogeneous state and Leo Strauss had convinced him that this coming civilization would be a terrible tyranny. Grant had put these thoughts to brilliant use in *Lament for a Nation* and in the address he delivered in 1964 to the Canadian Conference on Social Welfare, 'Value and Technology.' This talk is particularly interesting because it vividly portrays the effects of technology without much using the concept itself. The loss of meaning in society, Grant suggested, was a condition that challenged social workers to the limit of their capacity, or even beyond. As a teacher, Grant had encountered similar difficulties and so identified with the social workers. In his essay 'In Defence of North America' Grant pointed out that our continent is the dynamic heart of modernity, the spearhead of technique in the Western world, and he described the increasing difficulty we experience in our attempts to think outside it.

In 1966 he encountered the writings of the French social theorist Jacques Ellul, who in *The Technological Society* presented the character of modern technology in disturbing detail, and his review of this volume was important in extending Ellul's influence among Canadian critics of technology. Grant now understood much better the apparent meaninglessness of society. He was particularly moved by Ellul's account of how technique is self-augmenting and autonomous. 'Technical progress tends to act, not according to arithmetic, but according to a geometric progression.'[21]

For Ellul, technique was still a 'thing,' however dominant it had become. As Grant pondered the writings of Heidegger, however, he saw clearly what he had previously only intuited: technology had become a mode of being, the ontology of the age. Grant developed these thoughts in a speech he was invited to give to the Royal Society of Canada. His paper, 'Knowing and Making,' was addressed to the scientists who were the vanguard of technology. He warned them that they were quite likely to be creating a monster. A new relation had arisen between the arts and the sciences. Making, or art as it used to be called, had been transformed by the methods and discoveries of modern science. The interdependence (Grant called it co-penetration) of knowing and making had led to important scientific discoveries but at the same time had made these discoveries quite outside any consideration of human good. They claimed to be value free. The question that was driving Grant, and that he painfully tried to answer, was how it was possible even to think about goodness when the language with which we had invoked it had been taken from us. Biotechnology was a classic example of the feebleness of the language of good or justice in the modern world: through it human beings could transform human nature itself. Where was the standpoint from which we could assess this change, know that it was good – or evil? In this address to Canada's most distinguished scientists, Grant's appeal was passionate because it was inspired by a real and growing fear.

The next selection was written in the 1970s and presented in slightly different forms to many audiences before being published in 1986 in *Technology and Justice* as 'Thinking about Technology.' Unlike 'Know-

ing and Making,' it was intended to alert the thoughtful public, rather
than specialists. Its relevance in the 1990s is overwhelming. Those who
believed that it was still possible for human beings to control technology would issue calming reassurances such as 'the computer does not
impose on us the way it should be used.' Grant reflected on the
thought contained in that sentence. He took it apart almost word for
word, and the result is not easily forgotten. His conclusion is that computers can arise only in a particular type of society, and the fact of their
appearance against this background makes them far from neutral
instruments.

The last piece in this section is the little known 'Justice and Technology,' originally published in a large American anthology not readily
available in Canada. (It is reprinted here with corrections and addi-
tions Grant made to the original version.) Grant says that his intention
in this article is to discuss the relation between technology and two
statements about justice: Christ's 'happy are those who are hungry and
thirsty for justice' (Matthew 5:6) and Socrates's dictum that it is better
to suffer injustice than to inflict it (*Gorgias* 474b).

From some points of view, these two statements would be in perfect harmony with technology. Grant always acknowledged that one of
the reasons for technology's triumph was that many people, beginning with Francis Bacon, had believed that control over nature was
necessary in order to fulfil the biblical injunctions to be both good
stewards and good shepherds, to husband the resources of the earth
and make them prosper so that the sheep might be protected and
fed. Many of the achievements of technology did help make human
life better: penicillin healed the sick, the green revolution fed the
poor, labour-saving devices relieved people, especially women, of
much drudgery.

However, in this essay, Grant comes to terms with a terrible ambiguity about technology: it 'came into the world carrying a hope about justice, [but] has in its realization dimmed the ability to think about
justice.' One may ask: Why is it so important to be able to think about
justice when technology is bringing it about in the world? Who needs
an ontology of justice, or for that matter an ontology of anything? Why
does Grant so often call 'transcendence' a dangerous word?

It is not possible to dismiss such questions. Grant makes it clear that
the most important knowledge is given us in the ordinary occurrences
of daily life, and through the concrete more readily than through
philosophical abstractions. If a word like ontology – the science of

being – excludes the immediacies of justice here and now, it has become a dead object in the museum of our civilization, a dry academic phantom. If justice is, as both Grant and Plato believed, what human beings are fitted for, it must be an unchanging good, which meets us and calls to us to pay its price in the ordinary occurrences of space and time. This hard standard for our actions is quite alien to what is thought in technology about what is due to human beings.

The essay ends with a warning. Grant's frequent references to Plato do not imply a turning away from the present. We need to meet technology face to face, so that we learn to know it for what it is. This requires us to recognize what has been lost, politically and ethically, in the coming to be of technological modernity; and Plato can help us do that. But it is equally important to understand what good, if any, has been found in the genesis of technology. It is the same thought as that with which Grant ends *Time as History*: 'Nor should any dim apprehensions of what was meant by perfection before the age of progress be used simply as a means to negate what may have been given us of truth and goodness in this age.'[22]

The Beautiful and the Good

In this volume, it is a particularly smooth transition from the other sections to Grant's contemplation of the beautiful and the good. This section is not in any way separate from the preceding ones for, in most important ways, what Grant wrote in his more austere and negative pieces can be understood only in light of the ideas contained here. Perhaps a more obvious title for the section would be 'Religion,' but Grant did not like this term to describe faith. Religion, for him, was something public, worldly, political; it was the set of basic and accepted beliefs that held a society together. Nor did he ever write about his 'personal' faith. This silence allowed him to affect many readers who did not share his fundamental orientation, for they could accept his critique of technological modernity without feeling that they also had to be committed to his view of the transcendent. However, for Grant, reason, reverence, and love comprised a unity, and he did not write about 'his' religion because he did not think of Christianity as a personal possession. Nor did he accept the assertion that he subscribed to Christian 'values.' For him, Christianity was nothing less than the way he participated, albeit always imperfectly, in reality. Perhaps this is why so many of his sentences end rather awkwardly with a form of the verb 'to be,' as in such phrases as 'the understanding of what is.' The absence of personal affirmation might strike some readers as a mark of a cold intellectualism, a denial of the human; but Grant did not need to be reminded by Simone Weil that the God that Christians worship is the same one who causes the sun to shine and the rain to fall on the just and the unjust alike. He was aware always of what Plato calls 'the very real difference between the necessary and the good.'

The coupling here of the word 'beautiful' with the word 'good' should not suggest any hint of a religion of aestheticism, which was abhorrent to him. Nor is the 'beautiful' used in the subjective sense of approval, meaning little more than 'nice' or 'I like that.' Rather it is used in a precise Platonic way, either as a synonym for the Good itself (as in Plato's *Symposium*), or as an image of that Good (as in the *Phaedrus*). Because we are situated in a world where we cannot contemplate this Good directly and without distraction, it is necessary for us to approach it through its presence in the world as the Beautiful. One thing that is common to these pieces is the persistent note of hope, though it is a hope that recognizes that in the contemporary world the Good and the Beautiful are often most obvious in their absence, rather than their presence. Grant, as he always insisted, could never despair or be a pessimist, because such a stance towards existence was forbidden to a Christian.

Although Grant is known as a philosopher, he often experienced the world as a poet does, and some of his best prose has a poetic quality. The sonnet with which this section begins, however, is the only poem Grant published. 'Good Friday' celebrates the suffering and death of the perfectly just man. It treats the crucifixion rather than the resurrection of Christ. Grant thought that too many Christians celebrate Easter in a triumphalist mood. In contrast, Grant believed that it is not miraculous power that is of most significance to us, but the love with which the broken Christ asks his Father to forgive those who are torturing him. The amazingly concentrated line, 'His glance on Golgotha our sun for seeing,' is not an academic's reference to a Platonic metaphor (the Sun in the *Republic* 507–8), but Grant's instinctive use of Plato's imagery as the most comprehensive way he could find of summing up reality as he experienced it. Though written relatively early, this poem expresses a belief that lasted throughout Grant's life and which may be described as a theology of the cross. It is a celebration of the beautiful and the good, though in full awareness of 'the price of goodness in the face of evil.'[23]

With the next essay, 'A Platitude,' we return to the subject of technology. Why was it not put with the other writings on that subject? It is
here because of the lucid note of hope with which it ends. We live in
the dynamo of the technological world all around us. Yet many of us
are aware that we lack certain things that were once considered necessary to a fully human life. How can we be aware of such deprivations
unless we somehow remember the good that we now lack? As Grant
had put it in *Lament for a Nation*: '"I cannot but remember such things
were / That were most precious to me." In Mozart's great threnody,
the Countess sings of *la memoria di quel bene.** One cannot argue the
meaninglessness of the world from the facts of evil, because what could
evil deprive us of, if we had not some prior knowledge of good?'[24]
These intimations are precious and should be treasured, because they
may be the way that the good for human beings, unspeakable in public
terms in the contemporary world, may yet appear to us in the darkness
of our situation. They may even lead us to see the beautiful as the
image, in the world, of the good.

In the article 'Jelte Kuipers – An Appreciation' the Beautiful and the
Good is present in terms of one particular individual. This was a beautiful young man at the height of his potentiality for action and thought.
He married a woman of his own calibre and a few weeks later was killed
in a chance road accident. The distance between the necessary and the
good leaves us, as it often does, with unanswerable questions.

In an early writing Grant had put forward as descriptive of religion,
or of a religious experience, the act of loving someone (or something)
with a love that does not want them to be in the slightest degree different from what they are. He ended by asking: 'How do we make the religious act of not having it otherwise, that somebody we would not have
otherwise – should be mortal?'[25]

The book review of *Torture in Greece* might seem out of place here,
rather than in the section on politics and morality. Is it merely paradoxical to put it under the Beautiful and the Good? No, because Grant
understood clearly that torture is a thing supremely ugly, a thing in
which the Good does not participate in any way. Just as we could not
know what evil is without some idea of the good of which it deprives us,
so our vision of the good may be sharpened by remembering its most
appalling absence. In *Philosophy in the Mass Age*, Grant related a
thought experiment. Suppose a man had hidden a hydrogen bomb in

*'The recollection of that good.' Mozart, *The Marriage of Figaro*.

a large city, set to explode at a certain hour. If the police captured him, and he would not speak, should they torture his children if that would lead to his confession and would save thousands of lives?[26] Torture, whether for reasons of political prudence or for any other apparent necessity, passes beyond the limits of the permissible.

Although Grant recognized that goodness and justice are often experienced as absence in the modern West, he also knew that others had approached the Good less obliquely. Grant, only half-jokingly, described himself as standing on the extreme Hindu wing of Christianity, and he was delighted when his former student, Bithika Mukerji, asked him to write the foreword to her book *Neo-Vedanta and Modernity*. For Grant, Plato was the Western thinker whose thought was closest to the Vedanta, the ancient Indian scriptures. Dr Mukerji studied for many years the impact of Westernization on Indian thought and indeed on all religious and philosophical traditions from before the age of progress.

Grant was particularly interested in Mukerji's account of *Ananda*, usually translated as Bliss, which is a central attribute of the divine in the Vedanta. For us 'the ontology (or being) of *Ananda*' is a daunting phrase, because in our tradition bliss or joy is purely subjective and has no reality outside our feelings. Therefore, it is hard to think of bliss as having an ontology. Grant suggests that there is a need felt in our Western world for a joy that is more than transient and is somehow grounded in the nature of things. From this we may get a glimpse of what Mukerji thinks is threatened in her tradition. We may also get a glimpse of what Grant meant when he said that Mozart's music had a supernatural model. An extract from Grant's foreword appears under the title 'Bliss.'

We end this reader with Grant's most positive and powerful statement. As he explained to a young admirer: 'For the first time in my life I have tried to express Christianity [around] a wonderful sentence of Simone Weil's that "Faith is the experience that the intelligence is illuminated by love." I am sorry that some of my writings have made you "gloomy." Hope is a great virtue but I do not think it should be concentrated on the events of this world but on the eternal order.'[27] 'Faith and the Multiversity' is a deep meditation on Weil's sentence and it amounts to nothing less than a refutation of modernity understood as technology. Seen either as a mode of understanding or as a mode of being, technology is shown to be radically incomplete and fundamentally inadequate because it ignores the existence of love in the world.

This writing is also Grant's clearest account of why he so often prefaced the word Christianity with the qualification 'Western.' By the time one has fully assimilated this difficult essay, one has a better idea of what Christianity without the qualification meant to him. It brings together what he thought about love with his thoughts about the beautiful. His devotion to Plato's thought is reaffirmed, and so is his rejection of Nietzsche. His fundamental disagreement with Heidegger is, as usual, combined with a deeply respectful admission of his greatness.

In his last years, Grant was busy preparing to start his projected book defending Plato and Christianity from Heidegger's attack. Often he would write down the thoughts that occurred to him in preparation for the task. Most of these were in folders with the words 'Notes on the Good' scribbled on the front. Looking at these soon after his death, a friend observed: 'All his work could be summed up as "Notes on the Good."'

A Comment on the Texts

In editing the selections a number of minor stylistic changes were made to the original texts. In the case of previously published material, spelling, punctuation, and capitalization have been standardized. However, letters have been treated as historical documents and so generally retain all the original spelling, punctuation, and so on. The editors' notes are in the form of unnumbered footnotes, while Grant's original notes appear as numbered notes at the end of the selection.

NOTES

1 Eugene Forsey, *A Life on the Fringe: The Memoirs of Eugene Forsey* (Toronto: Oxford University Press 1990), 32.
2 A narrow local inlet of the ocean.
3 Highest good.
4 George Grant to Murray Tolmie, 29 March 1954, in *George Grant: Selected Letters*, ed. William Christian (Toronto: University of Toronto Press 1996), 185.
5 George Grant personal papers, Halifax, N.S.
6 Louis Greenspan, 'George Grant Remembered,' *Ta Panta*, vol. 6:1.
7 Quoted in William Christian, *George Grant: A Biography* (Toronto: University of Toronto Press 1993), 271.

8 Hugh Segal, *No Surrender: Reflection of a Happy Warrior in the Tory Crusade* (Toronto: HarperCollins 1996), 9.

9 George Grant, 'Religion and the State,' in *Technology and Empire* (Toronto: House of Anansi 1969), 43.

10 George Grant, unpublished talk to students at McMaster University, Grant personal papers.

11 George Grant to Maude Grant, spring 1952, in *Selected Letters*, 174–5.

12 George Grant, unpublished lecture, 1977–8, Grant personal papers.

13 Leo Strauss, 'What Is Political Philosophy?' in *What Is Political Philosophy and Other Studies* (Glencoe, Ill.: Free Press 1959), 55.

14 George Grant to Joan O'Donovan, 4 Jan. 1981, in *Selected Letters*, 312.

15 George Grant, *Time as History*, ed. William Christian (Toronto: University of Toronto Press 1995), 58.

16 George Grant to Joan O'Donovan, 1982, in *Selected Letters*, 324.

17 George Grant to Maude Grant, autumn 1951, Grant-Parkin Papers, MG 30 D59, National Archives of Canada.

18 George Grant to Maude Grant, 1952, ibid.

19 George Grant to Dennis Lee, 22 Dec. 1976, in *Selected Letters*, 296.

20 George Grant to Dennis Lee, November 1983, in ibid., 336. Though Grant never completed his book on Céline, interested readers should consult George Grant, 'Céline's Trilogy,' ed. S.V. Grant, in *George Grant and the Subversion of Modernity*, ed. Arthur Davis (Toronto: University of Toronto Press 1996).

21 Jacques Ellul, *The Technological Society* (New York: Knopf and Knopff 1965) 59.

22 George Grant, *Time as History* (Toronto: University Press 1995) 68.

23 George Grant, 'Faith and the Multiversity,' in *Technology and Justice* (Toronto: House of Anansi: 1986) 42.

24 George Grant, *Lament* (Ottawa: Carleton University Press 1997) 3.

25 Grant, private papers.

26 George Grant, *Philosophy in the Mass Age*, ed. William Christian (Toronto: University of Toronto Press 1995), 85.

27 George Grant to David Llwellyn Dodds, 11 Nov. 1986 in *Selected Letters*, 361.

PROLOGUE

Although Grant had studied at Oxford, the home of analytical philosophy, he always thought that philosophy was the study of the highest matters – the mystery of existence and how each human being should live his or her life. And although it was a difficult and demanding study, it was open to every human being to love the Good and to seek it.

What Is Philosophy? (1954)[*]

I want to try to describe what philosophy is. My job is to teach philosophy to youngsters. Just what is this subject that we try to teach them, and which is taught at all the universities of the world? Why is it that in all the great civilizations there have always been philosophers and that indeed we often judge the greatness of a society by the greatness of its philosophy?

The word philosophy comes from two Greek words, love and wisdom. Philosophy means the love of wisdom. Now most of us have some knowledge of what it is to love. Parents love their children – that is, the children are infinitely precious to them. Some of us at our worst moments love money in the same way. Money is what is infinitely precious to us. That is, to love somebody in the real sense, not the Hollywood sense, is to say that that person is not of relative but of absolute worth to one. People who love themselves think themselves of absolute worth. They are for themselves the centre of the universe.

But if it is fairly easy from our own experience to say what love is, it is far more difficult to know what we mean by the word wisdom. It is indeed quite easy to say what wisdom is not. It is not, for instance, knowledge in any specialized sense. We know people who have a great deal of knowledge about mathematics or medicine, of fixing radios or selling insurance, who despite that knowledge we would not call wise.

[*]Unpublished, 1954. George Grant personal papers, Halifax.

The great atomic scientist in the United States, Dr Oppenheimer,[*] obviously is a man of vast knowledge, but nobody who has followed his career could easily call him a wise man. Just like Einstein, outside his specialized knowledge field of physics he talks like a child. On the other hand, most of us have met people who have very little specialized knowledge and who one would yet call wise. For instance, I know a retired minister in Halifax who is no great specialist in any field but is one of the wisest men I have ever met.[†]

Now I think that gives us the clue to what wisdom is. We call people wise if they know how to live – if they know what is important in living. And when we speak about living we mean something to do with the whole of the person – that which goes to the very roots of an individual's life. And that is what we mean when we say philosophy is the love of wisdom. It is the desire to seek that which will give purpose and meaning and unity to life. That is the difference between philosophic and scientific knowledge. Scientific knowledge is always concerned with some part or aspect of life; philosophic knowledge is always concerned with the whole of human existence.

In other words, philosophy begins when we ask the questions: 'How should I live? What is life for? Why do I exist in the world?' Now of course for many people such questions as these do not arise as real questions. They think they know what life is really for. They think they know what is important. For instance, in North America today more and more people think they are certain what is of prime importance to living. It is to get more money, to buy a more expensive house, to have wider and more varied pleasures, to be a social success – that is what is known as getting on in the world. Once one has got a Chevrolet, get an Oldsmobile; once one has got an Oldsmobile, get a Buick. Among such people – and of course this kind of mood is present in all of us – there is little desire for wisdom, little desire to think what life is about. The practical getting on in the world is their philosophy – so they don't feel the need to think further.

In a nobler and deeper way the same thing is true of people who are

---

[*]Robert Oppenheimer (1904–67), director of the Manhattan Project and known as the father of the atomic bomb.

[†]The Reverend J.W.A. Nicholson, a retired United Church clergyman, who had earned, in Grant's eyes, a certain cachet because the United Church had once tried him for heresy.

held very simply by some clearly defined religion. If they take that religion seriously it tells them directly what is important about living. It gives them such certainty that they feel no need to think deeply about the meaning of life – that is, to ask philosophic questions. They live in tradition. And when I speak about religion I do not mean only as ancient and wise a tradition as Christianity. It is equally true of the great political religions of the twentieth century. In Soviet Russia, for instance, there is practically no philosophy, for the religion of communism provides for many people a simple Sunday school faith which tells them how to live.

Philosophy is for those who have moved beyond any simple certainty. It is for those who have come face to face with the mystery of existence and who have seen how profound a mystery it is. Philosophy is the attempt to fathom that profundity – that is, to find the wisdom which will enable us to live as we ought.

Now the sense of mystery arises for people in two ways; first from just plain wonder at the world around them, and secondly from the anguish of their own lives. That glorious man Plato – the greatest of all philosophers – said once that philosophy begins in wonder. We look at the immense spaces of the night – the worlds beyond worlds beyond worlds that the astronomers tell us about, and how can we not wonder what it is all for, where it all came from? We look at human history – at all the vast numbers of civilizations and billions of people who have existed, the traces of whom have entirely disappeared from the world – and we ask what human life is for. Certainly it exists in all children. When I say to my six-year-old daughter* that God made the world, she looks up in wonder to ask who then made God. When we meet a blind person my four-year-old son† asks why did God make some people blind – or why did God make mosquitos or sharks? Of course, the tragedy is that we kill that wonder in our children. We fill them with complacent conventional opinions and tame them to accept unquestioningly. We make them adjusted little members of the ant community. But still that spontaneous wonder in children is evidence that it is deeply in all of us. It is just our humanity that we desire to know, and that desire to know is the very root of philosophy.

---

*Rachel Grant.
†William Grant.

Of course, this sense of mystery comes to us not only in this natural spontaneous way – but also arises in the anguish and suffering which is so near the heart of all our lives. This anguish arises for us when people we love are dead or going to die – when we face the fact that inescapably we too must die. It faces us in all the suffering we undergo when we are disappointed in what we have desperately wanted. It arises for us most deeply in the guilt and shame we rightly feel when we have treated some other person cruelly or let some other person down. That is, when we see our shoddy little selves for what we truly are.

Most of us will try to do anything to avoid that anguish. We will do anything to forget that someday we shall die; we try to push aside the thought that we have treated people unfairly, by dubbing all our guilts 'neurotic.' We try to surround ourselves with pleasant thoughts – the next cigarette, the next dance, the next promotion, the next act of love. But inescapably the fact of our situation is there. At some moment – perhaps when we lie awake at night, perhaps when we are in pain, perhaps when we face the fact that somebody we love has no real care for us, perhaps even at our greatest moments of happiness when we know this happiness is bound to pass – at such moments we admit our situation and experience anguish. The whole mystery of human existence arises for us and we start to philosophize – to fathom that mystery in thought. For instance, these days if any of us really face what the cobalt bomb may mean – that human existence perhaps will cease to exist on this planet – that is, you and I and our children – we might really begin to face that mystery. Has the human story then been meaningless? Is my life, are my children's lives meaningless? It is in such moments that philosophy in its deepest sense arises.

Of course, the practical man will say, get on with the job – why think about such things – earn your living, bring up your family, do your duty, make the world more comfortable for other people. All one can say in answer to such practical people is that those who feel this anguish, meet this mystery, have no alternative to philosophy. It is what God has called them to do. Perhaps we may say even more. After all, an ape or a bee gets on with the job, earns his living, procreates and cares for his children, accepts his existence, adjusts to his society. Only man is capable of this attempt to understand the mystery of existence. It is only man who can rebel, feel anguish, think. Perhaps then in a very real sense, it is the ability to philosophize which gives man his real dignity, which makes him more valuable than a clever ape. One of the finest philosophers of all time, a Frenchman named Pascal,[*] once expressed this brilliantly. He said: 'Man is but a reed, the weakest thing in nature; but a thinking reed. It does not need the universe to take up arms to crush him; a vapour, a drop of water is enough to kill him. But, though the universe should crush him, a man would still be nobler than his destroyer, because he knows that he is dying, knows that the universe has got the better of him; the universe knows nothing of this.'

This means that philosophy is something inescapable to being a man. It is an activity rooted in the very nature of our humanity – not a pleasant academic exercise reserved for a few professors and students in a university. The farmer must find himself as much as the teacher; the businessman as much as the coal miner. It also means that philosophy is something that a man must do for himself. Nobody can make another man's philosophy for him. Other people can grow our food for us; other people can make our atom bombs for us; somebody else can cure us when we are sick – but nobody else can do our thinking for us. This is the ultimate truth of freedom. A man must do his own believing as he does his own dying.

This indeed takes me to one of the most commonly heard criticisms of philosophy – that there is no development in it, as, for instance, there is in the progressive development of the natural sciences. Science, it is said, is always growing in knowledge, philosophy is not. But to say this is to miss the whole point of philosophy – to fail to see what it is. It is not concerned with how men manipulate the public objects of the world – it is concerned with the journey of each individual's mind into the infinite. Therefore, philosophy must be lived through again and again in the life of each person. In science we are further ahead than the ancient Greeks or people at the time of Jesus. But philosophically our minds are not far ahead of the minds of Socrates or Jesus. Indeed, even the best of us only begin to touch at the hem of their garments. We must live through the same thought, the same agony they lived through, if we are to come to the majesty of their wisdom. That is why there is no progress in philosophy as there is in science. It is an activity which each new generation – indeed each new person – must live through for himself that he may find the ultimate vision for himself. This, again, is the very truth of freedom.

Another commonly heard criticism, related to this one and based on

---

[*] Blaise Pascal (1623–62), *Pensées*, §vi.347.

the same misunderstanding of the nature of philosophy, is the old cry: all philosophies contradict each other. Philosophy is blamed for being at once too diverse and too much the same. But in fact the major philosophies seldom contradict each other on fundamentals; the effect of doing so is a result of necessary differences of standpoints, emphasis, and idiom.

The way I have described philosophy has been as a very intimate and personal activity – something dealing with the core of the human mind. Of course, in the university it is presented to students in a more formal way. We try to put before the students what has been most illuminating in the great philosophizing of the past. The students study the writings that incorporate the fullest wisdom of the greatest philosophers. This study of the past is necessary, for, after all, each generation does not come into a new world – it comes into a world made rich by the tradition of the ages. Therefore, one of the things a man must do if he is to be wise himself is to partake of all that accumulation of wisdom. This study of the history of philosophy is the raw material out of which men can begin to build a philosophy of their own. Any man who has even elementary humility will want to find out what Aristotle and St Paul, Kant and Calvin said about a problem, and see in the great man's solution of that problem the beginnings of a solution of his own.

For instance, to such a central problem as 'what is truth?' we cannot expect any easy answer, and we need all the help we can get from those in the past who have had clearer minds and greater vision than ourselves. Do you remember Francis Bacon's wonderful description of the meeting between Pilate and Jesus. '"What is truth?" said jesting Pilate and would not wait for an answer.'[*] If we are not willing to wait for answers in philosophy, if we are not willing to learn from the wisdom of the past, how can we expect to get anything but a cheap answer to the problem 'What is truth?' And if we have a cheap answer to such a problem we are liable to have a cheap life. Indeed, it is the superficial flip way that we on this continent are bringing up our youngsters to have no respect for the wisdom of the past and to say that truth is what works and teaching them our rushing restless life, which makes one wonder what is going to happen to our society. In fact, one of our major tragedies is how little true philosophy there is amongst us. In our personal life, wisdom as an ideal is more and more replaced by success and wealth and adjustment. In our universities philosophy is being replaced

[*]Francis Bacon (1561–1626), *Essays*, I, 'Of Truth.'

by the study of natural science and useful techniques – studies that are popular because they lead to comfort and power. It is a sad fact but it must be admitted that we are a continent which has almost entirely given up the idea of philosophy.

Yet we must never despair for none of us is a slave to our society. The life of philosophy is open to all of us. And its reward is in truth infinite. For as we face the mystery of existence and pass in thought beyond a superficial view of the world, there will come to us, out of the mystery and the anguish, the certainty which is rooted not in foolishness but in truth. There will come to us indeed God – not God as he is so often thought of, as an insurance policy for the next world, or as a comforting drug – but God in his real and terrible presence. For that is finally what philosophy is – the practice of the presence of God.

Part 1

Politics and Morality

THE CHARACTER OF CANADA

Grant's grandfathers, Sir George Parkin and Principal G.M. Grant, were active in the Imperial Federation movement in the last two decades of the nineteenth century; they believed that Canada could not survive as an independent nation in North American without the counterweight of the British empire. Between 1943 and 1945, while Grant worked for the Canadian Association for Adult Education, he prepared two pamphlets exploring Canada's post-war future in a world that looked likely to be dominated by the superpower rivalry of the United States and the Soviet Union. These excerpts from The Empire: Yes or No? *explore many of the themes that he would develop in his political writings over the next twenty years, culminating in* Lament for a Nation *in 1965.*

The Empire: Yes or No? (1945)[*]

The origin of Canada as a nation is in the British North America Act.[†] And in the name of that Act we see indeed the main forces that have shaped our country. British, yes, and North American too; and from the amalgam of these two influences has come the Canada of today. The particular Canadianism, that we feel from the grey streets of Halifax to the foothills near Banff, from the wide horizons of the prairies to the lakes and rivers of the Algonquin Park, has been created from these two sources. Yes, Canada as a nation can truly be called British North America.

Today, however, there are in our midst certain English- and French-speaking citizens who decry the significance of our membership in the British Commonwealth. There are others, more numerous, who though paying lip service to the Commonwealth, belie their attachment to it in their activities or their apathy. It is necessary, therefore, that these Canadians who believe deeply in the value of the Commonwealth, for Canada and for the world, should reiterate their faith in it –

---

[*] George Grant, *The Empire: Yes or No?* (Toronto: Ryerson Press 1945).
[†] Now called the Constitution Act, 1867.

the faith that not only for the progress of the civilized world, but also for the existence of our nation as a free and democratic state, our membership in the Commonwealth is essential. Indeed, our reasons for remaining in the Commonwealth are not based on colonialism, or attachment to the past, but on the cold logic of the present. In this year 1945, every interest of Canada demands that we should remain intimately attached to the other British nations.

The first job in seeing our role in the British Commonwealth must be to look at what is happening in the world today. The first fact of the world today is that the United Nations have won complete victory over the forces of the fascist axis. This coalition of United Nations now comes out of the war as a possible nucleus for future world order. The gradual and organic development of the United Nations, from a mere coalition of powers in 1942 towards greater and greater unity, has spoken well for the sagacity of its leaders. In this the atomic age the failure of world order is too appalling to contemplate.

Imperialism

But though the first and most hopeful fact of the modern world is this developing new world order, let us not blind ourselves to the fact that the development of this world order into perfection will not happen overnight, and that every step of the way will be fraught with dangers and difficulties. Only if we recognize how difficult the job will be, shall we be clear enough and tough enough to accomplish it. The creation of the United Nations will by no means take us over into an ideal world. Friction between great and small powers will still remain. Self-interest and self-complacency will continue to beset nations and groups of nations, as they have beset individual men and nations in the past. Merely by vaguely inveighing against such words as imperialism and power politics we will not destroy them. By the very nature of life itself, power exists. By the very existence of life, it will be necessary to balance the stresses and strains of that power within the United Nations. Only if we recognize this will we be able to move forward gradually to the more perfect world order we desire.

The three great dominating powers of the world after the war will be three great empires. The two immense continental empires of the U.S.A. and the U.S.S.R, and the maritime empire of Great Britain.

There will be other powers. Perhaps in the near future France will return to its former noble stature, or China and India will become other great empires. But at the moment there is little doubt that these three are the mainspring of the United Nations. The U.S.A. will remain the dominant power in this hemisphere, and in most of the Pacific. The U.S.S.R. clearly is going to hold and expand its imperial sway from Central Europe to the Far East. The British Empire and Commonwealth will continue to encircle the globe. However much people may inveigh against such imperialism, in this spring of 1945, it is clearly the emergent pattern.

· · ·

The Necessity for a Third Power

But whereas the British Commonwealth and Empire help to mitigate continental regionalism by its world-wide nature, and at the same time cannot be just another power bloc, it is still in the realities of the present political situation the only group of nations with sufficient unity of purpose that can prevent a world organization from being totally dominated by the U.S.A. or the U.S.S.R. Without the British Commonwealth, the world organization will fall into two opposing camps.

For though the British Commonwealth is decentralized, it still has enough unity within itself to stand as a power between these two colossi. And power split three ways will surely be a much safer preserver of the peace than power divided between Washington and Moscow. The triumvirs of Rome in the dim past recognized that power was better divided three ways than two. For two always meant a division into two decided and hostile camps. Three means a more even balance.

So in the world we are coming into, it will be much safer to have, as well as Washington and Moscow, a third force like the British Commonwealth to stand with a firm heart in the councils of the world, and to keep it as strong as possible. For, it must be repeated, a world in which Washington and Moscow were supreme would be a world in which one empire controlled the Eurasian heartland and another the Americas, and no power on earth stood between them. It is as clear as crystal that we are moving in that direction today. Only the free maritime Commonwealth is sufficiently strong to prevent that division of power between them. Surely it is important that such a Commonwealth should exist as an effective body.

What Does This Mean for Canada?

It must be clearly stated that if the world is divided between Washington and Moscow (and the situation is sufficiently imminent not to be a mere bogeyman), nobody would have more to lose than Canada.

For if such an immense tragedy as conflict between these powers should take place, it would not take place in some distant corner of the globe, but on our own soil. Canada has indeed in the last years become the potential cockpit of the world, as Belgium was thirty years ago. As our north and south connections run to the U.S.A., so they run across the Pole to Moscow. As our east and west connections join us together, so they carry us towards Siberia and Asia in the east and to Great Britain and Europe in the west. We would be at the very centre of the conflict between the two great continental empires. It is clearly in our most direct and immediate interest to prevent that. If we do not, we will be caught like the nut in the nutcracker.

Our best means of preventing that tragedy is our continued membership in the Commonwealth. Cut off from the British nation, as an independent country, we would have little alternative but to join South American nations in the hemispheric empire of the U.S.A. And as part of that we would be strengthening the power of the U.S.A. to retire into isolation. We would be abetting its ability to establish an anti-Russian bloc. We would be increasing the chances for an American-Soviet conflict. On the other hand, as a member of the Commonwealth, we would be doing exactly the opposite. Friendly to the U.S.A., we would still not be her satellite. By our world-wide interest, we would, as her chief neighbour, be pulling her out of continental isolation and towards effective commitments to a world order.

• • •

Practical Decisions Must Be Made

Those people who wish Canada to retire from the British Commonwealth and Empire, and thereby greatly weaken that great organization, should think of a world in which it did not exist. What would such a world be like?

1. It would be a world in which the only free association of nations with membership in every part of the globe did not exist. A world where the only effective organization of free nations, cutting across regional and hemispheric boundaries, was destroyed.

2. It would be a world where the most effective experiments in the development of backward people towards political democracy and economic maturity did not exist.

3. It would be a world where the mainstay of Western Christian civilization did not exist. And Western Christian civilization, for all its faults, has developed in practice, more than any other, the practical concept of man's intrinsic and ultimate worth as an individual and the right of mankind to be free and to develop freely towards a higher and fuller destiny. And, as both André Siegfried[*] the Frenchman, or Cohen-Portheim[†] the Austrian have pointed out, Western Christian civilization has little chance of survival if the British Commonwealth and Empire goes down.

It was all very well for us in the 1920s and 1930s to think of the British Empire and Commonwealth as being dismembered, and to talk glibly of some uncertain perfection taking its place. But surely the terribleness of the last years has taught us that there is a good chance that what would take its place is not something better, but something a lot worse; that though the Empire and Commonwealth must be improved and many of its anachronisms wiped away, in 1940 it at least stood for a certain modicum of liberty, dignity, and decency when these values were all but swept away. And it bore this responsibility before either of the other two empires, the U.S.A. or the U.S.S.R. had accepted their responsibility for the maintenance of freedom.

• • •

Should We Preserve Our Nationhood?

The meaning and significance of Canada as a nation is that on the northern half of this continent a sovereign state has been created, friendly to the U.S.A. but essentially different. And the basic reason why

---

[*]André Siegfried (1875–1959), author of *The Race Question in Canada* (1907) and *Le Canada, Les Deux Races; Problèmes politiques contemporains* (1906).
[†]Paul Cohen-Portheim (d. 1932), author of *England, the Unknown Isle* (1935).

we are not part of the U.S.A. is because we have remained in the British orbit. The U.S.A. broke its ties with Western Europe. We never did. We kept our close connection, not alone with the United Kingdom, but with Europe in general. It is that difference that kept us separate from the U.S.A. It is that difference that made us a nation. It is that difference that preserved our individuality. Let us not fool ourselves. The same factors will continue to operate in our history in the future as they did in the past. If we have no link with the British Commonwealth we will soon cease to be a nation and become absorbed in the U.S.A. On the other hand, within the Commonwealth we will be able to develop the form of government and social order that we desire.

Those who want to destroy our membership in the British Commonwealth in the name of a greater Canadian nationhood are fooling themselves. They are really destroying our nation. Because without that membership no power on earth can keep us from being absorbed by the U.S.A. And with that we cease to be a nation.

. . .

What Is Canada?

Of course, in the final analysis this question boils down to what we consider Canada to be. There are now, and have always been in the past, two distinct versions of this. One is that it is only an unfortunate accident that we were ever created and that the sooner we join the United States, the better. The other (and what seems to the present writer a much nobler version) is the vision of Macdonald, Laurier, and Borden, that on the northern half of this continent has been created a nation, raised in a different tradition from the U.S.A. and dedicated to the extension of certain different political and social concepts.

But what are these concepts? It is always difficult to define such things in bald and general terms. We Canadians feel them in our daily lives, and we see them in intimate and immediate ways. We understand them in particular instances as they affect us, rather than rationalizing them into generalizations. But now that they are challenged they must be enunciated. The essential principle around which Canada has been established is embodied in the age-old struggle in human society as to how free each individual can be and yet live in an ordered society where that freedom is not so abused that it infringes on the freedom of others. Where does freedom for one person to do what he likes mean lack of freedom for other people? This conflict, so continuous in human life, can be expressed in many ways: the relation of the one to the many, of freedom to authority, of liberty to order. But it is the same old question. How do individuals live together in peace and harmony?

The main thought of Americans on this subject has emphasized the inalienable right of the individual to be free to do as he chooses, whatever effect it might have on society as a whole. We in Canada have put the balance far more on the side of order or the good of society. The individual has certain rights, but these rights must be strictly prevented from causing any disruption to the society as a whole. This stress on order in our society has been true of French as well as English Canada. In the opening of the west, also, we saw to it that the forces of law and order preceded settlement and did not follow it, as was often the case in the U.S.A. The RCMP was an instrument of the central government for maintaining order in the new territories, the like of which there never was in the U.S.A. or any other country of this hemisphere. Now, in modern times, on the question of wartime restrictions, for instance, there has been a widespread realization in Canada that because these restrictions were for the good of society as a whole they must be accepted, and they have been. In the U.S.A. there has been widespread attack on them as limiting the freedom of the individual.

It is unwise and presumptuous to say which balance is better – that of the U.S.A. or that of Canada. But let us admit frankly that it is important that this continent should have this diversity of social philosophy. The great question of the modern world is going to be to what extent, within the complicated pattern of industrialized civilization, freedom and authority can be truly integrated. How far in this new and intricate world will it be possible for men to have individual freedom without disrupting too many other men by their actions? How far will men have to be curbed by authority, so that they do not interfere with others? In 1929 the U.S.A. saw the results of complete freedom. Yet that nation still, more than anywhere else, deifies the right of the individual to do as he likes. In the U.S.S.R. the other extreme has been tried, wherein the individual has been subordinated to the good of society as a whole, and his acts are ruthlessly curbed for the sake of the general order.

• • •

We cannot judge the British Commonwealth from our petty interests alone (however well these are satisfied,) but on the highest criteria of political morality. For today in the modern world, with it more than with any other political institution, lies the hope of Christian man, of ethical man, of man the reasonable, moral being who stands before God and history. One can indeed say that ethical man, reasonable man, is a last remaining fragment of the dark ages, and that the new man is one ruled by marxian economics or Freudian sex – a man, in fact, who is brutal and unreasonable, unethical and material, and who is ruthlessly dominated by his appetites. Then we can disavow the British Commonwealth. But if we believe in Christian man, the finest flower of all that Western civilization has produced, then there can be no doubt that our chief hope in the survival of such values is in the survival of the British Commonwealth. Canada has a vital responsibility. Canada must choose.

MASS SOCIETY

Grant continued to believe in the importance of adult education after he took his teaching position at Dalhousie. William Grant, his father, had been active in setting up the annual Couchiching conferences, which brought together business people, academics, and politicians to discuss important contemporary political and social issues, and George Grant himself addressed the conference in 1955. On this occasion as on others, he demonstrated that among his many strengths as a philosopher was an ability to communicate complicated ideas. A member of the audience at Couchiching in 1955 recalled his reaction to Grant's talk: 'What I remember particularly was that this speech appeared to challenge many fundamental theological precepts of the Christian religion – although I felt at the end of his speech that I had never before listened to such a profoundly religious man ... It was the first time I had ever listened to anyone who seemed to be driven by spiritual, almost mystical, imperatives which profoundly affected his perception of the world around' (Paul Roddick to William Christian, 25 February 1991).

The whole of one's effort at everything seems extremely 'sub specie atomic bomb'; any effort must be directed to control of that. The bomb seems to stand over one like damnation.

– George Grant to Maude Grant, 1945

The Minds of Men in the Atomic Age 1955[*]

I don't intend to discuss whether we are going to be blown up or whether the human race is going to be sensible enough to survive. Whether we are going to destroy ourselves by Intercontinental Ballistic Missiles or slowly corrupt the very basis of our animal existence – I do not know ... I can imagine a prosperous society, without war, of healthy animals adjusted to worshiping their machines which could be so disgusting that one could will that it should be destroyed.

Therefore what I want to talk about is the quality of mind or soul which exists on this continent. In other words, if we aren't smashed in an all-out fight with the Asiatics, what kind of society is developing here at home?

The great fact of Canada today – indeed the great fact of the whole modern world – is that we are now living in the mass scientific society and this is something totally new in the experience of the human race. All the forms of our life – sexual, economic, political, artistic, moral, and above all religious – must be seen within this new situation – the world of the big city, automation, and the atom.

When I want to think of what the mass society is, and how much it has come to be in Canada, I think of Don Mills development in the north of Toronto. Thousands of comfortable, simple homes thrown up within a year from which hundreds of white-collared workers go forth to the new clean factories and offices. A community whose centres are an enormous Dominion store and Brewers warehouse – a community where families are co-operative enterprises to get the latest in electrical equipment and where children in mass schools are taught to be adjusted to their total life situation, watch the same television programmes, drink the same drinks, and go charging around in the same over-powered automobiles, the bumpers of which are now decorated with phallic symbols. Now of course, not all Canada is the mass world yet. But gradually and surely we move towards it. For instance, the farm community, as it once existed, is bound slowly to disappear – for even if people are farmers by profession they must become more and more town people with the automobile, the radio and television, the machine, and mass education. Indeed, of one thing we may be certain,

[*]'The Minds of Men in the Atomic Age,' in *Texts of Addresses Delivered at the Twenty-Fourth Annual Couchiching Conference* (Toronto: Canadian Institute on Public Affairs and the Canadian Broadcasting Corporation 1955; repr. 1985), 39–45.

the economy of organized obsolescence and high returns for the sales-
man, the broker, and the engineer, public technical education and
social standardization, mass stimulated sexual life and mass popular
entertainment, this is the world which must find an ever fuller incarnation in Canada. I do not know what forms of the human spirit this new
world will produce – but one thing I do know – no sensible person can
believe that the same kind of people are going to come out of this environment as came out of the old Canadian towns and farms.

Now there is no doubt that the mass society is here to stay – unless the
bombs really start falling. Nor have I any doubt about the great good it
has brought. It is obviously good that women should have automatic
washing machines; it is almost as good that we men should have cars.
The fact that machines do our work means we have more free time and
human freedom requires this time. In the old days leisure was something reserved for the privileged. Now it is open to more and more and
surely what we need for ourselves we must see as necessary for others,
and this possibility of leisure for all does involve the machine. Even
modern medicine, however much of a sacred cow it has become, we
must judge as good. Let anyone who has a child in pain doubt that.
Indeed, at the profoundest level we must welcome the mass scientific
society, despite all its horrors. For it has put us in a new relation to
nature. We can now as never before choose to make our world, to use
nature and abuse her, but less than ever before need we submit to her
as necessity. More and more life becomes an open decision of the spirit.

But let us also be certain what a terrible price is being paid all over
North America for the benefits of the mass society. And what that price
is can easily be stated. Economic expansion through the control of
nature by science has become the chief purpose of our existence. It has
become the goal to which everything else must be subordinated, the
God we worship. Indeed, for the last three hundred years there have
been a band of thinkers telling men to worship the world. Now at last in
North America this has become the dominant religion, which shapes
our society at nearly every point. What is wrong with this religion? The
plain fact that man's real purpose in life is not this. The goal of human
existence is not to be found in the world of nature – but in freedom.
Indeed, to be a man at all and not just an animal who looks like a man
but is not, is to strive to become free. And a free man is a person who is
not ruled by fear or passion – or the world around him – but by the eternal world of truth and goodness which is there to be realized by every
thought and action in our lives. The freest of all men once said: 'I have

overcome the world.'* And this is what life is for, to overcome the world, as we live in it deeply.

This is our human destiny, because our environment of nature depends upon an absolute environment – call it if you will God – and to live in the presence of that absolute and to judge the world by it is what it is to be free. I do not mean by this that a free man will turn away from the world in aloof isolation. After all, the man I have called freest lived in no ivory tower, but met the world most directly on a cross. What I do mean is that the free man is he who does not abandon himself to the mood of his age, who lives at the point where the passing moments of his life are met by the urgent present of the eternal. Such a man is not sheer animal or, worse, a machine.

Therefore, the price we have paid for the expanding economy is that by making it God men turn away from their proper purpose in this life. There is nothing wrong with automobiles and washing machines, but they must be known as simply means – means of richness of life for individuals and society.

But the expanding economy is no longer a means to us – a means for the liberation of the spirit – it has become an end in itself and as such is enslaving us. It so sets the tone and pattern of our society that the standards it imposes close people off from knowing what life is for. Look at the wives of our executives; look at the young men in the sack suits who have taken the vow to success; look at the girls in Woolworth's selling all day till they are exhausted and then being peddled a dream of heaven from Hollywood and NBC. The boom world creates like an aura its own standard of success – of what really matters in life – and that aura lies over everything, choking people with the fear of failure in terms of those standards, and cuts us off from any truer vision of life.

If you want to see just how much the expanding economy has become our God read a book called *Canada's Tomorrow*.† It is an account of a conference in the Westinghouse Company called together to discuss the future of our country. Leaders of all kinds from business and labour and government, from the universities and science and journalism were present. Well, the unanimous report of that conference was just more and more of the expanding economy – more trade, more production, more scientific research, more people. Its motto was

---

*Jesus, in John 16:33.
†Canadian Westinghouse, *Canada's Tomorrow: Papers and Discussion* (Toronto: Macmillan 1954).

the bigger the better; or size is greatness. The book should have been called *The Messiah Machine*. There was no attempt to look at what all the expansion is for or what kind of people are produced by such a world. It was just taken for granted that the true happiness of persons is always to be found in short-term economic gain. No questions of quality were asked; only questions of quantity. No ultimate questions were asked at all. If this is Canada's tomorrow, count me out of it.

And why I mention this book is that the people at this conference were the leaders of Canada – the men who are making our society and whose thoughts about our future are therefore really important. If these people think this way, this is the kind of Canada we are going to have. For let's have no soft democratic soap. It is the powerful and the influential who shape the short-term destiny of a country. If this 'the bigger-the-better' spirit prevails among these educated leaders, it gradually shapes all of us.

One comic side of this conference *Canada's Tomorrow* was that though there was the usual talk about the dangers of communism and Russia, the kind of society outlined at it doesn't seem very different from the society the Russian leaders are building for their people. If a conference of this sort had been called among Russian managers and university presidents and officials, the pattern of Soviet Tomorrow would probably have been very much the same – the same quantitative judgment of success.

Indeed, one of the communist myths which most of our businessmen and government leaders wholeheartedly accept – though they would loathe it to be known as a marxist myth – is 'seek ye first the kingdom of the boom and all shall be added unto you.' What they say is that economic development must come first and it will inevitably bring in its trail the pursuit of truth and beauty. Indeed, the very words 'truth and beauty' are seldom used now to denote realities, but rather a confused blend of sentiment and culture. Nice for those who have the time, but less real than the 'hard facts of life' – 'the business of living.' Just as it takes a while for the new rich to learn to spend their money with taste, so it will take time for culture to flower in our new rich society. Like much marxist theory, this is so much liberal illusion. What should be perfectly obvious is that if you pursue economic prosperity at the expense of everything else, what you will get is economic prosperity at the expense of everything else.

To see our minds in the atomic age, it is particularly necessary to look at our schools, our universities, and our churches. For the schools, the universities, and the churches are the chief institutions which can lead men to freedom in the truth. Love and art, thought and prayer are after all the activities which distinguish men from the other beasts, and it is the school, the university, and the church upon which we are chiefly dependent for stimulation of these activities. Our political and economic institutions have a function which is largely negative – they exist to prevent bad things happening: the schools and universities and churches have the positive role, they exist to stimulate the good.

Now our schools have been going through a terribly difficult period. When I criticize them I do not mean to lay all the blame on any particular shoulders. All of us, our ancestors and ourselves, are corporately involved in the guilt of what our schools have become. The mass democratic society has insisted on mass education. This, of course, has been the only possible and right course. But let us have no doubt that this process has meant a falling away of quality. What has happened is that the schools have been trying to carry on their job in a society which by and large does not think that education is important. What parents in the mass society are interested in is that their children should be fitted for success and adjustment, not educated. And what has been particularly sad is that so many educational administrators have not only given in to that pressure but have accepted the philosophy of worldly success and adjustment as a true account of what the schools are for. This is where I agree one hundred percent with Hilda Neatby.[*] The acceptance by so many educationalists of the philosophy of John Dewey[†] has in general meant the surrender by the teacher and the school of their proper function. If you say with Dewey that the intellect is solely a servant of social living, then you are saying that human beings have no transcendent purpose beyond society – no need for liberation of the mind. Indeed, such liberation is now no longer considered even a respectable goal. How can it be, since it is almost the exact opposite of the adjustment which the psychologists and the progressive educators teach us to aspire to? Nowadays, who really minds about prejudices, illusions, myths, and superstitions as long as they are the right ones, the

---

[*]Hilda Neatby (1904–75) called for a return to basics in primary school education in her controversial *So Little for the Mind* (1953).

[†]John Dewey (1859–1952), American educationalist and philosopher. He was a member of the pragmatist school, which treated education as a training for problem solving. His best-known works include *The School and Society* (1899) and *Experience and Education* (1938).

socially acceptable ones, the mentally healthy ones, the good Canadian ones?

What is meant by successful democratic living is conformity to the lowest common denominator of desire in our society. With such a philosophy the schools exist to pander to that mediocrity of desire rather than to lead children to know what is truly worth desiring. No wonder school teaching is a despised and underpaid profession. Teachers are seen as servants of the desires of the multitude.

To go a step downward, the surrender of the universities to the boom spirit is overwhelming. I watch it every day of my life. Universities are now places where young people can insure their entrance into the prosperous part of society by learning some technique, and where staff employees (once known as professors) increase the scope of some immediately useful technique. Intellect is respected, if at all, as a tool which can help one to do certain things in the world more efficiently. It is no longer valued for its relation to its proper object, truth. For there is no truth which it concerns us to know, there is only the truth with which we are concerned to do things. Indeed, three powerful forces in our society, business, government, and the democratic many, all have used their power to kill the university as a place of truth seeking and turn it into a successful technological institute. The businessmen who rule our universities naturally see them as places to perpetuate in the young the desires of the market place and of competition. Governments break down the balance of the university by encouraging those studies useful for defence and prosperity. It would be foolish, for instance, to blame the government for setting up the National Research Council – an institution perfectly valid in itself – but let us face the consequences of its existence for the university and the nation. It means we are channelling our ablest students into a narrow training in physical science and this will mean finally a nation which knows nothing else and believes there is nothing more to know but this. Perhaps the disappearance of the liberal university was an inevitable accompaniment of the expanding economy but let us not fool ourselves as to what this disappearance means to the kind of world that is coming into existence.

Last and saddest we come to the churches. Let me say immediately that when I speak of the churches I speak only of my own tradition, the Protestant. And here we come to the heart of the matter. For what men believe to be ultimately true is what makes them what they are and through them their society. And Protestantism is the basic issue because North America has been more deeply formed by Protestantism than by any other influence. Indeed, the central riddle of our history is why Protestantism, centred as it was on a great affirmation of freedom and the infinite, has been the dominant force in shaping a society which is now so little free and so little aware of the infinite. To answer that riddle is not possible here, but what must be said clearly is that whatever the present outward success of Protestantism, it is faced by a deep inward failure. That inward failure is seen in the fact of its surrender to become a tame confederate of the mass secular society. The ideal minister has become the active democratic organizer who keeps the church going as a place of social cohesion and positive thinking à la Norman Vincent Peale.[*] If he can promote building, increase organization, provide inspiration on Sunday and convince young people that there are more socially acceptable activities than sex and drinking, he is a success. Best of all, if he knows a little empirical psychology, he will understand that when a church member gets into real spiritual difficulties he should be sent to a psychiatrist (the man who can really get things done in the world of the spirit). What is, however, wrong about it is that it is a soft substitute for the real work of the church, which is to teach people through thought and prayer and worship to seek the ultimate truth, and to live by it. In my opinion, to this, their real job, the Protestant churches are largely indifferent.

I do not want to be pessimistic, but when asked to give a diagnosis, one must be honest. Nothing has done us more harm in Canada than that aura of self-congratulation with which we surround ourselves. 'This great country of ours' or the 'Kitimat[†] and democracy' routine which now goes the rounds in pulpits, service clubs, and political platforms. 'Take what you want, said God, take it and pay for it.'[‡] Let us not doubt what we have wanted, what we have taken, and *how we are paying for it.*

Of course, this is not to say that we can or should turn back from the technological society. What I am saying is that the great job in Canada now does not lie in further economic expansion and quantitative progress, but in trying to bring quality and beauty of existence into that

---

[*]An American popular psychologist and author of the best-selling book *The Power of Positive Thinking* (New York: Prentice-Hall 1952).
[†]Kitimat in British Columbia was the site of a major aluminum smelter built by Alcan.
[‡]In *Technology and Justice*, Grant describes this as a Spanish proverb. He first mentions it in his *Journal* of 1942. See *George Grant: Selected Letters*, ed. William Christian (Toronto: University of Toronto Press 1996), 106.

technological world – to try and make it a place where richness of life may be discovered. And of course some people in Canada are realizing this in their lives right now. I think of a brilliant architect who is not interested in making a fortune but in seeing how the city of Toronto can be more than an efficient machine of sewers and superhighways, rather a place in which human beings can lead a good life. I think of ministers who are making their churches places of adoration rather than issuers of eternal insurance policies. I think of the man who runs a small garage where the repairing of cars is made a work of excellence and interest rather than greed. I think of young people who have the courage to be schoolteachers when to the world it is a mark of their failure. I think of people in broadcasting and TV who use all their intelligence and integrity to see that these instruments are used for the dissemination of truth. I think of artists who give themselves to reality and beauty rather than quick financial success. I think of philosophers who practise the presence of God.

Whether freedom and love will be realized in the technological world who can tell? Or will our society pour into its emptiness the bare idea of pleasure in all its manifold, fascinating, and increasingly perverted forms – till force and mediocrity come entirely to rule us?

I do not want to be pessimistic. However, what is certain, beyond doubt, is that whether we live at the end of the world or at the dawn of a golden age or neither, it still counts absolutely to each one of us that in and through the beauty and anguish, the good and evil of the world, we come in freedom upon the joy unspeakable.

EQUALITY AND THE NDP

In 1960 Grant was invited to join with Michael Oliver, Pierre Trudeau, and others to help chart the direction of a new progressive political party to replace the Co-operative Commonwealth Federation (CCF), soon to be called the New Democratic Party (NDP). Together they produced a book, Social Purpose for Canada. *Although he was initially drawn to the party because it challenged the materialism and vulgarity of capitalism, his strong pacifist beliefs forced him to break with the NDP when it voted to defeat John Diefenbaker's Conservative government in 1962 on the issue of whether to accept nuclear weapons for Canada. And, while he welcomed a strong alternative to the capitalist parties, he never felt completely comfortable with the NDP since most of its members did not accept his view that equality had to be grounded in the equality of souls before God.*

An Ethic of Community (1961)[*]

In the last twenty years we Canadians have achieved the biggest economic expansion of our history. We have been able to impose our dominion over nature so that we can satisfy more human desires than ever before. We have moved from producing primarily raw materials to being an industrial society of mass production and mass consumption such as the United States. Every year a higher percentage of Canadians lives in the new environment of the mass society. This achievement has been due partially to special Canadian circumstances – the vigour and initiative of our people, the rewards from new resources on the northern frontier of this continent – but even more has it been due to the world-wide scientific and technological revolution of the twentieth century. The organizing genius of the American applied the scientific discoveries of the European with great vigour to the problems of production and so created the first mass consumption society in history. We now recognize that this form of society will spread to all parts of the world.

What is even more fundamental about our society than its structure of 'state capitalist' power is that it is a 'mass society.' The term 'mass society' is inadequate shorthand for the radically new conditions under which our highly organized technological society makes us live. These new conditions are experienced most profoundly in the growing urban conglomerations such as Toronto and Los Angeles, but nearly all the people in North America now have a share of them. The farmer listens to television and drives a car and may even organize his supply of rain; he may not experience the mass society quite so directly as does a resident of Toronto, but he still experiences it. What makes this aspect of modern life more fundamental than the capitalist structure of power is that this is the condition of life towards which all human beings are moving, whether their institutions are capitalist or not. Certain problems produced by these conditions are common to any mass society. Indeed, even if our capitalist structure disappears in Canada we will still live in a mass society. It seems imperative, therefore, to try to distin-

---

[*]George Grant, 'An Ethic of Community,' in *Social Purpose for Canada,* ed. Michael Oliver (Toronto: University of Toronto Press 1961), 3–26.

guish between those problems which are directly a product of our capitalist institutions and those which are indigenous to any mass society.

The term 'mass society' is used to summarize a set of conditions and
experiences so new and so different from the past that nobody can
describe them adequately or fathom accurately what is coming to be in
the world. Nevertheless, certain generalizations must be attempted.
This is a society in which high individual acquisition and consumption
of goods and services is increasingly open to most in return for comparatively short hours of work and in which an immense variety of commodities is ready to attract and to encourage a vast diversity of human
desires. It is a society which requires a high technical competence from
many to keep it operating efficiently and where therefore what is
demanded of most people is to be skilled at one small part of the whole
enterprise but not necessarily knowledgeable about the whole. It is a
society in which most people live within and under the control of massive organizations (private and governmental), the purposes and direction of which are quite external to them. The population is more and
more concentrated in the big cities, that is, in environments so complex that they must remain unfathomable to the individual and in
which the individual's encounters with other persons cannot always or
even frequently be with neighbours he knows, but are rather with
strangers who are likely to appear as impersonal units to him. It is only
necessary to compare shopping in a supermarket and in a country
store, or driving to work in a small town and on a metropolitan freeway,
to see the different human relations which arise in this new life.

The result of living in such a society is that individuals experience a
new kind of freedom and independence, and also a new kind of control
and dependence. The freedom is not only that in a high-consumption
economy a multitude of new choices and experiences is open to people, but also that in this environment the traditional standards of conduct become less operative. The high technical competence required
and the kind of education necessary to produce it takes men to the
point of technical reason where they see themselves as 'wised up' and as
not bound by the old ethical and religious standards. Authorities such
as the family and the church become less powerful so that individuals
are free to make their own standards. At the same time as the mass society produces this new sense of freedom, it also produces new impersonal authorities which bind the individual more than before, at the
level both of action and of opinion. In large cities the maintenance of
order in the vast tangle of conflicting egos requires a determined gov-

ernment and police force which must inevitably treat the individual arbitrarily and as a cipher. The individual is also coerced in what he desires and what he believes to be true by the instruments of mass communication which press on him from every side, presenting forcefully standards which suit the purposes of big organizations. Indeed, this control of action and opinion has been intensified by the fact that the cold war has made North America something of a garrison state.

What is central to this new experience and what distinguishes it from living in the old small town and rural worlds is that the individual is at one and the same time more dependent on big institutions and yet less organically related to them. This has meant inevitably a dying away of the individual's effective participation in politics. The institutions which control us are so powerful and so impersonal that individuals come to believe that there is no point in trying to influence them; one must rather live with them as they are. The result is that more and more people think of the state as 'they' rather than as 'we.' In great cities where so much of existence is public, individuals find their most real satisfaction in private life because here their freedom is operative, while in the public sphere they know their actions to have less and less significance. Thus, the mass society calls into question the possibility of democratic government, founded as it was on the idea that each citizen could and should exert his influence on the course of public affairs.

In general it can be said that the mass society gives men a sense of their own personal freedom while destroying the old orders of life which mediated meaning to men in simpler environments. Indeed, as men sense their freedom to make themselves, unhampered by the old traditions, they may find it difficult to give content and meaning to that freedom, so that more easily than in the past their lives can reflect a surrender to passivity and the pursuit of pleasure as a commodity. When men have no easily apprehendable law of life given them by tradition, the danger is that their freedom will be governed by an arbitrary and external law of mediocrity and violence which will debase their humanity rather than fulfil it. This relation between increased freedom and the lack of well-defined meanings is the essential fact with which any politics of the mass age must come to grips. The capitalist structure of our institutions undoubtedly gives this problem its own peculiar tint, but basically the same problem will be present in all societies, whatever their economic structure, once they have reached a mature stage of technological development.

Despite the inadequacies of present economic arrangements, a

greater cause for criticism of our society can be found in areas which
are not simply economic but extend over the whole range of human
well-being. In these areas it is more difficult to judge what is good and
bad in our society and thus more difficult for socialists to state clearly
and realistically how their goals differ from those now served. This can
be seen as soon as one compares the goals of socialism in a society of
scarcity with its goals in a society of affluence. On what grounds does a
socialist party ask people to vote for it under high-consumption conditions? It is clear, for example, that if there were a major economic catastrophe in North America the power of a socialist party would be vastly
increased. But no sane person desires such a catastrophe. Nor does it
seem likely. What seems likely is that technology will continue to bring
us growing prosperity and that our present institutions, though not
dividing that prosperity fairly, will do a sufficiently adequate job of
management to prevent any widespread or bitter discontent. In such a
society there may not be the goads of hunger to provoke dissent. This
being so, by what criteria of human well-being would the socialist criticize such a society?

It becomes more and more important for socialists to have a profound view of human good as society's most pressing problems become
less simply quantitative and begin to involve qualitative distinctions. If a
child is undernourished, if a family is living in one room, if a man has to
do hard or boring physical work for twelve hours a day, it is easy to see
what is needed for greater well-being: more food, more room, shorter
hours. There is still a multitude of such direct quantitative problems in
Canada and the old socialist ethic of egalitarian material prosperity is
the principle under which they can be solved. Nevertheless, it is clear
that as we move to greater technological mastery (a movement that can
only be stopped by war) the most pressing social questions will call
forth judgments as to which activities realize our full humanity and
which inhibit it. What can be done to make our cities communities in
which the human spirit can flourish? How far can we go in seeing that
in all work, particularly in large factories, construction jobs, and offices,
the dull or even degrading element is cut to a minimum and the creative responsible part brought to a maximum? How far can we make
the association of experts and power elites sufficiently open for large
numbers of people to take part in those decisions which shape their
lives? How can we stimulate education (in its broadest sense) so that
the new leisure will be more than a new boredom of passive acquiescence in pleasures arranged by others? How can we see that in right-

fully cultivating the fullest equality we do not produce a society of mediocrity and sameness rather than of quality and individuality? How can we produce an order and self-discipline in society which restrains the selfish and the greedy without becoming so authoritarian that individual initiative is crushed? How can we cultivate freedom for the individual without having it become identified (as it is now) with ruthless self-interest and the grasping of more than a fair share?

Any set of institutions is finally held together by a general conception of well-being which pervades them all. For example, in the last twenty years the chief Canadian ideal of manhood has become the ambitious young executive, aggressive in his own interests, yet loyal to his corporation, with a smart wife and two happy children. (He is sexually adjusted yet respectable, and never puts sex above the interest of the corporation.) He looks forward to a continually rising income and continually rising power and prestige. He will drive increasingly expensive cars and live in an increasingly expensive neighbourhood. He plays a part in respectable community activities (such as charities and art galleries), but sees that this does not interfere with the interests of his corporation or himself and keeps it clear that what really matters in life is business and ambition. He tries to make his opinions on all matters conform to what is considered 'sound' in the higher echelons of his corporation and knows he can only take part in politics or other activities insofar as his superiors approve. That such a young man should be increasingly the ideal of our society is inevitable: this ideal best serves our corporations and they do everything in their power to encourage and even create it. The advertisements of conspicuous consumption are addressed to these young aspirants and their idealized image comes back to us from the advertisements.

Such concepts of well-being (let the cynical call them mythology) are the visions in response to which the individual models and fashions himself. In developing such an ideal capitalism has not been without sense. The people who take up this ideal are full of the energetic spirit which assists certain forms of economic growth. Yet at what price in human well-being has this image and reality been created? For it is an ideal which can be achieved by very few. As a wise man has written about Canada: 'It needs only a simple exercise in arithmetic to show that at any given moment, all but a very small minority, even of employed adult men, have passed the age when they can expect any kind of promotion. Business ambition is available as motivation only for the few, even in Canada.'[1]

The result of this is the frustration of many who attempt to pursue the ideal; but beyond this is the sad fact that its pervasiveness prevents any widespread expression of other ideals of human conduct which are more universally fulfilling. It thus persuades too much of our best talent to direct itself along one route. The immense rewards it offers (plus its public identification with true success) have led too large a percentage of our energetic young people into this one activity at the expense of other socially necessary and desirable activities, for example, schoolteaching, public service, pure science, social work, the ministry, and the arts. When we recognize how much better comparatively the Russians are doing in elementary education than ourselves, we must face the fact that the Russian communal idea encourages respect for schoolteaching in a way that our capitalist ethic cannot.

Since reward in money and power are directed by state capitalism to those concerned with goods which can be produced privately at a profit, other activities tend to become pale shadows of business. The word 'business' is now tacked on to all our professions and pursuits: 'the medical business,' 'the legal business,' 'the entertainment business,' 'the education business,' the newspaper business.' ('The religion business' is more advanced in the United States than it is as yet in Canada.) Health, entertainment, information, order, beauty and truth are all commodities which individuals purvey at a profit and can only be socially justified if they can be 'sold' at a profit. The economic self-seeking of the individual is the only instrument available for the production of excellence. Yet this must frustrate excellence arising in many fields where the profit motive is not sufficient for achievement. These fields, where capitalist incentives fail, are the very ones where we most need success in the age of affluence.

Questioning of this capitalist ideal may be raised at an even higher level of morality. The type of young executive described can easily pass over from healthy competitive energy to ruthlessness in his own interests within his corporation, and ruthlessness in the relations of his corporation to the rest of society. Indeed, the ideal tends to encourage ruthlessness as the very mark of the manly. But such ruthlessness is the mainspring of that division of person from person which is the cause of all social disruption. It is the very denial of our membership one with another: a more insidious type of sin than the personal weaknesses we often exclusively identify with that word. A society is not likely to be a place of healthy loyalties and ordered cohesion if its members are taught to pursue first and foremost their economic self-interest and if its leaders are chosen from those who pursue that self-interest more ruthlessly.

Indeed, the most dangerous result of state capitalism is that our society recruits its chief leadership from the executives who have been most successful in living out the capitalist ideal. As later essays will show in more detail, the top executives of the corporations will not only control our economic life, but also decisively control other institutions of our society – our political parties, our universities, our churches, our charities. For example, the leaders of the great corporations are an overwhelming majority of the members of the governing boards of our universities. The higher education which they control must therefore be in the last analysis the kind which their vision of life dictates. Is it likely that men trained to manage corporations whose chief end is maximum profit will be people of wide social vision? Can it be hoped that they will fully understand the subtle problems that the mass society of high consumption now faces? Yet at every point where these new problems are arising the structure of our capitalism gives men with this limited view the deciding power in dealing with them. It produces a leadership impotent to take the obvious next step forward in our society. And this question of leadership applies not only to domestic issues, but to the relation of our society to the rest of the world. In 1945 the business elite in North America had in their hands the unquestioned leadership of the world. Because of their restricted vision that leadership is now passing more and more away from North America and more and more into the hands of a tough communist elite. With all its initial advantages the capitalist leadership could not compete against the also limited communist ideal, because it could only put up against it the motives of corporate and personal greed and the impulses for personal publicity and prestige hunting. It is, of course, not only the business community in North America which will pay for this failure of leadership, but all free men who care about the traditions of the West.

Our state capitalism is indeed more than a practical system for producing and distributing goods; it is also a system of ideas and ideals which determines the character of leadership and inculcates a dominating ethic in our democracy. When socialists criticize it, therefore, they must recognize that they are concerned not only with alternative governmental techniques in economic affairs but with profound questions of what constitutes right and wrong for persons and for society. They are maintaining that not only capitalist arrangements but the very capitalist ethic is quite unable to come to grips with the problems of the mass technological world. Therefore, when socialists pass beyond criticism to their proposals for the future, these proposals must be put forward not only as a set of specific economic and political techniques but as a higher conception of well-being – that is, as a morality. They must also be able to show that the social morality they propound comes to grips more cogently with our problems than does the present capitalist ethic. Socialist doctrine must be a morality and it must be a higher and more realistic morality than that which it is to replace.

Given the power of entrenched self-interest in individuals and institutions and the tendency to passive mediocrity among great numbers of persons, nobody can really believe that a just and creative society is emerging inevitably as our technological affluence increases. Neither can anyone believe that a new dawn will break after a great economic catastrophe, let alone after the absurdity of a violent revolution. Such ideas are the dreams of an innocent past. If we are to reach a better way of dealing with the problems of a mass society, this will only come about by the free choice of a multitude of Canadians who are highly conscious of true human good and determined on its wide social realization. In such a situation revitalized socialist theory is a necessary basis for effective socialist action. Only in terms of a consistent political and social morality will socialists be able to persuade Canadians that there is a better alternative to our present capitalist system and ethic. Such a morality can only be based on a profound vision of human well-being.

A moral view of socialism is contrary to a belief held by certain politicians and political theorists in Canada: that the art of politics is just the balancing and refereeing of the interests of various pressure groups. This is the Mackenzie King[*] theory of politics and it has been taken over by his disciples who may be found in both the Liberal and Conservative parties. In such a view of politics there is no need to appeal to ultimate criteria of human good. A socialist edition of this doctrine is that the job of a socialist party consists in marshalling together the short-term self-interest of those opposed to capitalism and through the power of that marshalling to realize those self-interests. Such a doctrine is supposed to be 'realistic' socialism. It is, however, not an alternative open to true socialists although it may be open to the slick and successful who were once Liberals and are now more likely to be Conserva-

---

[*]William Lyon Mackenzie King (1874–1949), leader of the Liberal Party, 1919–48, and prime minister of Canada, 1921–6, 1926–30, 1935–48, had become a symbol to opposition parties of unprincipled shifts of political position for partisan advantage.

tives. The political technicians of the old parties are in a position to say that they are simply 'honest brokers' and therefore need not think about issues of ultimate human good; actually their aim, of course, is to stay in power and work things out within the limits of the present capitalist structure. Indeed, they seriously delude themselves in thinking they are balancing in the name of democracy. What they are really doing is becoming servants of an ever more powerful corporate capitalism and what they call balancing is doling out minor concessions so that interests other than the capitalist will not make too great a fuss.

Socialists have now the alternative of this amoral theory of politics because what they are interested in is not simply power within the present system, but the art of using power to make men free. They cannot play the role of flatterers to a disappearing democracy, because they are the friends of a true and continuing democracy. A policy of drift in matters of theory about ultimate human good (which is the upshot of moral cynicism) has nothing to offer socialists because it simply serves to perpetuate the status quo.

The cement which binds together the ethical system of socialism is the belief in equality. It is the principle which tells us whom we are talking about when we speak of human well-being. We are not speaking of some rather than others, or of some more than others – but of each person. This assumption of equality may seem so commonplace in Canada that it hardly needs discussing as a principle. Is not equality an assumed article of faith for all true Canadians? Every political orator must speak of it; even our capitalism must justify itself by calling itself 'people's capitalism.' At a deeper level, is not the central achievement of modern political theory the enunciation of the principle of equality, as against the principle of hierarchy which was central to the classical world? The chief driving force behind the social reforms of the last two hundred years has been this principle. Is not, then, a discussion of equality the simple rehashing of a platitude which every decent man accepts and to which the indecent have to pay lip service?

Yet is this so? As we move into the mass world, how much is the belief in equality sustained in our thought or practice? It is indubitable that theoretical criticisms of equality are increasingly prevalent. Is not equality the enemy of liberty? Will not the striving for equality produce a dead-level society? Is not the search for equality something we should eschew economically, as making us unproductive by holding back the energetic, the responsible, and the intelligent? Has it not produced mediocrity in our education? Wealthy men with no knowledge of moral or political philosophy will bring out as a triumphant discovery (what one might have considered an obvious fact) that men are not equal in talent, and rush on to deduce from this that equality is a ridiculous doctrine. Nor is such ridicule met with only in expected quarters. In his attempt to drive the Russians to work, Stalin maintained that equality was a petty bourgeois ideal.

More influential than these theoretical criticisms is the fact that equality is becoming more at variance with social reality. The tendency to stratification and non-participation which threatens equality is more than a product of capitalism, but is related to industrialism itself, as can be seen from the fact that a new class system is appearing in the Soviet Union as much as in North America. The very structure of mass society produces impersonal hierarchies of power in which equality can have no substance, particularly equality of participation in economic and political life. This tendency in any industrial society produces added difficulties with our capitalism in which vast accumulations of economic power in private hands and inequalities of possession are the very substance of the system. In such a situation double-think about equality becomes manifest. The popular leaders of governments orate about the glories of equality on the hustings while enacting economic policies which establish intractable inequalities as the very essence of our social life. In such circumstances, talk about equality becomes more and more ritual emptied of belief – part of the equipment of the 'engineer of consent.'

It must also be recognized, of course, that the principle of equality has been interpreted in a particular way within North American history. In our past, it meant a combination of political equality (with all its rich content of the ballot, equality before the law, and so on) with equality of opportunity for economic advancement. It was believed that political equality would safeguard equality of opportunity in economic and social life from attacks by sinister interests. This combination of political equality and open careers for the talented would prevent the unfair 'conventional' inequalities, while leaving the 'natural' inequalities to work themselves out. In the early days when our country was a frontier individualistic capitalism, this edition of the equality principles worked pretty well. The question is now, however, whether such a theory of equality is adequate for the conditions of the stratified mass society. Can formal political equality still safeguard equality of opportunity from the attacks of vested interests? Does not equality of opportunity become more and more to mean the necessity of the ambitious to serve the corporations? In a world where the very complexity of our society makes us increasingly dependent on one another, do we not have to move forward to a richer conception of economic equality than equality of opportunity? Is this not particularly pressing for our democracy, in which the problem of leisure is as urgent as the problem of work?

In such circumstances it is no longer possible to take equality as a platitudinous article of faith which all may be assumed to assume. To those who would attack the principle, openly or covertly, we must try to express why exactly we believe in it. We must elucidate how it is related to other necessary principles such as the recognition of the diversity of talent. No satisfactory or systematic answer to these problems is, of course, possible in a short essay. What follows is only intended as an introduction to the question.[2]

Equality should be the central principle of society since all persons, whatever their condition, must freely choose to live by what is right or wrong. This act of choosing is the ultimate human act and is open to all. In this sense all persons are equal, and differences of talent are of petty significance. Any man who is fair in his dealings, any woman who treats the interests of others as of the same importance as her own, may in so doing have achieved the essential human act of loving the good as much or more than the cleverest or most powerful person who ever lived. Because of this fact, no human being should be treated simply as a means, like a tree or a car, but as an end. Our moral choices matter absolutely in the scheme of things. Any social order must then try to constitute itself within the recognition of this basic fact of moral personality which all equally possess.

It is clear that the foregoing is an essentially religious foundation for equality. Such a foundation will seem to the unbeliever too limited a basis for social principle. It must be insisted, however, that the idea of equality arose in the West within a particular set of religious and philosophical ideas. I cannot see why men should go on believing in the principle without some sharing in those ideas. The religious tradition was the biblical, in which each individual was counted as of absolute significance before God. This belief united with the principle of rationality as found in the Stoic philosophers. Among the greatest Western thinkers the conception of rationality has been increasingly unified with the religious principle of respect. To state this historical fact is not to deny that many men have believed in equality outside this religious and philosophical tradition. The question is rather whether they have been thinking clearly when they have so believed. This religious basis for equality seems to me the only adequate one, because I cannot see why one should embark on the immensely difficult social practice of treating each person as important unless there is something intrinsically valuable about personality. And what is intrinsically valuable about all persons except their freedom as moral agents? At the level of efficiency it is surely more convenient to treat some persons as having no importance, and thus to build a society of inequality in which some people matter and some do not. If individuals are only accidental conglomerations of atoms, why should we respect their rights when it does not suit our interests or inclinations to do so?

It is clear that marxism, as the dominant Western philosophy in the East, appeals to the sense of equality. The question is not whether this is good, but whether within marxist materialism there is any consistent place for this belief; whether, indeed, one of the reasons why the marxists in power have been so willing to sacrifice persons ruthlessly has not been that moral personality has no place in their theory. So also in the West ideals such as 'the survival of the fittest,' when taken over from biology and used about society, led to an undermining of respect for the individual. How often has one heard business people justify the results of the market by such an appeal to Darwin? What must be insisted upon is that in mass society the practice which sustains the rights of persons *qua* persons is very difficult to preserve. It will surely only be sustained by those who have thought clearly what it is about human beings which makes them worthy of being treated with respect.

To state this is, of course, in no way to imply that socialists who disagree as to the ultimate justification of equality cannot work together. Religious believers from various traditions will hold that in the hard pinches only such belief will make equality a possibility. The non-religious who are egalitarian may feel this is only superstition and have some other basis for their belief. But this need not prevent them working together. For, as the history of Canada manifests, common political ends can be sought without theoretical agreement.

It may still be argued (and has been) that although we should treat ourselves and others as of absolute worth, this does not imply equality in the day-to-day doings of life. A man is as free to save his soul in a slum as in a mansion, we are sometimes told, and therefore there can be no argument from this religious account to any particular worldly conditions. The truth of the first part of this statement may be admitted; the second part, however, must be categorically denied. The justification of equality must then make this denial. It is based on two facts about human personality which seem to the present writer indubitable. First, it is likely to be spiritually bad for any person to be in a position of permanent and inevitable inferiority in his relation with anyone else. Secondly, it is likely to be spiritually bad for a person to be in a position of unchecked superiority in his relations with another. That is, relations of superiority-subordination tend to thwart the true good of the people on either side (whatever petty pleasures of sadism or masochism may result and whatever mechanical efficiency may be obtained). Because this thwarting tends to occur, social policy should be directed always to the elimination of such relations. And this policy should be applied in the factory, the office, the family, the general social and political order. For example, families require discipline, but if that discipline is not to degrade children and parents alike, it must be directed to its proper end of leading the children to a freedom equal to that of their parents. Also in a factory or office there must be a proper ordering work by somebody in authority, but that authority must not deny the equality of those ordered, or their creativity and responsibility for the work done. The end which any society should be working for, however slow and difficult its accomplishment, is the elimination of these relations of superiority and subordination in all aspects of life.

Nearly all in Canada will grant some degree of equality before the law or at the ballot box, but when it comes to equality of participation in wealth, responsibility, and culture there is a violent anti-egalitarian reaction. Therefore, it must be insisted that a society which takes seriously its first principle that all its members are to be regarded as equal must give economic content to that regard. Men are living beings and if society does not allow them to sustain life it cannot be said to regard them. To have enough and to get it from reasonable hours of work is the condition not only of a comfortable and sensuously gratifying life (of which freedom from fatigue is not the least part) but of a life which can partake properly in love and play, art and thought, politics and religion. At the beginning of political theory Aristotle laid down that a free man must be a man with leisure – that is, a man who can get enough goods without working too hard. It is obvious that mothers with automatic washing machines are likely to have more energy to give to the cultivation of their children than those who must do the washing on boards, that a machinist who earns the same amount of money for forty as against sixty hours has more energy to go fishing, take responsibility in the union, or paint a picture.

It is now necessary to see how these arguments are related to the main argument against equality. This is based on an appeal to the fact of natural diversity of talent. It is said that men are unequal in talent and that therefore to base society on equality is to base it on an illusion which can only lead to social disaster in the form of stagnation and mediocrity. When society follows the facts of diversity of talent it naturally falls into a hierarchical structure. We so need the gifts of the talented that we must reward them greatly. It is obvious that this argument has cogency. Men do differ widely in talents. It is also obviously true that a wise social order will encourage certain talents for the sake of its continuing health and that any system of rewards must include the economic. Also, economic reward is not solely for the purpose of giving people things. Responsible officials, brain surgeons, and artists need a high standard of life to give them that peace necessary to their efficient performance.

Nevertheless, this is not all the story: the principle of hierarchy which arises from diversity of talents must be balanced against the principle of equality which arises from the absolute worth of all men. That proper balancing must be based on the moral distinction between the valuing of qualities and the regarding of persons. This distinction is the following: to be with any set of people is to be aware of valuing disparate qualities of intellect and physique, responsibility and imagination. But this does not mean that we should regard the interests of one of those persons less highly than that of any of the others. That is, qualities are valued, persons are regarded. To make this distinction is to put activities on different levels of moral importance. The regard which is due to persons is not dependent on the sum total of their qualities. We cannot score John 90 percent in qualities and Richard 40 percent and therefore say the regard due to Richard is limited by his low score. To do so is to deny the absolute regard which is due him. It is, of course, quite possible to give up the Judaeo-Christian truth. But if one holds it, then a hierarchy of talent and an equality of persons cannot be on the same level as principles for the ordering of society. How else have we learnt to scorn slavery? We scorn it because we do not find admirable a society whose leaders, thinkers, and artists bring forth their highest qualities in the freedom of being waited on by a slave class. We scorn it because the encouragement of these qualities cannot be measured in the same scale as the debasement of these other persons by slavery. The extreme case of slavery makes clear what is true in any circumstances. The value to be recognized in the highest artistic or scientific genius – in such men as Mozart or Einstein – gives me no reason to regard them more highly as persons than anybody else, or to fail to recognize that my duty to regard persons is a duty of a higher level than my valuing of the true, the noble, or the beautiful. For this reason, the hierarchy of talents must always be subordinate as a social principle to the basic equality of persons.

To say this is not to deny that there is a grave difficulty in balancing properly the claims of equality and diversity of talent in any society. Differences in human talent are inevitably so great that the differences in ways of life and degrees of power must also be great. A corrupt belief in equality which stood in the way of people knowing what it is to do something well would obviously be pernicious. Society must offer incentives to encourage people to do things well and to do the difficult jobs well. It is clear that some persons give to society more than they take, while others use society simply for what they can get out of it. Social policy must obviously encourage the givers.

Once having granted the real substance in the argument about incentives, it must be repeated that most of the talk along that line now heard in Canada is mainly a justification of the belief that the most important thing in life is to make a lot of money. This becomes clear when one asks the question: what are these incentives, and what social structure is to produce them? There are all kinds of varying systems to produce incentives towards differing social aims. And it must be insisted here that most people in our society who argue against equality in the name of incentives are arguing in the name of one particular structure of incentives – the structure which encourages men to assist profitable private production and distribution of goods. Moreover, the powerful instruments of opinion have tried to identify in the minds of the general public the capitalist model of incentive with all possible systems of incentive. They have tried (with some success) to convince people that only a capitalist society will maintain a proper care for incentive and that therefore an alternative form of organization will destroy initiative and energy. This is nonsense. What our present capitalism encourages is certain forms of activities at the expense of others.

It is often argued that by maintaining a wealthy and privileged class certain 'finer things' are kept alive. It is not necessary to discuss this argument in general, because it is so patently absurd to apply it to the privileged groups which exist in Canada. What are these 'finer things' that owe their survival to the rich, and which would not continue in a more egalitarian society? What valuable qualities of life do the very rich keep going in Canada with their pursuit of luxury (conspicuous or inconspicuous as their taste may be), their externalized culture and prestige seeking? Horse racing and collecting pictures are their greatest positive achievements. Among the moderately rich what noble culture is the product of Forest Hill and Westmount which might be threatened by greater equality? People who give their lives to the petty round of snobbery at home and relax playing cards in Florida in identical luxury hotels and mink stoles are hardly likely to be the vanguard of a Canadian renaissance.

Our capitalist system of incentives, then, can no longer be said to lead to that encouragement of diversity of talents which was its original justification. Equality of opportunity to serve General Motors or the Argus Corporation is not what earlier democrats meant by their doctrine. The incentives of capitalism no longer do what they are said they do. They no longer encourage that wide range of skillful activities which becomes increasingly our need in a mass society. In such a situation it is as much the function of a socialist morality to work out new and realistic schemes of incentive as it is to think out new means of sustaining and enlarging the equality of all persons against the threats of the mass age.

Two last points must be emphasized about the principle of equality in the technological society. First, it must be repeated that never before in history has it been open for the majority to have large amounts of goods with high degrees of leisure. This will be a growing possibility as techniques of automation increase, as the robots do more and more of the work in the factories and offices. Such equality to participate in leisure becomes moreover a pressing necessity of our economic health. Since 1939 a large percentage of the income of this continent has been devoted to defence. No sane man can want that to continue indefinitely. If the tension between the West and the communist world is reduced, however gradually, somehow the immense resources that have been put into the military effort will have to be used for peaceful purposes. This will only be possible if the old shibboleths of inequality are overcome. If our mastery of nature is to be used for peaceful purposes, a conscious policy of equality becomes a necessity. Such a policy within North America must, of course, be related to conditions in the rest of the world and our responsibility for and dependence on such conditions. How fast we should push for a realized society of leisure at home, and how far that should be restrained to help the Asians and Africans develop industrially, is a difficult question of balance and cannot be discussed in detail here. However, it merely suggests caution, it does not change the basic fact that the scientific economy of North America can only be healthy if it is set towards a basic policy of economic equality.

Secondly, and more important, the very form of human existence created by the mass society makes imperative a struggle for equality of participation in mind; imperative, that is, if we are to escape the civilization of the ant-heap. If it be probable that in the future human beings grow up in conditions where physical survival does not take most of their time, what then will give life its meaning and purpose? What is worth doing when the robots are doing the work in the factories? In a society of widespread leisure, aimlessness and boredom will be much more likely than in the past when leisure was the privilege of the few.

To meet such a situation, our democracy must consciously stimulate the equality of participation in mind, in ways that it has never dreamed of in the past. When leisure is open to all, then education must be open to all. To overcome the impersonality of the mass society, new relationships in work and leisure must be developed and lived out; indeed, new relationships at every level of existence – in art, in sex, and in religion. It would be folly, of course, to think that these new experiences will come easily or inevitably. Human sin is a historical constant, however much the forms of it may vary from era to era. Under any conditions it is hard for us to make a success of living. Nevertheless, one thing is certain. North America is the first continent called to bring human excellence to birth throughout the whole range of the technological society. At the moment, the survival of its capitalist ethic, more than anything else, stands in the way of realizing that opportunity. The only basis on which it could be realized is a clearly defined ethic of community which understands the dignity of every person and is determined on ways of fulfilling that dignity in our new conditions.

NOTES

1 Sir Geoffrey Vickers, 'The Unstable Society,' *University of Toronto Quarterly*, vol. 23, no. 4 (July 1959): 315–51.
2 Our present social and political theory is in grave need of a systematic discussion of equality. It is lacking, however, because the political philosophers and scientists sadly mirror the impersonality of our age by concentrating their energies on technical matters and on serving the society as it is.

CANADA AND NATIONALISM

Lament for a Nation *was the book that made George Grant famous and immediately established him as one of Canada's leading political thinkers. It is still the
work for which he is best known. In ninety-seven pages he wove together themes of
politics, history, philosophy, and religion. He was driven, he later said, by sheer
anger that Lester Pearson's Liberals had brought down Diefenbaker's government so that they could yield to American pressure and bring nuclear arms into
Canada. Although Grant foretold the demise of Canadian independence,*
Lament *inspired a generation of Canadians of all political beliefs to make one
last nationalist effort to save their country.*

I have written a piece called *A Lament for a Nation* of about 25,000 words. It is,
therefore, too long to publish in a quarterly. I write to know whether there is
any monographic publication in Canada for pieces this length. It would be
better to publish it in Canada than the United States as it is entirely about
Canadian life.

Its content may be such as to exclude it from your press, because it is the
Canadian established classes (particularly the Liberal party) who are considered most responsible in what I consider Canada's demise. Diefenbaker[*] is
criticized, but not from within liberal assumptions. Neither will it be favourably
received by any socialist as it does not presume the world is getting better and
better. It may be, therefore, that it is just too direct a publication for your
press, but I write to ask.

– George Grant to Frances Halpenny, 25 February 1964

Lament for a Nation 1965[†]

Never has such a torrent of abuse been poured on any Canadian figure
as that during the years from 1960 to 1965. Never have the wealthy and
the clever been so united as they were in the joint attack on Mr John
Diefenbaker. It has made life pleasant for the literate classes to know

[*] John George Diefenbaker (1895–1979), leader of the Conservative Party, 1957–67, and
prime minister of Canada, 1957–63. His government was defeated in 1963 on a parliamentary motion criticizing his defence policy, especially his refusal to accept nuclear
weapons for Canada's armed forces.
[†] George Grant, *Lament for a Nation: The Defeat of Canadian Nationalism* (Toronto: McClelland and Stewart 1965). Used with permission.

that they were on the winning side. Emancipated journalists were encouraged to express their dislike of the small-town Protestant politician, and they knew they would be well paid by the powerful for their efforts. Suburban matrons and professors knew that there was an open season on Diefenbaker, and that jokes against him at cocktail parties would guarantee the medal of sophistication ...

The tide of abuse abated after the election of 1963. The establishment thought that it had broken Diefenbaker and could now afford to patronize him. But Diefenbaker has refused to play dead. He has shown himself capable of something the wealthy and the clever rarely understand – the virtue of courage. The patronizing airs are turning once more into abuse; the editorials and the 'news' become increasingly vindictive.

It is interesting to speculate why Diefenbaker raised the concentrated wrath of the established classes. Most of his critics claim that he is dominated by ambition, almost to the point of egomania. They also claimed (while he was still in office) that he was dangerous because he was an astute politician who put personal power first. Yet his actions turned the ruling class into a pack howling for his blood. Astute politicians, who are only interested in political power, simply do not act this way. There must be something false or something missing in this description of his actions. To search for a consistent description is partly why I have written this book.

The search must be related to the title of this meditation. To lament is to cry out at the death or at the dying of something loved. This lament mourns the end of Canada as a sovereign state. Political laments are not usual in the age of progress, because most people think that society always moves forward to better things. Lamentation is not an indulgence in despair or cynicism. In a lament for a child's death, there is not only pain and regret, but also celebration of passed good.

> I cannot but remember such things were
> That were most precious to me.

In Mozart's great threnody, the Countess sings of *la memoria di quel bene.*[*] One cannot argue the meaninglessness of the world from the facts of evil, because what could evil deprive us of, if we had not some prior knowledge of good? The situation of absolute despair does not

---

[*]The recollection of that good.

allow a man to write. In the theatre of the absurd, dramatists like
Ionesco and Beckett do not escape this dilemma. They pretend to absolute despair and yet pour out novels and plays. When a man truly
despairs, he does not write; he commits suicide. At the other extreme,
there are the saints who know that the destruction of good serves the
supernatural end; therefore they cannot lament. Those who write
laments may have heard the propositions of the saints, but they do not
know that they are true. A lament arises from a condition that is common to the majority of men, for we are situated between despair and
absolute certainty.

· · ·

This meditation is limited to lamenting. It makes no practical proposals for our survival as a nation. It argues that Canada's disappearance was a matter of necessity. But how can one lament necessity – or,
if you will, fate? The noblest of men love it; the ordinary accept it; the
narcissists rail against it. But I lament it as a celebration of memory; in
this case, the memory of that tenuous hope that was the principle of my
ancestors. The insignificance of that hope in the endless ebb and flow
of nature does not prevent us from mourning. At least we can say with
Richard Hooker[*]: 'Posterity may know we have not loosely through
silence permitted things to pass away as in a dream.'

· · ·

The confused strivings of politicians, businessmen, and civil servants
cannot alone account for Canada's collapse. This stems from the very
character of the modern era. The aspirations of progress have made
Canada redundant. The universal and homogeneous state is the pinnacle of political striving. 'Universal' implies a world-wide state, which
would eliminate the curse of war among nations; 'homogeneous'
means that all men would be equal, and war among classes would be
eliminated. The masses and the philosophers have both agreed that
this universal and egalitarian society is the goal of historical striving. It
gives content to the rhetoric of both communists and capitalists. This
state will be achieved by means of modern science – a science that leads

[*]Richard Hooker (1554?–1600), British political theorist, author of the *Laws of Ecclesiastical Polity*.

to the conquest of nature. Today scientists master not only non-human nature, but human nature itself. Particularly in America, scientists concern themselves with the control of heredity, the human mind, and society. Their victories in biochemistry and psychology will give the politicians a prodigious power to universalize and homogenize. Since 1945, the world-wide and uniform society is no longer a distant dream but a close possibility. Man will conquer man and perfect himself.

Modern civilization makes all local cultures anachronistic. Where modern science has achieved its mastery, there is no place for local cultures. It has often been argued that geography and language caused Canada's defeat. But behind these there is a necessity that is incomparably more powerful. Our culture floundered on the aspirations of the age of progress. The argument that Canada, a local culture, must disappear can, therefore, be stated in three steps. First, men everywhere move ineluctably toward membership in the universal and homogeneous state. Second, Canadians live next to a society that is the heart of modernity. Third, nearly all Canadians think that modernity is good, so nothing essential distinguishes Canadians from Americans.

• • •

The impossibility of conservatism in our era is the impossibility of Canada. As Canadians we attempted a ridiculous task in trying to build a conservative nation in the age of progress, on a continent we share with the most dynamic nation on earth. The current of modern history was against us.

A society only articulates itself as a nation through some common intention among its people. The constitutional arrangements of 1791, and the wider arrangements of the next century, were only possible because of a widespread determination not to become part of the great Republic. Among both the French and British, this negative intention sprang from widely divergent traditions. What both peoples had in common was the fact they both recognized, that they could only be preserved outside the United States of America ...

Since 1945, the collapse of British power and moral force has been evident to nearly all the world. Its present position is the end-process of that terrible fate that has overtaken Western civilization in the last century. When the British ruling class rushed headlong into the holocaust of 1914, they showed their total lack of political wisdom. As much as anybody, they had been corrupted by the modern mania. Whatever the courage of Churchill in 1940, it must be remembered that he was one of those in the Liberal Cabinet of 1914 who pushed their nation into the intemperance of the earlier disaster. The best British and Canadian youth had their guts torn out in the charnel house of the First World War. To write of the collapse of Western Europe is not my purpose here, but one small result was to destroy Great Britain as an alternative pull in Canadian life.

The history of conservatism in Great Britain has been one of growing emptiness and ambiguity. A political philosophy that is centred on virtue must be a shadowy voice in a technological civilization. When men are committed to technology, they are also committed to continual change in institutions and customs. Freedom must be the first political principle – the freedom to change any order that stands in the way of technological advance ... As Plato saw with unflinching clarity, an imperialistic power cannot have a conservative society as its home base ...

• • •

Perhaps we should rejoice in the disappearance of Canada. We leave the narrow provincialism and our backwoods culture; we enter the excitement of the United States where all the great things are being done. Who would compare the science, the art, the politics, the entertainment of our petty world to the overflowing achievements of New York, Washington, Chicago, and San Francisco? ...

Before discussing this position, I must dissociate myself from a common philosophic assumption. I do not identify necessity and goodness. This identification is widely assumed during an age of progress. Those who worship 'evolution' or 'history' consider that what must come in the future will be 'higher,' 'more developed,' 'better,' 'freer,' than what has been in the past. This identification is also common among those who worship God according to Moses or the Gospels. They identify necessity and good within the rubric of providence. From the assumption that God's purposes are unfolded in historical events, one may be led to view history as an ever-fuller manifestation of good. Since the tenth century of the Christian era, some Western theologians have tended to interpret the fallen sparrow as if particular events could be apprehended by faith as good. This doctrine of providence was given its best philosophical expression by Hegel: '*Die Weltgeschichte ist das Weltgericht*' – 'World history is the world's judgement.' Here the doctrines of progress and providence have been brought together. But if history is the final court of appeal, force is the final argument. Is it possible to look at history and deny that within its dimensions force is the supreme ruler? To take a progressive view of providence is to come close to worshiping force. Does this not make us cavalier about evil? The screams of the tortured child can be justified by the achievements of history. How pleasant for the achievers, but how meaningless for the child.

As a believer, I must then reject these Western interpretations of providence. Belief is blasphemy if it rests on any easy identification of necessity and good. It is plain that there must be other interpretations of this doctrine. However massive the disaster we might face – for example, the disappearance of constitutional government for several centuries, or the disappearance of our species – belief in providence should be unaffected. It must be possible within the doctrine of providence to distinguish between the necessity of certain happenings and their goodness. A discussion of the goodness of Canada's disappearance must therefore be separated from a discussion of its necessity.

. . .

It has already been argued that, because of our modern assumptions about human good, Canada's disappearance is necessary. In deciding whether continentalism is good, one is making a judgment about progressive political philosophy and its interpretation of history. Those who dislike continentalism are in some sense rejecting that progressive interpretation. It can only be with an enormous sense of hesitation that one dares to question modern political philosophy. If its assumptions are false, the age of progress has been a tragic aberration in the history of the species ...

To many modern men, the assumptions of this age appear inevitable, as being the expression of the highest wisdom that the race has distilled. The assumptions appear so inevitable that to entertain the possibility of their falsity may seem the work of a madman. Yet these assumptions were made by particular men in particular settings. Machiavelli and Hobbes, Spinoza and Vico, Rousseau and Hegel, Marx and Darwin, originated this account of human nature and destiny. Their view of social excellence was reached in conscious opposition to that of the ancient philosophers. The modern account of human nature and destiny was developed from a profound criticism of what Plato and Aristotle had written. The modern thinkers believed that they had overcome the inadequacies of ancient thought, while maintaining what was true in the ancients.

Yet Plato and Aristotle would not have admitted that their teachings could be used in this way. They believed that their own teaching was the complete teaching for all men everywhere, or else they were not philosophers. They believed that they had considered all the possibilities open to man and had reached the true doctrine concerning human excellence. Only the thinkers of the age of progress considered the classical writers as a preparation for the perfected thought of their own age. The classical philosophers did not so consider themselves. To see the classics as a preparation for later thought is to think within the assumptions of the age of progress. But this is to beg the question, when the issue at stake is whether these assumptions are true. It is this very issue that is raised by the tragedies and ambiguities of our day.[1]

Ancient philosophy gives alternative answers to modern man concerning the questions of human nature and destiny. It touches all the central questions that man has asked about himself and the world. The classical philosophers asserted that a universal and homogeneous state would be a tyranny. To elucidate their argument would require an account of their total teaching concerning human beings. It would take one beyond political philosophy into the metaphysical assertion that changes in the world take place within an eternal order that is not affected by them. This implies a definition of human freedom quite different from the modern view that freedom is man's essence. It implies a science different from that which aims at the conquest of nature.

The discussion of issues such as these is impossible in a short writing about Canada. Also, the discussion would be inconclusive, because I do not know the truth about these ultimate matters. Therefore, the question as to whether it is good that Canada should disappear must be left unsettled. If the best social order is the universal and homogeneous state, then the disappearance of Canada can be understood as a step toward that order. If the universal and homogeneous state would be a tyranny, then the disappearance of even this indigenous culture can be seen as the removal of a minor barrier on the road to that tyranny. As the central issue is left undecided, the propriety of lamenting must also be left unsettled.

My lament is not based on philosophy but on tradition. If one cannot be sure about the answer to the most important questions, then tradition is the best basis for the practical life. Those who loved the older traditions of Canada may be allowed to lament what has been lost, even though they do not know whether or not that loss will lead to some greater political good. But lamentation falls easily into the vice of self-pity. To live with courage is a virtue, whatever one may think of the dominant assumptions of one's age. Multitudes of human beings through the course of history have had to live when their only political allegiance was irretrievably lost. What was lost was often something far nobler than what Canadians have lost. Beyond courage, it is also possible to live in the ancient faith, which asserts that changes in the world, even if they be recognized more as a loss than a gain, take place within an eternal order that is not affected by their taking place. Whatever the difficulty of philosophy, the religious man has been told that process is not all. '*Tendebantque manus ripae ulterioris amore.*'[2]

NOTES

1 The previous paragraph is dependent on the writings of Professor Leo Strauss, who teaches at the University of Chicago. For Strauss's account of political philosophy, see, for example, *What Is Political Philosophy?* (Glencoe, Ill.: The Free Press 1959) and *The City and Man* (Chicago: Rand McNally 1964). I only hope that nothing in the foregoing misinterprets the teaching of that wise man.

2 Virgil, *Aeneid* (Book VI): 'They were holding their arms outstretched in love toward the further shore.'

THE VIETNAM WAR

Grant was a pacifist during the early stages of the Second World War and he returned to his pacifism in the 1950s. As American involvement in Vietnam escalated, so did Grant's outrage and he soon found himself in active alliance with fellow academics and students of the New Left. The speech he gave to a 'teach-in' at Varsity Arena at the University of Toronto in 1965 was his most powerful and effective public presentation. However, it soon became clear that the students in the New Left disagreed with Grant about tactics. Grant did not accept the need for civil disobedience in a parliamentary regime that was still open to reasoned opposition.

In the November issue, in which you published a speech of mine,* you also said, 'In effect, he (G.P. Grant) seems to be suggesting that real change will only come about within the power structures of society, not over against them.' It amuses me how such a deduction could be drawn from my words. I certainly think that real change is going to take place within the power structures, but it is going to be changed for the worse. I was not saying to the protesting young that they should not fight the present power structures. To imply that the present power structures will change for the good is to misjudge completely their present activity in Vietnam. What seems to be implied in your editorial is that change for the good (e.g. progress) must happen. This proposition I would entirely deny.

> – George Grant to the editor, *Christian Outlook*, 29 December 1965

I enclose a draft letter which has been jointly worked out by some students (members of the Student Union for Peace Action) and myself. It will be the basis for a presentation to all members of parliament in the week starting Monday, February 28. We are going to have a silent vigil of 48 hours at the beginning of that week in front of parliament for its presentation. This letter is asking you whether you would sign this document[†] (or something very close to it) and indeed whether you would take part in that silent vigil. I am going to do both.

The reasons for doing this seem to me something like the following:
(1) For whatever motives, it seems to me that the U.S.A. has got into a position where it is massacring masses of Vietnamese. Canada is more and more implicated in this, and the thought of us being implicated in a long and growing war between Asia and North America is too terrible to contemplate. (2) I think it is important that those of us of the older generation who are Canadian nationalists should join these young people and show them that there are some older people in this country who are willing to speak about this matter – and not simply the older radicals.

> – George Grant to Kenneth McNaught, 11 February 1966

A Critique of the New Left (1966)[‡]

I speak as a Canadian nationalist and as a conservative. It is necessary to

---

*George Grant, 'Realism in Political Protest,' *Christian Outlook*, vol. 21, no.2 (November 1965): 3–6.

[†]A pamphlet.

[‡]George Grant, 'A Critique of the New Left,' in *Canada and Radical Social Change* (Montreal: Black Rose 1966).

start here for the following reason. To speak of the moral responsibility of the citizen in general is impossible; the question entirely depends on the kind of regime in which one is a citizen. The United States is a world empire – the largest to date. Its life at home is controlled by mammoth corporations, private and public, and through these bureaucracies it reaches out to control a large proportion of the globe and soon beyond the globe. The nineteenth-century idea of the democratic citizen making the society he inhabits by the vote and the support of political parties must have less and less meaning. In local matters, the citizen of an empire can achieve some minor goals. But he cannot shape the larger institutions or move the centres of power. Democratic citizenship is not a notion compatible with technological empires. Now Canada moves more and more to being a satellite of that empire. And Canadians live much of their lives under the same imperial bureaucracies. The institutions of Toronto are much the same as those of Detroit. Yet despite this there is a sense in which we still have more citizenship here than in the U.S.A. because we have some political sovereignty, if we fight for it. Traditional democratic means – the vote and support for political parties – have more meaning in our smaller sphere. Political choice is both more real and more possible in Canada. This might be truly useful to the world, if we in Canada could use it to see that North American relations with Asia did not always simply follow Washington.

But to pass to the broader question of what it is to be a citizen in North America in this era, let me start from the position of the New Left in North America, that is, the movement which has public significance because of what it did in the civil rights struggle. I find myself in agreement with the account the leaders of this movement give of the inhumanity of the institutions of North America. When I read Professor Lynd[*] in *Liberation* speaking of what the institutions of his society do to human personality both at home and abroad, I agree with his account of those institutions. When I hear what Mr Savio in Berkeley or Mr Drushka[†] in Toronto write about the inhumanity of our multiversities, by and large I agree with them. How can a conservative not feel sympathy with their outrage against the emptiness and dehumanization that this society produces?

But when the New Left speaks of overcoming these conditions by

---

[*]Staughton Lynd, an American anti-war activist who spoke at the 'teach-in' at Varsity Arena in 1965.
[†]New Left students and anti-war activists.

protest, I think they are indulging in dreams and dangerous dreams. The moral fervour that accompanies such dreams is too valuable to be wasted on anything but reality. When they speak as if it were possible by marching and sitting to turn North American society away from being an empire protecting its interest in the world by violence, I just do not know how they can think this. When some of them speak as if the empires of the East were not moving in the same social direction as the United States, I think they are deluding themselves. When they propose that our modern universities can be overcome and turned into human sources of enlightenment, I think they have not looked at our society closely enough.

Their politics of hope and of Utopia – indeed with some of them another outbreak of the traditional form of the politics of the apocalypse – seems to me a kind of dream from which analysis should awaken them. They seem to think that these massive institutions which stifle human excellence can be overcome, and I think this arises from a profound misinterpretation of modern history. For several centuries the chief energies of Western society have been directed to the mastery of nature – at first non-human nature and now human nature. We now live in the era where that process moves quickly to its apotheosis. The motive of this pursuit was that by it men should be made free. Freedom was its rallying cry. And it is in the pursuit of this dream of freedom that we have built the mammoth institutions, international and national, in which we live. This pursuit of the mastery of nature has gained men great victories over natural necessity. Who can doubt that? But at the same time as it has produced these victories, it has subjected men to the forces of the artificial necessities of the technological society. 'The further the technical mechanism develops which allows us to escape natural necessity, the more we are subjected to artificial technical necessities. The artificial necessity of technique is not less harsh and implacable for being much less obviously menacing than natural necessity.'[1] This is the crucial question about citizenship in this era: what is it to be a citizen in this new society ruled by its technical apparatus?

What I do not see is why anybody should believe that by some dialectical process of history there should suddenly spring out of this technological society a free and humane society. First, Western men and now men everywhere in the world are driving with enormous speed to the building of this technological straitjacket. This is a society which by its very mammoth nature must destroy the idea of the responsible citizen. What evidence is there for believing that this system can by protest be turned towards the ends of human excellence? What reason have we for believing that the vast imperial structures will act towards each other and towards their neighbours in a nobler way than empires have in the past? The empires may restrain themselves from fright, but the small nations who are unfortunate enough to be caught between them will be ground between the millstones. And to speak about the institutions I know best – the universities – what reason is there to believe that they can be diverted from the very purpose for which they exist? The modern universities exist above all to provide personnel to feed the vast technological apparatus. That technological apparatus is now autonomous and produces its own needs which are quite detached from human needs. Are such institutions which are of the very fabric of the modern quest to be diverted from this end?

The supreme example of the autonomy of technique is surely the space programme. If it is possible for man to do something it must be done. Vast resources of brains, money, materials are poured out in the U.S.A. and U.S.S.R. to keep this fantastic programme proliferating. And it is accepted by the masses in both societies not only as necessary but as man's crowning glory. One leader of the US space programme said that as we cannot change the environment of space, we will have to change man. So we are going to produce beings half flesh – half electronic organs. If it can be done, it must be done and it surely will be done. This is what I mean by the autonomy of technique. The question whether technique serves human good is no longer asked. It has become an end in itself.

There is a lot of talk among the New Left about the present system of society collapsing because of its internal contradictions. What signs are there of that collapse? The American system with its extension into Western Europe seems to me supremely confident and to have the overwhelming majority of its citizens behind it – the same seems true of the Russian system and will be increasingly true of the Chinese system.

One immediate reason why I think the New Left is deluded about what is happening in North America is because it has misinterpreted the events which took place in the southern United States. It says today: look at our triumphs in the South; we will now carry these triumphs of citizen action into new fields of social revolution. What has been forgotten is that the powerful among the people and institutions of North America were more than willing that the society of the white South should be broken. The civil rights movement had behind it all the powerful forces of the American empire. It marched protected by federal troops, it had the blessing of the leading government figures. It was encouraged night after night by NBC and CBS. There was violence from the white South, but the white South is not an important part of the American power elite. It will surely be a different matter when the protests are against some position which is dear and close to the American liberal establishment. We have only to think of how much is immediately accomplished by protests about Vietnam, the Dominican Republic, or nuclear policy. Anyway, dissent and protest are themselves bureaucratized in our society. They are taken into the system and trivialized. They are made to serve the interest of the system they are supposed to be attacking, by showing that free speech is allowed.

I am not advocating inaction or cynicism. Nothing I have said denies for one moment the nobility of protest. Nothing I have said denies that justice is good and that injustice is evil and that it is required of human beings to know the difference between the two. To live with courage in the world is always better than retreat or disillusion. Human beings are less than themselves when they are cut off from being citizens. Indeed one of the finest things about the present protest movements in North America is that they try to give meaning to citizenship in a society which by its enormity and impersonality cuts people off from the public world. Anybody who lives within a university must know that the students who care enough about the world to protest are much finer than those who are interested in public affairs simply because they want to climb within the system and use it to gain recognition for their egos. Indeed, how much finer are those who protest than those who crawl through the university simply as a guarantee of the slow road to death in the suburbs. In our monolithic society, the pressures upon the individual to retreat from the public sphere are immense. The new politics of protest have tried to overcome those pressures and to give new meaning to citizenship. Nobody should attack them for that.

What I am arguing against is the politics based on easy hopes about the future human situation. The hope, for example, that some future transformation of power in North American is going to overcome the implicit difficulties of the technological apparatus, that North American society can in the future be radically changed in its direction. Hope in the future has been the chief opiate of modern life. And nobody is more responsible for dipping out that opiate than Marx. Its danger is that it prevents men from looking clearly at their situation. It teaches them to dream instead of coming to terms with facts. The most dangerous quality of the politics of Utopia is that it can easily turn into despair.

If people have vast expectations of hope about a society such as ours, they are going to be disappointed and then their moral fervour can turn rancid and bitter. Moral fervour is too precious a commodity not to be put in the service of reality.

If protest is to be effective in this era, if we are to be successful in creating space for human spontaneity in the iron maiden of the technical apparatus we have created, then it is essential that those who are in the forefront of protest must combine with their actions the deepest and most careful thought. Action without thought will be an impotent waste of time. In this ferocious era, if we are to keep ourselves human and to be effective citizens, then our first obligation is to be free. And by free I mean knowing the truth about things, to know what is so, without simplifications, without false hope, without moral fervour divorced from moral clarity. The central Christian platitude still holds good. 'The truth shall make you free.' I use freedom here quite differently from those who believe that we are free when we have gained mastery over man and over nature. It is different even from the simple cry for political liberty: 'Freedom now.' For in the long pull freedom without the knowledge of reality is empty and vacuous. The greatest figure of our era, Gandhi, was interested in public actions and in political liberty, but he knew that the right direction of that action had to be based on knowledge of reality – with all the discipline and order and study that that entailed.

Truth seeking is of course hard to accomplish in this society. Our universities have at many points retreated from it into fact gathering and technological mastery, what is now called the knowledge industry. Most of our social scientists have used the idea of a value-free social science to opt out of the battle of what constitutes the good society, and spend their time in discovering techniques for adjusting people to the system. The philosophers have often opted out to play clever professional games. Much of the religious tradition seems a worn-out garment and not able to help in the search for truth. Above all, what may hold people from the search for the truth is that the human situation in the totally realized mass world may be so unpalatable that we simple do not want to face it. If we do not face reality we may be able to avoid the great evils of despair and pessimism, but we also cut ourselves off from any chance of maturity and effectiveness.

I have concentrated on North America, because we in North America are inevitably in the forefront of the world. We are the society that has most completely realized the dominance of technique over every aspect of human life. Every year we are moving with prodigious speed to the greater and greater realization of that system. All other societies move at various speeds to the same kind of society we are creating. We are the first people who will have to learn what it is to be citizens in a society dominated by technique. Because that system is most fully realized with us, we are the first people who can look it in the face and we are called upon to see it for what it is and not fool ourselves about it. We must face the laws of its necessity – its potential to free men from natural necessity, its potential for inhumanity and tyranny. We must not delude ourselves and we must not throw up our hands. We must define our possible areas of influence with the most careful clarity. Where in this mammoth system can we use our intelligence and our love to open up spaces in which human excellence can exist? How can we use the most effective pressure to see that our empire uses moderation and restraint in its relations with the rest of the world? I end where I began, that our greatest obligation as Canadians is to work for a country which is not simply a satellite of any empire.

NOTE

1 J. Ellul, *The Technological Society*, trans. John Wilkinson (New York: Knopf 1964).

Although Grant did not believe in civil disobedience in the Canadian context, he strongly believed in the right and the duty of every person to take a public stand on important moral issues in the hope of influencing public opinion.

The Value of Protest (1966)[*]

The desire to stop the war in Vietnam should not be limited to people of any political party or any political philosophy. It should be common to all men who hate crime and injustice. And as Senator Fulbright[†] has

---

[*] George Grant, 'The Vietnam War: The Value of Protest,' an address delivered on 14 May 1966 in Toronto at a demonstration for peace in Vietnam.
[†] American Senator J.W. Fulbright (1905–95) at first supported the Vietnam war; however, by the beginning of 1966 he had begun to criticize the war and by 1967 was openly in opposition.

made clear, it should be common to all North Americans who have the long-range interests of this continent in their minds.

All decent people, if they look at the facts, must know that what is being done in Vietnam by President Johnson[*] and his legions is the waging of an unjust war, by atrocious means. It is war which can only be won by the terrible means of genocide. What the American government is saying to a country, thousands of miles from their shores, is that Vietnam must do what we want or it will be destroyed. Let us remember that the bombing of the northern half of the country is not as terrible as the bombing of the southern half. In the current year twice as many bombs as were dropped in the whole of the Korean war are going to be dropped in the southern part of Vietnam – the country the Americans are supposedly saving. A few months ago I met some American professors who were in favour of their country's policy, and I asked them what was their policy for Vietnam and they said 'We are going to pave it.' That is, rather than let it out of the American grip, they will totally demolish its civilization.

All the complex problems of international politics – the confrontation of the American and Chinese empires, the meeting of industrial and non-industrial cultures – do not cloak the central fact about the Vietnam War, which is this: we of this continent have in the last year unequivocally embarked on a policy which means the extermination of masses of the Vietnamese people. It is this which makes this war the most horrible thing that has happened in the world since the destruction of the European Jews. It is this fact which requires that all North Americans of good conscience should protest and protest till this war is brought to an end. The horrors of the twentieth century have been manifold; but this must be the worst one for North Americans because we are doing it.

Canadians cannot escape from their involvement in this crime. Obviously, most Canadians want to use what independence we have left to keep ourselves from being any more directly implicated in that war than we already are. But morally our position is a queer one. In the same week that our prime minister makes a cautious move towards peace,

[*]Lyndon B. Johnson (1908–73), president of the United States, 1963–9. Johnson succeeded to the presidency on John F. Kennedy's assassination. Although he was a proponent of an expanded welfare state in his domestic policies, his presidency became increasingly entangled in the Vietnam War and his unpopular policies eventually forced him to withdraw from the 1968 presidential campaign.

another member of the government demands that Canada be given a greater share in the continental defence production. Indeed, Canadians may emphasize their independence, but such independence cannot deny our long-term deep involvement in the injustice which is being perpetrated. Canadians are finally and inescapably North Americans – members of Western society. That society as a whole – not only the United States – is losing any honourable reputation it had with the rest of the world, because of the conduct of this war. The longer this war continues the more terrible will be the whirlwind that Western men will reap because of it. You don't have to be an anti-American to see this. That great American patriot, Senator Fulbright, has shown this in crystal clarity for all to see. The longer this terrible war is continued, the deeper and deeper becomes the legacy of hatred that Asians are laying up against all of us North Americans. Canadians who see beyond the ends of their noses should see this – whatever their political persuasion. Both conscience and self-interest should, therefore, unite to make us protest the continual escalation of this war.

Canadians seem to be getting used to this war. Fifteen months ago the truly massive American escalation started. As it grows and grows, we seem more and more willing to take it for granted. To a society which wants continual new excitements it becomes more important whether two entertainers are kicked off a television show than whether we are massacring Asians. Who slept with whom nearly a decade ago seems to engage our prime minister's attention more than this terrible calamity. Newspapers and television seek the new sensation in a society that cannot long pay attention to anything. And this lack of care seems worse in Canada than in the United States. For even as we seek a greater share in defence production, we say that Vietnam is not really our business; we can turn aside. One of the worst things about the affluent imperialism we live in in North America is that masses of people can be led easily from acquiescence to indifference about the terrible things that their society is perpetrating in other parts of the world. A country which will scream its head off about a television programme and be silent about Vietnam is surely sick.

Of course, there are many who care deeply about what is happening in this war – but who say to themselves 'What is the use of protesting?' Our protests do nothing and can do nothing against the determination of those who have the power in Washington. Look at what has happened in the last year. The teach-ins and marches and demonstrations of a year ago haven't stopped the escalation of the war. Even the courage of Senator Fulbright and Senator Morse,[*] in the greatest American legislative body, hasn't done any good. The number of American troops and planes grows; the ferocity of the bombing in both the northern and southern parts of the country has increased in the last weeks. Even the demonstrations by the people of Vietnam in their own country do not seem to have swayed President Johnson. He is determined to get his way even if it means making the country a desert.

More and more people say that in a technological society such as ours the actions and thoughts of the individuals do not count and as the central executive in Washington is set on massacre there is nothing that can be done. But who can be sure that this is true? Let us look at what has happened in the last year. Who can say that if there hadn't been widespread protests there would ever have been the hearings in the Senate or that those hearings would have been televised? And those hearings have evidently got through to a lot of voters and Johnson for all his consensus still has to face elections in November. Who can say that as powerful a figure as Senator Kennedy[†] would have come out for negotiations with the National Liberation Front if he wasn't aware that right throughout society there were people who hated the war and were aware of some of the facts of that war? Without the protests there would have been far fewer of such people. Even in Canada who can tell how much further this country would have been directly implicated in the war if politicians were not aware that there was deep suspicion of the American government's motives right across this country? And let us never forget that there are powerful forces in this continent who push for Canada to be more deeply implicated in the prosecution of the war. The pain and impotence that one feels as the war mounts in ferocity must not blind us to the fact that without protest, we might be in an even worse position than we are. In every situation in human life it always matters what you do and this is a situation where protest must go on.

Obviously, the first reason for protest is to try to stop the terrible things that are being done in Vietnam. But there is another reason for

---

[*]W.L. Morse (1900–74) sat in the U.S. Senate from 1945 to 1969, first as a Republican, then as an Independent, and finally, from 1956, as a Democrat. His opposition to the Vietnam War brought about his defeat in 1968.

[†]Robert F. Kennedy (1925–68), brother of John F. Kennedy. Attorney general from 1961 to 1964, and a senator from 1965, he was assassinated in 1968 during his campaign for the presidency.

protest even if you can't change events. We must keep alive in our society the recognition that there is a difference between lies and truth. Ours is a society where the most enormous pressure can be brought to hide the truth and to make lies seem like truth. The weight of television, press, and radio can be used to convince people that lies are truth. The liberal society keeps itself going above all by propaganda, by submerging people with propaganda. A society that feeds on propaganda soon cannot tell the difference between lies and truth. The kind of people who get to the top politically in a liberal society are those who have learned that if it helps their cause to say something they will say it even if they know it not to be true Nowhere has this been more evident than in the speeches of Secretary of State Rusk* and Vice President Humphrey.† When one hears some of the things they have been willing to say about Vietnam, can one believe that they think they are telling the truth? Perhaps Humphrey is dumb enough and corrupted enough by his years of liberal rhetoric, but that cannot be the case with Rusk. Let me take the simplest fact about Vietnam. By the Geneva accords it was not meant that Vietnam should long be divided into southern and northern sections. Yet the American officials have continually spoken as if North and South Vietnam were separate countries and most people in North America now believe this.

A society in which the difference between truth and lies disappears is a society doomed for debasement. Because you can't make even fairly reasonable decisions if you can't sort out facts from illusions. In private life this is what we call madness, when people can't distinguish facts from illusions. And it is just as much madness when it applies to whole societies as when it applies to individuals. This is what happened in Germany, enough people came to believe illusions about the Jews. This is one service the protest movement must perform in this society. It must break through the curtain of lies and half-truths and tell what is really happening in Vietnam. For we will be truly lost if we bring up our children in a society where lies are not called lies.

To finish, the worst thing about Vietnam is the terrible suffering of the Vietnam peasants; the second worst thing is the lies and perversion of the truth which is eating away at the soul of our society.

---

*Dean Rusk (1901–89), American secretary of state, 1961–70. Rusk served under presidents Kennedy and Johnson and was a dedicated opponent of communist expansion. He was closely associated with the American involvement in Vietnam.
†Hubert H. Humphrey, Jr (1911–78), vice-president of the United States under Lyndon Johnson 1965–9. He lost the 1968 presidential election to Richard Nixon.

THE UNITED STATES AS A
TECHNOLOGICAL SOCIETY

Lyndon Johnson ran for presidency of the United States in 1964 on the slogan 'The Great Society,' a domestic program that was to include the Civil Rights Act of 1965 and Medicare and Medicaid in 1965. However, for Grant, American domestic achievements paled beside U.S. military actions in Vietnam. In 1967 he returned to Couchiching to take his warnings about the Vietnam War and what it implied for the United States to a larger and more mainstream audience than student radicals.

As a Canadian I have always believed in the use of the national state as a means of protecting Canadian independence. On the other hand, in the general economic situation of North America I dislike the concentration of power that is taking place in the hands of Washington. I would not have found it impossible as an American to have voted for Senator Goldwater[*] on domestic, but not on international issues. I unequivocally would have voted for General Eisenhower[†] in both elections.   – George Grant to George Hogan, 26 April 1965

It is easy to be against nationalism when one is a member of a nation which is the centre of a great empire. But think of the other side: may it be a good thing to be nationalist when one is defending a communal existence against that empire? The alternative to nationalism for small communities is not internationalism but a dominance of their existence by empires. This seems to me as true of communities near the Russian empire as it is those near the American; though the ability of a capitalist empire may be more insidious than the more blatant means of a communist empire.

– George Grant to John Robertson, 9 October 1969

The Great Society 1967[‡]

First, what is meant by the Great Society? It is a vision of a society of free

---

[*]Barry Goldwater (1909–) was the conservative Republican candidate for the presidency in 1964. He was soundly beaten by Johnson.

[†]Dwight Eisenhower was Republican president of the United States, 1953–61.

[‡]George Grant, Comments on the Great Society at the 35th Annual Couchiching Conference, in *Great Societies and Quiet Revolutions*, ed. John Irwin (Toronto: Canadian Broadcasting Corporation 1967), 71–7.

and equal men, to be realized through the application of certain principles. These principles are to be taken seriously because they are enunciated by President Johnson as determining the policies of the American government. These basic principle are, in essence, two:

(1) By the application of those sciences which issue in the mastery of human and non-human nature, it will be possible to build a society of free and equal human beings.

(2) The application of these mastering sciences should be carried out by a system which can be quickly described as 'state corporation capitalism'; that is, by the co-operation of the public and private corporations.

In stating these two principles it is useful to add that this continent is much the most advanced in the application of the sciences which result in the control of human and non-human nature. The chief reasons for this are that the dominating immigrant groups came from Western Europe, and it is in Western Europe that modern science and its mutually interdependent political ideas arose. The people with these ideas took over a continent of vast resources and unified the wealthy part of it under a modern system of government. When the second and greater wave of the technological revolution began to crest after 1945, the continent had not been ravaged by war and was ready both materially and in spirit to build a society based on this technology. In short, North America is far ahead in building a universal and homogeneous society of free and equal men, and since 1945 such a society can be considered not simply a dream but a possibility.

One might proceed by pointing out the actual results of the application of the Great Society principles in our society, and trying thereby to judge the principles themselves. To support distrust of these principles one could point at domestic and international phenomena which give one pause. One could describe the quality of life which is arising in the great *megalopoleis*; what life is like in the bureaucracies of the public and private corporation; the ruthlessness of the society to those who cannot succeed by the standards of prestige and acquisition; the impersonality and vacuousness of its educational institutions; the pursuit of titillation and shock in its artistic and sexual life; the derootedness of mobility and the impossibility of effective citizenship, etc., etc. It could be pointed out, also, that this society seems increasingly violent and masterful in its dealings with the rest of the world. I say this because I think it quite appropriate to judge the Great Society, not only by its domestic, but by its international actions. But as my job is to concentrate on

North America, I must avoid any implication that all the evils of the international order can be laid at the door of Washington. I do not intend to minimize the difficulties that any government of the American empire would have in its confrontation with the Soviet and Chinese empires. It must be recognized, however, that as the Great Society develops it exercises extreme violence in its relations with the rest of the world. Look at the growing number of military regimes among the satellites of the American empire in South America and Africa. Above all, we cannot disassociate what is happening in Vietnam from the principles of the Great Society. That ferocious exercise in imperial violence must surely be part of our pointing. Mastery extends to every part of the globe.

Nevertheless, it is not through looking at these particular applications of principles that we come to a final judgment of these principles. Not only could the supporters of the Great Society point to certain good results, which would turn the debate into a simple listing of black and white, but with more force its supporters could claim that the bad results of the Great Society are but temporary aberrations or faulty applications of the principles, and will be overcome at a later stage on the road of progress. For example, if these supporters of the Great Society were marxists (and even Johnson's speeches are often good marxism coated with Billy Graham[*]) they could say that once the Great Society frees itself from the anomalies of the old capitalism, it will rid itself of many of its domestic evils. Again, they might claim that the impersonality of the big cities will be overcome by the more careful use of social science. We need more social science to cure the ills which science has created. Or, if they are liberals, they could say with the vice-president that once America is freed from the necessity of standing up against the aggression of a relentless communist imperialism, it will be possible for it to enjoy the full glories of the Great Society both domestically and internationally. In short, the argument from results does not allow us really to get at the principles of the Great Society and to judge them as they are in themselves.

The true issue in this discussion turns around the first principle of the Great Society as I enunciated it earlier. That was the claim, that, by the application of those sciences which lead to the mastery of human and non-human nature, we will be able eventually to build a society of

---

[*]Billy Graham (1918–), a charismatic evangelical American clergyman who used radio, television, and movies to reach a large audience.

free and equal men. This is the proposition that must be discussed. Before doing so, let me say two things about it. (1) That proposition embodies the religion of this society. Religion means what men bow down to, and the great public religion of this society is the bowing down to technology. It is never easy to discuss the truth or falsity of a society's religion when in the midst of that society. (2) This religion, which is most completely realized in North America but which is coming to be in all parts of the world, has deep roots in the most influential thought of the West in the last centuries. It is the essence of modern liberalism and that liberalism has been the dominating influence of modern thought for three or four hundred years. We are living in the era when the great thoughts of Western liberalism are being actualized. For these reasons the question I am asking about this idea of technological progress and mastery is not whether it is going to survive. Certainly the mass of men cannot be turned back from the realization by argument. To debate whether this principle should dominate the future would be like debating whether water should run downhill. What I am questioning is whether societies dedicated to this pursuit of technological control are going to find it indeed a means to their final end; whether the application of this principle can in fact result in a Great Society of free and equal men, a society that promotes human excellence; or whether the nature of the means will not determine an end of quite another complexion.

We may be born with Downs Syndrome. We find ourselves in a world where we are the victims of chance, chance which limits the possibility of our partaking in human excellence. Modern science which issues in mastery arose above all from the desire to overcome chance. Let me say here what I mean by human excellence. There are two purposes to human existence: to live together well in communities and to think. These two ends are distinct, because thinking is not simply a means for living together. I will not go into the conflict that often in actuality arises between these two ends. I mean by human excellence the realization in people of the various virtues necessary to the achievement of these two purposes. It is no accident that the modern experiment should have arisen in the religious ethos it did, in the sense that modern science is so closely related to charity. Science was turned from contemplation to mastery so that by the overcoming of chance the good life would be made open to all. Yet we should contemplate the ambiguity that in the achievement of that mastery we have built a monolithic apparatus which becomes ever more tyrannous. Tyranny is, of course, the greatest political foe of excellence. It denies both the chief ends of man – living well together and thinking.

Let me illustrate. To overcome economic chance we have built our economic system. This leads to the birth of enormous numbers of people. The need arises to limit the population, both in what we call underdeveloped nations in the first stage of industrialization, and also in highly developed nations. Beyond quantitative proliferation, there is also the question of quality. Why should we leave to chance (and indeed as we all know to some very strange chances) the quality of people coming into the world. Modern scientific studies mean that sun and man need no longer generate men haphazardly. But both quantitative and qualitative control must mean enormously powerful institutions to exercise that control. Is a man who has to get a licence to have children a free man? Of course, what is replied here is that the modern masters will not control others by force (except when absolutely necessary) but by the use of social sciences will adjust people so that they will want the socially useful. It is claimed that it will be possible to avoid tyranny by the inculcation of the truths of social science through mass communication. 'This Hour Has Seven Days.'* But will not this central thought control be just as tyrannous as the old methods? If one believes that the needs of the soul are the most important it will be more tyrannous. And beyond that the question remains whether adjustment to socially useful attitudes can be equated with the goodness once defined as the cultivation of the virtues. Can living together well be produced by mass propaganda or can it only be achieved by free men pursuing virtue through their own motion? Beyond living well together, the mass stimulation of socially useful attitudes can certainly not be conducive to the other end of man – thinking. To put the matter generally: can men live well together within the enormous institutions necessary to the massive overcoming of chance? To take but one point: I assume that one aspect of human excellence is to take part in the major political decisions of one's community. Is this possible under modern institutions? Professor McLuhan suggests that the new democratic politics will consist in men learning the facts on an issue over television, and then regularly, perhaps daily, registering a plebiscite on a great computer system. This does not seem to me at all the same thing as the traditional partaking by free men in political activity. Who will control the televisions? Who will decide what are the facts?

*A satirical Canadian current-affairs television program, which ran from 1964 to 1966.

Solitary men living in *megalopoleis*, not being able to know their leaders, pushing computer buttons are not free men, or equal men. To sum up: the overcoming of chance to which we are committed builds institutions which more and more negate the freedom and equality for the sake of which the whole experiment against chance was undertaken. And the ambiguity goes deeper: the building of the universal and homogeneous state by mastery was the chief ideal of Western liberal theory. If the achievement of that end can now more and more be seen as the achievement of tyranny, then the theory can no longer be accepted.

I cannot, in a short space, deal with the difficulty in which we are left. Man has to overcome chance to some degree to form communities at all; yet the drive for the total overcoming of chance leads to tyrannies. What degree of the overcoming of chance is necessary for the good society? The anthropologist Lévi-Strauss[*] says that the best order for man was what we call the neolithic era in which man had gained sufficient control to build organic communities and to give him time to contemplate. I do not know what the answer is.

Despite my diagnosis of potential tyranny, I am not advocating the dreaming of anti-social dreams. The immoderation of technique cannot be met by the immoderation of retreat from society. At all times and in all places it always matters what we do. Man is by nature a social being, therefore it is a kind of self-castration to try to opt out of the society one is in. There are going to be many wounds to be bound up in our world. Who cannot admire those young people who work among the Métis or who work for almost nothing in poverty projects, or who care for truth in the multiversity? When I read the new journal *This Magazine Is about Schools* produced in Toronto by young men who care desperately that education be more than our provincial efficiency nightmare, and who are willing to forgo the world of acquisition and prestige to produce such a magazine, I cannot doubt that such things are worth doing. Just because our fate is to live in a concrete empire – half garrison and half marketplace – we cannot opt for that mysticism, LSD or otherwise, which tries to reach the ultimate joy by bypassing our immediate relations and responsibilities in the world.

Finally I would tentatively suggest that the virtue most necessary for this era is what I would call openness. This quality is the exact opposite of control or mastery. Mastery tries to shape the objects and people

[*] Claude Lévi-Strauss (1908–), French anthropologist and the founder of structuralism.

around us into a form which suits us. Openness tries to know what things are in themselves, not to impose our categories upon them. Openness acts on the assumption that other things and people have their own goodness in themselves; control believes that the world is essentially neutral stuff which can only be made good by human effort.

Openness is a virtue most difficult to realize in our era as it requires daily the enormous discipline of dealing with our own closedness, aggressions, and neuroses, be they moral, intellectual, or sexual. To be open in an age of tyrannical control will above all require courage.

Professor Grant, in reply to questions:

Technology is creating a global situation, very similar whether it be in Russia, in time in China, perhaps in India, as in the United States. I see the United States as the most advanced industrial society on earth. Therefore, what is coming to be in the United States is what is coming to be in the rest of the world. Now I do not see how you can have decentralization of power when you need enormous institutions to run things. I do not think you can produce General Motor cars without something like General Motors, whether it is privately owned or publicly owned.

Now, let me say that tyranny is a very pressing problem, because in my view of life, the world is eternal, not created, and tyranny is a danger coeval with the world, with man, as cancer is a danger coeval with man. I think that there is no danger in stressing that. Now I do not, therefore, see how any revolution could replace centralized power in highly technological societies. I just do not see how it is going to happen.

Modern Western man has been committed for three hundred years to the building of an enormous technological apparatus which is now spreading into the rest of the world. I think you can live perfectly well in a tyrannical regime. I am just saying that the technological era is coming and is going to be a tyranny. Now I would try and do everything I could to limit that tyranny. I do it by trying to teach things about ancient religions and philosophy at university. Other people do it by writing or going and working with the Métis. I would personally be much more interested in politics if I lived in French-speaking Canada but as I live in English-speaking Canada, which is a satellite of the Great Society, about all I can do is carry out my private duties and think my private thoughts. There is not much that anybody can do to stop this tyranny from being; one simply has to live through it.

Let me say that I think that if you have a highly technological society it has to be very largely corporate. This is why I have very great sympathy for what is going on in Quebec.

I would point out that the Great Society is an idea that really grew in the United States. Let us start in 1932 with Roosevelt. Since 1932 the United States has become the greatest empire in world history, greater than Rome. In the last few years, it has been able to upset the government of Brazil, the government of the Argentine, been able to upset governments all over Africa – do you not call that an empire? It seems to me to be indubitably an empire, although obviously a different kind of empire from the colonial empires the English and French had. *The Nation* magazine calls U.S. action in Vietnam, 'welfare imperialism.'

We surely must face the fact that, as Marx said and as I have observed, social progress in America has always been impeded by great outbreaks of nationalism.

On the other hand, a society that is committed to technology is committed to continual change. This is why other societies like the English do not commit themselves to technology; they do not want continual change. In the three religions I know best, Hinduism, Buddhism, and the Greek religion, the intellectuals turned their backs on technology. The Greeks were aware there was such a thing as algebra, which is the basis of technological training, but they literally refused to allow it into their society. I imagine you would find similar objections from some of the Buddhists in Vietnam. They are terrified by what is coming, obviously, terrified of the technological society.

PIERRE TRUDEAU

In the late 1960s the Quebec terrorist organization, the Front de libération du Québec, began to accelerate its campaign for Quebec independence. It kidnapped a British diplomat and a Quebec cabinet minister in October 1970, and Prime Minister Pierre Trudeau put the country under martial law. Grant opposed this assault on civil liberties, which he thought was a manifestation of Trudeau's technological understanding of the world. His hostility to Trudeau increased over the years.

Trudeau has always seemed to be a gentlemanly kind of person. I distrust his distrust of traditional French Canada and I fear his naivety about the nature of English-speaking society.

– George Grant to Hugh MacLennan, 27 March 1969

The [forces] of independence – whether traditional or radical – are really little waves on the surface. Trudeau is a kind of Canadian Kennedy – a shallow politician who makes people think this vulgar society has a slick patina to it.

– George Grant to Derek Bedson, 26 July 1974

As for Trudeau, he incites me to rage. It is very good that now all the provinces, except Ontario, know that he is trying to destroy their autonomy as societies.

– George Grant to Gaston Laurion, 19 March 1981

Nationalism and Rationality (1971)[*]

The politics of technologized societies are an open field for demagogic tactics. Politics is the working out of public disagreement about purposes. But politics is now increasingly replaced by administration, as disagreement about purposes is legitimized away by the pervasive assumption that all which publicly matters is the achievement of technical 'rationality.' Elections become increasingly plebiscites in which the masses choose between leaders or teams who will be in charge of the administrative personnel. In plebiscites it is necessary to have leaders who can project their images through the various media, and so catch the interest of the masses who are bored with politics, except as spectacle and as the centralizing organization for technologized life. The plebiscitary situation calls forth from the privileged classes leaders who have the will to project their personalities and as these men are increasingly the product of the modern 'value-free' university, they are likely to be willing to use any means when it suits their interests. A negative example of this thesis is Mr Nixon. It is inconceivable that he could have been elected President in 1968 without the administrative disaster of the Vietnam War which exposed the blatant failure of the Democratic personnel to provide what was wanted at the home of the empire. For all his administrative reliability and talent, he simply lacked the image for the plebiscites in comparison with his Republican predecessor or his Democratic alternatives.

[*]George Grant, 'Nationalism and Rationality,' *Canadian Forum*, January 1971, 336–7.

In recent Canadian events there have been two successful plebiscitary leaders – Mr Diefenbaker and Mr Trudeau. Mr Diefenbaker had,
however, one grave disadvantage. He had certain residual loyalties (for
example, to the independence of Canada) which acted against the
demands of 'rationality' and administration. Therefore, despite his
ability to transmit his image he came into conflict with the sheer needs
of the private and public corporations – that is, with state capitalist
'rationality' itself. He could not continue to get votes in the parts of
Canada which were most enmeshed in that continental administrative
system, and where the voters were most at the mercy of the legitimizing
powers of that system. But Mr Pearson lacked the plebiscitary appeal so
that he could not get an outright majority even although his actions
were acceptable to continental administrative 'rationality.'

Mr Trudeau combines plebiscitary appeal with acceptance of the
assumptions of the state capitalist 'rationality.' He must therefore be
seen as a formidable figure in our public life. In his writings he has
unequivocally stated that he believes the best future for French Canadians is to be integrated into the Canadian structure as a whole, and that
the Canadian structure should be integrated into the whole Western
system (if not in an overtly political sense, at least economically and
socially). Throughout his career his appeals have been to universalism,
and universalism in a Canadian setting means integration into a
smooth functioning continental system. It is this union in Mr Trudeau
of charisma with the acceptance of the purposes of corporation capitalist efficiency which made Mr Denis Smith's article about his policies so
telling. The idea that Mr Trudeau was changing our political framework from a parliamentary to a presidential system involves more than
a change from Canadian to American traditions. This change in political structure would fulfil the needs of a society in which administrative
rule is bolstered by plebiscites about personnel.

In Mr Trudeau's writings there is evident distaste for what was by tradition his own, and what is put up along with that distaste are universalist goods which will be capable of dissolving that tradition. Indeed, this
quality of being a convert to modern liberalism is one cause of his for-
midability. Most English-speaking liberals have lived in universalism
much longer. They have not come to it out of something different, but
have grown up in it as their tradition. They are apt, therefore, either to
accept it automatically or even to start to be cynical about its ability to
solve human problems. On the other hand, Mr Trudeau's espousal has

behind it the force of his distaste of its opposite against which he is reacting. Recent converts are especially effective exponents of a system because they have the confidence of believing they are doing right.

Mr Trudeau combines, then, administrative reliability with the power to project his image in the plebiscites. In 1968 this image was partially a revamped Kennedy one – openness to youth and freedom, a marvelous expectation about the potentialities of our system (no interference in the bedrooms of the nation etc.). This was effective in the Canada of Expo,[*] especially because there was an awareness that things were not going as well in the U.S.A. as the Americans had expected at the beginning of the Kennedy era. Tacitly behind this part of this image, and clearly related to it, was the sense, in English-speaking Canada, that here at last was a French Canadian who would deal with Daniel Johnson[†] and De Gaulle.[‡] Mr Trudeau came to power by a brilliant use of television around that constitutional encounter. Indeed, many of the smartest media men who now deplore his recent actions had helped him to organize that use. At its worse, Mr Trudeau was for many English-speaking Canadians that happy phenomenon 'A Frog who could deal with the Frogs.' In his recent actions he has fulfilled for them that promise. As he said in October, 1970, 'Just watch me.'

I leave aside the intriguing question of why the Trudeau administration embarked on the War Measures Act and I do so having taken for granted that the government had sufficient power, without its invocation, to deal firmly with what was happening in Quebec. The question then arises: Does his employment of these powers make Mr Trudeau a more or less effective plebiscitary leader in Canadian life? As far as French Canada goes, a useful answer could only be made by somebody with great knowledge of Quebec from the inside. How deep is the desire on the part of many French Canadians to exist as a Franco-American community in the midst of the homogenized English-speaking sea? Is the French-Canadian question truly a political one, in the sense that the powers of administrative rationality cannot dissolve it?

Obscurity is increased by the fact that two different voices of opposi-

---

[*]The Montreal world's fair of 1967 coincided with Canada's centenary and was the focus of the year's celebrations.
[†]Daniel Johnson was the Union Nationale premier of Quebec, 1966–8, and a strong defender of Quebec's powers against federal encroachment.
[‡]Charles De Gaulle (1890–1970), president of France, 1958–69.

tion to Mr Trudeau seem to be coming out of Quebec. On the one hand, there is the voice of nationalism, expressed particularly by members of the elite, who care about the continuance of their community and who know that Mr Bourassa's[*] slogan 'American technology – French culture' cannot be an adequate basis for any real survival. On the other hand are the inchoate voices of those who are the particular victims of the fact that Quebec came late into the American technological expansion – e.g. the people of east Montreal and the students who cannot get jobs. These voices seem to employ the mode of popular marxism. What is the relation between these two forms of opposition? It has often been possible for marxists to appear as supporters of nationalism, for example as resisters of western invasion in Russia or China. But clearly at its heart marxism is a universalist and not a nationalist doctrine, and just as much as Mr Trudeau's liberalism, it puts the development of technique as its priority. Also, since Quebec is at the very heart geographically of the Western empire, it is going to be modernized within the setting of capitalist rationality – not marxist. Within that setting marxism will be simply an ideology for the sympathetic, an opiate for the unfortunate. The responses of the student population will be crucial. Can enough of them be won over from their nationalism, as Mr Trudeau has predicted, if Quebec is effectively oriented into the American system and enough managerial jobs are provided for the educated? Has capitalist rationality the means of bringing about that integration quickly enough?

In English-speaking Canada it seems that Mr Trudeau's status will remain high. He has come through on his promise to deal strongly with separatism. That he deals with it quite outside the principles of constitutional liberties does not seem important, because although these traditions of law were the best part of British tradition, they are not something that can hold masses of voters' minds in the age of technological rationality. Civil liberties can be a supplementary issue in times of bad employment or in connection with other failures of the system, but they cannot be a determining issue for many voters who live within modernity.

Indeed, in the extreme circumstances of the War Measures Act, the two main political questions of Canadian life come together for those

[*] Robert Bourassa (1933–96), premier of Quebec 1970–6, 1986–93, a moderate nationalist who was more interested in modernizing and rationalizing the Quebec economy than pursuing constitutional reform.

of us who must oppose what the Trudeau administration has done. The possibility of some freedom in the American empire is mutually interdependent with some potential *modus vivendi* between English-speaking and French-speaking Canadians. But it is hard to move from this relation to practical judgments about immediate Canadian politics. On the one hand, it is obvious that any indigenous English-speaking Canadian society requires the help of Quebec. Yet how can this be advocated in a way that is not simply asking French Canadians to be led along to their doom as a community? In other words, are the French not best to be separatists in the face of the North American situation? This dilemma for English-speaking nationalists is even more evident because of the events of the autumn. Before these events, a certain nationalist spirit seemed to be growing in English-speaking society. This was encouraged by the obvious social failures of the United States, and also by the economic consequences of being a branch-plant society, which were coming home to many Canadians at a time of American retreat. Yet during the crisis in Quebec, a large English-speaking majority readily acquiesced in an attack not only on terrorism but on constitutional French nationalism. In the light of this, French Canadian nationalists would perhaps do well to concentrate on the possible means of their own cultural survival and to accept that English-speaking culture is only a Trojan horse for the 'rationality' of the North American monolith. What effective alliance can English-speaking nationalists offer their French compatriots? How would it be expressed in immediate political terms? What advantage has it to offer those who seriously desire that Franco-American culture survive in a more than formal sense? Mr Lévesque's[*] question to English-speaking nationalists stands, and has been made more urgent by the present crisis.

JUSTICE AND THE RIGHT TO LIFE

Grant was invited to deliver the 1974 Wood lectures at Mount Allison University in Sackville, New Brunswick. Over the next three years he revised the manu-

---

[*]René Lévesque (1922–87), a former Quebec Liberal cabinet minister who formed the Parti Québécois in 1968 and led it to successive election victories in 1976 and 1980.

script for publication and the result, English-Speaking Justice, *was his most sustained piece of political and philosophical analysis to date. He brought together what he saw as the decay of liberalism in the United States with his increasing concern for the right to life. The event that stimulated this analysis was the American Supreme Court decision* Roe v. Wade *(1973), which virtually legalized abortion on demand. Grant was particularly worried by Mr Justice Blackmun's decision, which denied any legal status to the foetus. From this time on, the right-to-life movement was one of Grant's leading concerns and the right to life was one of the shibboleths of his politics.*

I would like to write-out at the moment the reasons why the 'contractualism' which lies at the basis of English-speaking liberal moral philosophy seems to me a failure and why one must try and understand morality as natural rather than contractual. This would be a general lecture but it would centre around a book which is very influential in the English-speaking world at the moment. The book is called *A Theory of Justice* by John Rawls – professor of philosophy at Harvard. It is a brilliant attempt to talk of moral philosophy within the analytical tradition. I would like to take this book as a starting point and move out to talk about what was good and what was inadequate in the tradition of English-speaking liberalism. Would this be an appropriate lecture?

– George Grant to Alex Colville, 24 May 1973

English-Speaking Justice (1974)[*]

English-speaking contractualism lies before us in the majority decision of the American Supreme Court in *Roe vs. Wade.*[†] In that decision their highest court ruled that no state has the right to pass legislation which would prevent a citizen from receiving an abortion during the first six months of pregnancy. In that decision one can hear what is being spoken about justice in such modern liberalism more clearly than in academic books which can be so construed as to skim questions when the

[*] George Grant, *English-Speaking Justice*, the Josiah Wood Lectures, 1974 (Sackville, N.B.: Mount Allison University 1974; repr. 1985 by House of Anansi and University of Notre Dame Press with an 'Introduction' that states: 'The text is essentially the same as the Mount Allison edition, except for the expansion of certain citations in the footnotes'). Excerpt. Used with permission.

[†] In *Roe v. Wade* (1973), the American Supreme Court ruled by a 7–2 majority that women have a constitutional right to abortion and that the foetus is not a person within the meaning of the American constitution.

theory cuts. Theories of justice are inescapably defined in the necessities of legal decision.

Mr Justice Blackmun[*] begins his majority decision from the principle that the allocation of rights from within the constitution cannot be decided in terms of any knowledge of what is good. Under the constitution, rights are prior to any account of the good. Appropriately he quotes Mr Justice Holmes[†] to this effect, who, more than any judge, enucleated the principle that the constitution was based on the acceptance of moral pluralism in society, and that the pluralism was finally justified because we must be properly agnostic about any claim to knowledge of moral good. It was his influence in this fundamental step towards a purely contractual interpretation of their constitution that has above all enshrined him in American liberal hagiography. In the decision, Blackmun interprets rights under the constitution as concerned with the ordering of conflicting claims between 'persons' and legislatures. The members of the legislature may have been persuaded by conceptions of goodness in passing the law in question. However, this is not germane to a judge's responsibility, which is to adjudicate between the rights of the mother and those of the legislature. He adjudicates that the particular law infringes the prior right of the mother to control her own body in the first six months of pregnancy. The individual who would seem to have the greatest interest in the litigation, because his or her life or death is at stake – namely the particular foetus and indeed all future American foetuses – is said by the judge not to be a party to the litigation. He states that the foetuses up to six months are not persons, and as non-persons can have no status in the litigation.

The decision then speaks modern liberalism in its pure contractual form: right prior to good; a foundational contract protecting individual rights; the neutrality of the state concerning moral 'values'; social pluralism supported by and supporting this neutrality. Indeed, the decision has been greeted as an example of the nobility of American contractarian institutions and political ideology, because the right of an individual 'person' is defended in the decision against the power of a majority in a legislature.

[*] Harry A. Blackmun (1908–), appointed by Richard Nixon to the Supreme Court of the United States in 1970. He wrote the majority opinion in *Roe v. Wade*.

[†] Oliver Wendell Holmes Jr (1841–1935), one of the great American Supreme Court justices whom Grant had much admired in his youth.

Nevertheless, however 'liberal' it may seem at the surface, it raises a cup of poison to the lips of liberalism. The poison is presented in the unthought ontology. In negating the right of existence for foetuses of less than six months, the judge has to say what such foetuses are not. They are not persons. But whatever else may be said of mothers and foetuses, it cannot be denied that they are of the same species. Pregnant women do not give birth to cats. Also, it is a fact that the foetus is not merely a part of the mother because it is genetically unique *ab initio.*[*] In adjudicating for the right of the mother to choose whether another member of her species lives or dies, the judge is required to make an ontological distinction between members of the same species. The mother is a person; the foetus is not. In deciding what is due in justice to beings of the same species, he bases such differing dueness on ontology. By calling the distinction ontological I mean simply that the knowledge which the judge has about mothers and foetuses is not scientific. To call certain beings 'persons' is not a scientific statement. But once ontological affirmation is made the basis for denying the most elementary right of traditional justice to members of our own species, ontological questioning cannot be silenced at this point. Because such a distinction has been made, the decision unavoidably opens up the whole question of what our species is. What is it about any members of our species which makes the liberal rights of justice their due? The judge unwittingly looses the terrible question: Has the long tradition of liberal right any support in what human beings in fact are? Is this a question that in the modern era can be truthfully answered in the positive? Or does it hand the cup of poison to our liberalism?

This universal question is laid before us in the more particular questions arising from the decision. If foetuses are not persons, why should not the state decide that a week-old, a two-year-old, a seventy- or eighty-year-old is not a person 'in the whole sense'? On what basis do we draw the line? Why are the retarded, the criminal, or the mentally ill persons? What is it which divides adults from foetuses when the latter have only to cross the bridge of time to catch up to the former? Is the decision saying that what makes an individual a person, and therefore the possessor of rights, is the ability to calculate and assent to contracts? Why are beings so valuable as to require rights, just because they are capable of this calculation? What has happened to the stern demands

[*] From the beginning (Latin).

of equal justice when it sacrifices the right to existence of the inarticulate to the convenience of the articulate? But thought cannot rest in these particular questionings about justice. Through them we are given the fundamental questions. What is it, if anything, about human beings that makes the rights of equal justice their due? What is it about human beings that makes it good that they should have such rights? What is it about any of us that makes our just due fuller than that of stones or flies or chickens or bears? Yet because the decision will not allow the question to remain silent, and yet sounds an ambiguous note as to how it would be answered in terms of our contemporary liberalism, the decision 'Commends th'ingredients of our poison'd chalice / To our own lips.'[*]

The need to justify modern liberal justice has been kept in the wings of our English-speaking drama by our power and the strengths of our tradition. In such events as the decision on abortion it begins to walk upon the stage. To put the matter simply: If 'species' is an historical concept and we are a species whose origin and existence can be explained in terms of mechanical necessity and chance, living on a planet which also can be explained in such terms, what requires us to live together according to the principles of equal justice?

For the last centuries a civilizational contradiction has moved our Western lives. Our greatest intellectual endeavour – the new co-penetration of *logos* and *technē*[†] – affirmed at its heart that in understanding anything we know it as ruled by necessity and chance. This affirmation entailed the elimination of the ancient notion of good from the understanding of anything. At the same time, our day-to-day organization was in the main directed by a conception of justice formulated in relation to the ancient science, in which the notion of good was essential to the understanding of what is. This civilizational contradiction arose from the attempt of the articulate to hold together what was given them in modern science with a content of justice which had been developed out of an older account of what is.

It must be emphasized that what is at stake in this contradiction is not only the foundations of justice, but more importantly its content. Many academics in many disciplines have described the difference between the ancient and modern conceptions of justice as if it were essentially concerned with differing accounts of the human situation.

---

[*] *Macbeth.* Act 1, Sc. 7.
[†] The Greek words for knowing and making, from which our word technology derives.

The view of traditional philosophy and religion is that justice is the overriding order which we do not measure and define, but in terms of which we are measured and defined. The view of modern thought is that justice is a way which we choose in freedom, both individually and publicly, once we have taken our fate into our own hands, and know that we are responsible for what happens. This description of the difference has indeed some use for looking at the history of our race – useful both to those who welcome and those who deplore the change of view. Nevertheless, concentration on differing 'world views' dims the awareness of what has been at stake concerning justice in recent Western history. This dimming takes place in the hardly conscious assumption that while there has been change as to what can be known in philosophy, and change in the prevalence of religious belief among the educated, the basic content of justice in our societies will somehow remain the same. The theoretical differences in 'world views' are turned over to the domain of 'objective' scholarship, and this scholarship is carried out in protected private provinces anaesthetized from any touch with what is happening to the content of justice in the heat of the world. To feel the cutting edge of what is at stake in differing foundations of justice it is necessary to touch those foundations as they are manifested in the very context of justice.

The civilizational contradiction which beset Europe did not arise from the question whether there is justice, but what justice is. Obviously any possible society must have some system of organization to which the name 'justice' can be given. The contradiction arose because human beings held onto certain aspects of justice which they had found in the ancient account of good, even after they no longer considered that that account of good helped them to understand the way things are. The content of justice was largely given them from its foundations in the Bible (and the classical philosophy which the early Christians thought necessary for understanding the Bible) while they understood the world increasingly in terms of modern technological science.

The desire to have both what was given in the new knowledge, and what was given us about justice in the religious and philosophical traditions, produced many conscious and unconscious attempts at practical and theoretical reconciliations. It is these attempts which make it not inaccurate to call the early centuries of modern liberal Europe the era of secularized Christianity. It is an often repeated platitude that thinkers such as Locke and Rousseau, Kant and Marx were secularized

Christians. (Of the last name it is perhaps better to apply the not so different label – secularized Jew.) The reason why an academic such as Professor Rawls has been singled out for attention in this writing is as an example of how late that civilizational contradiction has survived in the sheltered intellectual life of the English-speaking peoples.

Indeed, the appropriateness of calling modern contractualism 'secularized Christianity' may be seen in the difference between modern contractualism and the conventionalism of the ancient world. Although the dominant tradition of the ancient world was that justice belonged to the order of things, there was a continuing minority report that justice was simply a man-made convention. But what so startlingly distinguishes this ancient conventionalism from our contractualism is that those who advocated it most clearly also taught that the highest life required retirement from politics. According to Lucretius, the wise man knows that the best life is one of isolation from the dynamism of public life. The dominant contractualist teachers of the modern world have advocated an intense concern with political action. We are called to the supremacy of the practical life in which we must struggle to establish the just contract of equality. When one asks what had been the chief new public intellectual influence between ancient and modern philosophy, the answer must be Western Christianity, with it insistence on the primacy of charity and its implications for equality. Modern contractualism's determined political activism relates it to its seedbed in Western Christianity. Here again one comes upon that undefined primal affirmation which has been spoken of as concerned with 'will,' and which is prior both to technological science and to revolution.

This public contradiction was not first brought into the light of day in the English-speaking world. It was exposed in the writings of Nietzsche. The Germans had received modern ways and thought later than the French or the English and therefore in a form more explicitly divided from the traditional thought. In their philosophy these modern assumptions are most uncompromisingly brought into the light of day. Nietzsche's writings may be singled out as a Rubicon, because more than a hundred years ago he laid down with incomparable lucidity that which is now publicly open: what is given about the whole in technological science cannot be thought together with what is given us concerning justice and truth, reverence and beauty, from our tradition. He does not turn his ridicule primarily against what has been handed to us in Christian revelation and ancient philosophy. What was given there has simply been killed as given, and all that we need to understand is why it was once thought alive. His greatest ridicule is reserved for those who want to maintain a content to 'justice' and 'truth' and 'goodness' out of the corpse that they helped to make a corpse. These are the intellectual democrats who adopt modern thought while picking and choosing among the ethical 'norms' from a dead past. Justice as equality and fairness is that bit of Christian instinct which survives the death of God. As he puts it: 'The masses blink and say: "We are all equal. – Man is but man, before God – we are all equal." Before God! But now this God has died.'[*]

Particularly since Hume, the English moralists had pointed out that moral rules were useful conventions, but had also assumed that the core of English justice was convenient. Hume's 'monkish virtues' – the parts of the tradition which did not suit the new bourgeoisie – could be shown to be inconvenient; but the heart of the tradition could be maintained and extended in the interests of property and liberty. It could be freed from its justification in terms of eternity, and its rigour could be refurbished by some under the pseudo-eternity of a timeless social contract. But Nietzsche makes clear that if the 'justice' of liberty and equality is only conventional, we may find in the course of an ever changing history that such content is not convenient. He always puts the word 'justice' in quotation marks to show that he does not imply its traditional content, and that its content will vary through the flux of history. The English moralists had not discovered that realm of beings we moderns call 'history,' and therefore they did not understand the dominance of historicism over all other statements. Their social contract was indeed a last effort to avoid that dominance, while they increasingly accepted the ways of thought that led ineluctably to historicism. The justice of liberty and equality came forth from rationalists who did not think 'historically.' For whom is such justice convenient when we know that the old rationalism can no longer be thought as 'true?'

However, it is Kant who is singled out by Nietzsche as the clearest expression of this secularized Christianity. Kant's thought is the consummate expression of wanting it both ways. Having understood what is told us about nature in our society, and having understood that we will and make our own history, he turned away from the consequence of those recognitions by enfolding them in the higher affirmation that

---

[*]Friedrich Nietzsche, *Thus Spoke Zarathustra* Book, I.v., 'Of the Higher Men,' trans. R.J. Hollingdale (Midddlesex, U.K.: Penguin 1961), 297.

morality is the one fact of reason, and we are commanded to obedience. According to Nietzsche, he limited autonomy by obedience.
Because this comfortable anaesthetizing from the full consequences of
the modern was carried out so brilliantly in the critical system,
Nietzsche calls Kant 'the great delayer.' Kant persuaded generations of
intellectuals to the happy conclusion that they could keep both the
assumptions of technological secularism and the absolutes of the old
morality. He allowed them the comfort of continuing to live in the civilizational contradiction of accepting both the will to make one's own
life and the old content of justice. He delayed them from knowing that
there are no moral facts, but only the moral interpretation of facts,
and that these interpretations can be explained as arising from the historical vicissitudes of the instincts. Moral interpretations are what we
call our 'values,' and these are what our wills impose upon the facts.
Because of the brilliance of Kant's delaying tactics, men were held
from seeing that justice as equality was a secularized survival of an
archaic Christianity, and the absolute commands were simply the man-
made 'values' of an era we have transcended.

Nietzsche was the first to make clear the argument that there is no
reason to continue to live in that civilizational contradiction. Societies
will always need legal systems – call them systems of 'justice' if you like
the word. Once we have recognized what we can now will to create
through our technology, why should we limit such creation by basing
our systems of 'justice' on presuppositions which have been shown to
be archaic by the very coming to be of technology? As we move into a
society where we will be able to shape not only non-human nature but
humanity itself, why should we limit that shaping by doctrines of equal
rights which come out of a world view that 'history' has swept away?
Does not the production of quality of life require a legal system which
gives new range to the rights of the creative and the dynamic? Why
should that range be limited by the rights of the weak, the uncreative,
and the immature? Why should the liberation of women to quality of
life be limited by restraints on abortion, particularly when we know
that the foetuses are only the product of necessity and chance? Once
we have recognized 'history' as the imposing of our wills on an accidental world, does not 'justice' take on a new content?[1]

Against this attack on our 'values,' our liberalism so belongs to the
flesh and bones of our institutions that it cannot be threatened by
something as remote as ontological questioning. The explicit statements of the American constitution guard their system of justice; the

British constitution guards the same shape of rights in a less explicit but in a more deeply rooted way. These living forces of allegiance protect the common sense of practical men against the follies of ideologues. Anyway, did not the English-speaking peoples win the wars against the Germans, and win them in the name of liberalism, against the very 'philosophy' that is said to assail that liberalism?

It is also argued that the very greatness of American pluralism, founded upon the contract, is that out of it have come forth continuous religious revivals which produce that moral sustenance necessary to the justice of their society. Is it not a reason for confidence that in the election of 1976 the two candidates competed in allegiance to the traditions of religion, and that there is a renewed interest in religion among the young in the contractual society? Where is the atheism of the right in the United States? Does not the greatness of the American constitution lie in the fact that the general outlines of social cooperation are laid down and maintained by a secular contract, while within those general rules the resources of religious faith can flourish, as long as such faiths do not transgress that general outline? The greatness of the system is that the tolerance of pluralism is combined with the strength of religion. God has not died, as European intellectuals believed; it is just that our differing apprehensions of deity require that the rules of the game are defined in terms of the calculation of worldly self-interest; beyond that, citizens may seek the eternal as they see fit.

Indeed, any sane individual must be glad that we face the unique event of technology within a long legal and political tradition founded on the conception of justice as requiring liberty and equality. When we compare what is happening to multitudes in Asia who live the event of technology from out of ancient and great traditions, but without a comparable sense of individual right, we may count ourselves fortunate to live within our tradition. Asian people often have great advantages over us in the continuing strength of rite; our advantage is in the continuing strength of right. Also, our liberalism came from the meeting of Christian tradition with an early form of modern thought, so that our very unthinking confidence in that liberalism has often saved us from modern political plagues which have been devastating in other societies. At the practical level it is imprudent indeed to speak against the principles, if not the details, of those legal institutions which guard our justice.[2]

Nevertheless, it must be stated that our justice now moves to a lowered content of equal liberty. The chief cause of this is that our justice is being played out within a destiny more comprehensive than itself. A quick name for this is 'technology.' I mean by that word the endeavour which summons forth everything (both human and non-human) to give its reason, and through the summoning forth of those reasons turns the world into potential raw material, at the disposal of our 'creative' wills. The definition is circular in the sense that what is 'creatively' willed is further expansion of that union of knowing and making given in the linguistic union of 'technē' and 'logos.' Similar but cruder: it has been said that communism and contractual capitalism are predicates of the subject technology. They are ways in which our more comprehensive destiny is lived out. But clearly that technological destiny has its own dynamic conveniences, which easily sweep away our tradition of justice, if the latter gets in the way. The 'creative' in their corporations have been told for many generations that justice is only a convenience. In carrying out the dynamic convenience of technology, why should they not seek a 'justice' which is congruent with those conveniences, and gradually sacrifice the principles of liberty and equality when they conflict with the greater conveniences? What is it about other human beings that should stand in the way of such convenience? The tendency of the majority to get together to insist on a contract guaranteeing justice to them against the 'creative' strong continues indeed to have some limiting power. Its power is, however, itself limited by the fact that the majority of that majority see in the very technological endeavour the hope for their realization of 'the primary goods,' and therefore will often not stand up for the traditional justice when it is inconvenient to that technological endeavour. The majority of the acquiescent think they need the organizers to provide 'the primary goods' more than they need justice.

In such a situation, equality in 'primary goods' for a majority in the heartlands of the empire is likely; but it will be an equality which excludes liberal justice for those who are inconvenient to the 'creative.' It will exclude liberal justice from those who are too weak to enforce contracts – the imprisoned, the mentally unstable, the unborn, the aged, the defeated, and sometimes even the morally unconforming. The price for large-scale equality under the direction of the 'creative' will be injustice for the very weak. It will be a kind of massive 'equality' in 'primary goods,' outside a concern for justice. As Huey Long[*] put it: 'When fascism comes to America, it will come in

---

[*]H.P. Long (1893–1935), Louisiana governor and U.S. senator, who in 1934 seized almost dictatorial powers in his home state. He was assassinated the next year.

the name of democracy.' We move to such a friendly and smooth-faced organization that it will not be recognized for what it is. This lack of recognition is seen clearly when the president of France says he is working for 'an advanced liberal society,' just as he is pushing forward laws for the mass destruction of the unborn. What he must mean by liberal is the society organized for the human conveniences which fit the conveniences of technology.

As justice is conceived as the external convenience of contract, it obviously has less and less to do with the good ordering of the inward life. Among the majority in North America, inward life, then, comes to be ordered around the pursuit of 'primary goods,' and/or is taken in terms of a loose popular Freudianism, mediated to the masses by the vast array of social technicians. But it is dangerous to mock socially the fact of contradiction. The modern account of 'the self' is at one with the Nietzschean account. This unity was explicitly avowed by Freud. With its affirmation of the instrumentality of reason, how can it result in a conception of 'justice' similar to that of our tradition? In such a situation, the majorities in the heartlands of the empires may be able to insist on certain external equalities. But as justice is conceived as founded upon contract, and as having nothing to do with the harmony of the inward life, will it be able to sustain the inconveniences of public liberty?

In the Western tradition it was believed that the acting out of justice in human relationships was the essential way in which human beings are opened to eternity. Inward and outward justice were considered to be mutually interdependent, in the sense that the inward openness to eternity depended on just practice, and just practice depended on that inward openness to eternity. When public justice is conceived as conventional and contractual, the division between inward and outward is so widened as to prevent any such mutual interdependence. Both openness to eternity and practical justice are weakened in that separation. A.N. Whitehead's[*] shallow dictum that religion is what we do with our solitude aptly expresses that modern separation. It is a destructive half-truth because it makes our solitude narcissistic, and blunts our cutting edge in public justice.

Above all, we do not correctly envisage what is happening when we take our situation simply as new practical difficulties for liberalism,

---

[*]A.N. Whitehead (1861–1947), British mathematician and philosopher and co-author with Bertrand Russell of the *Principia Mathematica* (1910–13).

arising from the need to control new technologies, themselves external to that liberalism. Such an understanding of our situation prevents
us from becoming aware that our contractual liberalism is not independent of the assumptions of technology in any way that allows it to
be the means of transcending those technologies. Our situation is
rather that the assumptions underlying contractual liberalism and
underlying technology both come from the same matrix of modern
thought, from which can arise no reason why the justice of liberty is
due to all human beings, irrespective of convenience. Insofar as the
contemporary systems of liberal practice hold onto the content of free
and equal justice, it is because they still rely on older sources which are
more and more made unthinkable in the very realization of technology. When contractual liberals hold within their thought remnants of
secularized Christianity or Judaism, these remnants, if made conscious,
must be known as unthinkable in terms of what is given in the modern.
How, in modern thought, can we find positive answers to the questions: (i) what is it about human beings that makes liberty and equality
their due? (ii) why is justice what we are fitted for, when it is not convenient? Why is it our good? The inability of contractual liberals (or
indeed marxists) to answer these questions is the terrifying darkness
which has fallen upon modern justice.

Therefore, to those of us who for varying reasons cannot but trust
the lineaments of liberal justice, and who somehow have been told that
some such justice is due to all human beings and that its living out is,
above all, what we are fitted for – to those of such trust comes the call
from that darkness to understand how justice can be thought together
with what has been discovered of truth in the coming to be of technology. The great theoretical achievements of the modern era have been
quantum physics, the biology of evolutionism, and modern logic. (All
other modern theoretical claims, particularly those in the human sciences, remain as no more than provisional, or even can be known as
simply expressions of that oblivion of eternity which has characterized
the coming to be of technology.) These are the undoubtable core of
truth which has come out of technology, and they cry out to be
thought in harmony with the conception of justice as what we are
fitted for.

The danger of this darkness is easily belittled by our impoverished
use of the word 'thought.' This word is generally used as if it meant an
activity necessary to scientists when they come up against a difficulty in
their research, or some vague unease beyond calculation when we

worry about our existence. Thought is steadfast attention to the whole. The darkness is fearful, because what is at stake is whether anything is good. In the pretechnological era, the central Western account of justice clarified the claim that justice is what we are fitted for. It clarified why justice is to render each human being their due, and why what was due to all human beings was 'beyond all bargains and without an alternative.' That account of justice was written down most carefully and most beautifully in *The Republic* of Plato. For those of us who are Christians, the substance of our belief is that the perfect living out of that justice is unfolded in the Gospels. Why the darkness which enshrouds justice is so dense – even for those who think that what is given in *The Republic* concerning good stands forth as true – is because that truth cannot be thought in unity with what is given in modern science concerning necessity and chance. The darkness is not simply the obscurity of living by that account of justice in the practical tumult of the technological society. Nor is it the impossibility of that account coming to terms with much of the folly of modernity, e.g. the belief that there is a division between 'facts' and 'values'; nor the difficulty of thinking its truth in the presence of historicism. Rather, it is that this account has not been thought in unity with the greatest theoretical enterprises of the modern world. This is a great darkness, because it appears certain that rational beings cannot get out of the darkness by accepting either truth and rejecting the other. It is folly simply to return to the ancient account of justice as if the discoveries of the modern science of nature had not been made. It is folly to take the ancient account of justice as simply of antiquarian interest, because without any knowledge of justice as what we are fitted for, we will move into the future with a 'justice' which is terrifying in its potentialities for mad inhumanity of action. The purpose of this writing has been to show the truth of the second of these propositions. In the darkness one should not return as if the discoveries of modern science had not taken place; nor should one give up the question of what it means to say that justice is what we are fitted for; and yet who has been able to think the two together? For those of us who are lucky enough to know that we have been told that justice is what we are fitted for, this is not a practical darkness, but simply a theoretical one. For those who do not believe that they have been so told it is both a practical and theoretical darkness which leads to an ever greater oblivion of eternity.

In the task of lightening the darkness which surrounds justice in our era, we of the English-speaking world have one advantage and one great disadvantage. The advantage is practical: the old and settled legal institutions which still bring forth loyalty from many of the best practical people. The disadvantage is that we have been so long disinterested or even contemptuous of that very thought about the whole which is now required. No other great Western tradition has shown such lack of interest in thought, and in the institutions necessary to its possibility. We now pay the price for our long tradition of taking the goods of practical confidence and competence as self-sufficiently the highest goods. In what is left of those secular institutions which should serve the purpose of sustaining such thought – that is, our current institutions of higher learning – there is little encouragement to what might transcend the technically competent, and what is called 'philosophy' is generally little more than analytical competence. Analytical logistics plus historicist scholarship plus even rigorous science do not when added up equal philosophy. When added together they are not capable of producing that thought which is required if justice is to be taken out of the darkness which surrounds it in the technological era. This lack of tradition of thought is one reason why it is improbable that the transcendence of justice over technology will be lived among English-speaking people.

NOTES

1 To put the matter politically: the early public atheism of Europe generally came from 'the left.' Its adherents attacked the traditional religion while taking for granted almost unconsciously that 'the right' would continue to live with its religious allegiances. 'The left' could attack religion partially because it relied on 'the right' having some restraint because of its religion. Philosophers cannot be subsumed under their political effects, but with Nietzsche the atheism of 'the right' enters the Western scene. One definition of national socialism is a strange union of the atheism of 'the right' and of 'the left.'

2 It is well to remember that the greatest contemporary philosopher, Heidegger, published in 1953 *An Introduction to Metaphysics* in which he wrote of National Socialism: 'The inner truth and greatness of this movement (namely the encounter between global technology and modern man).' One theoretical part of that encounter was the development of a new jurisprudence, which explicitly distinguished itself from our jurisprudence of rights, because the latter belonged to an era of plutocratic democracy which

needed to be transcended in that encounter. Such arguments must make one extremely careful of the ontological questioning of our jurisprudence, even in its barest contractual form.

CANADA AND QUEBEC

In 1976 René Lévesque led his separatist Parti Québécois to power in the Quebec provincial election, a victory that represented the greatest threat yet to the survival of the Canadian state. Grant often spoke out publicly in the next few years in an attempt to moderate English-speaking Canadians' response to the hopes and fears of their French-speaking compatriots.

I saw a map (Europe &) the world from the U.S.A. – black for fascism, white for democracy. Quebec was grey.
– George Grant to Maude Grant, 1937

We drove into Magog through the wonderful township country with the hills all around. Glorious countryside in the two essentials: it is lived in, fertile & with the mark of man's touch and at the same time it is powerful, strong & wild. Magog was a typical French town, recently industrialized, enjoying its Sunday. (The townships that used to be 3/4 English, 1/4 French, are now 80% French.) We had an ice cream cone & then went to the meeting. The platform was on the steps of the main RC church with microphones planted in the west windows & the Bourbon fleur-de-lis & cross everywhere & the tricolor draped around the front of the platform. The priests looked on (six or eight of them from the upstairs gallery of the presbytery next door). A large crowd spread around and out into the street – a crowd of both industrial workers & farmers. A lovely gay French crowd, with its humour and stupidity, its highly respectable farm women and its tart like industrial ones. Well, first the candidate from Montreal–Cartier spoke, then Choquette[*] for Stanstead – both dull and short. Then Barré[†] ... spoke as you would never hear (or at least rarely hear in

---

[*]J.-A. Choquette (1905–?), president of the Union catholique des cultivateurs, elected to the House of Commons in the Stanstead by-election of 9 August 1943 for the Bloc Populaire Canadien.

[†]Laurent Barré (1886–1964), farmer and politician, first president of the L'Union catholique des cultivateurs (1924).

English Canada) with humour, wit at first, then gradually bringing it all up to a climax – far better than we can do. Then, suddenly, in the middle of one of his rising polemics, a honking of horns & in an open car – the old man [Henri Bourassa]* arrived. Against all my judgment it was the most moving moment I have ever had in Canada. The first feeling of being a Canadian since returning from England. He stepped from the car – the old man helped along by a young man. His fine Gallic face – white beard – and the crowd – not very excited up to that – going wild – & wild with a feeling that this was their man & they really loved him. He walked down the centre aisle – shaking hands with an elderly cultivateur here & another one there – and as he reached the platform they sang (& mind you everybody sang O Canada, deeply moved). Compared to the fat King or the pompous Bennett,† this really was a man. He was not only a leader of a party – who had kept power, to whom power was real. This man had an idea. A bad idea, a pernicious idea, but at least an idea. He was some-thing in the realm of morality, not merely a man whose end was office. Woods-worth‡ was the only other Canadian who has ever given me that feeling & these people believed in him. He represented in some basic way the aristocrat of 'leur pays.'

A young man got up to introduce him. Here was a danger. A young fellow called Laurendeau,§ editor of *Action Catholique*, bitter, Catholic, the real fascist, evidently the brains behind the Bloc. Far too urban, too smooth, too passionate without solidity, for the agricultural audience. Obviously deeply moved at the last meeting of the grand old man of their movement.

Then Bourassa. Again wild cheers. An old man's voice – 'Je viens de la cama-raderie de vous voir'¶ – tired, but what a show – up and down the platform – gesticulating – and humour. Magnificent entertainment. King being seduced by the Queen – feeding her cognac, but being duped. 'Je respecte le roi – mais le roi du Canada – pas le roi d'Angleterre.'** The Queen departs bored stiff with poor old King a real royalist, etc., etc. King is only an expert on farming

---

*Henri Bourassa (1868–1952), nationalist Quebec politician and founder of *Le Devoir*.
†R.B. Bennett (1870–1947), Conservative prime minister from 1930 to 1935.
‡J.S. Woodsworth (1874–1942), clergyman, social worker, and leader of the Co-operative Commonwealth Federation (precursor of the New Democratic Party) from its founding in 1932 until his death.
§J.-E.-A. Laurendeau (1912–68) became provincial leader of the Bloc Populaire in Febru-ary 1944 and was elected to the Quebec assembly. In 1963 Lester Pearson appointed him as co-chair of the Royal Commission on Bilingualism and Biculturalism.
¶I come to see you out of friendship.
**I respect the king, but the king of Canada, not the king of England.

with the sheep he has in Parliament. [illegible] wild, great cheers, the biggest of
the afternoon other than Bourassa's arrival. Then 'ce brave Paulliot' – what
scorn. Then back to King. He had a grandfather, I had one – 'Louis Joseph
Papineau'* – wild cheers. King has deserted his grandfather. I have remained
loyal to mine. Foreign policy, for years dictated by G.B., 'mais maintenant plus
servant à Washington.'† (Solitary cheers from George Grant.) King going to
London via Washington, to Washington via London, but [pour] le Canada
jamais etc., etc. Then suddenly and very effectively from melodramatic humour
and exaggeration to dramatic seriousness – quietly and with terrific force, 'I
have never lied to my people.' Wild cheers. We must look to our rights – we
must be Canadians etc., etc.

Then, he sits down amid prolonged applause – we left hastily.

I think because this particularly county is 40% English they stressed the
Canadian nationalism rather than the French-Canadian. But what impressed
me most – this was a show – a mixture of festival in honour of the great man and
a circus for entertainment. This was alive, real, vital. Whatever party wants to get
anywhere in Quebec, it seems to me, must put on such a show. Thirdly, where
the CCF were allowed to rent the RC parish hall for their candidate, who is the
RC mayor of Magog, these people had the steps of the church with microphones from inside.

– George Grant to Maude Grant, summer 1943

I simply do not get near what is happening in Canada at the moment. Living
in a vulgar Americanized institution I have some sympathy for nationalism in
Quebec, but the more one watches the new government it seems to want to
just produce further modern vulgarity, but just speaking French. I was in
Montreal for a couple of days after Xmas staying with some priests. They are
rather vague nationalists, but the impression I got above all was that they were
just living their lives (men of between sixty and forty) with little sense of the
continuance of their order when they are gone. At the best one could say that
after the quiet revolution they were reculer pour mieux sauter,‡ but they
seemed to be reculering for ten years and with little sense of what went
beyond.

– George Grant to Derek Bedson, January 1977

---

*L.-J. Papineau (1786–1871) was leader of the 1837 rebellion in Lower Canada against the
British. Mackenzie King's grandfather, William Lyon Mackenzie (1795–1861), led the
rebellion in Upper Canada.
†But now more subservient to Washington.
‡Drawing back in order to jump better.

On National Unity[*] (1977)

I am honoured to be asked to say a few words at this gathering.

Canadian politics has had two main questions: (i) how to maintain some independence while sharing this continent with the most powerful modern empire; (ii) how to maintain workable relations between the French and English-speaking communities. Those two very complex questions can only be thought about clearly if they are thought about together.

This country was made up of two founding groups who weren't very friendly to each other, but who made a contract because they thought such a contract would help each of them achieve their own particular ends – but they were different purposes.

The present constitutional crisis has arisen because some of the Quebec elite has received the backing of many voters, particularly young voters, under the affirmation that that contract does not serve their purposes and therefore must be terminated or perhaps clarified.

What is the proper response of English-speaking people to such an event? I am sure that it shouldn't be what has been all too common since that election. Namely – let's see how we can get those people back into line. Namely – we've got a clever fellow up there in Ottawa who promised us in 1968 that he could keep them in line and who was willing to use troops in 1970, and used those troops while most of English-speaking Canada cheered.

Rather than that approach, I think our constitutional crisis should lead us to three steps:

(i) to try and understand clearly why these people are saying that the contract does not work;

(ii) to think clearly – above all, do we really want a country on the northern half of this continent?

(iii) If we answer that question honestly in the affirmative, how can we reach a revised contract that will suit them and us?

Let me emphasize that if we really aren't interested in having a country, there is little point in trying to reach a renewed contract.

Why isn't the contract working in the mind of many French people?

Let me take just one issue - language. Up until recently the French did not go in for concentrated technological education but continued

[*] George Grant and Maurice Lamontagne, *On National Unity* (Cemasco Management for Constellation Life Assurance Company of Canada 1977).

Catholic education. (I do not say that as a sneer, for as a fellow Christian I have a great sympathy for Catholic education.)

Now that they are with technological education, they find the following:

(i) they are behind;

(ii) the universal language of the most powerful technology is English;

(iii) the only choice they have for control over the technological life of their country is to hold onto French as the language of that country. Why?

(iv) their language is the only advantage they have in trying to redress the balance of what has been English-speaking control of their technology;

(v) that advantage might give them ten years to catch up in technological education. – I know the people around Dr Laurin[*] and know that that is what they are thinking. Nobody in English-speaking Canada ever seems to say this or even understand this.

Do we have sympathy to allow them to use that one advantage to redress the balance of technological education or do we say we are simply the instruments of institutional business and we are going to prevent them taking advantage of that advantage?

For that is clearly one thing that they have said to us unambiguously. They say: the federal government has been keeping Canada's prosperity going – by selling our natural resources cheaply and piling up an enormous indebtedness in the international community. (Just look at the rate of growth of our international indebtedness since the Trudeau government came to office.) What the P.Q. government seems to be saying is that they will take charge of selling our resources, James Bay,[†] etc., because the federal government has not made a very good job of it. Is that so different from Premier Lougheed[‡] – who seems to me a very sensible man?

What I fear from my own community is that we will see the present crisis in the following way: We will assert that we all believe in the future of our country and that all we have to do is to struggle for the

---

[*] Dr Camille Laurin (1922–), psychiatrist and Parti Québécois cabinet minister.

[†] A major hydroelectric project, much of whose output was destined for sale to the United States.

[‡] Peter Lougheed (1928–), Conservative premier of Alberta, 1970–85.

hearts and minds of Quebec. I don't think you come to sensible contracts from out of such self-delusion.

The first priority for English-speaking Canadians is to think what we
want, and first in that is to think whether we want to be a country in
the northern half of this continent and what we need to do if we want
to continue as such a country.

(Let me say forcibly in parenthesis that I do not think that the only
difficulty here is the business community, for scientists and other aca-
demicians have been just as equivocal in their relation to their country
as have some business people. Universities in English-speaking Canada
have increasingly tried to model themselves on Michigan State or Cal.
Tech. or Yale with little sense of the responsibility to anything unique
this country has to offer.)

I just do not know what the consensus of English-speaking Canadians will be to this question. Do we care to contract to be a country in
the light of this constitutional crisis?

I do know that if English-speaking Canadians do have enough sense
of wanting to be a country – then we have to get down to reaching a
contract with Quebec in which what both parties need can be put
together.

In that process what will be required above all will be moderation. I
do not mean by moderation – weakness. Moderation is clear firmness.
It is the opposite of intemperance and confrontation.

Let me give you an example of how intemperance fails: The federal
government and its leaders at several TV reported meetings went in for
confrontation with premiers Daniel Johnson and Bertrand[*] of Quebec. They made a lot of political capital out of these confrontations
with these moderate nationalists. In November 1976 the sons[†] of both
premiers, Johnson and Bertrand, were elected as Parti Québécois
members. I think that is a lesson about confrontation that needs to
sink it.

Moderation is not only needed from our political leaders – but from
the rest of us. I admire the Globe and Mail, but when its chief corre-
spondent in Quebec heads its lead story with the words: 'Premier
Lévesque from his bunker in Quebec City' – my heart sinks. The

[*]Jean-Jacques Bertrand (1916–73) succeeded Johnson as Union Nationale leader and
premier until his defeat in 1970 at the hands of Robert Bourassa's Liberals.
[†]Pierre-Marc Johnson led the Parti Québécois from 1985 until 1987 and was premier in
1985. Jean-François Bertrand was elected in 1976 and was a member of the Parti Québécois cabinet from 1978 to 1985.

leader of a few million French surrounded by 250 million English-speaking people – identified by the bunker with a maniac!

I am more hopeful about moderation since reading the recent paper on language from the federal government, although my hope is modified by the fact that this government has been one of confrontation in the last ten years and has not succeeded by these means.

I am also hopeful about moderation because I think both the people of Quebec and indeed even Premier Lévesque are not *ideological* separatists. I think he wants to achieve certain purposes and if some of these purposes are achievable within a new contract, I think he would go for such a contract.

In short, if you want this country, I can see no alternative to the procedures of clear moderation. I am not always optimistic that we will follow such a course for to put it plainly the twentieth century has not been exactly a moderate century and there are many people around including important ones who may find that they have much to gain personally and immediately by being immoderate.

CLASSICAL LIBERALISM

Grant respected the political and juridical achievements of nineteenth-century liberalism, which he considered a highly practical, though not necessarily philosophical, achievement. However, he considered these achievements under threat in the late twentieth century because the institutions that had arisen in liberal societies did not have adequate philosophic grounding. Some of the blame for that inadequacy, Grant thought, lay with John Stuart Mill, liberalism's most influential Victorian expositor.

It was not easy for me to leave the Canadian academic establishment and it was not easy to face the intolerance of that establishment – particularly as that intolerance claimed for itself the name of 'liberalism.' I think the most savage words ever spoken to me by an older man I had respected were said by W.A. Mackintosh[*] and I identified his opinions with your own. For an ambitious person such as myself, it is easier to take such remarks today when one is secure

---

[*]W.A. Mackintosh (1895–1970), professor of economics at Queen's University and civil servant.

than at the time they were made, when I was without a job. When English-speaking liberalism seemed to have the world at its feet in the 1950s, it was not tolerant of anything which lay outside its vision and nowhere was it more intolerant than in its academic manifestations.

– George Grant to J.A. Corry, 17 February 1972

John Stuart Mill (1977)[*]

It is appropriate that the University of Toronto should be issuing the definitive edition of the collected works of John Stuart Mill. The formative ideas of that university in its heyday were essentially Millian. In his introduction to these volumes, Professor A. Brady points out again and again that Mill was a 'rationalist.' What he is saying is that Mill's account of 'reason' is the same as that which dominated the University of Toronto. That is what 'rationalist' is. Indeed, university life in Canada, before the American invasion of the sixties, was largely congruent with Mill, the archetypal British bourgeois philosopher. This was true, not only of our intellectual life, but of our politics. Just think of people like Mackenzie King, L.B. Pearson,[†] O.D. Skelton[‡] – progress as technology, liberty as individualism and property ...

These two volumes (XVIII and XIX) are made up of Mill's writings on politics and society, except for his *Principles of Political Economy* which is in a separate volume. The two central pieces are his long essay *On Liberty* (1859) and his book *Considerations On Representative Government* (1861) – the most influential writings about politics coming from Britain at the height of its power in the nineteenth century. Many other shorter pieces are made easily available in these volumes. Above all, it is good to find Mill's two long essays on *De Tocqueville on Democracy in America*. Here is Mill coming to terms with a great writer of his age. At a time when those of us of British tradition are called on to reassess our past, it is useful to have the writings of its most influential

---

[*] George Grant, review of *John Stuart Mill: The Collected Works, vols. 18 and 19*, ed. J.M. Robson (Toronto: University of Toronto Press). *Globe and Mail*, 6 August 1977, 31.
[†] L.B. Pearson (1897–1972), deputy minister of external affairs, 1946; secretary of state for external affairs, 1948–57; winner of the Nobel Peace Prize, 1957; leader of the Liberal Party from 1958 and prime minister from 1963 to 1968.
[‡] O.D. Skelton (1878–1941), Queen's political scientist and under-secretary of state for external affairs from 1925 until his death.

secular expositor laid before us in such clear and handsome form. Professor J.M. Robson is to be congratulated as the chief textual editor of this collected edition. All the labour of presenting the works efficiently and accurately has been well done. The volumes have been completely and pleasantly printed by the U of T Press. They are not expensive, considering the price of things these days.

It is all too easy for a person of my temperament, thought, and convictions to describe J.S. Mill as a figure of high comedy. Through the decades from 1830 to 1870 he lectured the English people on how they must improve themselves. This is, of course, a very familiar role for 'intellectuals' in a society with Protestant traditions, and would not alone make Mill a figure suitable to the talents of Aristophanes or Jane Austen. Rather, it is that he dons the robes of justice, while at the same time his account of the whole leaves no reason why anybody should take seriously an appeal to justice. The mantle of the tireless preacher is worn without any seeming recognition that if what he is preaching is taken seriously there is no reason why it is good to be just. Mill is indeed the very archetype of the secularized Protestant. He wants it both ways. He is part of the long tradition of English empiricism, and affirms that pleasant life in space and time is what matters; at the same time he affirms a call to justice as right, which comes forth from the very Protestantism which he rejects theoretically. Indeed, in his attempt to have it both ways, he decently tried to improve the utilitarianism of Bentham and his father, in which he had been educated.

In their utilitarianism, happiness meant the sum of pleasures, and pleasures were to be calculated quantitatively. Although the anointed successor of this doctrine, Mill cannot quite accept it, because to him some pleasures are to be encouraged in society, while others discouraged. He therefore introduces into his utilitarianism the doctrine of higher and lower pleasure. But by wanting at the same time both a teaching about higher and lower pleasures and his empiricism, he becomes inconsistent. He is too secularist to give up utilitarianism; he is too Protestant to give up higher pleasures. The comedy is for a philosopher to sacrifice consistency to decency. He continually inveighs against the reactionary results stemming from the dogmatic religion of his country (that is, Protestantism), while his intuitive and imaginative responses are tied to the very religion he inveighs against. The pedantry of his expository style combines the exhortations of the pulpit with the flat substance of secularism, so that he achieves the very difficult result of making de Tocqueville[*] appear a bore. Indeed, the comedy appears not only from his thought but from his life.

Here is a man who affirms that the purpose of life is maximizing pleasure, and yet may never have achieved intercourse in his long years with Harriet Taylor. Marriage blanc is a strange enough conception even within the more austere reaches of Christianity and Judaism, but it is even stranger in a man who lectured his compatriots on maximizing pleasure.

Nevertheless, to approach Mill as a figure of comedy is worse than inadequate, it is intellectually irresponsible. Here is a man who articulated the political thinking of the dominant class of the dominant society of his era, and at a time when that class stood at the height of its world influence. One is not implying the truth of Hegelianism, if one states that the philosophy of a world historical class must be looked at with high seriousness. By seriousness I mean that one must first look for what is true in such an articulation. Any class which has been greatly influential in the world has incorporated some aspect of political truth in the formulation of its mission. A century before Mill, that shrewd political philosopher, Montesquieu, had said that the highest regimes of the Western world had been the Athenian and the English. The modern was higher than the ancient, because the English had wisely substituted the pursuit of commerce for the pursuit of honour as the pulsating heart of their constitutional regimes. The pursuit of commerce was the best foundation of a free political order.

It may be that the earlier voices of English secular liberalism, Locke in particular, were more comprehensive, more consistent, subtler than Mill in formulating the principles of the regimes that Montesquieu so praised. But in Mill the articulation comes forth when this class was fully realizing its destiny, and it includes the idea of progress in a way that Locke did not. Therefore, one must try to look at what is being said of truth in Mill's thought. Moreover, whatever needs to be thought about the inadequacy of bourgeois liberty, the regimes that have blossomed as later forms of modernity, for example communist and nationalist socialist regimes, have been so much worse than the plutocratic democracies that one cannot but look with some sympathy at Mill's articulations. Whatever barrenness there was among the bour-

---

[*]Alexis de Tocqueville (1805–59), a French nobleman and social critic whose *Democracy in America* is considered a classic liberal analysis of American society.

geois English in such forms of activity as music and contemplation, politically they have been the best that modernity has to offer.

Indeed, for those of us who live in English-speaking regimes, there is a particular need to think about Mill's principles. Despite the disintegrations and contradictions of our regimes, liberal principles are the only political principles we've got. What other principles could possibly give more cogency to our processes than something quite close to what Mill is talking about?

And beyond the practical, it is true that 'the owl of Minerva only begins to stretch its wings in the dusk.' If our dusk is the twilight of our liberal regimes then the stretching of any remaining philosophical wings must include letting those principles lie before us.

In his essay *On Liberty* Mill states clearly the central affirmation of all modern liberal regimes:

> The object of this Essay is to assert one very simple principle, as entitled to govern absolutely the dealings of society with the individual in the way of compulsion and control, whether the means used by physical force in the form of legal penalties, or the moral coercion of public opinion. That principle is, that the sole end for which mankind are warranted, individually or collectively, in interfering with the liberty of action of any of their number, is self-protection. That the only purpose for which power can be rightfully exercised over any member of a civilized community, against his will, is to prevent harm to others.

To many of the best people in our society that principle is fundamental to our politics, and so self-evidently true that it is outside thought – the foundation stone of liberal regimes. What is necessary is not to think about it, but to see how it can best be implemented in full recognition of the difficulties in advanced technological societies. It is so self-evident that to think about its truth is a silly waste of time, worthy of irresponsible professors who should be kept busy with some productive research. Yet the passion of astonishment perhaps cannot finally be destroyed even in America. To let this principle lie before one and ponder its truth is first to ask what is being said in it about human beings. Why are human beings such as to merit regimes of freedom? It was indeed these kinds of questions that Mill did not ask, largely it seems because his confidence in his world excluded him from the passion of astonishment. He could combine his secularism with his care for the rights of the individual without being astonished at that combination. In our era, however, when the individual is so terribly threatened (literally torn from the mother's womb), that combination appears more astonishing. The questions of the fundamental principles of a decent regime arise in a more primal way than they could for Mill.

One is grateful that the University of Toronto is bringing out the texts of a significant ancestor. Scholarship is not thought and indeed is generally in our current multiversities the enemy of thought, because it is used as a substitute. But scholarship can sometimes be a propaedeutic to thinking. If these volumes lead some people to think about the fundamental propositions of our secular liberalism, they will have been worth producing.

CONSERVATISM

John Diefenbaker remained in Parliament for sixteen years after his defeat in 1963. In spite of Grant's criticisms of Diefenbaker's administration, Grant was seen by the media as one of the few Canadians academics who had anything at all good to say about the former prime minister. When Diefenbaker died in 1979 Grant was asked to write this brief assessment. He found Diefenbaker profoundly flawed as a politician and statesman, but he still admired the prairie politician's great political courage.

I have never felt such political loyalty as I feel for Green and Dief. Whatever the PM lacks, he spoke unequivocally for Canadian independence. When Macmillan purred while he was being raped; Dief. fought. And of course Green has deeply cared for the most important political cause of all – disarmament – and has been willing to risk the wrath of big business on this issue. Whatever Dief's failings, he has in the clinch spoken for Canada. All this leads me to loyalty to the Conservatives.

– George Grant to Derek Bedson, 1962 1

I feel such a debt to the Conservatives for sticking up for Canada's independence. Whatever else Dief has done – this has been fine. So many people around here just talk as if Canadian independence was a romantic notion from the past.

– George Grant to Derek Bedson, 1 October 1963

A Democrat in Theory and in Soul (1979)[*]

Why did so many Canadians love John Diefenbaker? Watching his funeral on television, I had to ask myself why I should feel such affection for him, such a sense of debt for what he represented.

The trust of his countrymen had enabled him to break the long smooth reign of the Liberals from 1935 to 1957 and had been the basis of the enormous electoral victory of 1958. In those elections he had the full weight of the powerful classes against him (including its members in his own party) and was still able almost single-handed to prevent the Liberals from forming majority governments. This was probably his most remarkable political achievement, and certainly a mark of the affection he could summon forth.

This affection was not something shared by the clever or the rich or the slick of our society. When he was in power they feared him because he might take Canada off the smooth course they had charted since 1935; when he was out of office they despised him as a silly survivor from a well-forgotten past who did not know the score.

A young scion of great wealth in English-speaking Montreal said in 1965: 'Oh George, how can you support such a vulgarian? Pearson is such a gentleman compared to that yahoo.' The remark illustrated what the definition of gentleman had become in our society.

Of course, there was something in what the rich and the clever said about Diefenbaker. His rhetoric was indeed antediluvian; his egocentricity often seemed to transcend his principles. He often sounded the note of messianism without content. Above all his appalling choice of French colleagues suggested that he did not know the first principle of Canadian politics: no party can properly rule in Canada for long without solid support in Quebec. Why then did he continue to summon up such affection from so many Canadians?

The first fact of Diefenbaker's greatness was that he reached that part of our population which feels excluded from politics. There are about 25 per cent of our population who think of politics as something carried on by 'them' for 'their' benefit. (Perhaps in a technological era this percentage will grow, particularly among the dispossessed young.)

In some mysterious fashion Diefenbaker reached those excluded

[*]George Grant, 'Diefenbaker: A Democrat in Theory and in Soul,' *Globe and Mail*, 23 August 1979, 7.

and inarticulate people and persuaded them that he was on their side. What was surprising to political analysts was that he did this as leader of the Conservatives when socialists were not able to achieve that identification. He did this despite the formality of his dress and manners in public. He still wore Homburg hats and elegantly formal suits. I suppose he did it finally because he really did care for all kinds of people in their authentic individuality. The excluded and the inarticulate recognized this and responded. He was indeed an honest politician; he was a democrat not only in theory but in his soul.

Diefenbaker's principles were grounded in primary loyalties, and loyalty is the great virtue for political leaders. That it is a virtue is often denied in modern political thinking. Intellectuals are apt to believe that leaders should have well thought out 'philosophies,' which have arisen by putting all primary loyalties in question. But this is nonsense for the following reason. The virtues necessary for the political life are not altogether the same as those necessary for the contemplative life. The latter requires that one be open to everything, and this includes putting everything in question.

In the practical life one is continually faced with making moral decisions, and in doing so one must not put one's fundamental principles in question, because that only leads to callous opportunism. Diefenbaker's strength was that his fundamental principles were loyalties which he did not put in question. He did not debate his beliefs in freedom within the law, patriotism, social egalitarianism. He just lived them out as best he could. People therefore knew where they stood with him and loved him for it.

In the fast changing world of calculation, 'loyalty' is often considered outdated and useless for administration. It is therefore becoming a rare virtue in our society. But people were wise to recognize it in Diefenbaker and knew they could rely on him.

Diefenbaker's loyalties came straight out of our particular Canadian tradition. Take his populism as an example. It has been said that Diefenbaker was simply a Canadian William Jennings Bryan,[*] with his appeal to 'the people' against the big interests in the east. But that misses the distinctly Canadian flavour of Dief's populism. It misses the fact that he combined his populism with the British tradition of the primacy and nobility of law.

---

[*]W.J. Bryan (1860–1925), Democratic presidential candidate in 1896, 1900, and 1908, Bryan was a populist politician known affectionately as 'The Great Commoner.'

In the opening of the west, individuals went first in the United States and made their own law. In Canada, the federal Government went before the immigrants, and the immigrants inherited a tradition of law. Diefenbaker was part of our tradition. He advocated populism, he believed in the rights of individuals, but always within the primacy of law. This was why he gave such strong loyalty to the crown and to Parliament. Like Macdonald he did not see our democracy as a pale imitator of the American, but as something richer, because it understood better the dependence of freedom upon law.

Diefenbaker's nationalism was not ideological; he just took it for granted. It was something given – just as parents are given, both for good and for ill. Because it was not something he constructed as he went along, it had real bite. After all, the nuclear arms crisis of 1963 was the first time since 1935 that a Canadian government really offended the Government of the United States so that it directly entered Canadian politics. (The next time could be if a Canadian government were to find itself forced over energy.)

But Diefenbaker was speaking honestly when he said 'I am pro-Canadian, not anti-American.' He was much too aware of what a dangerous and complex world it is to be ideologically anti-American. He was much too rooted in everyday life, in Prince Albert and Ottawa, not to belong to the continent we share with the Americans. He just assumed that Canada is our own, and that the United States is not. He assumed that if we have any pride in our own we must be in some sense sovereign.

When John F. Kennedy told Diefenbaker in Ottawa that Canada could not sell wheat to China – and he meant 'could not' quite literally – Diefenbaker replied: 'You aren't in Massachusetts now Mr President.' He was expressing that Canadians must take for granted their sovereignty or else have no pride. This was of course a much less worldly-wise assumption than Pearson's recognition that we are finally part of the American empire. Nevertheless, it is a necessary basis if we mean anything more than rhetoric about Canada being our country.

Because Diefenbaker's nationalism was a given loyalty, it often showed inadequacies when he tried to express it in office. He was not able to formulate feasible policies necessary to that nationalism in a technological era. But to be fair to him: Who since his day has been able to formulate such feasible policies? Even the wisest patriot of this era, de Gaulle, was not able to prevent France from being integrated into the homogenized modern culture.

The great criticism of Diefenbaker was always that he was 'out of date.' In his last years when he had become a respected elder states-man, no longer to be feared, this criticism became a kind of patroniz-ing of him as a fine old dear who was really irrelevant. I always found it unpleasant that Trudeau used to patronize him from this superior standpoint.

But what does 'out of date' mean? It is the language of those who think that our humanity can be made totally intelligible in terms of such concepts as 'progress,' 'history,' 'evolution.' What such words generally come down to in practice is that anything that is technologi-cally and administratively necessary is also good. This expresses that oblivion of eternity which now defines the West.

But Diefenbaker's loyalties were not defined within such a context of calculation. Indeed, it is not surprising that his greatest political humiliation should have been arranged by a public relations executive – the very type of job which incarnates the absoluteness of calculation.

This is why Diefenbaker was so loved by many of my generation – particularly by those of us less clever and less successful. Despite all his bombast, all his egocentricity, all the wild failures of his judgment, one sensed in him a hold on certain principles which cannot be 'out of date' because their truth does not depend upon dates. Despite his almost juvenile engrossment in the day to day excitement of the politi-cal scene, one sensed some deep hold on certain good things that do not change. About such good things there has to be calculation, but their essence is beyond all bargaining. It is to be hoped that the politi-cal scene will continue to allow such men to be produced.

The cadence of Milton's poetry is not the greatest in the English lan-guage, but it is very good. It can catch the rhetoric, the tensions and the nobilities of the battling Baptist lawyer from the prairies.

> Among the innumerable false, unmoved,
> Unshaken, unseduced, unterrified.

Not everybody is false in the modern world, but there are great pressures on all of us in that direction. At the political level Diefen-baker was always a lesson. Whatever else he may have been, he was not false.

BRITISH CONSERVATISM

Sir John A. Macdonald had built Canada, in Grant's view, under the inspira-
tion of the conservatism of Benjamin Disraeli, the great mid-Victorian British
Conservative prime minister. Disraeli's Conservative Party stood for modera-
tion, fairness, and good sense, and these were the virtues, as Grant had
explained in The Empire: Yes or No? *that distinguished Canada from the*
United States. Yet, however admirable Disraeli's conservatism may have been,
Grant thought that it lacked the strength to withstand the new combination of
liberalism and technology that was becoming the sole public value.

Gladstone & Disraeli were titans, absolute titans. I started with a great bias for
Gladstone, but now I have absolutely no idea whom I prefer. I read four of Disraeli's[*] novels and one of his political writings; the great life (abridged slightly)
by Monypenny & Buckle. I think for a while Disraeli was the great Victorian
statesman and Gladstone the highly limited and bigoted politician. Then I read
something about Gladstone and I say he was the colossus, he was the great
statesman who dominated England with supreme greatness; then I think Disraeli was a crafty opportunist politician. *What giants* they were. Colossuses. I
practically burst into tears when I read the story of Bismarck at the Congress of
Berlin in 1878 and he turned to someone and said, 'Der alte Jude, der ist der
Mann.'[†] A superb story.

But then the polemic of Gladstone on ideals and Armenian massacres. Ideals
rather than necessity and selfishness in foreign policy. Ireland and his conscience. Power and the Midlothian campaign.

Then Disraeli laughs (oh so humanly) at the utilitarians who tried to form
society around a formula, a principle. Philanthropic Disraeli.

– George Grant to Maude Grant, spring 1938

Benjamin Disraeli (1982)[‡]

First, a word of high congratulations is in order. The editors have done
a magnificent job, searching diligently to make this collection as com-

---

[*]Benjamin Disraeli (1804–81), 1st Earl of Beaconsfield, author of *Conningsby, Contraini*
Fleming, Lothair, and *Sybil, or the Two Nations.*
[†]'What a man the old Jew is.'
[‡]George Grant, review of *Benjamin Disraeli: The Early Letters,* ed. J.A.W. Gunn et al., *Globe*
and Mail, 8 May 1982, E15.

plete as seems possible, and then laying the letters before the reader
with all the aids of scholarly clarity so that they are a delight to read.
The University of Toronto Press has produced beautiful books at a reasonable price for these expensive days. This is scholarship at its best.
When one thinks that these two volumes only take Disraeli up to his
entrance into Parliament in 1837, and that the great man goes on until
1881, what a treat awaits us. These volumes are not only useful for people who want to study the nineteenth-century European world professionally, they will be a delight for anybody who wants to contemplate
the life of a great political leader.

Politics is, as Plato showed, the royal art. In the golden afternoon of
England's authority as the first of the industrialized nations, she was
fortunate to have such outstanding practitioners of that art as William
Gladstone and Benjamin Disraeli. When one compares their level of
education and character with that of the people who run our societies
today (Canada included), one may have a word to say for aristocracy as
against the undiluted triumph of capitalist democracy. For my part, I
put Gladstone slightly higher because he had the perspicacity to try to
limit English imperialism at the height of its power.

But Disraeli was also a splendid politician. Even more than Peel, he
was the founder of the modern Tory Party, and through all the cata-
clysms and aberrations of the modern era, that party more often than
not has stood for good sense. That is a lot to say of any institution. To
take a small influence: one cannot understand the conservatism of
Canada (Macdonald, Whitney, Borden, Ferguson, Bennett, Diefenbaker) without thinking of Disraeli. This may be a tradition that has
decayed in Canada before the ravages of capitalist liberalism, but it was
a great part of this country. Another Canadian connection in these volumes is that there is a nasty picture of Lord Durham, whose report did
much harm in Canada by failing to recognize the French for what they
were. These two volumes only take us through the early years, culminating in the disappointment of the unfair failure of his maiden
speech in Parliament. A sweet letter from his school in Blackheath is
followed by accounts to his sister of trips around Europe and the
Levant. These are followed by letters in which he tries to establish himself in the literary and political scene of the New World that is coming
forth after the Reform Act of 1832. He has difficulties with his publish-
ers, he has continued failures at the polls, but he never flags in his
determination to establish himself in the ruling class. Why shouldn't
he? Neurotic ambition can be a corrupting vice, but Disraeli's ambi-

tion seems singularly free of the neurotic. He just wants to get on and achieve what he knows himself capable of, in a country which he thoroughly likes. Compared to Gladstone again, he does not start with an established position. He has to make his place in the world and he does so in a direct and healthy way.

What comes forth from these letters is a very worldly human being. By worldly, I do not mean a non-religious man. He seems to take religion for granted, as something quite given in the nature of things and to be properly respected. What I mean is that he likes the riches of experience. This comes out in his long letters from abroad. He describes what he has been doing and seeing with external gusto – often in a way that may bore us moderns who are more used to subjective analysis. But this love of the surface and of the immediate is the mark of his health. Many successful politicians are often neurotic insofar as they pursue power to assuage their subjectivity, but the best politicians are those who like the world. One trusts Disraeli because his shrewd and interested acceptance means that he is not a hater. It seems natural that he should be the fellow countryman and near contemporary of the delightful and insightful Jane Austen.

One particular mark of his health is how much Disraeli loved women. I do not mean by this that he was in pursuit of the continual Giovannian orgasm which in our age is often implied when one says that somebody loves women; such pursuit is for much less sane human beings than Disraeli. What I mean is that he writes to all kinds of women with a delicious interest in their doings and his own. Some of the best letters in the first of these volumes are to his sister Sarah (he addresses her sweetly as Sa), and there is a halcyon quality about their obvious mutual affection. Clearly from the later letters, he used his aristocratic mistress Lady Sykes to advance his career, but there is no sign that there was anything particularly nasty in this. It is often said that Disraeli manipulated Queen Victoria for his own purposes. We will obviously have to wait for the later letters to see whether this was the case.

But from these letters, I doubt whether manipulation is the right word. Interest in and understanding of other people is the basis of intimacy. Disraeli had interest and understanding for many ladies, from his grandmother to his sister and a wide variety of intelligent and aristocratic women. To take that as manipulation is to miss the point that he had empathy for their worlds. To state the obvious: it is surprising to consider how few human beings really like the members of the opposite sex.

Yet it must be insisted that these volumes depend on what lies ahead. Nobody would be publishing these letters if they were not a preparation for what is going to happen in the future. They are of interest because they come from the young man who will try in 1878 to prevent Europe from tearing itself apart in war. Perhaps one begins to see in this loving and ambitious young man the later man to whom Bismarck would pay his great compliment. Perhaps one begins to see why a great aristocrat, Lord Salisbury, given above all to the defence of the Church of England, would work so happily as his second in command.

Shrewd men are often not likeable; likeable men are often not shrewd. As a young man, Disraeli is obviously both. Above all, he has loyalties (not principles) which quite transcend his own ambitions. He loves his country, the landed aristocrats, and his family. Loyalties rather than principles are the mark of the conservative. This is one reason indeed why conservatism is so difficult in a technological age. It cannot be said too often that fast technological change goes with fast moral and religious change. Disraeli's loyalties were strong enough to see him through.

I await with eagerness the volumes which follow when he becomes a great practitioner of the royal art.

LIBERALISM AND TYRANNY

When the Canadian Supreme Court struck down Canada's law governing abortion, Grant concluded that another step had been taken in the decay of the liberal tradition of justice. He began increasingly to fear that the universal and homogeneous state was approaching more quickly than he had previously thought. Normally he was an advocate of moderation in politics, but in this selection Grant's anger flames forth as he compares the philosophical basis for the pro-choice movement to the essential element that drove the Nazis. However, there is little doubt that Grant genuinely believed that the coming technological state would be a tyranny.

We have just had a Supreme Court decision here on abortion. The majority was, if possible, worse than Roe v. Wade but luckily we've a health care system where the money comes from the federal government but where administration is in the hands of the province. Some of the provinces have refused to allow their hospitals to finance non-medical abortions. But you can imagine how the press is attacking them as 'rednecks' etc., etc. What is so extraordinary about our politics is that some of the left-wing politicians who speak most often about rights are just those who speak most loudly in favour of abortion on demand.

– George Grant to David Bovenizer, 6 March 1988

The Triumph of the Will (1988)[*]

The decision of the Supreme Court concerning abortion could be seen as comedy – if it did not concern the slaughter of the young. Any laughter is quelled by a sense of desolation for our country. Yet the comedy too must be looked at to understand our political institutions. The comedy arises from the fact that the majority of the judges used the language of North American liberalism to say 'yes' to the very core of fascist thought – the triumph of the will. Their decision is a good example of Huey Long's wise dictum: 'When fascism comes to America it will come in the name of democracy.' The court says yes to those who claim the right to mastery over their bodies, even if that mastery includes the killing of other human beings.[1]

Indeed, the advocates of abortion have shown since the decision how much they are believers in the triumph of the will, when they 'demand' that the government 'must' immediately guarantee access and payment for all abortions. That is, the state must pay for these processes, even when they are not medically necessary. The triumph of the will realizes itself when its advocates understand that the individual will is only liberated to its full power when it can dominate the state.

The imputation of fascism to those with whom one disagrees is indeed a dangerous game. People of the left call Mrs Thatcher a fascist, when, whatever she may be, she is not that. People of the right call Castro a 'fascist,' when, whatever he may be, he is not that. To speak of incipient fascism in the present case requires that one discuss what fascism is. That is a useful public task, because fascism is a growing possibility in advanced industrial countries. If one does not look clearly at such phenomena, one cannot think how to deal with them.

The English-speaking liberals quite correctly saw the European

[*] George Grant, 'The Triumph of the Will,' in *The Issue Is Life: A Christian Response to Abortion in Canada*, ed. Denyse O'Leary (Burlington, Ont.: Welsh Publishing, 1988).

examples of fascism as despicable tyrannies. What they could not express was the difference between such totalitarian tyranny and most of the tyrannies of the past. The marxists saw clearly the partial truth that fascism was made possible by a late stage of a decaying capitalism. They had no explanation for the fact that certain fascists spoke so violently against Western capitalism. The Americans and the Russians united to defeat National Socialism in battle. As Stalin so rightly put it: 'The Americans gave money, the British gave time, the Russians gave blood.' But the defeat in battle has not enabled us to understand what fascism was. Its core was a belief in the triumph of the will. The result is that when the triumph of the will manifests itself politically in our societies, we just cannot know it for what it is.

What is meant by the seemingly simple word 'will?' In the pre-modern world it had a certain meaning which was particularly emphasized in Christianity, because the words which were spoken in Gethesemane – 'Yet not My will but Thine be done' – were paradigmatic for Christians. It meant appropriate choosing by rational souls. With the coming of modernity, it has come to mean something different. When 'will' is thought modernly it means the resolute mastery of ourselves and the world. To understand this modern illumination of the word 'will,' it is necessary to put aside entirely that old faculty psychology, in which will was understood as a power or faculty of the soul, having to do with free choices. Rather, will is the centre of our aiming or seeking, the holding together of what we want. That greatest modern definer of will, Nietzsche, said that everything was 'will to power.' This has often been misinterpreted by traditionalists as if he was substituting power for happiness or pleasure, as that which was worth aiming at. But in the phrase 'will to power,' he is not describing what we aim at – something outside the will. Rather, he is saying that will is power itself, not something external to power. What makes Nietzsche such a pivotal thinker in the West is that he redefined 'will' to make it consonant with modern science. 'Will' comes to mean in modernity that power over ourselves and everything else which is itself the very enhancement of life, or, call it if you will, 'quality of life.' Truth, beauty, and goodness have become simply subservient to it.

How did this new conception of 'will' come to be central in Western civilization? Obviously, first as science. Modern science is a particular form of science – that which issues in the conquest of human and non-human nature. This is why it is right to call Western science 'technological science.' Technology produces 'quality of life.' This science understands nature as outside the idea of purpose. Nature is understood as a product of necessity and chance – not of purpose. That is, modern science laid nature before us as raw material to be used as we dispose. How then should we dispose? In the early years of our science, Christian purposes were still operative, and later the purposes of various kinds of secularized Christianity. (Propriety forbids me a bow to Mme Justice Wilson[*] for her decision in the present case.) These secularized Protestant purposes were above all expressed in the English-speaking world as the greatest happiness of the greatest number through capitalist technology. In the marxist world these purposes were expressed as the building of the classless (and therefore egalitarian) society, through the communal ownership of the means of production. But both these ethical systems depended on something outside 'will' itself. Why should I aim for the greatest happiness of the greatest number? Why should I 'will' the classless society? These aims were outside will and therefore inhibited enhancement of life by imposing on will aims from outside will itself. Therefore, the deepest movement of modern thought was to take the great step that our aim was the power of will itself. That is what is meant by 'the triumph of the will.'

The Triumph of the Will is, of course, the title of Leni Riefenstahl's[†] documentary about the National Socialist Party's convention at Nuremberg, a brilliant title for a brilliant documentary. Is it not absurd, therefore, to relate the apotheosis of such an occasion to the freedom of women to have abortions as they deem it desirable? Is it not particularly absurd when the height of the Nazi occasion is essentially masculine, and women are shown by a woman in the stance of adulation? Several points, however, need to be made about fascism (call it, perhaps more accurately, National Socialism).

In the film, Hitler is seen, not as the liberator of his own will, but as the man who through his own liberation can make possible the liberation of each individual will in his nation. From the moment that he descends from the skies in his airplane and walks hesitantly forward, he is the ordinary German who through his own liberation apotheosizes the liberation of all Germans.

It must be remembered that National Socialist doctrine despised the

---

[*]Bertha Wilson (1923–), justice of the Supreme Court of Canada from 1982 to 1995.
[†]Leni Riefenstahl (1902–), German actress and filmmaker who became notorious for her Nazi propaganda films, especially The Triumph of the Will (1934), one of the most powerful propaganda films ever made.

submergence of the individual will in the rationalized collectivism of communism, as much as it did the impotence of the individual in capitalist democracies. The doctrine was that each individual will would find its liberation in unity within the National Socialist Party. Anything that was 'given' in a situation, so that it could not be changed, was seen as an unacceptable limitation on the triumph of the will. The Jewish community was strong in German-speaking lands. The Jews were thought of as internationalists and cosmopolitans. Therefore, according to the national socialists, they stood in the way of the triumph of German will. And so these masses of human beings, this given part of Germany, who stood in the way of what National Socialists considered to be the quality of German life, had to be exterminated. When the National Socialists gathered that they were being beaten in war, this terrible extermination was speeded up in the name of their will's revenge. Nothing given could stand in its way – even the givenness of other human beings.

Is it not true, however, that National Socialism is a thing of the past and therefore pointless to bring into debate about today's issues? It was a revolting regression from the modern age of reason, a finished nightmare to be put aside. I am saying something very different.

When one strips away the particularities of the German situation after the intense defeat of 1918, one finds that that situation was a particular possibility for the manifestation of the triumph of the will. That doctrine expresses very closely what human beings think to be true in modernity, when they seek to express their search for meaning in a universe which is known as purposeless. This doctrine has therefore continued to be present in the English-speaking world which has been dominant since 1945. It has particularly expressed itself in the dealings of the U.S. with its empire abroad. It was evident in the determination of the American leaders to have their will by air power right around the world in Vietnam. It can be seen at home, for example, in the work of medical research to find means of mastery over the reproduction of the species.

It is not surprising that leaders of the women's movement, seeking to overcome the injustices of a long-standing patriarchal tradition, should express themselves in the modern language of the triumph of the will. As the presentation of modernity to itself, it is in all of us at some level explicit. It is to be expected that this language should become dominant among the leaders of the women's movement, because they are so aware what it is to live in modernity.

Of course, ever since patriarchal society began all women have had to face the fact that the enjoyment of sexuality left them with the prodigious possibility of pregnancy, while men could go forth free from that enjoyment. Perhaps this was even resented by some women in matriarchal times, in which the whole society turned on the recognition of birth as central. (We just do not have the records of matriarchal society and its overthrowing.) In earlier patriarchal societies, religious control had some effect sometimes, in forcing men to assume some responsibility for pregnancy. Where land was the essential cause of wealth, owner families had a very great interest in forcing men to bear responsibility.

In modern technological society, most bourgeois women, and those who wish to become bourgeois, find themselves in a position where at one and the same time the emancipation of sexual desire is advocated from the earliest age, and yet where, if they are to be anything socially, they must go out to work in the world where what matters is the emancipation of greed. This is achieved under corporate capitalism through mastery over oneself and other people. How can such modern women put up with unexpected pregnancies (whether within marriage or without) which can demolish their place in the corporate market and push back their ambitions in relation to the ambitions of other people at the same level? Abortion on demand, then, appears a necessity under the conditions of corporation capitalism, as it presumably also does under corporation communism. Indeed, women's position as potential mothers becomes particularly pressing in all advanced industrial societies, because their skilled or unskilled labour, their low or high ambitions are wanted in the marketplace. This happens at a time when the overcoming of the unfairness of their sexual position seems at last possible.

It is no wonder, then, that the leaders of the women's movement take on the language of the triumph of the will when they are seeking to get the state to fulfil their purposes, and when they are opposed by those who must be against abortion on demand for the clearest reasons. The ambiguity is that the famous feminist phrase 'biology is not destiny' must be true for all Christians, because we have been told that in Christ there is neither male nor female. At the highest reaches of human life and love, gender is simply unimportant. The question is, at what levels of life and love *is* gender important, and how should that difference manifest itself?

It is not that the women's leaders say that to be truly free, women must get rid of their gender. They do not seem to want to build an entirely androgynous society. It seems rather that, in their desire for liberation, they want not only to keep their gender, but also to use it as they will. But their ability to use their gender, and not to be controlled by it, requires their life and death control over beings other than themselves. For the 'given' which their wills need to control is those individual members of their own species within their bodies. 'Otherness' which must be dominated has always been that thing in terms of which the language of the triumph of the will arises. In this case, the need for liberation arises not against the absence of the vote, or inequality in the marketplace, but against developing infants. This is the terrible pain which leads certain women to the language of the triumph of the will. They feel trapped by their gender but the means of liberating themselves from this entrapment must often include killing. The language of the triumph of the will is a means of escaping from that trap, because it frees one from the traditional restraints against killing.

What is saddest for the modern future is that belief in the triumph of the will seems to bring with it an intensity of propaganda in which the general public is prepared for the killing which is to ensue. For a decade the National Socialists had been saying that the Jews were not truly human, that they were parasites living off the healthy society. It hardly needs saying that the Jews are as truly human as the rest of us. Nevertheless, the fact that the opposite was a lie did not prevent its dissemination and influence. Those who disseminated it believed it. The most effective dissemination of lies is by those who believe them. So in the coming of mass abortion in our society untruths have been spread by those who do not know they are untruths. Current scientific knowledge tells us that a separate human life is present from conception, with its own unique genetic pattern, with all the chromosomes and genes which make it human. It is of the very heart of fascism to think that what matters is not what is true, but what one holds to be true. What one holds to be true is important because it can produce that resolute will tuned to its own triumph.

However, it must be said that where the clarity about truth which belongs to modern science has allowed us to know what the fetus is in a matter-of-fact way, more difficult implications arise when modern science is used as if it provided the whole truth about life. This has sometimes led to a belittling of human life and to the arising of the doctrine of the triumph of the will. All this has often been denied or refused by advocates of abortion on demand. It has been said that the fetus is a few cells attached to a woman's body that can be easily clipped away. It has been said that it is simply a parasite which has attached itself to a woman's body. Lies have been told or truths neglected to loosen up people to be prepared to accept the mass feticide which now characterizes our society.

Post-Darwinian biology has set before us an account of all animals essentially understandable as matter in motion. What is made final for all animals is that they are driven by the necessities of the struggle for existence. To say the least, such an account of life makes it problematic whether there was something about human beings which should make us hesitant to kill them. National Socialist ideology was impregnated at its heart with Darwinian biology. In terms of such an account of life, why should we care about the life of a fetus when it conflicts with the will of a fully developed woman? But then, of course, we are led inexorably to the next stage. Why should we care about the lives of human beings outside the womb if they are only an accidental conglomeration of cells, and if they stand in our way? The science which explains everything in terms of necessity and chance has been the basis of our obvious progresses, but at the same time its intellectual victory over all other kinds of thought has left Western human beings questioning whether their own life has meaning other than in terms of the triumph of the will.

After the Supreme Court decision, the victorious advocates of abortion on demand paraded with signs, on some of which was the slogan 'Abort God.' They were right to do so. What they meant was 'abort the idea of God because it has held human beings back from liberation.' What is given us in the word 'God' is that goodness and purpose are the source and completion of all that is. Only in terms of that affirmation can we dimly understand why our lives and others' partake in a meaning which we should not hinder but enhance. It is in the name of the fact that the human fetus is a member of our species, called to partake in meaning, that in the past we have turned away from abortion, except in extreme cases. All this was affirmed not only in the teachings of Christians but in the Hindu Vedanta – that greatest Eastern teaching. Those who see life simply as a product of necessity and chance are inevitably more open to feticide, because they do not see the destiny of meaning to which human beings are called. This is the prodigious predicament that the intellectual triumph of modern science has cast upon us human beings.

To say all this is not to imply that North American society is yet close to fascism as a form of government. There are many influences in our society which hold us back from that. Obviously, all sane people hope that these influences will continue to prevail. What I am implying is that these influences are fragile in the face of the doctrine of the triumph of the will. Nor am I saying that North American fascism would be, in outward appearance, much like the National Socialism of Europe. The trappings of romanticism in North American fascism would be quite different from the trappings of German romanticism.

It is interesting that, alone among Western countries, West Germany has a law which gives the fetus a legal right to life, with some conditions. The Constitutional Court says that this is to make plain the German historical experience and 'the present spiritual-moral confrontation with the previous system of National Socialism.' In 1988 West Germany has forbidden surrogate motherhood and the production of human embryos for research. The Germans have the great advantage over us of *already* having faced the political incarnation of the triumph of the will.

I am, however, saying two things: The triumph of the will as an individual view of life passes over into politics, and even in government, in advanced industrial societies, when those societies see themselves as threatened or fading or even at the point of defeat. It was certainly the smashing of Germany by the Allied powers in 1918, and the ruthlessness of the defeat imposed upon them, which led to fascism in Germany. The unequivocal victory of American capitalism in 1945 meant that we had no need of fascism. But if in some unpredictable future the power of American capitalism seems to be fading before the power of Japan and China, and if the economic powers in America recognize the consequences of that threat, then very different forms of government might arise within the bounds of their democratic constitution.

Secondly, the living forth of the triumph of the will among the strongest advocates of complete liberty for abortion does not imply that such advocates are in any sense a core for fascist politics. They simply give us a taste now of what politics will be like when influential groups in society think meaning is found in getting what they want most deeply at all costs. They illustrate what pressure this puts upon a legal system rooted in liberalism, whose leaders have not been educated in what that rootedness comprises. Even in its highest ranks the legal system in its unthinking liberalism simply flounders in the face of those who find meaning in the triumph of the will. This has been shown in both of the liberally appointed American and Canadian judiciaries. When society puts power into the hands of the courts, they had better be educated.[2]

Fast technological change is always accompanied by fast moral and religious change. It is good, therefore, for Christians to look clearly at what the advocates of abortion on demand portend in the way of unrestrained politics. The politics of the triumph of the will are less and less controlled by any considerations of reason, let alone by tired liberal reason which expresses itself only in terms of a contract. However important these questions about politics, more immediate is the massive slaughter of the innocent which goes on and on.

(Note: Another long article would be required to spell out the causes in legal and general education which lead to the jurisprudential shallowness among the judges. As much as abortion, this question goes to the very roots of modernity.)

NOTES

1 Note: I do not intend to show in this writing that the fetus is a developing individual of our species from conception. This was shown beyond doubt in the testimony of the famous French geneticist, Jerome Lejeune, before a committee of the American Senate.
2 The more the justices quote philosophy or religious tradition the less they give the sense they understand what they are dealing with.

FREE TRADE

In 1988 the Conservative government of Brian Mulroney completed a free-trade agreement with the United States. Although Grant had, with little enthusiasm, generally supported the Mulroney regime, he was not prepared to accept more rapid Canadian integration with the United States or the debasement of Canadian culture that free trade seemed to threaten. In the last few months before his death, this was an issue that more and more attracted his attention.

The sadness of English-speaking nationalism in Canada is that so much of it wants nationalism, but wants to be the same American capitalism, with a [illegible] maple leaf flag put on top. You rarely meet people who are outside the determining power of that American dream. It is for this reason that I detest [NDP leader Ed] Broadbent's supposed nationalist rhetoric. It is just the Democratic Party North. As Mulroney is the Republican Party North.

– George Grant to Gaston Laurion, 21 July 1988

The Fate of the Willing (1988)[*]

This book comprises statements by forty-seven thoughtful Canadians who oppose the Canada–U.S. free-trade agreement. The contributors vary widely: from Margaret Atwood to Frank Stronach, from David Suzuki to Peter C. Newman. It is divided into three sections: 'What We Think,' 'What We Know,' 'What We Feel.' Most of the contributors are people who believe that free beings ought to be able to decide rationally what will happen in the world. That is, the good-mannered and liberal left predominates. Different voices deal with different problems: many with the economic issues, some with the social, cultural, and political issues. Taken all in all, this is a powerful statement of what a turning point the free-trade deal will be in Canadian life, and why it bodes ill for our nationhood.

Much of the argument deals with the practical issues directly: why Canada would be better served, for prosperity and independence in a technological age, by other strategies ... Several of the writings argue that Canada will be forced to give up social programmes that have expressed community solidarity. They will have to be given up so that we can maintain cost-competitiveness with the Americans. Here the appeal has been strongly made by such labour leaders as Shirley Carr and Bob White. But I think the best understanding of this matter is found in Denis Stairs's article. He understands that community responsibility, and indeed the continuing basis of Canada, has lain in the primacy of the political in our national life.

He states: 'The treaty is only partly about securing access to the American market and subjecting Canadian industries to the salutary cleansing of the cold shower. It is also about "deregulating" Canadian society – that is, about diminishing (after the American model) the

---

[*]George Grant, review of *If You Love This Country: Facts and Feelings on Free Trade*, ed. Laurier LaPierre (Toronto: McClelland and Stewart, 1987) in *Books In Canada* vol. 17, no. 1 (January–February 1988), 18–19.

role of the state in Canadian life.' Or again: 'The fact remains that the proposed treaty not only embodies but, if implemented, will further encourage a conception of government and society different from the one that Canadians currently enjoy. Canada will be a less relaxed, a less gentle, a less tolerant place in which to live.' He of course realizes that this is not an absolute difference between Canada and the United States. I wish he had carried over his splendid argument about the primacy of the political into how the three Canadian parties destroyed their nationalist wings: the squashing of Walter Gordon[*] by Lester Pearson when the former annoyed the business community; the removal of the Waffle[†] from the NDP when it angered the unions; the destruction of Diefenbaker and his followers by Camp[‡] and the business Tories. At the level of the immediate issues, Stairs's statement about the necessary primacy of the political over the economic should be central to any argument about free trade.

There is one statement in the book that moves quite outside the careful assumptions of practical decision. This is Farley Mowat's. He is not concerned with how we should deal immediately with the Americans. He recognizes the arrival of cosy totalitarianism at the centre of the American empire, and hates it. This is the statement with which I feel the greatest sympathy. It is not filled with progressive talk about free human beings being able to make the world as they choose. He sees what corrupts the possibility of politics at this stage of raging technological change. His statement just expresses clear hatred. Hatred is not a typical Canadian emotion or one that Canadians admire – greatly to their credit. Nevertheless, some things deserve to be hated – the friendly tyranny of corporation capitalism and the consequent *Bodenlösigkeit.* (The English word *rootlessness* catches less well what is happening than does the German.) Love and hate are necessary to each other except among the saints.

There is one phrase that recurs in this book that I find unwise: 'Our two countries.' This is what might be called the rhetoric of Broadbent – the rhetoric he has used since he was used to drive the nationalists out of the NDP. But it is also the 'liberal' rhetoric by which American

---

[*]Walter L. Gordon (1906–87), minister of finance in the liberal government of Lester Pearson, 1963–5.

[†]A left-wing, nationalist movement within the New Democratic Party, purged from the Ontario NDP in 1972, it had disintegrated by the mid-1970s.

[‡]Dalton L. Camp. (1920–). Conservative Party president 1964–9; in this capacity he was intrumental in the removal of John Diefenbaker as party leader in 1967.

journalists legitimize themselves to themselves. They proclaim themselves a country and eschew the word *empire*, while their battleships try to impose their will in the Persian Gulf. I would have wished, in this book, for a sharper understanding of what imperialism means, and particularly the workings of capitalist imperialism. This is necessary even if we are perhaps faced by a fading Western empire. I think there should have been more understanding in the book of how the central stage of world history now moves from Europe to Far Asia, as China is developed with Japan. What does this mean for Canada, living on the very periphery of that Western empire? In our present case, some of our shrewder capitalists may be calling for continental solidarity as a necessity of this situation. Truth cannot be much spoken in the public realm. *Fata volentem ducunt, nolentem trahunt* [fate leads the willing and drags the unwilling]. What is great about this book is that its writers are splendidly stating their unwillingness to be dragged. It is surely a nobler stance to go down with all flags flying (even our present Canadian one) and all guns blazing than to be acquiescently led, whether sadly or gladly, into the even greater homogenizing of our country into the American mass.

Part 2

Philosophy and Education

PHILOSOPHY AND THE PERFECTION OF GOD

Grant was asked to write an essay on the state of philosophy in English-speaking Canada for the Massey Royal Commission on the Arts, which had been established to make recommendations on the state of Canadian culture. Though he never doubted the truth of his bold assertion in the opening sentence of this essay, he had cause to regret having written it since it earned him the enmity of many of the most senior and influential philosophers across the country, not least the formidable Fulton Anderson, head of the department of Philosoohy at the University of Toronto.

Philosophy (1951)[*]

The study of philosophy is the analysis of the traditions of our society and the judgment of those traditions against our varying intuitions of the Perfection of God. It is the contemplation of our own and others' activity, in the hope that by understanding it better we may make it less imperfect. At the centre of the traditional faith of the West has been the understanding that there are two approaches to reality, the contemplative and the active, and that only in the careful proportioning of these can individuals and societies find health. The contemplative life, whether mystical, artistic, or philosophic, has therefore been encouraged by societies not only for the good of the contemplative himself but because its influence upon more active members was considered of value. Philosophy was therefore encouraged as the rational form of such contemplation.

Such a definition of philosophy asserts that it is in no sense limited to being a technical subject confined to specialists in universities. It is an activity necessary for all sorts and conditions of men – politicians and saints, artists and businessmen, scientists and farmers – if such

---

[*]George Grant, 'Philosophy: An Essay Prepared for the Royal Commission on National Development in the Arts, Letters and Sciences 1949–1951' (Ottawa: Edmond Cloutier 1951). This material originated in the Privy Council Office and is reproduced with the permission of the Minister of Public Works and Government Services, 1996.

men are to relate their particular functions to the general ends which society desires.

Philosophy is not, then, confined to a subject found in university calendars. Yet at the same time universities are the focal points upon which will depend in large measure the state of rational contemplation in the rest of society. In the universities, society allows scholars the time and the freedom to contemplate the universe, to partake of the wisdom of the past, to add their small measure to the understanding of that wisdom, and to transmit the great tradition to certain chosen members of the younger generation. If the universities are not rich in the practice of philosophy it is unlikely that less favoured parts of the community will be much touched by it. Therefore, what follows will be concerned with the teaching and practice of philosophy as it is carried on in our universities.

In writing of this question it is only realism to pose the problem pessimistically. Why do our universities fail in providing a place where young Canadians are encouraged to think about their world in the broadest and deepest way? That the universities are not providing such a place is but to state a truism. Can it be doubted that Canadian universities today exist essentially as technical schools for the training of specialists? They turn out doctors and physicists, economists and chemists, lawyers and social workers, psychologists and agriculturalists, dieticians and sociologists, and these technicians are not being called upon in any systematic way to relate their necessary techniques to any broader whole. Even the traditional humane subjects such as history, the classics, and European literature are in many cases being taught as techniques by which the students can hope to earn their living, not as useful introductions to the sweep of our spiritual tradition.

Indeed, behind the character of our classrooms lies the fact that this production of technicians is being encouraged by the dominant forces that shape society. The general voting public (that is, the parents of the young) think of the university as a place where the child can become a specialist and so equip himself to enter or to remain in the more economically fortunate part of society. Governments – provincial and federal – use their influence to see that practical training is encouraged, so that the society will not be ill-equipped in any necessary technique, whether that technique be appropriate to a university or not. Anyone who has sat on a faculty of graduate studies knows well that the ablest students are being encouraged by our government (in that clearest form of encouragement – the financial) to become technicians. Students who want to become physicists, biochemists etc. know that if they are at all promising they will receive help from the National Research Council, the Department of Defence, etc. Students in such fields also know that there will be lucrative jobs waiting for them when their studies are finished. On the other hand, those students who are studying in the general humane tradition know that financial help in their fields is small and that jobs will be hard to find when they are through. Finally, it must be said that the university authorities themselves do little to control this tendency. In some universities in English-speaking Canada, there are four times as many people teaching physics as teaching philosophy, and three times as many people teaching animal husbandry.

These general facts about our universities must be mentioned, for it is clearly impossible for the study of philosophy to flourish in such an atmosphere. Philosophy is not in essence a technique. Its purpose is to relate and see in unity all techniques, so that the physicist for instance can relate his activity to the fact of moral freedom, the economist see the productive capacity of his nation in relation to the love of God.

The prime reason, no doubt, for this state of affairs in Canada is the fact of our short history, most of which has been taken up with the practical business of a pioneering nation. Such a society must put its energies into those pursuits that will achieve material ends. The active rather than the contemplative life perforce becomes the ideal. Anything that will effectively overcome hardship must be welcomed with enthusiasm. That concentration of material ends and admiration for the man of action continues for a long while after it has ceased to be a necessity.

In a subtler way our pioneering background has affected our taste for rational contemplation. A pioneering society in which there are obvious material accomplishments open to all men of average intelligence leads to an optimism about the universe much like the optimism associated with youth. The tragedy and complexity of maturity are not so evident as in an ancient and more static society. When the spiritual difficulties of maturity arise, the cry of 'Go west, young man' can help individuals to avoid them. It is out of a sense of tragedy and uncertainty more than anything else that the need for philosophical speculation arises. A young nation in its sureness and confidence is thus basically unphilosophical.

Yet, lest our short history be used as a sufficient justification of our lack of interest in the contemplative arts, it is humbling to remember that two or three generations ago when the country was small and poor, Canada in proportion to its size was far more ready to support the 'impractical' studies than it is today. Both within the Protestant and Roman Catholic traditions of English-speaking society the small and poor community struggled to establish universities in which chairs of classics, philosophy, and theology were considered the essentials. The traditions of Christian Europe which the early settlers brought with them did not allow them to believe that man lives by bread alone, even when bread was far more scarce than it is today. It is therefore necessary to look beyond the mere fact of our youth for the causes of the materialist concentration in our universities.

It is but another truism to say that Canada has come to maturity, not in isolation but as a member of the Western society of nations. Our spiritual climate is largely formed by our partaking in the ideas of that civilization, which during the years of Canada's development was being transformed by the new mass industrialism. With that industrialism went certain dominant ideas that effected an almost incalculable spiritual change in the West. In the light of the amazing power of science, men no longer doubted that they could easily perfect their societies. In the field of knowledge the slogan was 'knowledge for power,' in the expectation that with such power all would be well. In the field of education there arose the egalitarian slogans with their contempt for the 'impractical' and the 'academic.' Men often forgot the need of those disciplines that once had been considered a potent influence in preventing us from becoming beasts. The more Canada has become part of the scientific world of the West, the more it has partaken of ideas such as these, and the tragedy of its youth has been that the bonds of tradition have been less strong with us than elsewhere. What can the place of the philosopher be in the mass world, when by definition, philosophic knowledge is not open to the stereotyped mass, and when the philosopher cannot believe that salvation is achieved by techniques? What is the role of the philosopher in the universities which have in general accepted the aspirations of their societies – aspirations that leave little place for the practice of contemplation?

Tragically, the scandal must be admitted that, with rare exceptions, philosophers in Western society have joined in the aspirations of the scientific age. The lie that knowledge exists only to provide power has been as much in the soul of philosophers as in the rest of society. The chief schools of thought in Canada among energetic philosophers in the 1920s and 1930s were pragmatism and positivism. What do such positions mean but that ideas are true insofar as they help men manipulate their natural environment? Along with marxism (on the whole less potent among Canadian philosophers) they tend towards the position that all men's problems may be solved by scientific technique. Canadian philosophers indeed have joined as fully as any part of the Western world in making philosophy the servant rather than the judge of men's scientific abilities. Young Canadians have quite logically drawn the correct conclusion from such an attitude. If philosophy is merely the servant of science, then they are better occupied studying with the master rather than with the servant.

Associated with the philosopher's willingness to make his subject serve the interest of physical science has been the dream of modern philosophy – that it might free itself from its traditional dependence upon the theological dogmas of faith. Canadian philosophers have shared in this secular hope as deeply as have their fellows in the rest of the Western world. This hope has been connected intimately with the gradual secularizing of those universities founded within the Protestant tradition. Philosophy was thought of as a secular study to suit the modern world and the secular university. It is not possible here to enter in any adequate way upon the ancient controversy as to the proper relation between philosophy and theology – between the discoveries of reason and the discoveries of faith. Yet it would seem that unless philosophy is to become a purely negative discipline, it must have some kind of dependence on faith – whatever faith that may be. Reason not guided by faith cannot but find itself in the position of destroying everything and establishing nothing. And though one of the roles of philosophy must be destructive and critical, if that be its only role it cannot hope to have any profound or abiding influence on society. Active men depend upon faith of some sort for their very existence. It is not surprising that the destructive philosophy that characterized Western universities after 1914 led students to give up the study of philosophy as pointless. When philosophers are jejune enough to deny in the name of secularism and science the possibility of rational faith, then young men and women in their need of faith will simply bypass the philosophers. Society will suffer the tragedy of men looking for their faiths outside the rational discipline that is the function of philosophy to provide in the search for faith. Society suffers the tragedy of their youth finding faith in such childish hopes as marxism, in such unbalanced cults as the Jehovah's Witnesses. It would seem clear, then, that only as philosophy finds its roots in religious faith will it once again have a profound influence on young Canadians. The teaching of philosophy in our Canadian universities is not only bound up with the question of what our universities are to be but also with the larger question of what our churches are to be.

To face as the primary thesis of this essay that philosophical studies are in no healthy state in Canada must not prevent mention of the good things that have been done and are being done. The Roman Catholic tradition in English-speaking Canada may be mentioned first because it has always been numerically smaller and because it has maintained relatively unbroken its traditional attitude to the role of philosophic speculation. It has always maintained its ancient trust in the activities of speculative reason for certain carefully chosen of its members, so long as that speculation is carried on within the limits of its closely defined faith. The Roman Catholic colleges and universities have always insisted that their best pupils go out into the world with some grounding in the traditions of scholastic philosophy – that is, in the reasonable framework of the theology of their church. They have been insistent that the training of rational Roman Catholics was at least as important as the training of efficient economists or physicists. Often the technicians have made the claim that students from these universities have not as adequate a technical knowledge as students trained elsewhere. The philosopher can but ask whether this lack of technical width (if it be a fact) is not more than counterbalanced by the other ends that their education has served.

A notable step in Roman Catholic philosophic activity was the recent establishment of the Pontifical Institute of Medieval Studies. This institution is connected with St Michael's College and through it to the University of Toronto. It calls together Roman Catholic scholars of the first magnitude to pursue their studies in the fields of medieval history and political thought, medieval philosophy and theology. To it come postgraduate students who can pursue their own studies in this field under scholars of first-rate calibre. Concentration is laid on the study of St Thomas Aquinas, so that students have the possibility of mastering a great system of thought. From such an institution as this, well-disciplined teachers go back into the undergraduate fields equipped to pass on something of the unity of their particular tradition. Other institutions have much to learn from places such as this, from which undergraduate studies receive their life-blood and in which different studies are so intertwined as to learn the values of each other.

It is more difficult to understand what has been accomplished in philosophy among those institutions that belong to the Protestant tradition. Protestants, whether in Canada or elsewhere, have been less certain in their formulation of the relation of philosophy to faith than have the Roman Catholics. They have never been willing to maintain such ecclesiastical discipline as could preserve a consistent stand on the matter. On the one hand, Luther's great affirmation that the Word of God is sufficient for the Christian has ever made certain branches of the Protestant church wary of speculation as a pagan activity that adds nothing to the faith by which men are saved. On the other hand, the liberal elements that have become increasingly dominant within the Protestant churches have sought a close alliance between philosophy and theology so that the church would have a rational apologetic with which to face the world. Yet again certain secularist elements that have increasingly sheltered within traditionally Protestant institutions have gone so far as to seek the freeing of philosophy from any dependence upon faith, even in those very institutions founded and supported by men of the Protestant faith. The results of the first and third of these tendencies have, though contradictory, led in the same direction. Philosophy has been, by and large, taught in the universities of non-Catholic Canada as a secular study not necessarily connected with the progress of faith. As a result of this anomaly, a subject such as philosophy, which deals with the wholeness of existence, has been in no way related to the faith from which the universities sprang, and indeed is sometimes in direct contradiction to that faith. This anomaly has been left largely undebated both by men who are avowedly Protestants and by the secularists.

What has happened to the universities and colleges that originally sprang from the Protestant tradition? Do these universities in any sense continue to think of themselves as servants of that tradition or do they think of themselves as secular? Clearly, on the answer to that problem will depend the character of the philosophy which will develop in our colleges. This history of Queen's University may be taken as an example of what is involved in this problem. About half a century ago Queen's decided to sever its official connection with the Presbyterian Church

from which it had sprung. It did this in the hope that it could thereby
play a wider role in the national life. Did the men responsible for this
decision visualize that philosophy would then be taught as a study
unconnected with the faith? In looking at the documents of the time it
is difficult to suppose that the men who advocated this course did so
intend. Yet half a century later the content of the teaching in the Faculty of Arts at that university is found to be almost entirely secular. The
universities controlled by their respective provincial governments raise
another problem. If to be non-denominational means to be non-religious, is philosophy (as a general university subject) to be taught as a
secular study?

The churches themselves have a great stake in this question of the
teaching of philosophy. In the past presumably they have thought of
the universities to which they have sent their young members (whether
laymen or incipient members of the clergy) as institutions closely
related to the Church. Yet in the past, the study of philosophy in these
institutions has just as often served as a destroyer of the faith rather
than the creator of the rational groundwork to that faith. It must be
admitted that the Protestant churches have been remarkably uncon-
cerned with a state of affairs which has done much to vitiate their
strength.

Indeed, the prime difficulty in estimating what our philosophic ideas
have been is that Canada during the period that those ideas were forming has witnessed the change among influential sections of the population from being Protestants to being secularists. Though this has not
been true of the majority of Canadians, it has been true of a large percentage of the intellectually gifted people who shape our society and to
whom reasoning is a possibility. Such a remarkable and deep-seated
change in our national life has naturally confused our philosophizing.

Despite the difficulties of understanding what philosophy has meant
within the Protestant tradition, certain real achievements must be recognized. These have been generally accomplished by men of Great
Britain, educated in the Christian and classical studies of that country.
Many of these scholars did noble work in revealing the value of such
studies to many generations of Canadians. Two fine examples of this
kind of teaching may be singled out: the work of Professor Watson[*] at

---

[*]John Watson (1847–1939), Canada's foremost philosopher of his time. He began teaching at Queen's in 1872 and served under Grant's grandfather. Grant was a student at
Queen's when Watson died and he served as a pallbearer at his funeral.

Queen's around the turn of the century, and the work of Professor Brett* at Toronto University in the third and fourth decades of this century. Because these men had been trained in European philosophy with its faith in human reason's pursuit of the Good, they could bring a tradition to Canada far more profound and ordered than the pragmatisms which were influencing us from the south. They had been brought up in societies that had been for centuries Protestant and so could help keep alive in Canada those ideas out of which the English-speaking forms of our society had been born.

One difficulty of having Englishmen as our leading teachers of philosophy must, however, be mentioned. As has been said earlier, these men were teaching at a time when the conception of the contemplative arts was being radically assailed in Canada. The fact that the men who were deeply involved in keeping this conception alive were generally men bred in Great Britain often meant that they were unable to transpose the vital issue of philosophy into sufficiently Canadian terms to make them of burning interest to young Canadians. This failure became increasingly important as the forms of life in Canada became more differentiated from those in Great Britain. To say this is in no sense to stand on the dogmas of a narrow Canadian nationalism, or to imply that Canadians have not important things to learn from men trained in Great Britain. It is, however, to say that a philosophy department must not only have the conservative aim of acquainting students with ideas from our past, but also the prophetic aim of showing what those ideas mean in our actual present existence. It is certainly true that in any Canadian department of philosophy there is ample room for teachers from Europe who will almost certainly understand the past of Europe better than will Canadians. But their work must be carried on within a context of Canadian teaching impregnated with our history and the form of our institutions and ideals. Often in the past, philosophy has seemed a pursuit which turned out cultured Europeans, but hardly an absolutely necessary activity for Canadians.

During the last years there have appeared the first signs of an indigenous Canadian approach to the problem of philosophy. All over the Western world, the multiplying tragedies that have occurred since 1914 have turned more sensitive minds to a new assessment of human existence. The dimming of the optimistic hopes that characterized that first

---

*George S. Brett (1879–1944), a classics professor at the University of Toronto who joined the philosophy department, of which he was chair from 1927 until his death.

industrial expansion has led men to seek a faith that has a fuller answer to the tragedies of experience. In this world there was little need to speculate deeply. As optimism declines, there is more reason to do so.

The evidence for this new awakening to our problem is indeed hard to assemble. Yet it is impossible to be with young Canadians and not feel an eager and questioning curiosity, a dissatisfaction with easy answers, out of which a truly Canadian philosophy might be born. This possible awakening is seen at a further level in the scholarly writings that are appearing. Canadian scholars are beginning to produce works of a profounder nature than studies of the wheat trade and the development of responsible government in Canada. It must be noted that these new works are not so much coming from men in the philosophy departments proper as from men whose studies are in one of the specialized fields. Such studies have led men to understand the limits of their fields seen in isolation, and so to an attempt to relate that field to the problem of human existence as a whole. Thus, their thought has become philosophical. Too often those in the philosophy departments proper have not been to the same degree challenged by the modern world so as to face the problems of philosophy in this living way.

The work of the late Professor C.N. Cochrane of Toronto may be taken as a noble example of this new Canadian interest in the problems of philosophy at their most profound and necessary level. His *magnum opus, Christianity and Classical Culture* (1940),[*] shows how interest in a particular field of human study drives the sensitive thinker out into the very midst of those spiritual problems that beset the modern world. In his early writings it is clear that he considered the historian's job was simply to say what had happened and to leave to other men the deeper judgments as to the meaning of history. As in most of this scientific investigation, the values that sustained the society were assumed, by an implicit faith, to be certain, and therefore not the concern of the scholar to defend. Yet in *Christianity and Classical Culture* Cochrane goes far beyond this 'objective' tradition and raises the profoundest questions about human destiny. He questions the very possibility of the aloof scholarship that he had once practised. To read the work is to understand that the history of the ancient world has been illuminated for him by the predicaments of his own society, and that he uses the example of the ancient world to throw his light towards the solution of the modern predicaments. A work such as *Christianity and Classical Cul-*

[*] See George Grant, 'Charles Cochrane,' in Part 3.

ture is not one to fall under the heading of light reading, even to the trained mind. It is the kind of work that will not influence large numbers at one time, but will influence and continue to influence the few. Such indeed must always be the role of significant philosophy – to affect the spirits of the intellectually gifted and through them to filter down into society as a whole.

One may cite other examples of specialists who in moving beyond the limits of their techniques see the broader questions of knowledge. In Professor Frye's[*] recent work on William Blake – *Fearful Symmetry* – full recognition is given to the fact that Blake's writing cannot be understood through the criteria of literary criticisms alone, but must be judged within the wider reference of the interpretation of experience that Blake attempts. Thus, his work is not limited in interest to the scholar of English literature, nor does it merely maintain that a cultured man should be interested in poetry. Rather, through the study of one poet it raises basic problems about the nature of man with which all are concerned whether they will it or not. Yet another example is Professor Woodhouse's *Puritanism and Liberty*.[†] Even Professor Innis,[‡] who in his early work rigidly confined himself to technical questions of economic history, has expanded his recent lectures on *Empire and Communications* (1950) to relate the questions of economics to their wider philosophical background.

These examples of Canadian thinkers who have shown themselves willing to go beyond scholarship to more general questions of human importance are encouraging to those who would hope for a native tradition of Canadian philosophy. They are signs that Canadians are no longer willing simply to accept from the more important nations of the Western world their assumptions about human life. There is the beginning of a recognition by Canadian scholars that we cannot count on our spiritual tradition remaining alive automatically. There is a realization at the intellectual level that Canadians can no longer afford to play

[*]Northrop Frye (1912–91) was a Canadian literary critic who taught at Victoria College at the University of Toronto and whose work achieved international renown. His first important book was *Fearful Symmetry* (1947). See Grant's later review of *The Great Code*, Part 4 of this volume.

[†]A.S.P. Woodhouse (1895–1964), head of the department of English at University College, Toronto, 1944–64, and author of *Puritanism and Liberty* (1938).

[‡]Harold Innis (1894–1952), Canadian economist and communications theorist, headed the Department of Political Economy at the University of Toronto 1935–52. See Grant's later discussion of Innis in Part 4 of this volume.

the role of debtor nation to the Western tradition, but must play their part in conserving and enlivening that tradition. Even more so, there is the understanding – and here the work of Cochrane must be especially noted – of how much the wisdom of that tradition has already been trodden under foot in our concentration on developing the mass society. Cochrane makes clear that only in realizing how close the intellectual life of Canada has come to losing the wisdom of a pre-scientific age will the strength and vitality be found to work towards the rediscovery of such wisdom.

At the more immediate level, these examples of a renewed interest in philosophical and theological wisdom point to some conclusions as to how philosophy could better fulfil its unifying role among our various necessary techniques. First and foremost it lights up the fact that most of our ablest teachers and students must perforce be technical specialists. Those who recognize the need for philosophical studies in Canada must work within the limits that are imposed by the hard facts of our situation. To put it historically, it is not possible in Canada to recreate the medieval idea of the university, or to copy the form of Classical Greats which held so great an influence over the education of the privileged classes of Great Britain in the nineteenth century. If philosophic studies are to be revived, it must be by reviving them among students and teachers whose first duty is the pursuit of some specialism such as law or history, economics or medicine. The hope is that specialists may see the interdependence of their specialty and the general questions of human existence. This philosophic interest must not be confined to those who are going to be academic practioners of their specialism, but must include those students who are to become more active members in society, whether as judges, doctors, civil servants, or scientists in the great industries. The tragic split between the men of action and the men of contemplation must be overcome; the philosophers must recognize the relation of philosophy to the problem of society, and the spirit of philosophy must be infused into those who must act. Such an end is clearly an ideal impossible of achievement but a move towards it is the only hope of reviving the contemplative life.

At the undergraduate level, something in this direction is already carried out in most Canadian universities. A majority of students who are studying for the BA are at one time or another exposed to some philosophy. To a lesser degree this is true of those working towards a BSc. Courses in philosophy for engineering and medical students are becoming more of a commonplace in our calendars. It may be said, however, that often these classes in philosophy serve as a pleasant cultural appendage rather than as something central to the business of living. The main difficulty still remains that those students in BA and BSc courses who are really capable of sustained and systematic thought are being encouraged to specialize. Our arts faculties are a series of unrelated departments, so that the students receive little sense of the unity of human knowledge. In the sciences this is perhaps understandable; in the arts it is a tragic disgrace. Our technical tradition in the arts is a narrowing circle. The students we train in that specialist tradition in time become teachers themselves and thereby further atomize the arts faculties. This narrowing circle is tightened by the fact that professors have a tendency to compete like prima donnas and to use their influence to persuade students to specialize with them rather than to help them to gain a broader education.

The question is, how can the narrowing circle be broken? With the present state of Canadian universities it does not seem possible that the return to a more unified conception of education can be achieved by reforms in our undergraduate arrangements. Rather, our hope must be to broaden our graduate studies so that the graduates thereby produced may one day be in a position to do something about our undergraduate teaching. Today it must be recognized that our society and its universities are so organized as to admit large numbers to higher education who are not capable of advanced thought, and that therefore undergraduate studies must perforce be limited in their scope and expectations. Those students who have shown themselves able to continue their studies at the graduate level in a specialized field are just the members of society who will benefit from the unifying discipline of philosophy. Also, they will be older, and as Plato and Aristotle both point out, philosophy can best start when men have some experience on which to philosophize. The chief aim of philosophy in Canada, then, should be to see that graduate students continue their studies not simply in an ever narrowing field of specialism but within some kind of philosophic framework. Nothing else could do more to increase the strength of the contemplative tradition in Canada. It may be said that if something were accomplished in this direction the title 'Doctor of Philosophy' might once again signify what it is supposed to signify.

How can something be done towards this end? First is the question of how those who teach these advanced techniques may be brought to realize the value of their students beholding their studies within a wide whole, and may be persuaded to allow them to spend some of their time on work towards this purpose. Secondly, there is the question of how the general public may come to recognize that this is an end on which time and money must be spent. In both cases it is only sensible to admit that any movement away from our present situation will be slow. A change in the attitude of society seems improbable unless the first move be made by the university authorities – both the teachers and the boards of governors. So often our university authorities have seen themselves as the servants rather than the teachers of the public. They have given way to the pressures of popularity. If the universities give a lead in this matter, they must be willing to pay the price of such a lead. The price in a democratic and industrial society such as ours will be the accusation of being 'academic' and 'impractical.' Also, it may be said that the lead must probably come from the wealthier universities in the larger centres who are more able for financial reasons to resist outside clamours.

One step would be a change in the curriculum of our graduate schools, so that advanced degrees would not be granted unless the student shows some grip of the tradition. This would require some real philosophic study. Since the curriculum of the graduate schools is in the hands of the academic personnel, a change in this direction would be an immediate possibility. How can the PhD have any meaning as a degree, or any right to its title, if it be granted to students who are not required to show any formal understanding of the relation of their subject to the questions of human existence as a whole? Toronto University does something in this direction. However, when one reads technical theses which have been accepted for the doctorate at that university, and which are devoid of the primary element of philosophic thought, one can only be dubious of what is being accomplished. It has often been the way of modern men to laugh at the medieval student for discussing how many angels could stand on the point of a needle. Our modern laughter must be humbled by reading theses on the excreta of rats for which PhDs have been awarded.

The concern of the governors of our universities is the sheerly quantitative question of number of teachers. Most philosophy departments are now staffed as if philosophy were one of the less important techniques taught at the university. If it is to be more than that, if its role is to provide some unity between various studies, then the governors must be willing to spend enough money to make this possible. Sheer quantity of teachers will by itself achieve nothing. It is nevertheless a *sine qua non*. A tradition of rational speculation is not something that a society can buy cheaply – a pleasant extra that coats the real business of improving the standard of living.

More important than sheer numbers are the subtler questions of what kind of teachers one wants and how they may best be trained. The teachers of philosophy, if they are to have influence, must be men who are not only steeped in the wisdom of the past but who are also aware of society as it is. Above all, they must be aware of the meaning of the various other studies in the university. Only in this way can they fulfil their special responsibility for making clear to the university community that their subject is not another specialism but related to all studies. Nothing has done the practice of philosophy more harm than the idea of some scientists that philosophy is another science of the same kind as theirs. The narrow vocabulary and approach of certain philosophers has been largely responsible for that illusion. Therefore, our teachers must be men able to expose that illusion by teaching philosophy in a broad and living way.

A chief step, then, must be in the setting up of graduate schools in which this narrow approach to philosophy can be broken down. Here the Pontifical Institute of Medieval Studies must once more be referred to. For all institutions now existing in Canada, it seems to point most surely in the right direction. There one sees a graduate institution which approaches the activities of the human spirit in a unified way, and all in relation to a particular tradition. Philosophy is not seen as an isolated technique but as something related to the other facets of the Catholic life – history and theology, art and liturgy. To repeat, the students from such an institution have a wholeness about their attitude to learning not found among many of the students who have done their work in the atomized graduate schools of our country.

Immediately the question arises about the cost of establishing such institutions. One advantage of the Roman Catholic Church over others is the economic saving of a celibate priesthood. But the cost in other traditions should not be prohibitive, especially when it is compared to the money spent on the researches of physical science. The enormous money spent on guaranteeing the physical health of our society would not be necessary in establishing institutions such as these which would guard our spiritual health. The question is simply whether a society gains more from its M.I.T.s or from its Institutes of Medieval Studies.

The difficulty immediately arises of whether these institutions in non-Roman Catholic education should be secular or professedly Christian. This, however, need not be a difficulty. Those universities which now admit they are simply secularist will probably be quite content with their graduate schools as they already are. If not, they could set up Institutes of Humane Study or some such title. Protestant universities or colleges that maintain their Christian affiliations could set up schools for Christian study very much like the Institute for Medieval Studies. From what has been said earlier there can be no doubt which of these two types of institutions the present writer would expect to be the more effective. The dependence of philosophy upon theology makes such a conclusion necessary. From such institutions a start might be made in seeing that our spiritual traditions were once more in close relation to the life of actions. Thence would come the vitality which might recreate our universities into what they should always have been – centres of rational thought about the universe.

Inevitably in such a young country as Canada, one must write about the teaching of philosophy in the spirit of things hoped for, not in the pride of what has been accomplished. Upon what is likely to be accomplished, it would be folly to speculate. As in all the slow intangible accomplishments of the human spirit, its quality will depend on whether men look for the long-term or the short-term results. In the short view, the advantages are clearly with the continued production of technicians by our higher education. The question will be decided by whether our political leaders and civil servants, our businessmen and educators come to see more clearly the long-term advantages of training our able youth in a contemplative as well as an active approach to life. It will depend indeed on whether they see the incalculable advantages that will pertain to any society which has a contemplative tradition strong enough to act as a brake on the rightly impetuous men of action. In the world we live in, the need of such an influence should become increasingly apparent.

The tragedy must be admitted that, just as the controlling forces in our Western world are beginning to understand how deeply our spiritual traditions need guarding, and that some of our energy must be diverted from technology towards that purpose, our society is being challenged to defend itself against a barbaric empire that puts faith in salvation by the machine. This must inevitably mean that a large percentage of Western wealth be spent on the mechanism of defence.

As this essay is addressed to a Royal Commission, something must be said in closing of how interdependent is the progress of philosophy with the progress of the arts. The practice and enjoyment of the arts has only flourished in the past among men who have had some understanding of the wholeness of life, and who therefore could see the true purposes of art in relation to the other necessary activities of human existence. A supreme artist such as J.S. Bach could use the techniques of his craft to the full because he understood the purpose of his art within the wider range of human function. Equally, the community for which Bach wrote could appreciate his music because they had some vision of what music meant in the total progress of the human soul. Philosophy cannot produce that intuition of the beautiful out of which art arises, but it can help to promote that unity of mind in which such intuition will best flourish. The same may be said of letters. Though it is suggested in this essay that applied science is already overdeveloped in Canada, philosophy can give that unity of mind out of which the speculations of pure science arise. The development of the philosophical disciplines in our universities would provide the kind of integrated minds among educated Canadians through which the arts of civilization could flourish in some balanced proportion.

In closing, the present writer has no alternative but to repeat once again his conviction that the practice of philosophy (and for that matter, all the arts of civilization) will depend on a prior condition – namely the intensity and concentration of our faith in God. It is a great illusion that scepticism breeds thought and that doubt is the producer of art. The sceptic fails in that courage which alone can buttress the tiring discipline of being rational. Why should those who believe there is so little to know spend their energy in the hard activity of contemplation? As the late A.N. Whitehead wrote, it is in the ages of faith that men pursue truth and beauty. It would be impudence indeed in this essay to suggest how and when we Canadians will reach a fuller and more balanced intuition of God. It is not impudence, however, to point out that without such faith it will be vain to expect any great flowering of our culture in general and of our philosophy in particular.

THE ROLE OF EDUCATION

Ever since working with the Canadian Association of Adult Education from 1943 to 1945, Grant was passionately interested in education. He rarely declined an opportunity to speak to teachers' groups and he constantly reminded them of the dangers of losing sight of the fundamental truths that gave teaching its importance.

You mentioned before I went to the 'old country' that I might look around for somebody (preferably Scottish) to help teach philosophy. I came across nobody who seemed suitable. Indeed the more I saw of young European philosophers the more I wondered how they would understand and fit into the Nova Scotian pattern. Science is so objective and certain that the background of the teacher is not of its essence. Philosophy because it deals with such personal mysteries does depend on the teacher understanding and sympathizing with the background of his pupils. So many of the young English and Scottish teachers I have met were able, but I doubted their ability to transfer that ability to a Canadian setting. This is not to say that I do not believe that Canadians have endless things to learn from the great tradition of European life and thought – but it does seem to me that somebody who was a Canadian and yet knew Europe would be better in the university teaching philosophy than somebody from the United Kingdom.

– George Grant to A.E. Kerr, late summer 1950

University education, if it is to be worth anything, must be aristocratic. (Aristocratic, of course, not in the sense of birth, but of capability.) I do also know that the most aristocratic part of a university must be a philosophy department. Under the mysterious providence of God, not many men or women are intended to understand life *sub specie aeternitatis.*[*] We must grant that in their strange way those students who do may become the most important members of society. While at college they need the close and careful attention of teachers.

– George Grant to A.E. Kerr, 29 February 1952

The Paradox of Democratic Education (1955)[†]

What do I mean by the paradox of the democratic educator? The paradox seems to me this: On the one hand, there is much in democracy to

---

[*]In the context of eternity.
[†]George Grant, 'The Paradox of Democratic Education,' *The Bulletin* (published by the Ontario Secondary School Teachers' Federation), vol. 35, no. 6 (November 1955), 275–80. (Second Ansley Memorial Lecture, delivered on 1 October 1955 at Assumption University, Windsor.)

which we must give loyalty; on the other hand, isn't there something in democracy which we must fear as the enemy of true education?

It is of course impossible in short space to give a close definition of democracy. In the present context I mean simply the kind of society we have here in Canada. By so defining it, I do not intend to describe all the forms of our society as democratic, for that is clearly contradicted by our economic forms. Nevertheless, in a general sense we can speak of our society as democratic.

Now, to state the one side of the paradox, I for one am clear about giving loyalty to that democracy, particularly as it is seen against possible alternative systems of society abroad in the world. This allegiance must be limited, of course, for it is idolatry to give more than limited allegiance to anything as relative as the ordering of society. And when I speak of loyalty to that democracy, I do not only mean to its political forms, but to its social forms as well. For instance, the idea of social equality, which is so much a product of the North American as against the English tradition, is something to which I give wholehearted allegiance.

It is necessary to make this distinction between social and political democracy, for these days there is a new conservatism abroad which supports the political forms of democracy while attacking its social forms. This conservatism has a great appeal, for it is based on the truth that men are not equal in talents. And this truth certainly needs stressing as against certain vacuous talk of our more naive progressive democrats. It has, however, been the genius of Christianity, at its richest, to hold together in tension both sides of the truth at this point. It has remained clear that men are not equal in talents and yet has insisted on the more mysterious truth that all persons being called by God to salvation are equal before His majesty. If I may say a word in praise of the Puritans, who have been so cheaply abused in recent years by the humanists, it was this mystery of equality that they so well understood.

It is, indeed, at this point as much as any that I find the secular democrat difficult to understand. If, as they do, one holds that man's destiny is only in this world, how is it possible to believe in equality? In a worldly sense, men are so obviously unequal. Therefore, if one is a consistent secularist one should certainly not believe in social democracy. Social and educational democracy is a doctrine which only has meaning when seen to be rooted in a theological mystery. That mystery is the recognition of both sin and love. Aristocratic forms of government are rejected because the Christian is at once cynical of the ability of the ruler to free himself from corruption, and hopeful of the possibility of the love of God in the life of the ordinary person. The value of the ordinary person, socially and educationally, is recognized because he is an object of the divine love. A tradition which knew that the Saviour of the world was a crucified Palestine carpenter and his disciples certainly not aristocrats, was one which recognized that the love of God can pour into the hearts of the many. It is ultimately in terms of this idea alone that any allegiance to social democracy can be maintained.

Nevertheless, once this side of the paradox has been stated, it seems to me that the other side must be stated too. Is it not equally true that democracy can openly and obviously be an enemy of true education? I think this side of the case can be put most clearly by stating what Plato says about the matter in his *Republic*.

You will remember that at the end of the *Republic* Plato describes the decline of society and the soul. Having described the ideally good society and the ideally good soul, he now describes the ideally bad, which he calls despotism. He does not believe that the ideally good or bad are possible in this world. They are described simply as ethical principles of attraction and repulsion. And in the scale between the good and the bad he places the democratic society and soul very low – as indeed the last step before the descent of man into the depths of despotism. He describes democracy as that state in which the lowest common denominator of desire rules and where every institution is dominated by this lowest common denominator of desire. By lowest common denominator of desire, he means that the desires arising from the appetites have taken over the person, and have become the ruling principle. Reason has been dethroned. Democracy must therefore destroy itself because it will become a chaos. It will become a chaos because, as people give themselves ever more and more to the pursuit of the immediate claims of appetite, the ordering power of reason disappears. In short, by definition democracy is the purest and most blatant love of the world as an end – that is, secularism.

And surely once we look at the present education situation in Canada, don't we see how true is what Plato says? I have not time here to describe in detail the situation in our schools and universities as I see it. Of the universities, suffice it to say that in general they have become servants of the expanding economy. They are places where our youngsters go to be taught certain techniques which will allow them to enter or remain in the more prosperous part of society. They are largely servants of that appetite which is dominant in the cleverer part of our society – namely greed. Any idea of education which transcends that is the merest minority report. And though I cannot speak of the schools from inside knowledge, my view of them, certainly those in Nova Scotia, is that in large measure they are places where youngsters are taught to adjust themselves to the lowest common denominator of achievement.

I will allow myself simply one example to illustrate how our modern education leads us to take this distrust of democracy seriously: the degree to which the philosophy of John Dewey has been influential. Only a society which already accepted a very low view of human nature and destiny would have responded the way it did and does to what Dewey said about human existence and the purpose of education. For whatever is valid in Dewey at the level of practical techniques, the philosophy which underlies it is nothing more finally than that worship of the lowest common denominator of appetite which Plato describes. This is explicitly spelled out in Dewey's position. The world of space and time is seen as the ultimately real. Reason is, therefore, defined as the instrument whereby we learn to adjust ourselves to that world. And if adjustment to the world can in effect mean anything else than adjustment to the lowest common denominator of desire, then I wish somebody would show me. What Plato sees as the tragedy of democracy, namely the gradual abdication by the higher faculties of their rule over man, Dewey accepts as the true end of education. About one thing I am crystal clear: if, as the Deweyites claim, their philosophy of education is the truly democratic view, then democracy is a state of society in which true education cannot flourish. And what I must emphasize again is that the very fact that pragmatism should have had such power over the minds of so many people influential in our democratic school system could only have been possible if our view of man had already degenerated under democracy; and that shows us how seriously we must take the claim that such a low view is implicit in the system.

To return to the paradox: what I have said I hope illustrates how much it is a real paradox and not just a dilemma I am putting up to knock down. The more I think about the question, the harder it is to find reconciliation either at the level of thought or action. How does one reconcile one's deep loyalty to the tradition of democracy with the undoubted debasement of education that our democracy brings?

Of course, one can get out of the dilemma in two ways – by dropping either side of the difficulty. One can simply just not recognize the tendencies towards debasement and to see the democratic system as a glorious progressive affair – broadening down from precedent to precedent. This is what so many school and university teachers and administrators do. They simply get on the bandwagon of vulgarity and ride it with varying degrees of success. On the other hand, one can solve the dilemma by simply discarding all faith in democratic education. But that is wrong in principle because it surrenders for all practical purposes the Christian mystery of love. It is also apt to mean that one just retreats out of the modern world and to do that is to forget one of the supreme principles of ethics, namely that though we may dislike the world in which we are placed, it is the only one we've got – that is, it is the society into which God has called us to act. The only alternative, therefore, to escaping the paradox is to live in its tension.

. . .

I want to illustrate this paradox further in relation to a certain philosophy of the modern democratic school which seems to me to exert great influence in our midst. In the mixture of truth and falsity which that philosophy represents, I think one sees more clearly what democratic education is.

I heard this theory expressed over and over again this summer at a conference on the philosophy of education held by the Ontario Teachers' Federation which I had the great good fortune to attend. The exponents of this theory say something like the following:

> The democratic society of North America is based upon certain moral values which were first formulated in the Judaic-Christian tradition. Therefore, because one of the chief aims of our school system is to teach allegiance to the democratic society, we must try by any means appropriate to inculcate those values into the minds of our youngsters. Nevertheless, this must not mean that the schools should touch the field of ultimately reality – that is, the field of religion. This is a personal matter with which the schools cannot interfere. Indeed, it would be against true democracy to teach about religion, for as people disagree as to what is ultimately real, to teach about it would be to infringe the personal freedom of the individual to reach his conclusions on this matter. In short, ethical values are a common ground where the public schools can act with authority – that is, endeavour to inculcate; religious truth, however, is a personal matter and thereon the public schools must not be allowed to speak.

. . .

Now, the position outlined in this report recognizes certain unfor-

gettable truths about our society. The mass society is here and therefore we are committed to the problem of mass education. Moreover,
the report maintains that we should be committed to that task in joy
because of the value of each person, and as I have said earlier I entirely
agree with that. It predicts that technological advances will give the
majority more leisure than ever before in history. It recognizes that in a
society of such varying traditions it is inevitable that the state, as the
only common institution, should play a central role in education. I
have not time to discuss in detail the extraordinarily subtle question of
church and state in a society which is religiously pluralist, and though I
disagree with much that the report says on this matter, it is still right
when it says that North American democracy is committed to pluralism
and that therefore the state schools must respect it. This respect will
insure that the school shall not encroach on the duties of the church
and the home. Lastly, we can even admit that this document expresses
one side of the truth when it says that one's religion is a personal matter. This is true in the sense that final reality, being spirit, can only be
encountered in a free act of the spirit. However, that is only half the
truth as traditions, education, institutions, and authority are, of course,
also necessary to that encounter.

Nevertheless, as soon as one has stated the truth in this report, it is
necessary to state with full force its basic falsehood. I am going to illustrate this falsity in two ways: (i) with regard to the proper ordering of
studies; (ii) with regard to the divorcing of values from reality.

First, then, why is this position shown to be false when we look at the
question of the proper ordering of studies? To prove this I will have to
lay down certain basic propositions. The school is the chief instrument
in our society for the cultivation of the human reason – particularly the
theoretical reasons as distinct from practical reason which is cultivated
at all points in our life. Now, why do we count it good to cultivate the
theoretical reason in ourselves and others? There are many subsidiary
purposes for that cultivation, but the fundamental purpose is, as Aristotle says, that all men desire to know the real and that therefore the final
object of the cultivation of reason is that we may know what is ultimately
real – that is, God. Now, this proposition, which is obviously central to
the philosophy of education, cannot be justified at length here. It is the
ultimate truth of human existence and therefore the hardest truth to
prove to oneself or to others. I may say, however, and this will seem to
some of you extreme arrogance, that I do not count this truth to be
mere opinion, something of which I am not certain. I am certain of it in
the sense that, though I cannot prove it to be true, I can prove all dif-

fering positions to be false and therefore must assume this as necessary. It is a truth which is assumed in all rational activity – scientific, philosophic, artistic, or moral.

But if this proposition is true, then it will shape our schools at all points particularly as to the proper ordering of studies. How can we do a proper job of education unless we have some clarity as to what education is for? How can the purpose for which we study not determine what studies are carried on?

Let me illustrate this from contemporary education. There doesn't seem to be much doubt from anybody in education that careful study of certain traditional subjects, whether at the university or school level, is dying out. Now, the progressive educators tell us, and I think rightly, that this is not a necessary result of the new methods. The traditional subjects can be well taught under the new methods. So much of the old discipline in the school and the home was quite wrong. But when the progressive educators have said this they have not freed themselves from the charge of being deeply responsible for the decline of the old studies. Their responsibility is not, however, at the level of practical method but of theory. Their philosophy is that the purpose of education is successful living in this world: they deny any transcendent end to education. This is explicitly and continually stated in Dewey. Therefore, as the end is different, different studies are necessary.

Why was classical language and history studied in the old schools? It was not studied only to give exactness in language or to give examples from history so that men would be the better able to manipulate their present. After all, as the progressive educators have said time and again, these purposes could be equally well served by modern language and modern history. It was studied so that the ablest in our society – those who were going to have responsibility in church and state and education – would be able later to learn those philosophic truths which are found in the classical thinkers. These truths indeed were known to be basic to any later understanding of Christian theology, the knowledge of which was recognized as the pinnacle to which all education aspired. Mathematics was not taught primarily so that we could have enough capable engineers but because through it the intellect could learn to isolate concepts and so be ready later to ascertain universal truth at a higher level.

Now, of course, when you think there is no transcendent truth to be ascertained, no God to be known, when you think as Dewey does that the purpose of education is adjustment to this world, then the emphasis of your curriculum will be entirely different and what students think important to study will be entirely different. I am sure you all see this every day of your lives as I do. One of the reasons for the existence of the university in which I work is that it is a great exporter of commercial lawyers to the temples of Bay Street in Toronto. Now, to be successfully adjusted to the world of Bay Street you do not need any knowledge of classical history or philosophy (a certain attenuated culture may be necessary but that can be picked up at a session of the Harvard School of Business Administration and by careful attention at cocktail parties). Therefore, classics and philosophy are not considered important either by the administration or by students. The same example could be given by our export of research physicists or chemists to the government laboratories in Ottawa.

How are we to speak to students clearly outside some philosophy as to what is ultimately real? Are we to encourage students to study this or that and yet not be able to tell them the purpose of studying this or that? Now, of course, the answer we give to younger students may have to be of an indirect or even allegorical kind. We may have to say to them you can't yet see why mathematics is important, if one is to advance to higher studies, but trust me that it is. Yet all the same we have to be clear in ourselves or else the brighter the student the more he will see education as pointless and chaotic.

There is a popular modern position which tries to escape any statement about ultimate reality by that wonderful platitude that the purpose of the school is to teach people to think. A dean of education from western Canada was down in Halifax saying this to our teachers last week and I hear it from many quarters. This position has the advantage of seeming to be a compromise which appeals to both the traditionalist and the progressive. But, of course, it entirely breaks down as soon as one asks the simple question – why is it good to think? Won't I be happier if I don't think, if, for instance, I don't go near the study of philosophy? And when one tries to answer that question one is forced to some view of what really matters in life. Either one says one should think because it will help one to get on in the world and that is what matters; or think because it will teach you what is real, it will give you the vision of God. And I would point out again that only the second answer has any value in persuading youngsters to study any subject which takes one beyond the palpably useful.

What I have been saying is that a philosophy is necessarily implied in the schools. Students will study subjects, institutions will teach subjects according to their view of reality. This is an inescapable fact of education. People who believe what Dewey says are in fact shaping the curriculum by their metaphysics; my criticism of them is simply that they have a false metaphysic. Therefore, when this report says that the democratic school must not be based on any view of what is ultimately real, aren't the writers of it just fooling themselves or trying to fool the public? For surely what the report is saying is rather that the schools must indeed take a view of reality but a very inadequate one; namely reality as it appears to the common sense of the mass. And if this is so, then doesn't the report illustrate exactly what Plato says, that democracy is the rule of the lowest common denominator and as such an enemy of true education?

This indeed takes me to my second point concerning values in which the central fallacy of the position advocated in this report is exposed. As in regard to the ordering of studies, so in this question the falsity of the theory is inseparable from its disastrous results in practice.

Values depend on what is real. It is a simple fact that what actions we think to be good depend on what we think is ultimately real. Therefore, to have right values we must have a right apprehension of the real. To put it technically, ethics depend on metaphysics. For example, if a man believes that the struggle for animal existence is the underlying truth of all nature and history, obviously the virtue of brotherhood will not seem valuable. Or again, if we believe that persons are but instruments of the life force, then of course chastity is not the supreme value of the sexual life. For Christianity, the highest activity possible for man is redemptive love, which of necessity includes in itself suffering. But we cannot see why such an activity is valuable unless in some sense we recognize the truth of Christian theology about the purposes of the divine love in the world. If indeed in some sense we do not see history in this pattern then remedial suffering will seem to us just queer – as the psychologists say, the kind of thing which masochists indulge in. To repeat, what one believes to be ultimately true, not what seems nice, will determine what actions one really thinks valuable.

I see this fact in the universities. For example, in the Dalhousie medical school there are many professors who themselves believe and imply in all they teach that man can be totally understood as animal. Yet these professors are horrified when one of their students cheats, or when they see the old medical ethics breaking down before the growing love of money among the doctors. But why should they be? If man is simply an animal, morality is an illusion and then why shouldn't students cheat, why shouldn't one try to amass more nuts than the other squirrels? And what always seems most amazing to me in this is how little these professors see that what they have been teaching students over the years about ultimate reality (namely that man can be fully known as a biological object) has had a direct effect in producing the kind of doctors they now dislike.

Obviously, the same thing applies in the schools. If you have schools where the best teachers assert that what is real is the world of space and · time, as so many teachers do, then it is foolish to try and impose in that school a set of values which come from a very different view of reality. All you do then is to produce chaos. The clever children see the inconsistency and the stupid are meanly tricked. One is saying to them that brotherhood matters in terms of this world. When they go out into the world they soon find that brotherhood does not bring success in worldly terms – that it just means they get taken. Then the inference from that is that the value of brotherhood is just part of that pious nonsense which schools put over but which nobody means.

This is the basic failure of this document of the National Education Association. Its failure is at the level of philosophy and theoretical consistency. There is nothing wrong with the document at the level of practical virtue. (It has, indeed, more pious exhortations to virtue per square inch of print than any other document I have ever read.) But the proposition that we can hope to inculcate Judaic-Christian values while eliminating any systematic teaching and thought about what is real must be criticized philosophically. For if what I said is true: namely that values are the flowers, the roots of which are our affirmation about metaphysics, then this document is telling us that the flowers can be kept alive when they are cut off from their roots. If you can believe that, you can believe anything.

But though this is what this report states explicitly, really what is implied is a deeper philosophy than that. What is implied in every line of this document is a profound irrationalism. Positively, this irrationalism takes the form of saying that the natural and social sciences are the way we find out what is real, while religion and values are concerned with subjective preferences arising largely from the emotions. Religion is thought of as a kind of emotional certainty and volitional commitment à la Billy Graham, and values are thought of as the right emotional attitudes the democratic society wants to inculcate. Reality is thought of as the sensuous world of space and time, and truth about reality as the accumulation of facts through the sciences. Negatively, that is, the document denies the basic proposition of Western thought that the reason, practical and theoretical, is the faculty by which man apprehends ultimate reality and that therefore that reality is supersensible. The assumption throughout is that values and religion are matters of opinion, not matters where truth can be discovered by proper use of the mind. The position is something like this. On the one side you have a world of facts of reality gained by the sciences; on the other hand you have an emotional world of value and religion. The human being is broken down the middle. Reason operates for dealing with the world but not for giving one truth for how one should act or what one should worship.

In other words, however much this report tries to escape any accusation of Deweyism, by an avowed friendship to religion and values, it really is in exactly the same position. For the basic proposition of Dewey is still there – namely that reason is only an instrument for manipulating the world. The religious, ethical, and metaphysical questions of mankind are a realm where reason cannot operate. And, of course, if this presupposition of the document is true then all its practical proposals logically follow. But this proposition cannot possibly be justified in thought. You cannot by reason show that reason has no power.

I have spoken of the position advocated in this report at length because it illustrates a truth which tends to be forgotten in a society such as ours. That truth is this: a position which, practically, seems both decent and feasible in the short run, may still be false philosophically and so can only be disastrous in the long run.

But, of course, if the philosophy of education is to be of service it must not put itself outside the awful responsibilities of time. And that means that the short run and the long run must be brought together. In relation to the position in this report the tension of our minds must be to see in unity its short-term truth and its long-term falsity. How are we to recognize that mass democracy is here and that in love we must care about it? How are we to take that seriously and still recognize that the purpose of education is the movement of the mind to God and that therefore all activities in the schools must be seen in that context?

And as I have said, this question presents to me no easy solution. I do not see any coordinated plan of group action (the kind of thing that we in North America are so fond of) that can take us off the hook of this predicament. It is a tension which all of us have to live through. Therefore, I am in no position to end this talk by introducing some *deus ex machina.*[*] A fellow, who is now very prominent in universities circles in central Canada, always seems at this point to come up with the proposition 'Give me five million dollars and I will save Western civilization.' I do not mean to say anything of that sort. For one thing nobody can know how others will live out the tensions and agonies of this life. And how this situation is met in North America will depend on how thousands of us live out those agonies.

There are, however, two things which do not seem to me pretentious to say. First and foremost, I must repeat the platitude that what matters above anything else in this is that there should be teachers who know deeply what education is for and whose wills are committed to what their intellects have seen. Only such people can lead the young to reality. Only such people will have the courage to be teachers in a world which does not take the intellect seriously and which therefore thinks teaching is unimportant besides medicine or engineering, stock-broking or salesmanship. And the first consideration of such teachers must be to be steeped in the reality they teach about. Those who teach mathematics or literature or classics or history or natural science must know deeply the reality with which these subjects are concerned. That is why method must be known as subordinate to subject matter. Of course, methods are important but to lift them up as sacred cows is obviously to lose sight of what they are for. They are a means through which young people may be brought to partake in reality as given in the subject taught.

But the teacher must have more than simply a knowledge of reality at the level of his subject. He must see reality at that level in its proper subordination to what is ultimately real. He must have given his mind over seriously to the philosophy of education. And this is necessary, because if reality is only known in segments, the segment which is known cannot help but be distorted. For, if the teacher of literature, however much he is steeped in the poets, has not thought about the relation of poetic beauty to the final beauty, his teaching is liable to end up in a rather insipid aestheticism. And even more important, if the teacher of science does not see that the reality of nature must be seen in its relation and dependence on other realities, the teaching of science can lead youngsters to the cheapest kind of materialism. And as soon as one has said this, it is clear that the teacher must have thought about philosophic truth. I do not mean by this simply a few pleasant aphorisms

[*] A god from a machine; saved in a contrived and lucky manner (Latin).

picked up on the side (for this I am afraid is what the philosophy of education comes down to in many of our colleges of education) but that he must strive to think things as a whole not only as a student but throughout his life.

This seems to me particularly important in these days. All of us in the modern world are dominated far more than we know by the world view given us by empirical science and pragmatic philosophy. It distorts our thought at all points, and we find it of incredible difficulty to think beyond it – let alone outside it. Now, I do not want to say that philosophy is the only way of preventing that world view from gradually taking us over completely, because art and love, prayer and worship, are also important. Nevertheless, philosophic thought is crucial. If we can take the domination by this world view up into our rational mind by seeing it in the light of the great philosophers and theologians of the past and present, we can then hold this scientific, pragmatic world view in perspective – see it for what it is, a partial and inadequate truth which is not final and therefore something which must not become an idolatry. Only if we ourselves are not swamped by the modern world view can we hope to lead youngsters to the truth which is beyond that view.

I know this is not easy. All of us are pushed hard at work and the better the youngsters we have the more our minds are pushed to keep up with them. We are pushed to make a go of it economically for ourselves and our families. We are pushed to wash dishes and spend time with our own children. We are taken up into the busyness and social life which is typical of Canadian communities. Despite all these other duties, however, one thing is clear: to be a good teacher one must have a private life of study and thought of one's own. Otherwise we are simply pulled into the mediocrity we are trying to change.

We must have, then, a life of loneliness. One of the clearest statements in the Old Testament is: 'Be still and know that I am God.' Indeed, one of the dangerous half truths of progressive theory is its attack on the idea of loneliness. I often meet teachers who take so seriously the emphasis on the group and on social adjustment that they criticize the more aloof children as immature for not participating in the group. That aloofness may be a mark of maturity, of having discovered at even a very young age the riches of loneliness. This is not to deny the idea of community – but if the community is to be more than a beehive it must be made up of individuals who are in themselves something. A group is not by definition good. We must remember that a group of a million could still be nothing. For nothing plus nothing plus nothing (even a million times) is still nothing. That is, as teachers we must cultivate our aloneness so that when we come to a group, we come as somebody.

Secondly, I would like to say that the temptation we must watch above any other is despair. In England there is a tombstone of a seventeenth-century Puritan divine who lived through the agonies of the civil war and on his tombstone is written: 'He did the best things at the worst times and hoped for them in the most calamitous.' Let that be written on ours. Despair for the teacher these days may so often lead to what I would call a Brahmin view of education – that is the view that we can touch a few choice spirits, but that the rest of the world is lost in ignorance.

A figure out of our history whom I like to contemplate in this connection is St Augustine – the African philosopher and theologian. Augustine lived at a period when it was hard to believe that history was to some purpose – the dissolution of classical society was all around him. He saw clearly that the principles abroad in that society necessarily meant its degeneration into increasing chaos. But in that situation he did not despair; nor, what is more important, did he take a wrongly otherworldly view. It was, indeed, in this terrible crisis of the classical world that Augustine affirmed with greater clarity than had ever been stated before that God is not alone the God beyond the world, but is also working in each moment of the historical. So from this hope the seeds of new meaning *in* the world as well as *beyond* it were planted not only for himself, but for others. He knew that despair was wrong, because despair always assumes that the issue of history lies finally with ourselves. But clearly it is not with ourselves that the ultimate issue lies. Our hope lies rather in One who is power and reason and love, Who has indeed most manifestly shown us that power and love and reason are in Him, One – eternally.

RESIGNATION FROM YORK

In late 1959 Grant accepted a position as head of the philosophy department in the newly created York University in Toronto. However, he resigned before taking up his position. He considered that control over the curriculum was essential for a university teacher, and he refused to have the content or the textbooks for his courses chosen by others. This letter outlines the reasons for his decision. Although it was not published, Grant intended it as a formal statement.

Letter of Resignation (1960)[*]

14 April 1960

Dear President Ross,

This is just to say that after long thought I have decided it would be wrong on my part to introduce youngsters to philosophy by means of Professor Long's textbook[†] and that as there seems no alternative to such a procedure at York, I must with regret submit my resignation to you.

As this is an important matter of academic principle I would like to state my objections to this procedure. (a) Professor Long's textbook pretends to be an introduction to philosophy which does not take sides, but introduces the student objectively to the problems of the subject. This is, however, not the case. To illustrate why it is not the case, let me take as an example the basic question of the differences between classical and modern philosophy. Professor Long's book is based on the presupposition that the assumptions of nineteenth century philosophy are true in a way that implies that those of the classical philosophy are not. As an obvious example, the book is prefaced by a quotation from Lessing which is taken as true and which implies that Plato and Aristotle largely wrote untruth. It is, of course, not my purpose here to debate the very vexed and difficult questions of the quarrel between the ancients and the moderns, but simply to say that one hardly has an objective textbook when it is based on such an assumption. What makes these assumptions particularly unobjective is that they are not made explicit in the work. (b) When I say that Professor Long's book is based on an implied assumption of the truth of modern philosophy, I do not mean contemporary philosophy, but the philosophy of the late nineteenth century in Great Britain and the early twentieth in the U.S.A. His book is oblivious to nearly all contemporary philosophy. For instance, there is no mention of Wittgenstein in his book – certainly the most influential modern philosopher in professional philosophic circles in the English-speaking world. (c) Apart from the assumptions of the book, its very method seems to me inimical to the proper teaching of philosophy. It is about philosophy; it is not philosophy. The result of this approach is to encourage sophism among youngsters – that is, it

[*]From William Christian, ed., *George Grant: Selected Letters* (Toronto: University of Toronto Press 1996).
[†]Marcus Long, *The Spirit of Philosophy* (1953).

encourages them to say here are a lot of opinions about this subject and that, but it does not encourage them in the real task of trying to make true judgments about those matters.

I would like to include a paragraph about Professor Long's relation to religion and my own, because I am sure you have heard it said that I confuse religion and philosophy and that you will now hear it said that my objection to Professor Long's book comes from my religion. Let me make it clear that I consider the practice of religion and the practice of philosophy two distinct human activities. I do not think that philosophy can prove or disprove Christian doctrine. My position on this matter is illustrated by the fact that the philosopher I admire most in North America is Leo Strauss at Chicago. He is a practising Jew and I would have no hesitation in saying that he is a better philosopher than any practising Christian I know on this continent. Some of my best graduate students have been practising Jews and I have had no difficulties with them on this score. Of course, though religion and philosophy are distinct activities, their relation is a philosophic question of magnitude and Professor Long inevitably deals with it. Unfortunately he does not deal with it accurately. If, for instance, you turn to what Professor Long says about the relation between philosophy and the idea of revelation in certain religions on p. 23 of this book, I do not think one could find any trained philosophers who are either believing Protestants or Catholics or Jews who would say that it is an accurate or adequate account of the matter. I did not ask that the textbooks I use should be directed towards the spread of my religion. (I suggested the works of Plato and Russell neither of whom are in any way identified with the Christian church and neither of whom are in any way identified with the true.) But I could hardly be expected to use a textbook which misrepresents the religion of my allegiance. I would also point out that though Professor Long deplores the influence of faith on certain philosophers, he has no hesitation in closely identifying the claims of his faith with the facts of the case. It is in my opinion just this which above all makes Professor Long's book so poor an instrument for introducing youngsters to philosophy most of whom will have been born since 1940 in modern industrial Canada. Professor Long's faith was obviously formed by the experience of his break with a limited Calvinism in light of certain philosophic and scientific ideas. This was a very moving and formative experience for the English of the 1890s, for the Americans of the early 1900s, and for Canadians in the 1920s, but it has little bearing on the situation of Canadians growing up in Ontario at the moment.

Some of my friends have suggested that I should get up in class and quietly say where I think the required textbook is inadequate. This would indeed be fun; but it would also be unjust. It would leave the beginners with two conflicting accounts and an exam to be faced. This might be good for the clever, but it would be radically unfair for the weaker brethren. Also I would hope that if my teaching were good the better students would understand the inadequacy of the book. Then they would surely ask (if I had the right relation with them) why I employed it as a textbook. To that question I would have no just answer – beyond appealing to the necessity of earning my living, my liking for my home town, etc. Such considerations would not stand up against the unflinching moral judgments of which youngsters are capable.

Professor Anderson[*] told Professor Long to write to me about details, where his own letter covered the matter unequivocally in terms of general policy. Professor Long told me I could use other textbooks. He included a list of these which Professor Anderson would consider suitable. I do not see, however, that this makes possible any solution because if the York students have to write Toronto exams, marked by Toronto examiners, the use of an alternative textbook would cause an unfair burden on York students. Professor Long's textbook is sufficiently idiosyncratic that I do not see how students could answer questions chosen from it by studying from some other textbooks. The burden here would particularly fall on the marginal student, of which there are bound to be some at York.

I am sorry that this resignation has been left so long, but it has only become clear to me gradually in the last months the degree to which York is going to be tied to the U of T and the consequences that this would have on my teaching at York ...

With all best wishes,
George Grant

THE MULTIVERSITY

During the 1960s the secularizing trends in Canadian universities picked up speed. Grant began to refer to the universities as 'multiversities' because he

---

[*]Fulton Anderson, University of Toronto philosopher.

thought that they had lost any sense of a unity of knowledge. And did not believe that the growing fragmentation of knowledge was an innocent trend: it served the interests of the dominant elites in North American society.

The University Curriculum (1975)[*]

The chief purpose of the curriculum in our universities is to facilitate the production of personnel necessary to that type of society. Because there is such agreement about the chief goal of society, there is a vast consensus about the principles of the curriculum. Debates take place about the government of the university, about humane existence within it, etc., but not about what it concerns a human being to know. So monolithic is the agreement of society about ends, so pervasive the ideology of liberalism which expresses that agreement that the question about knowing cannot be raised seriously. (I mean by liberalism a set of beliefs which proceed from the central assumption that man's essence is his freedom and there-fore that what chiefly concerns us in this life is to shape the world as we want it.) When a student first arrives at university, the curriculum may appear a set of arbitrary and incoherent details. This is so only at the surface. In fact, it can be understood in terms of the powers and purposes of our society.

The chief job of the universities within the technological societies is the cultivation of those sciences which issue in the mastery of human and non-human nature.

. . .

It would, of course, be absurd to deny that the pure desire to know is present in many modern scientists. In my experience, such a desire exists in the community of natural scientists more than in any other group in our society. Also, I would assert on principle that such a desire belongs to man as man. What I am saying is that in science the motive of wonder becomes ever more subsidiary to the motive of power, and that those scientists still dominated by wonder have a more difficult

[*] George Grant, 'The University Curriculum and the Technological Threat,' in *The Sciences, the Humanities, and the Technological Threat*. ed W. Roy Niblett (London: University of London 1975), 21–35. Written first in 1968.

time resisting the forces of power which press in upon them from without their community.

• • •

Within the last hundred years it has become increasingly clear that the technological society requires not only the control of non-human nature, but equally the control of human nature.

• • •

For the social scientists to play their controlling role required that they should come to interpret their sciences as 'value-free.' This clarification has been carried out particularly by sociologists, and, indeed, it is inevitable from its very subject matter that this science should be magisterial among the social sciences. The use of the term 'value' and the distinguishing of judgments about values from judgments about facts enables the social scientist to believe that his account of reality is objective, while all previous accounts (which were not based on this distinction) were vitiated by their confusion of normative with factual statements. It is not appropriate in this writing to describe the history of the idea of 'value-free' social science as it came to be in the European tradition, particularly under the influence of Kant and Nietzsche, and was so elegantly formulated by Weber. Nor is it necessary to describe how it has been reformulated in liberal Protestant terms by such men as Parsons[*] and Lasswell[†] to suit the American scene. What is important to understand is that the quantification-oriented behavioural sciences which have arisen from this methodological history are wonderfully appropriate for serving the tasks of control necessary to a technological society. Indeed, where the fact-value distinction was originally formulated by Weber as a means whereby the academy could hold itself free from the pressures of the powerful, it has quickly become a means whereby the university can make itself socially useful. Social sciences so defined are well adapted to serve the purposes of the ruling private and public corporations.

Indeed, the distinction between judgments of fact and judgments of value has been thought to be favourable to a pluralist society. The

[*] Talcott Parsons (1902–79), Harvard-based American sociologist, one of the most influential theorists of the twentieth century.
[†] H.D. Lasswell (b. 1902), distinguished American political scientist.

common or objective world would be that of facts known scientifically, leaving men free to choose their values for themselves. However, this distinction has worked in exactly the opposite direction towards the monism of technological values. From the assumption that scientific method is not concerned with judgments of values, it is but a short step to assert that reason cannot tell us anything about good and bad, and that, therefore, judgments of value are subjective preferences based on our particular emotional makeup. But the very idea that good and bad are subjective preferences removes one possible brake from the triumphant chariot of technology. The rhetoric of pluralism simply legitimizes the monistic fact.

The 'value-free' social sciences not only provide the means of control, but also provide a large percentage of the preachers who proclaim the dogmas which legitimize modern liberalism within the university. At first sight it might be thought that practitioners of 'value-free' science would not make good preachers. In looking more closely, however, it will be seen that the fact-value distinction is not self-evident, as is often claimed. It assumes a particular account of moral judgment, and a particular account of objectivity. To use the language of value about moral judgment is to assume that what man is doing when he is moral is choosing in his freedom to make the world according to his own values which are not derived from knowledge of the cosmos. To confine the language of objectivity to what is open to quantifiable experiment is to limit purpose to our own subjectivity. As these metaphysical roots of the fact-value distinction are not often evident to those who affirm the method, they are generally inculcated in what can be best described as a religious way; that is, as a doctrine beyond question.

I do not mean to imply any insincerity on the part of those teachers who preach this doctrine. Throughout history the best preachers have often been those who thought they were talking about universally self-evident facts. Nor should it be implied that our multiversities ought not to fulfil this legitimizing role. Class liberalism is the ideological cement for a technological society of our type. Its sermons have to be preached to the young, and the multiversities are the appropriate place. That the clever have to put up with this as a substitute for the cultivation of the intellect is a price they must pay to the interest of the majority who are in need of some public religion. And the fact-value distinction is the most sacred doctrine of our public religion.

. . .

In the last hundred years in Europe, a series of justifications of humane study arose in the light of the crisis produced by the age of progress. Each of these passing justifications made certain particular studies dominant for their particular hour. For example, Dilthey's[*] distinction between *Naturwissenschaft* and *Geisteswissenschaft*[†] led to the enormous concentration on the study of history as that which would fulfil the role which once had been played by the traditional philosophy and theology. By studying history men could understand the alternatives of the past, see where they were and be enlightened to choose where they were going. The humanities became the sciences of the human spirit which culminated in that new subject, the philosophy of history. This position was in turn destroyed by Nietzsche when he showed that history could not, any more than God, provide men with a horizon within which to live. In terms of this critique, Weber taught that a humane and scientific sociology could fulfil the magisterial role. Over the century these various justifications have had their necessary moment, but as they have succeeded each other, the humanities have become smaller and smaller islands in a rising lake. The drowning lake was the ever more clearly formulated assumption that all the important questions can be solved by technological means.

. . .

Indeed, in many liberal minds widespread university education was seen as fulfilling the role which had been played by revelation in the once dominant Calvinist Protestantism. When revelation no longer appeared to be a fact to the powerful classes, the hope appeared among some that the humanities in the universities would teach men the best purposes. This popular hope could never be realized for the following reason: those who knew the humanities professionally were aware of what was going on in Europe. The best of them knew that social thought was methodologically dominated by 'historicism' and 'the fact-value distinction.' Historicism was the belief that the values of any culture were relative to the absolute presuppositions of that culture which were themselves historically determined, and that therefore men could not in their reasoning transcend their own epoch. The fact-value distinction led generally to the conclusion that there was no rational way

[*]Wilhelm Dilthey (1833–1911), German psychologist and philosopher.
[†]The study of nature and the study of human actions.

of knowing that one way of life was nobler than another. Those who studied the humanities were led to a great uncertainty about what constituted the good life, and whether this was a real question at all. The public hope that the humanities would fulfil a positive moral role was, therefore, vitiated by the fact that the best professionals of these disciplines did not see their activity in this way. Indeed, it is a fact of North American history that the spread of professional teaching in the humanities has been a means whereby the scepticism of Europe has penetrated the more innocent traditions of North America.

The professional practitioners of the humanities have justified their studies quite differently from the popular rhetoric. They have increasingly said that the humanities are non-evaluative sciences. The cruder form of this justification has led those disciplines to become highly research-oriented, so that they could cover themselves with the mantle of science and Protestant busy-ness. An enormous amount of energy and money has been channelled into research projects. In English literature there are many great factories pouring out editions, commentaries, and lives on all but the minuscule figures of our literature. (The equivalent of the expensive equipment of the scientist are the rare manuscript libraries.) If one has a steady nerve, it is useful to contemplate how much is written about Beowulf[*] in one year in North America. One can look at the Shakespeare industry with perhaps less sense of absurdity; but when it comes to figures such as Horace Walpole[†] having their own factory, one must beware vertigo. The difficulty in this research orientation is that whereas research in the progressive sciences produces discoveries which the public see as useful, this is not so in the humanities. The historian may claim that all the careful work that goes into small areas can be justified as useful in that it makes up the totality of a mosaic from which those who are educated in the discipline may better know the past and so make more prudent judgments in the present. He may even claim that the formal discipline of Namerian[‡] history is in itself a good training for potential rulers. Both these justifications may be true, although the proof of this would require a discussion of the place of historical judgment in the training of rulers. What is, however, paradoxical at the practical level about the vast appa-

---

[*] The great Anglo-Saxon saga.

[†] A minor English literary figure of the eighteenth century.

[‡] Sir Lewis Namier was a British historian who believed that history could best be explained by reference to the personal motives of individuals.

ratus of modern historical scholarship is that it exists in an age when it is increasingly believed that the race has little to learn from human existence from before the age of progress. We may be grateful that this contempt for the past has not yet penetrated the ranks of academic historians, who therefore remain the chief brake on the simply modern in our multiversities. Nevertheless, the role of brake is a very minor one compared with the pre-progressive role of the humanities.

. . .

Non-evaluative analysts see their activity as essentially self-justifying. They are moved by the pure desire to know; for example, the sheer joy in mastery over such a diverse field as literature. This gives the humanities freedom from the crude pressures of society, as can be seen by comparison with the popular justification of the humanities which has been described earlier. In the popular account, the natural scientists were supposed to know so that they could provide material techniques; the teachers of humanities were supposed to know so that they could be purveyors of values. In both cases, the pure desire to know was considered subsidiary to some public end outside the subject itself. Non-evaluative analysis has exalted cognitive power and has brought back into the disciplines rigour which was often lacking when professors of literature and philosophy were surrogate preachers. Although it must be granted that non-evaluative analysts can, at their worst, fall into the snobbishness of an impractical mandarinism, they have saved the humanities from an empty antiquarianism. They are interested in the understanding and mastery of literature as a living activity and in the practice of linguistic clarity as important in the present.

Nevertheless, the consequences of this approach must be insisted upon. Non-evaluative analysis cuts men off from openness to certain questions. Let us imagine a student who is studying the works of Tolstoy and de Sade under the guidance of an intelligent and sensitive practitioner of non-evaluative analysis. He can be taught to understand much about their writings, what is being said and how it is being said and the dependence of these on very complex traditions. As in some sense both authors are writing about the proper place of sexuality in human existence, the student can be taught to anatomize the similarities and differences in what the authors say about sexual 'values.' From such study the student will learn what two remarkable men have thought about the place of sexuality in human life. Yet, because the study is a non-evaluative science, what would seem to be the most important question cannot be raised within the study: that is, whether de Sade or Tolstoy is nearer the truth about the proper place of sexuality. In the same way in 'philosophy' the study of ethics tells one much of how language is used and can be used consistently in ethical discourse. But it no longer claims to be concerned with what are the highest possibilities for men. Such studies are impotent to lead to what was once considered (perhaps and perhaps not naively) the crucial judgments about 'values' – whether they are good or evil. Their scholars have gained their unassailable status of mastery and self-justification by surrendering their power to speak about questions of immediate and ultimate meaning – indeed generally by asserting that such questions only arise through confusion of mind. Such a position provides immunity within the academic fortress, but it can still be asked whether the impotence of mind towards meaning is man's necessary condition.

Be that as it may, the central role of the humanities will be increasingly as handmaiden to the performing arts.

· · ·

When truth in science seems to teach us that we are accidental inhabitants of a negligible planet in the endless spaces, men are forced to seek meaning in other ways than through the intellect. If truth leads to meaninglessness, then men in their thirst for meaning turn to art. To hope to find in the products of the imagination that meaning which has been cast out of the intellect may, in the light of Socrates, be known to be a fruitless quest. Nevertheless, it is a thirst which is the enemy of tyranny.

· · ·

If we are to live in the modern university as free men, we must make judgments about the essence of the university – its curriculum. If such judgments are to be more than quibbles about detail, they must be based on what we think human life to be, what activities serve human fulfilment, and what place higher education should play in encouraging the realization of these activities.

As soon as this is said, however, the tightness of the circle in which men find themselves in modern civilization becomes evident. For on one side of the picture, most men have given up not only the two great accounts of human excellence in the light of which Western men had understood the purpose of existence (the one given in philosophy, the other in revealed religion) but also the very idea of human existence having a given highest purpose, and therefore an excellence which could be known and in terms of which all our activities could be brought into some order. It is now generally assumed that the race has meaning (call it if you will purpose) only on the condition that we view ourselves as purposive and that none of these views are truths concerning the nature of things, but only ideologies which we create to justify our man-made purposes. There is no objective purpose to human or non-human nature which men can come to know and in terms of which the various occasions of life can be ordered. Purpose and value are the creations of human will in an essentially purposeless world.

Yet it is not simply this absence of the idea of objective human excellence which constitutes the tightness of the circle in which we live. For on the other side of the picture, it is not to be thought that just because the dominant intellectual position of the age is that there is no highest purpose, the public realm is in fact able to do without such a conception. The political aspect of the liberal critics of human excellence was the belief that unfettered by 'dogmatic' and '*a priori*' ideas of excellence men would be free to make the world according to their own values and each would be able to fulfil his individuality. Ideas of purpose and indeed of a highest activity were superstitious strait-jackets – the enemies not only of an objective science but of the free play of individuality. Their elimination through criticism was the first step towards building a pluralist society. Yet pluralism has not been the result in those societies where modern liberalism has prevailed. Western men live in a society the public realm of which is dominated by a monolithic certainty about excellence – namely that the pursuit of technological efficiency is the chief purpose for which the community exists. When modern liberals, positivist or existentialist, have criticized the idea of human excellence, they may have thought that they were clearing the ground of religious and metaphysical superstitions which stood in the way of the liberty of the individual. Rather, they were serving the social purpose of legitimizing the totally technological society by destroying anything from before the age of progress which might inhibit its victory. Modern liberalism has been a superb legitimizing instrument for the technological society, because at one and the same time it has been able to criticize out of the popular mind the general idea of human excellence and yet put no barrier in the way of that particular idea of excellence which in fact determines the actions of the most powerful in our society. The mark of education is claimed to be scepticism about the highest human purposes, but in fact there is no scepticism in the public realm about what is important to do.

• • •

The tight circle then in which we live is this: our present forms of existence have sapped the ability to think about standards of excellence and yet at the same time have imposed on us a standard in terms of which the human good is monolithically asserted. Thus, the university curriculum, by the very studies it incorporates, guarantees that there should be no serious criticisms of itself or of the society it is shaped to serve. We are unable seriously to judge the university without judging its essence, the curriculum; but since we are educated in terms of that curriculum it is guaranteed that most of us will judge it as good. The criteria by which we could judge it as inadequate in principle can only be reached by those who through some chance have moved outside the society by memory or by thought. But so to have moved means that one's criticism will not be taken seriously from within that society.

It would be presumptuous to end by proposing some particular therapy by which we might escape from the tight circle of the modern fate. The decisions of Western men over many centuries have made our world too ineluctably what it is for there to be any facile exit.

• • •

It is possible, nevertheless, to assert one criterion by which all the potential therapies may be judged. Do they mitigate the division which comes forth from the modern vision? Do they help to overcome the way that we envision ourselves as 'creative' freedom and all else as objects either useful, threatening, or indifferent? In its political context that division had led us, in our very drive to universalize freedom, to build the acme of the objective society which increasingly stifles the spontaneity of those it was built to free. The division widens so that it has almost killed what little remains of those mediators – common sense, reverence, communities, and art (perhaps even finally sexuality) – which are the means for us to cross the division separating ourselves and our habitations. At any time or place it is a strange destiny to be a 'rational animal' – and indeed strange that there should be such – but the loss of these mediators makes that strangeness almost unbearable by tearing apart that which we are – rational animals. Socrates's prayer for the unity of the inward and the outward was spoken in an antique world, the context of which it could not be our historical business to recreate. Yet the fact begins to appear through the modernity which has denied it; human excellence cannot be appropriated by those who think of it as sustained simply in the human will, but only by those who have glimpsed that it is sustained by all that is. Although that sustainment cannot be adequately thought by us because of the fragmentation and complexity of our historical inheritance, this is still no reason not to open ourselves to all those occasions in which the reality of that sustaining makes itself present to us.

RESEARCH AND RESIGNATION

After twenty years at McMaster, Grant grew tired of fighting losing battles against what he called 'research.' His resignation started a national controversy, and this article in the Toronto Globe and Mail *was meant to clarify what he thought had gone wrong at research-driven universities.*

The Battle between Teaching and Research (1980)[*]

Most of us try to act from what we know or think we know. Therefore, if we are to understand society, we must understand our educational institutions.

In the Sixties a great change took place in the universities of Ontario. They were expanded in numbers, size, and wealth by the government. Like most things in Ontario, this change was initiated because of what was happening in the United States. This change should be associated with the name of President John F. Kennedy.

The question was asked in terms of Sputnik: Can it be possible that American education has fallen behind that of the Soviet Union? If so, we must immediately do something about it. Beyond this response, there

[*]George Grant, 'The Battle between Teaching and Research,' in *Globe and Mail,* 28 April 1980, 7.

was also the nobler positive affirmation: Let us see that everybody in society can reach his highest potential through education; let us expand the frontier of knowledge; let us build a noble technological society of highly skilled specialists who are at the same time people of vision.

It came to be believed that the university would become central in building a humane and liberated technological society. Ontario naturally followed the continental pattern and established a great network of universities.

The new university system came into existence at a time when the account of knowledge which had dominated the Western world for three centuries had reached its height of influence. Every civilization has produced its own account of what constitutes knowledge, and has been shaped by that account. Such accounts spring forth from a particular aspiration of human thought in relation to the effective means of its realization. Our dominant account of knowledge in the West has been positive and progressive science. The aspiration of thought from which it sprang was, above all, the desire to overcome chance so human beings would be the controllers of nature.

The effective condition for its realization was what we now call research. Research is the method in which something is summoned before the court of human reason and questioned, so we can discover the causes for its being the way it is as an object. Research made its appearance on the public scene of history when Galileo ran balls down an inclined plane. Now research is applied to everything from matter to human beings, from modern society to past societies.

The amazing achievements of research are before us in every lived moment – in the achievements of modern medicine and communications, of modern food production, and warfare. If one ever has doubts about the goodness of many of its achievements, it is well to remind oneself of penicillin. It is the method of scientific research that had made Western civilization a world civilization. It is at the heart and core of our lives, and as such at the heart and core of our education.

Yet there are great questions which present themselves to all thinking human beings and which cannot be answered by the method of research. What is justice? How do we come to know what is truly beautiful? Where do we stand towards the divine? Are there things that can be done that should not be done? One just has to formulate these questions to see they cannot be answered by research. Yet thinking people need to be clear about such questions and therefore they cannot be excluded from the university.

Education about these questions was carried on for centuries by the method of dialectic. Dialectic just means conversation – sustained and disciplined conversation. It takes place between students and students, between students and teachers. It takes place by means of the spoken and the written word. (If one writes an essay for a teacher, one is having a conversation with him.)

We have to talk with the great minds of the past. To think deeply about justice requires sustained conversation with Plato and Kant. This method of dialectic demands a different form of education from that required when the product pursued is research. It is a much more erotic kind of teaching than that which has to do with knowing about objects – erotic because what is to be known about justice or God or beauty can only be known when they are loved. This is why I have such a sense of failure as a teacher.

The older forms of education took place in Arts faculties. But the research paradigm of knowledge is becoming so powerful in those faculties that the tradition of dialectic is gradually being driven out. Energetic professors soon come to know that prestige is to be gained from research, and therefore pursue it. The reward system of the institutions teaches young professors that if they are to get on they must produce. This not only turns them away from the business of teaching, but it also turns them away from educating themselves in a broader context. What was necessary for the traditional form of education was to become an educated human being through a sustained life of study.

Obviously there is need of research in the humanities. Who could not be glad that C.N. Cochrane from Toronto wrote the great book *Christianity and Classical Culture*? But Cochrane was not first and foremost a specialist; he was first an educated man who looked at the ancient world from out of his long life of sustained self-education.

Of course, in the older Ontario universities such as Queen's and Toronto, the tradition of dialectic has more continuance. This is also true of Trent, which was modelled on the Canadian pattern of the colleges at Toronto. But in the universities whose ethos developed in the 1960s, the dominance of the new paradigm of knowledge becomes stronger and stronger.

It is around this question of principle that the large influx of American professors into our universities should be understood. Germany was the country where universities were first oriented around research. American higher education was more influenced by German patterns than by any other source. Flexner[*] is the man most associated with that influence. On the other side, dialectical education was stronger in England than anywhere else, largely because of the powerful influence of Oxford and Cambridge. Canadian higher education was more shaped before 1945 by English influences than by any other. The influx of American professors in recent decades has brought a powerful push toward the research-oriented university. The nature of that influence does not turn on the particular nationality of particular people. No decent human being should judge another solely in terms of the accident of where he was born. But the problem still remains. The influx of American professors brought with it certain German ideas which have greatly cut across many of our traditions.

When I was growing up in university circles in the 1930s, it was taken for granted that Canadian universities were probably better than (at least different from) their American counterparts. Since 1945, Canadian confidence in its own traditions has continually weakened, because of our belief that the American model is determinative.

This abstruse question of educational principle may seem far away from the realities of life. Yet it is not. You cannot have a free and vibrant society unless there are free and vibrant people in it. Obviously there are large numbers of free people in Canada who have no touch with higher education. Their freedom has other sources. Nevertheless, it is important for the health of any society that there are people in it whose sense of freedom is sustained by having thought in a disciplined way about the supreme questions of human life.

When our Arts faculties are centred around research they produce a culture which is essentially a 'museum culture.' Museums are places where we see past life as objects – as flies in amber. We do not see them as existences which light up our existence.

Never has so much money been spent on the organized study of the past, and never has the past had less meaning in shaping the real life of our present. Art and religion and the passion for justice will continue, but they will be more and more cut off from the rationality that the universities should offer them. Technological excellence plus museum scholarship are not enough. When they are considered sufficient, the mass of students will become listless. Scholarship is a means to thought, not a substitute for it.

[*]Simon Flexner (1863–1946), American scientist and head of the Rockefeller Foundation, 1920–35.

Part 3

Thinking Their Thoughts

PLATO (427–369 B.C.)

For Grant, Plato was a thinker much too profound merely to write about. Through Plato's dialogues, Grant glimpsed an eternal and transcendent reality. He gave frequent lectures and seminars on Plato and Plato's influence on Grant's own writings was pervasive. It lay behind almost everything he wrote, but was implied rather than formally stated. Grant was not an antiquarian and he did not believe that it was sufficient merely to reconstruct Plato's thought. He needed Plato as a guide who might help him see reality through the mist of the modern world.

Now, in terms of an acceptance of what I take to be the Platonic position, when one speaks of the separation of good and necessity one is speaking of that separation as it must appear to us here below. It does not imply that the order of necessity and the order of morality do not both proceed from the Good. Presumably, the beauty of the world which is manifested both in the order of necessity and the order of morality may to the follower of Plato teach us more about the ultimate unity of those orders than Kant in his wonderful *Critique of Judgment* would say we are vouchsafed.

– George Grant to Rod Crook,[*] 19 July 1965

Introduction to Plato (1973)[†]

... Let me start with a simple remark. What I find is most perfect in Plato is that there is a total union in his thought of what is in lesser philosophers either separated or part of which is not present. That is, he combines in a staggering unity the cosmological approach with the ethical-religious approach. What I mean by these two is the following: the cosmological approach is the question: 'What is the nature of the universe – what is real and how can I know what is real?' Or, to use other language, it puts the philosophic question as 'What general

---

[*] R.K. Crook, author of a substantial review of *Lament:* 'Modernization and Nostalgia: A Note on the Sociology of Pessimism,' *Queen's Quarterly*, vol. 73, no. 3 (1966): 269–84.
[†] unpublished lecture, 1973.

and universally valid conclusions about the cosmos can I draw?'
On the other hand, the ethical-religious approach starts from the
question: 'How shall I live? What is worth doing? To what shall I
pay my allegiance, my reverence? How shall I find happiness?' And
if you want, as I certainly do want, to use directly religious language,
'How can I come to know God and to be like Him, or as Plato says, His
friend?'

Now, many philosophers either concentrate on one of these sides
but not on the other, or separate them. But what happens when they
are separated?

If the cosmological is taken alone, philosophy becomes an abstract
remote discipline which has no connection with our life and our existence. And this is what has happened in an age when philosophical
analysis has become the handmaid of the natural sciences and when
philosophy becomes more and more logic and particularly the logic of
the sciences. It is against this that that wonderful philosophic movement, existentialism, has made its protest. As existentialism says, I start
from my existence and try to find its meaning. It is for this reason that
Kierkegaard – that early existentialist and the first exalter of Christianity against philosophy – could still have such enormous respect for
Socrates, whom he described as 'a passion of inwardness in existing,'
and we will indeed come to this when we come to discuss *Phaedo* next,
where Socrates talks of how he turned from the scientific philosophy
of his day to the effort to know himself.

On the other hand, if the ethical-religious sacrifices the cosmological, philosophy is also lost, because the questions 'How shall I act?
What shall I reverence?' must be concerned with the nature of things
as they are, and the effort to know those things as they are. We can
only know how we should live if we know what kind of a universe it is.
And that is where existentialism, for example, fails. It is not concerned
with science – that is, with the desire to know systematically the nature
of things and of the cosmos as a whole.

What is so wonderful in the Platonic writings taken as a whole is the
holding together of the cosmological and systematic view of philosophy with the ethical-religious view.

Now, in this class we are first of all concerned with dialogues which
clearly fall in their emphasis on the side of the ethical-religious. Particularly the *Symposium* and *Phaedo* are the dialogues of life and of death
and are passionately existential – though in them the cosmological is

not far away. In the *Phaedrus* we are nearer the unity of the two, so we shall study it last. But we are not studying the great cosmological dialogues of which the *Sophist* and the *Parmenides* are, in my opinion, the greatest. Nor are we studying the last great dialogues in which the cosmological and the ethical-religious are at one – the greatest of which in my opinion is the *Philebus* – that supreme philosophical writing. Nor should we think that the immense generality of metaphysics is higher than the practical – because the last work of Plato, *The Laws*, is concerned with such concrete subjects as how much wine a man should drink at different ages, and at what age one should marry.

Now, I have said this to begin to talk about the Good, and to point out that the Good as seen in the *Symposium* is seen as the supreme object of desire.

But let us remember that the Good and the One are the same.

In the *Republic* the argument for the speculative life – the argument from knowledge for God's existence – is combined with the argument from desire so that the Good is not only seen (a) as the highest object of desire, but also (b) the cause of knowing, that is, that which makes the world intelligible and our minds intelligent, and also (c) as the cause of being, that is, the cosmological and ethical-religious are very closely bound together.

In the *Symposium* we are chiefly concerned with desire. But in the *Symposium*, though what we concentrate on is desire or love, we must always be aware that the Good is both the supreme object of desire and of knowledge. They are at one. The One and the Good are the same.

Let me say also that I interpret Plato as unequivocally believing in the One or the Good as transcendent – that which is the supreme object of our love is absent. Let me quote to you the *Republic* 508–9.

To make this clear I would have to comment on *Parmenides* at great length and, as that is impossible, let me only say this. What does it mean to say that the highest object of desire and of the intellect is ultimately unknowable?

Philosophers mostly agree that it belongs to the nature of mind to seek unity. Now, they seem to disagree at this point as to the nature of that unity – or see it from the side of desire to seek meaning.

Those who I may quickly characterize as the immanentists would say

– 'though it is difficult to understand what meaning the world has, we do, however, know in principle the kind of meaning that complete insight would reach' – though of course the immanentist would admit that what we know in principle we cannot know in detail.

What the believer in transcendence would say is that this unity which we seek we can neither know in principle or in detail. To put it in theological terms, God's essence is unknowable. Read Dionysius in *The Descent of the Dove*, p. 61.[*] This is the idea that the One or the Good or God is beyond knowledge.

[half page missing]

That fundamental awareness that makes experience possible for us is dormant, potential, and its actualization requires an external stimulus. But this is only a stimulus, it does not produce that awareness. The human soul has by nature, by being a human soul, the truth within itself. There is a natural harmony between the human mind and everything that is, between the human mind and the whole. Man has a kinship with the whole, that is to say with the good of the whole, with what makes the whole the whole. The good of the whole makes intelligible the place which man occupies within the whole. This is the singular dignity of man, the fact that man is a singularly privileged being, and at the same time not the highest being, for his privileged position is not his work but given to him. This we can say was the basis of classical philosophy, and not only the classical, because it is of course also the view of the Bible.

Plato and Augustine (1952)[†]

Last summer I made a giant step forward in beginning to understand Plato and the result has been a greater ability to think clearly. My main difficulty was that for a long time the habits and tradition of liberalism, in which (thank God) I was brought up, proved inadequate during the war and during my time in adult education. To break loose from a set of habits and traditions proved impossible for my temperament without a period of reaction. Luckily circumstances have given me the chance to have time to go beyond simple reaction and come

---

[*] Charles Williams, *The Descent of the Dove* (London: Faber and Faber 1950, 1963).
[†] George Grant to Margaret (Grant) Andrew, after May 1952.

back to find that the basis of liberalism, if carried far enough, was the right basis for action. In other words, what Plato is teaching me is not that I disagree with the tradition of liberalism in which I was raised, but that the tradition in which I was raised hadn't really sufficiently examined itself to find on what principles it did exist.

Well, after this preliminary, an historical note. I thought it unfair in your letter to mention T.S. Eliot and Augustine in the same connection. Eliot seems to me a quite good poet (though capable of extreme cheapness, e.g. *The Cocktail Party*), but a man hardly capable of systematic thought, and one who simply accepts the Catholic position with particular emphasis on the givenness of revelation. This is indeed the picture of Augustine that, for differing motives, certain Catholic and sceptical writers have put abroad. But it is an untrue picture. Augustine, for instance, said several times that the whole of Christian truth was present in Plato and the best of the Greek philosophers. In fact, the whole of his system is a defence of the unity of reason and revelation as against the position (which one finds perfectly expressed by St Thomas) that there is a gulf between what we know by our reason and what is thrust upon us (they are never clear how) by God.

I mention this only because it seems to me that it was on the ground of this reason that Augustine sought some measure other than convenience by which to judge that thoughts were true or false, actions right or wrong. When you say that this tradition exalts some transcendent, unknowable power over against man, and thereby denigrates man, I do not think that is what people who believe in the final unity of the world are doing. It is because of the form of human life – not to escape from the form of human life – that they say that Reason, Love – call it if you will God – is the measure, and not the pleasure or convenience of man. And this answer arises from two questions and two questions alone. (1) What is knowledge? That is, what is the difference between truth and falsehood, or, to put it better, knowledge about which we are certain and opinion which varies from minute to minute. E.g. The Pythagorean theorem is within certain assumptions always true, it is knowledge; while the opinions of most Nova Scotians about politics is not knowledge. (2) What standards can we find by which our reason can judge whether our actions are right or wrong? That is the question of morality. That is, the question of God's existence arises entirely from an attempt to answer those two primary questions. What is knowledge? What is morality? And these really boil down to one: What is the place of reason in our lives, whether speculatively in knowledge or practically in action?

I think the whole classical and modern tradition would here agree that for knowledge to be possible, there must be some unity between our minds and the external world we know, for otherwise our minds could know nothing of the world. Yet science shows us that we do. Therefore, the world and our minds must be at unity. So equally with reason in action, for there to be any standards on which we can act. Our reasons must be able to apprehend in some dim sense their place in the order of the world. For what else is morality but fulfilling one's proper purpose? (Of course, the place of reason in morality raises other difficulties of a kind that do not appear in the case of knowledge.)

Now here is where I think the great split comes in the history of thought (whether classical or modern, eastern or western.) There are those who say an immanent principle of unity is sufficient to account for the existence of knowledge and morality (e.g. Spinoza, Hegel, and, I think, Aristotle) while others say that the principle of unity is transcendent (e.g. Plato, Plotinus, Augustine, Kant). I would stand here. Now my argument for the transcendence of unity as against its immanence would be based on any number of arguments by taking the contradictions between various categories and showing that they can only be reconciled in terms of such a transcendent unity – e.g. mind and body, universals and particulars. But finally, my chief argument against those who find an immanent principle of unity sufficient would be that they cannot properly account for human imperfection. If the world is a unity in itself, why, then, is that unity broken by nearly all of us in our actions – selfishness, ignorance, etc.? Men like Spinoza answer that, of course it is not that human imperfection is an illusion, or, as Hegel said, the individual evil is the universal good. But such phrases just seem to me paradoxes, not explanations, and they still leave one with the fact of human imperfection; and that drives one to say that the unity of the world finally rests upon a unity which is transcendent ...

Now, you may well ask with this philosophy, where does the specifically Christian tradition fit in? First and foremost, I would say that where the Christian tradition substantiates the philosophical one is in its greater and profounder understanding of the problem of how all men can come to see the unity of the world and their proper partaking of that unity. That is the great point where I find [St] Paul sees more deeply than Plato. How all men are within this unity and, therefore, must freely be brought to it; and that all men learn in direct ways as well as the inferential way and, therefore, the language of primitive Christianity is so supremely open to all men. Of course, the greatest symbol to any of us is another human being's life and, therefore, you have at the centre of Christianity a symbol or image of the final unity of the world in a concrete life through which men can come to find that unity for themselves. This is what I think Jesus's life must have meant to men like Paul (who must have been trained in Platonic thought, and, for that matter, the Mosaic thought which in so many ways is like Platonism): the giving to men in concrete pictorial way that end or unity towards which they strive and in terms of which men alone can find happiness, health, or call it if you will, salvation.

Now I would agree as much as anybody that the difficulty of this symbolic, imaginative part of Christianity is that it so easily gets cut off from its real basis and gets turned into a lot of nonsense that may do a lot of people harm. I think a great deal of the Roman church's system of rewards and punishments is just that. And, of course, at the moment, the Christian tradition of European Protestantism is largely worn out. What it was saying, basically, in its day was of eternal significance, but so much of the eternal has been lost and only a weak frame is left. But some frame has to be found both at the basic philosophical level and at the level of corporate religious institutions that will pass on the tradition. Tradition does not seem to me the end; it is simply a ladder we use when we are young and which we must finally pass beyond as our knowledge of perfection is always greater than its incorporation in any particular tradition. Yet because our existence is at a low level of biology and, therefore, of continuity, we need these traditions to sustain us and prevent us becoming beasts ...

ST AUGUSTINE (354–430 A.D.)

Grant was profoundly influenced by St Augustine. From family friend and University of Toronto classics professor Charles Cochrane (1889–1945) he learnt of Augustine's synthesis of classical philosophy and Christianity and hence of

Augustine's central position in the history of Western thought. After he read Philip Sherrard's The Greek East and the Latin West, *he continued to believe in Augustine's centrality, but he also came increasingly to think that Augustine had been the source of certain fundamental errors that had led to the decay of the Western tradition of Christianity and its replacement by technological civilization.*

Charles Cochrane (1954)[*]

Profound thinking is not an activity which we associate with Canada. Our country is certainly not organized for the encouragement of thought. The type most typical of our early days was the pioneer and the explorer; the type of our modern society is the engineer – business-man – politician who pushes on at economic expansion and does not think much beyond it. It is not surprising, therefore, that where our economic success has been great, our spiritual contribution to human history is almost nil.

It is therefore a great pleasure to speak about a Canadian who did achieve greatness of the spirit in thought – indeed, who, in my opinion, is the most remarkable thinker Canada has produced and as the movement of the mind to the ultimate reality is the most important human activity. I, therefore, place him as one of the rare men of our country. His name was Charles Cochrane.

As is true of men who give themselves to the spirit, the externals of Charles Cochrane's life sound commonplace enough. He was born in western Ontario, went to the University of Toronto and then to Oxford in England. Like so many of his generation, he was caught up in the holocaust of the World War of 1914. Between that war and the next big one in 1939 he taught at the University of Toronto – taught history of Greece and Rome. He died at the end of the Second World War.

Most people who met Charles Cochrane probably said: Here is a pleasant professor living out his life inoffensively in a backwater of Toronto University – quietly married, raising his children – a nice and witty hangover from older days. Because that is what most people think

---

[*] This talk was given by George Grant in the series *Anthology*, broadcast on the radio station CBL to the Trans-Canada Network, 26 October 1954.

of classics professors – archaic survivals. During his lifetime indeed his genius was not recognized even in the Canadian university world. Only men of rare perception, such as Harold Innis, realized that here was greatness. I have heard it rumoured that a university in central Canada (I am too ashamed to mention its name) turned Cochrane down for an honorary degree; and when one thinks of some of the people who have received honorary degrees from that institution one is indeed left breathless.

But, as usual, the judgment of the world was wrong, for in that seemingly quiet life was going on a supreme struggle for the truth – in that backwater the very foundations of human existence were being examined at the limits of judgment.

We know now that this was the case because in 1940 Cochrane published a book called *Christianity and Classical Culture*. It is about that book and its indubitable greatness that I want to speak this evening.

Christianity and Classical Culture is an account of the impact of Christianity on the classical world of Greece and Rome. Looked at in even a superficial way, the story to be told is a fascinating one. The faith centred around a crucified Palestine peasant penetrated to the very centre of the powerful and sophisticated civilization, and by doing so moved on to dominate the early years of our civilization. The history has been written about often, but never, in anything I have read, with the penetrating insight which Cochrane brings to it. For he recognized that what happened in those first four centuries after the death of Jesus could only be made meaningful if it was seen not simply as a battle of organizations but as an attempt by human beings to fathom the meaning of our existence. That is, he raises up the simple facts of history into the highest questions of philosophy and theology and knows that they can only be illumined in those terms.

What Cochrane sees in Augustus, the first Roman emperor, is the effort to create a civilization that should be an end in itself – a community which would be eternally safe and secure in the world. Already a very noble civilization had been built in the Roman republic, and Augustus hoped by creative political action to turn Rome into an everlasting community in which all civilized men could cultivate the good life. This was, of course, not only the hope of a politician such as Augustus but was the dominant ideal of the philosophers of that time. Their ideal was that wise men should strive to build a perfect earthly city through political action. This ideal was incorporated in its richest form in the poet Virgil. He used all the seductive power of his art to convince men that the destiny of eternal Rome was to build this perfect earthly city. That is, men such as Augustus and Virgil claimed for Rome a uniqueness and finality – that it was the incarnation of the divine purpose in the world.

The history of Christianity is in Cochrane's eyes largely a criticism of those claims of Rome. It was quite impossible, said the Christians, to attain this perfection through political action and trust in political leadership. 'To them the state, so far from being the supreme instrument of human emancipation and perfectibility, was a strait-jacket to be justified at best as a remedy for sin. To think of it otherwise they considered the grossest of superstitions.' Against the idea of eternal Rome – the city of the world – they raised up the city of God. A city which could not be brought in by the superficial methods of politics, but by the wills of men as illumined by God through the vision of the crucified Jew.

But Cochrane sees that this difference between classical and Christian thinkers about political questions originated in a difference that was far deeper than politics. It lay in the very difference between the two visions of the nature and destiny of man. It lay in what Cochrane calls the defective logic of classical naturalism – the view of man and his place in nature constructed by classical science. What the Christians claimed was that the Roman world was defective at the very deepest level – the level of first principles – and what they demanded was a revision of those first principles.

As Cochrane writes: 'The basis for such a revision they held to lie in the meaning of Christ, conceived not as a revelation of new truth but of eternal truth – and saw in it the illumination which would be the basis for a new physics, a new ethic and, above all, a new logic – the logic of human progress. In Christ, therefore, they claimed to possess a principle of understanding superior to anything existing in the classical world. By this claim, they were prepared to stand or fall ...' They formulated this principle in the doctrine of the Trinity which they saw as no obscurantist mystery (as do most of our present-day theologians) but as that in terms of which all else could be understood.

The main part of Cochrane's book is concerned with the gradual formulation of this principle and its use as an instrument whereby to criticize the failures of the Roman Empire as they became increasingly apparent. He traces the story from the early cruder thinkers such as Tertullian – through the attempt of Constantine and his advisors to use Christianity to buttress the empire – to its consummation in the thought of Augustine. In Augustine the principles of Christianity are laid down in a philosophic system of the first magnitude, in which the first principle of Christ is seen in all the subtlety of its relation to every aspect of human existence – ethics and art, cosmology and science, politics and history. The last three chapters of Cochrane's book are just an analysis of Augustine's philosophical system. Though it has been the practice in recent years of optimistic and simple-minded American psychologists such as William James[*] or Gordon Allport[†] to berate Augustine as an abnormal personality – even a psychotic – it is surely truer to see Augustine as one of the two or three greatest minds in all the history of the West, and I do not know where else the essentials of his position are as brilliantly expounded as in Cochrane.

Of course, the story is not all of conflict between Christian and classical ideas. For, on the one hand, the Roman world was more and more forced to turn to the Christian community for support. On the other hand, the Christians, if they were to expound their position beyond the barest outline, had to turn beyond the Bible to the more sophisticated language of classical philosophy and in using that language the great truths of classical philosophy were incorporated into Christianity. That indeed is the accomplishment of Augustine, that he did not scorn truth wherever it was to be found but took the truth of Platonism and gave it new illumination through the light of Christ. If I have one criticism to make of Cochrane it is that he draws the line between classical and Christian philosophy too sharply. There was such a line, and a distinct one at that – but Cochrane seems to underemphasize the side of Augustine which was ready to say that Plato, through he lived four hundred years before Jesus, still knew the whole of Christian truth except that the Word had been made flesh.

Now you may well say, yes, this is probably a very learned book about the past, but why should it be considered so important for us who live with our own difficulties in the twentieth century? How can a book

[*]William James was an American psychologist and philosopher, a pragmatist who believed that truth was measured by the extent to which it serves human freedom.
[†]Gordon Allport was an American psychologist who argued that behaviour patterns are set within the individual.

about events so many centuries ago be as important as you say it is? The answer to that lies in the very condition of our present civilization. It is surely true that our civilization – the civilization of the West – has reached a point where the signs of its intellectual, religious, and moral disintegration are present at every point. Internally we have only to look at the breakdown of our educational and religious traditions – our desperate trust that the problems of the human spirit can be faced by psychological manipulation or political arrangement. Externally we are threatened by determined opponents who, on the whole, we must class as barbarians. What a ring the word 'twentieth century' once had and think what it sounds like now.

The Moving Image of Eternity (1986)[*]

I have no doubt at all that Western Christianity made some great errors in its origins, and here – and I say this with great hesitation, because he is a genius – I blame St Augustine. I think it was Augustinian Christianity that came in to shape both Catholicism and later Protestantism, which led to this Christianity, which in turn led to this extreme secularized form of itself as progress. And you know I have no doubt that Christianity is true, and I think it has to be reformulated out of this – I think Western Christianity is, in a sense, through. And I think that it has to be reformulated, getting rid of this Western interpretation of it that led to these strange modern phenomena. I think that this kind of Procrustean, triumphalist Christianity led Western civilization to go out into the world, thinking it could do anything to other civilizations; and it was even more terrible when it had become secularized Christianity.

IMMANUEL KANT (1724–1804)

Grant had an abiding interest in Kant's thought and taught courses on him at both Dalhousie and McMaster. For Grant, Kant's importance lay in his understanding of the inwardness of morality and the importance of moral freedom.

---

[*] CBC Radio *Ideas* broadcast.

These phenomena lay, for Grant, at the heart of the modern world and consti-
tuted great achievements and even greater dangers.

Kant and the Separation of Good and Necessity[*]

Does the distinction between necessity and good really lead to the fact-value distinction?

This seems to me the question: are all dualistic ways of thought the same?

I think we can best start from what one thinks the moral judgment to be. My immediate difficulty is that I do not understand how Weber analyzed the making of moral judgments. (You could help me here with an account and with references.) I do think I understand what Kant says. What is the difficulty in that account for me (and with as great a thinker as Kant, one has to say that the difficulty may be that one has not grasped the doctrine) is that I do not understand the relation between freedom and reason in his teaching. On the one hand, the very idea of reason presents itself to us so that we know directly that certain actions contradict that very idea. It presents itself to us in the imperative mood; he indeed expresses that presentation with the word *Achtung.*[†] Yet, at the same time, we self-legislate this commanding law of reason, and are capable of disobedience, that is, we are free in the sense that Weber means (?). Did Weber take from Kant the idea of freedom without the idea of reason?

As I see it, the great advantage of any dualistic system (Kant's e.g.) is that it squarely faces the problem of suffering and does not swallow it up in any easy explanation. By this I mean that any position must start from a recognition that to exist is to suffer and in human terms it is to learn that we cannot have what we want. (See Plato, Christ, Freud, etc.) In other words, from the human standpoint the first thing a philosopher must try and understand is what is the purpose (if any) in the fact that our immediate desires are broken and trampled on from the earliest age. Kant's answer of duty, that is of putting aside one's immediate desire in the name of universal purpose, seems to me a very great

---

[*]Letter to Rod Crook, 19 July 1965, in *George Grant: Selected Letters*, ed. William Christian (Toronto: University of Toronto Press 1996).

[†]Respect (German). I owe this translation to one of the University of Toronto Press's anonymous readers.

answer, and, of course, puts him in some sense squarely in the Christian tradition, the overwhelming power of which was to bring suffering into the Godhead, to be in fact the religion of slaves.

(Let me say in parenthesis that your very wise criticism of a debauched Protestantism could, it seems to me, lead you off certain tracks, important for the truth, if it leads you away from understanding the strength of Christianity as the religion of suffering. For, not only Christianity, but all the great religions, have great insights about the negation of desire as part of the human condition.)

Of course, this account of the moral judgement for Kant had to go with the possibility of science, and that for Kant meant a nature freed from purpose. Therefore, reason commanded us rather than nature giving us the law.

Now, it is at this point that I would like to write down why I cannot give a satisfactory answer to your question. I hope that it will not simply be of interest as my stage, but raising some important questions.

Looking back from Kant to Plato and Aristotle (for reasons part of which will be evident in the foregoing, but part of which would take too long in a letter) I am faced with an ambiguity. I think (but am not sure) that there is in Plato a much greater understanding of the suffering of man than in Aristotle. The transcendence of the forms the criticism of which in Aristotle is badly parroted by nearly every modern student of philosophy with one year's training ('Plato hypostatized concepts, etc, etc.') does appear to me very similar to Kant in the sense that the good by which we act comes to us somehow from beyond nature – call it if you will by that hated word supernaturally – and demands the death of worldly desires. All the psychological or sociological reductions of that position in the name of accusing it of repression, aberration and perversion does not seem to me to get around its appeal for two reasons: (a) the meaning of the whole does not seem to be understandable in the light of evil in an immanent way; (b) the question of the meaning of the whole cannot easily be put aside either existentially or scientifically.

The ambiguity this presents to me may be put historically in two ways: (a) I am not sure I am interpreting Plato correctly; (b) I am at last realizing that there are certain arguments on the Aristotelian side, which I have not met and which means that I have to study at a more than student level Aristotle's *Ethics* and *Politics*.

(a) The interpretation of Plato. At the beginning of the *Republic* there is the statement of Glaucon about the sufferings of the just man;

I have always taken that to be a straight affirmation of the transcendence of the Good. Yet, in a recent book of Strauss's he mentions (and he has some weight with me) that this is in Glaucon's mouth and is an exaggeration because we must not say that absolute justice and suffering go together. I presume he is speaking as an Aristotelian and that he implies that for them to go together would mean that there would not be an immanent political science of A's variety and that it leads to that sharp distinction between law and right, which is so characteristic of Kant and indeed of Protestantism. I see the point, but consider it a more important point to repeat that in the light of the human condition the ultimate purpose must be transcendent. In other words, the traditional interpretation that what Plato was concerned with was the justice of the wise man, while Aristotle was concerned with the justice of the wise man and the natural justice of common sense, I can see.

This is, of course, very closely related to the fact that seems to me indubitable (however one interprets the ambiguous dialogues), that Plato differs from Aristotle in believing that theory can never be detached from the moral life, while Aristotle affirms the independence of theory from moral virtue. In a rather different way this same distinction seems to me possible to make between Kant and Hegel; and, of course, I am on the Platonic and Kantian side. Why? Because I do not think it is comprehensible that one could come to understand the ultimate purpose of things except in this way; otherwise is one not shallow about evil? A circle? Yet, at the same time I am at the moment very much helped by the argument 'how can one have political philosophy, if you take the Platonic side – that is, transcendence?' I would recognize the terrible tendencies towards obscurantism in any doctrines of transcendence. Yet, once again, without such a doctrine I do not see that one is not led by the facts of evil to give up the idea of ultimate purpose.

Now, in terms of an acceptance of what I take to be the Platonic position, when one speaks of the separation of good and necessity one is speaking of that separation as it must appear to us here below. It does not imply that the order of necessity and the order of morality do not both proceed from the Good. Presumably, the beauty of the world which is manifested both in the order of necessity and in the order of morality may to the follower of Plato teach us more about the ultimate unity of those orders than Kant in his wonderful *Critique of Judgment* would say we are vouchsafed. But if my interpretation of Plato is right, he stands quite close to Kant as an agnostic. Socrates 'the philosopher

is the man who knows that he knows not.' Also Pascal: 'We know too
much to be sceptics; we know too little to be dogmatists.' Kant certainly says that in the preface to the 2nd edition of the 1st Critique.
Beyond this – and here I know nothing; it is evidently possible according to the mystics to come to an understanding of the beauty of necessity as we submit to its afflictions and love others who are so submitted.
But about that I must repeat that I know nothing. In my book (which
was a popular book) I make clear that I spoke simply from the position
of the person who must proceed in the practical life from the position
that the order of morality and the order of necessity cannot be known
as proceeding from the Good.

George Grant to Simone Pétrement (1975)[*]

I make another point concerning Kant simply for the sake of interest
and in no way to take away from the genius of Simone Weil or from the
nobility of your book. Kant was the thinker who first explicitly made
the autonomy of the will central to western moral philosophy. Such a
doctrine is clearly denied in Plato and is not even present in Aristotle.
Kant says directly that Greek philosophy fails because it does not
understand the autonomy of the human will. Also I can see great contradictions between Simone Weil's account of society and Kant's. Kant
is unflinchingly contractualist. As he writes in the first supplement to
Perpetual Peace. 'The problem of organizing a state, however hard it
may seem, can be solved even for a race of devils, if only they are intelligent.' I have had to think through the basis of European contractualism and its baneful results because no societies have so suffered from it
as ours in North America. Also if one takes into account Kant's continual references to his debt to Rousseau, it becomes clear that he is
entangled in all that has harmed the modern world in the conception
of 'history' and which Simone Weil has so wonderfully criticized. I take
it as a fact that the origin of the concept of 'history' is first clearly
expounded in its modern sense in the 2nd Discourse of Rousseau.
Admittedly Kant is to be preferred to Hegel who carries this way of
thinking further into that strange enquiry 'the philosophy of history.'
Nevertheless, the seeds of Hegel are already in Kant. He has journeyed
very far from Plato. Indeed *The Critique of Pure Reason* is dedicated to

---

[*]Letter, 3 April 1975, *George Grant: Selected Letters*, ed. William Christian (Toronto: University of Toronto Press 1996).

Francis Bacon and ends with a section entitled 'The history of pure reason.'

Lecture (1977/8)[*]

Thinkers such as Bacon, Hobbes, Locke, and Hume seem to be emancipating human beings from the past because they turn from the eternal to something immediate and ordinary – self-preservation, survival, control of nature, etc., and this seemed an enormous emancipation from the old tradition. But here in Kant, the emancipation is much more fundamental than those earlier emancipations because it is not based on something ordinary like self-preservation. It is an emancipation that deals with the highest things in human beings – morality, freedom, etc.

This is what sometimes makes Kant difficult to understand. Because people see that Kant is showing the absoluteness of morality as control, they do not see what a radical emancipator he is. That the very purposes of the absolute morality are the very basis of that emancipation, which is far more radical than those of Bacon, Locke, etc.

I remember after the war being intoxicated by Kant's absolute morality. My position, brought up as I was in liberal pragmatism, could not go with the war. I was longing to understand the absolute, the unconditioned, and therefore was intoxicated by Kant's account of morality. It freed me from all the vulgar liberal pragmatism, and this made it very difficult for me to see what a radical emancipation of man was being stated ... the good will being the only good without qualification.

Lecture (1977/8)[†]

I now see Kant as a supreme moment in defining what *is* in terms of the liberation to the new freedom, which is the essential fact about modernity; and this holds together what Kant is saying about objective knowledge with what he says about the autonomy of the will.

Let me say categorically that to see the modern as essentially this liberation for new freedom is not to affirm or deny at first whether this liberation has been for good or ill. That is a later question ... The first

---

[*] Lecture notes, McMaster University, 1977/8, George Grant personal papers, Halifax.
[†] Ibid.

purpose is to see what the liberation for this new freedom is. Only when it is entirely before one could one speak about whether its unfolding, its coming to be, has been for good or ill ...

To be immediate, this says something about philosophy and life as we have to live it. For example, in our practical life we are faced now in every lived moment with the unfolding of that liberation to a new freedom. A very good example of that liberation is recombinant DNA research. Insofar as such research is our business, then we can practically say 'no' to the unfolding of that new liberation. But to do that is a different thing, though part of the same life, from knowing philosophically whether that liberty's unfolding is for good or ill. In short, we can neither say that philosophy and life are separated, nor can we affirm the unity of thought and practice ...

But what lies behind this? What was the primal affirmation from which both Descartes and Bacon arose? Suffice it to say here that the subject (human beings as subject) became that before which must be led everything which is, and through which everything that is is justified for what it is. The human being (call it if you will in the generic sense 'man') based on his own authority becomes the foundation and the measure of all that is ... The world is represented to us as an object that we as subjects interrogate and over which we have jurisdiction. One must see that this is a new way of representing the world to us, and we could see this well if we were to compare it with the older receptive views of perception in the ancient tradition.

Modern science and morality came out of this new view of the sovereignty of man as subject. As I have said, the unfolding of all this, man as subject, the world as object, is the liberation of man for a new liberty. As I have also said, the fundamental basis of this human event from which pours forth the new liberty is not clear to me, as I have tried to say in what I wrote about in *English-Speaking Justice*.

But what can be seen with clarity is that the account of reason so brilliantly expounded in the *Critique of Pure Reason*, which holds the world before itself, representing it to itself as object, which is the basis of truth – positive truth – is the basis of the new liberty which is going to establish its domination over the whole earth. Man establishes himself as sovereign over the totality of all that is. What Kant says in the *Critique of Pure Reason* and what he says about the autonomy of the will in the *Grundlegung* are at one, as they are both man taking his fate into his own hands. Henceforth, man sets out from himself and for himself.

It could be said at a certain level that for Kant 'to know' and 'to will' are held apart. We are commanded to will the categorical imperative in the midst of a world we do not know for what it is in itself (which can only know as appearances; that is, we can only know that relation between appearances, so that justice is something commanded us and quite other to what we know with certainty). Yet on the other hand, it must be said that at a deeper level 'to will' and 'to know' are not held apart, because in the very archetype of knowing for Kant, modern science, what is the Copernican revolution but the summonsing of objects before us to give us their reasons, and that summonsing makes the very act of knowing a kind of willing. What is modern science but an act of the subject's willing?

Now of course this understanding of the new liberty, in the sense of an autonomous legislation on the part of humanity as the basis of truth, first had to assert itself as liberation from the certitude of Western Christianity and, because it asserted itself first against Christianity, it seems in its expression in relation to Christianity, a relation that is determined by itself, as rejection of Christianity. But (and this is an enormous 'but') in looking this way we must remember that when people talk of modernization as the transfer into the world of what is Christian, it must be remembered that 'the world' into which Christianity is taken is something absolutely other than Christian. It is only in the core of such a world that secularization could install itself and develop itself. Of course, at the core of any account of truth is the truth about justice, and the liberation of the new freedom can only finally justify itself in terms of a new view of justice.

Now it seems to me that this is what is so fascinating about Kant. As much as anybody, he lays before us the new essence of truth in which humanity as subject interrogates all that is, and in which humanity installs itself as sovereign over all that is, and in which humanity understands itself as autonomous legislator to master all that is, and to enact what the world will be like. But then at the height of that new system of representation, namely in the question of justice, he does not cross the Rubicon to the new account of justice that is required by the new account of truth, proceeding from the new account of reason. He offers the categorical imperative, that morality is the one fact of reason. He offers a fundamental equality of persons, that is an account of justice that comes out from the older account of truth, which was based not on the first principle of subjectivity, but on the eternal order.

In saying what I have said I do not mean in any sense to imply that I have caught Kant out in some kind of contradiction. I think it is the greatness of Kant that he turns back at the point of his doctrine of justice from the consequences of the modern essence of truth; and indeed since his day that turning back has been a central fact of the intellectual and practical life of the best. I tried to say in the piece I wrote about English-speaking justice why that was for the Western world the very incarnation of that turning back.

When Nietzsche calls Kant the great delayer, one can well reply: Does one not want to delay the realization of the account of justice in Nietzsche? (Not indeed that the account of justice in Nietzsche is the perfect statement of what is implied in the modern account of the essence of truth, but it moves in that direction.)

Why one is filled with foreboding concerning the doctrine of justice given in the modern account of the essence of truth is of course another question ...

KARL MARX (1818–83)

Grant's Philosophy in the Mass Age *was broadcast as an experiment in the educational use of radio, in the first CBC* University of the Air *radio lecture series. The talks were an immediate hit. Grant's interpretation of Marx was influenced by his reading of the philosopher and social critic Herbert Marcuse. Grant had little sympathy for Marx's materialism. In contrast, he treated Marx almost as a religious writer and admired him as a great social theorist who protested against the immoralities of capitalism.*

As well as reading for my work I have read a life of Karl Marx with long extracts from the writer. I find that I try to answer his questions to prove that he is wrong. I cannot. I am not advanced enough. But, at the same time, I am positive that one cannot answer certain statements that he makes. That if one is not prejudiced by a 'good upbringing' one must believe *some* of the things he says.

– George Grant to Maude Grant, 1938

Philosophy in the Mass Age (1959)[*]

In the thought of Karl Marx the meaning of the change described in the last chapter is brilliantly illuminated. Through his thought more

[*] For a new edition of this work, see George Grant, *Philosophy in the Mass Age*, ed. William Christian (Toronto: University of Toronto Press 1995), 49–61. Used with permission.

than anyone else's, the Western spirit of progress has gone out into the countries of Asia and has become the dynamic religion of the East. Study of this thought is, therefore, pressed upon us in the West. Yet just as this understanding of marxism is most important to us, it has become most difficult, because in the last decades there has been a campaign of vilification against Marx and of suspicion of those who study his thought in any systematic manner. He has been attacked as the prophet of the worst abuses of the Soviet empire; as the subverter of the achievements of capitalism; as the enemy of godliness and morality. Although this campaign has draped itself in the flags of patriotism and of religion, it is not surprising that it has been inspired largely by those whose basic interest was the maintenance of our present property relations. [I remember when his picture was put on the cover of *Time*. The resulting misrepresentation is what we have been led to expect from *Time* when it wants to blacken a reputation. The story inside was of a jealous, half-educated, ambitious and neurotic man driven to his hatred of capitalism by the pain from the carbuncles on his behind.]* The contradictory nature of this attack stems from the mixture of fear and contempt with which it has been motivated. Why should the blackeners of Marx try to prevent systematic studying of his writings, if they consider these such a jumble of nonsense? What is especially strange in the behaviour of those who attack Marx in this wild way is that they have generally asserted their faith in God. Do they not believe then that this faith includes the belief that the truth will make men free and that therefore only in careful study can the chaff be divided from the wheat?

The contempt for Marx has not been confined to the irresponsible rich and their demagogues. It is heard from responsible businessmen and government officials and from their servants in the universities. This educated contempt is more dangerous to Western interests because it takes the form not of abuse but of patronizing aloofness. These people claim that the important thing is Russian and Chinese imperialism, not the spread of marxism. To those who pride themselves on their realism, Marxism need not be taken more seriously than any other faith. They assert that what matters is power and not ideas. This position naturally appeals to the civil servants of Washington, London, and Ottawa who like to be considered too sophisticated in the ways of

---

*The material in square brackets has been restored to the published version from the radio lectures.

the world to take theory seriously, and believe that history is ultimately shaped by the *ad hoc* decisions that make up their lives. This supposed realism is, however, one-sided and short-sighted. If the word power is to mean anything, the social and ideological structure of that power must be analyzed and understood. It is the pettiest view of human history to believe that the intellectuals of Asia are moved by a philosophy that is simply a tissue of wild imaginings. We must understand Marx as well as the power of Russia and of anti-colonialism if we are to understand the continued victories of communism in Asia. We must understand, indeed, how much marxism has contributed to the present political and technological power of Russian society.

It must be insisted, however, that Marx is worth studying not only because of his influence in the history of Asia, but also because of what he is in himself: a social theorist of the first rank, who reveals to us the diverse currents that make up the progressivist river. Indeed, it must be recognized that marxism is a much profounder river than the limited canals of theory dug by the officials of the Communist Party in the East or West. As has been the inevitable fate of great prophets, his disciples have consistently neglected and misinterpreted those aspects of his thought that did not serve their purposes. This process started even with his intimate friend Engels, who is inclined to interpret Marx as a disciple of Darwin. The narrowing was carried even further by such men of action as Lenin and Stalin. Marx must be studied not so much as a political-economic propagandist than as a theorist who brought together the varying streams of the humanist hope and in whose synthesis, therefore, the value of the doctrine of progress is most clearly exposed to us.[1]

Marx is essentially a philosopher of history, that is, one who believes he knows the meaning of the historical process as a whole and derives his view of right action therefrom. In a certain sense the philosophy of history is the modern equivalent of what in olden days was known as theodicy, the vindication of the divine providence in view of the existence of evil. The search for meaning becomes necessary when we are faced with evil in all its negativity. In Marx's search the starting point is the indubitable fact of evil. Reality is not as it ought to be. Men are not able to live properly, because their lives are full of starvation, exploitation, greed, the domination of one man by another. Our present society is not such that it permits men to fulfil themselves. As Marx says: 'Men are for other men objects.' No thinker ever had a more passionate hatred of the evils men inflict on each other, nor a greater yearning that such evils should cease. It is perhaps not surprising that he should have been so aware of evil, living as he did in the early years of the industrial era, when new ways of work were instituted with little respect for those who did the work. What is more surprising is how few of his contemporary intellectuals rebelled against the crimes that were being committed against working men, women, and children.

Marx proceeds from the present evil to criticism of the religious solution of that evil. He says that the religious solution is to maintain that all is really well, despite the evident evil. This solution has prevented men from dealing with the evils of the world. The idea that there is a God who is finally responsible holds men from taking their responsibility sufficiently seriously. If there is going to be pie in the sky when you die, then the evils of the world are not finally important. In this sense, religion is the opium of the people. Religion and its handmaiden, traditional philosophy, have said that reconciliation can be found in the here and now – if men will only seek God. In fact, they say that evil is not what it seems and that despite it, all is well. But this is not the case: all is far from well. To pretend anything else is simply to disregard the sufferings of others. Therefore, the first function of thought must be the destruction of the idea of God in human consciousness.

As Marx wrote: 'The philosophers up to now have been concerned with understanding the world; we are concerned with changing it.' What he means is that the philosophers have sought the meaning already present. They have sought God. He is not concerned with the meaning already present; he is concerned with the creation of meaning in the future by man. He is concerned with the practical overcoming of the suffering he sees all around him. Therefore, man must take his fate into his own hands and to do that he must overcome the idea of God.

Marx's criticism of religion, however, is more profound than that of others who have said the same thing. For he recognizes that if man is to pass beyond belief in God, religion must not only be denied, but also its truth must be taken up into the humanist hope. The truth of religion for Marx was the yearning of the human spirit to overcome its evil – or, in his language, to overcome its own alienation. By 'alienation' he means that man's situation in society estranges him from the proper fulfilment of his freedom. He has never been able to live as he ought in society. Marx claims that he has freed this religious yearning for the overcoming of evil from any supernatural connotation, and shown how it will be fulfilled by man in history.

In the previous chapter, the centre of Biblical thought was defined as the idea of history being the divinely-ordained process of man's salvation. Marx takes over this idea of history as the sphere for the overcoming of evil. Therefore, Christianity is for him the absolute religion, in that as far as religion can go, Christianity takes it. The supreme insight in Christianity, according to Marx, is the doctrine of the Incarnation, which means that God is no longer other to man, because he has become man. But according to him, Christianity had never understood the consequences of its own doctrine of the Incarnation. In a world of scarcity it could only hold the idea of 'the God-man' as an ideal once achieved, but not to be made universally concrete. It is Marx's claim that he has taken what is true in Christianity and liberated it from this limitation. He has taken the doctrine of God become man, freed it from its other-worldly associations, and shown how it can be universally realized in the time process. In denying supernatural religion he believes that he has taken its truth into his philosophy.

Marx's philosophy of history is, however, not only the perfection of humanism, because it makes the religious hope serve a humanist purpose, but even more because he sees the most representative activity of the modern world, natural science, as the chief means of conquering evil. More than any other philosopher, he places the activity of the natural scientist in a setting of ethical redemption. Marx's recognition that natural science is central to the humanist hope has led many scientists to see the meaning of their activity in terms of marxism. Even today in the Western world, when many scientists do not wish or do not think it wise to espouse a systematic Marxism, their real religion remains very much like it. To show this more fully, it is necessary first to describe what Marx thinks is going on in history.

This can only be understood in terms of Marx's debt to German philosophy in general and to the philosopher Hegel in particular.[2] When Marx is thinking about history, he is thinking in Hegelian terms. History is the sphere in which spirit is realizing itself in the world. It is realizing itself always in relation to nature. Here appears the distinction between spirit and nature. Nature is what it is and is not what it is not. A stone is a stone and not something else. But man is self-conscious, and self-consciousness is divided against itself. Man can always stand above himself and make himself what he is not. Every action is a project to the future, in which we negate what we are now. Therefore, man both is and is not what he is. Spirit, then, has a different logic from the logic of identity proper to nature. History is the coming to be of spirit in the world. Marx takes over this Hegelian way of thought, and limits it by finding the whole meaning of history in the relation of human freedom to nature. There is for him no nature without human significance; there is no significance to human freedom apart from the domination of nature.[3] To Marx, therefore, the way that men have organized their economic relations is the key to history. In the economic organization that expresses our relation to nature, he sees the cause of human evil in the past; in the creation of a new relation he sees the overcoming of that evil.

To state this in more detail: from the earliest days of history, men found themselves in a position of scarcity. There was just not enough food, shelter, and clothing for everybody to have an abundance. Because of this a society of class dominance was necessary. A minority group in society gained control of the economic life, the means of production. And as they controlled the means upon which everybody depended for sustaining life, they controlled society as a whole, and set the pattern of its government, its art, its religion, its morality. In other words, in a world of scarcity, society was necessarily divided into classes. Class in Marx is defined in a strictly economic sense, in relation to control or lack of control over the means of production.

This division of society has meant class struggle between those who wanted to maintain their control over the source of wealth and their consequent position of privilege, and the majority, who were excluded from that control. But at the same time as one dominant class has been imposing its control over society through its control of the means of production, people have also been seeking greater power over nature through technology, and therefore introducing new forms of social wealth. This continually changing relation of men to nature has prevented any one class from long being able to impose its dominance over the means of production, and so over society as a whole. The new forms of wealth have produced new classes to challenge the power of the old rulers. For example, in medieval society the means of production were chiefly land, and therefore the ruling class was the landlords. But as there came to be more and more commerce and simple manufacturing, the new middle class arose in the new towns. This class challenged the power of the landowners. The times of quick and radical change in history have been when a new class, produced by new economic conditions, has come to sufficient power to challenge the old ruling class, which in turn does all it can to retain its dying supremacy.

Marx also believed that as man's control over nature becomes more complete, so the dominant classes who come to power progressively serve a more universal interest of mankind. They serve the gradual emergence of freedom in the world. In the modern era it has been the historic role of the capitalists and their capitalist society to bring technology and economic organization to the point where, ideally, the conditions of scarcity might be once and for all overcome. The achievement of the capitalists has been to destroy the old natural world in which human freedom could not come to be. They have rationalized society.

At the same time, however, as capitalist society has created the conditions of liberation, it has intensified the conditions of enslavement. The very form that the ownership of the means of production takes in capitalism sharpens the class struggle to its peak. For as capitalism solidifies, it moves, because of the profit motive, to the concentration of economic control into fewer and fewer hands. The mass of mankind are cut off from control over the conditions of their own work as they are cut off from any control over the means of production. The contradiction that capitalist society creates is that it has produced the possibility of overcoming scarcity – that is, the conditions for overcoming class dominance and inequality have arrived; yet at the same time it has chained the mass of men to uncreative labour, work for which they have no responsibility. It has taken to the extreme the division between the owners of the economic apparatus and servants of that apparatus. In such a situation where liberation is possible and where alienation is actual, there can be only one result. The mass of men will not allow themselves to be excluded from the liberation that technology has now opened for them. They will take the means of production out of private control and place them under social control. They will destroy capitalism and create socialism. In this new society the basic cause of evil will be overcome. Men will no longer be for each other objects of economic exploitation. Human beings will be able to give themselves over to the free play of their faculties, to the life of love and art and thought.

The mass of people who are increasingly separated from control over their own work and over the economic apparatus as a whole, Marx calls the proletariat. Few conceptions in Marx generate so much confusion. People think that the proletariat means the hungry, the ragged, the destitute. As today in North America there are not many people who are destitute, the inference is drawn that Marx has been proven wrong about capitalism. Of course, Marx hated the grinding poverty and the degrading division between physical and intellectual work that characterized the capitalism of his day. He said that industrial workers were turned into the living counterparts of a dead mechanism. But the idea of destitution is not necessary to the idea of the proletariat. The proletariat consists of those who have no creative responsibility for the society through their work, because they do not own the means of production with which they have to work. They are employees serving the private interests of their employers. For Marx, the proletariat is not one class amongst other classes, one class against other classes. It is the universal condition in which the vast majority of men find themselves in the age of the machine, when the machines and the machines that make machines serve private interests. The proletariat cannot liberate itself by producing another class society, but only by destroying the very existence of economic classes themselves. The mass of society are driven to recognize that in a machine age all work is social and rational and that therefore what must be created is an appropriate economic apparatus, not one given over to the irrational ends of private profit.

Those people who first become conscious that this is the historical position of the age will become the leaders of that liberation, the proletariat conscious-of-itself. They are the Communist Party, the party that will direct the bringing in of a classless society of equality. Thus, the sufferings of the proletariat are seen as the Christian sees the passion of Christ, necessary to the redemption of mankind. It is this idea (at some level of explicitness) that has enabled countless ordinary people to endure suffering – with such high fortitude – for the sake of the communist cause. The suffering is seen as meaningful.

It is not possible to assess here this remarkable vision of human history. There are many things to be said about it both as economic and philosophic doctrine. For instance, to assess it as an economic doctrine it would be necessary to discuss its dependence on the labour theory of value; to assess it as a philosophic doctrine, discussion of the causes of human evil would have to be introduced. Nor is it possible to describe the development of marxist doctrine in the last century or the question of how far the Russian Revolution and the consequent regime of the Soviet Union can be said to be the socialist society of which Marx was talking. It is, for instance, arguable that it is with us in North America that the conditions that Marx prophesied are most clearly fulfilled, and therefore Marx is more the prophet of North America than of Russia. These are intricate questions to which no short answer can be given.

What must be insisted on, however, is that Marx's philosophy has been the most powerful of modern humanisms, for two reasons above all. First, it was a humanism of universal salvation, and secondly, it seemed very concrete and practical about the means to that salvation. With regard to the first point: the marxist hope is not for the isolated individual but for society as a whole. His humanism is not for a few rare, fine spirits in exceptional positions, but promises the good life for all. So often humanist liberalism has been made ridiculous by its individualism that disregarded the dependence of the individual on the community, and seemed little concerned with the way the mass of men lived. But how can the human spirit find any moral fulfilment in such individualism? There can be no perfected freedom in a world where others have not found it. What kind of a heaven can be enjoyed while others are in hell? The power of marxism has lain in the fact that it foretold a concrete overcoming of evil in the world, which would be for society as a whole. Here Marx's dependence on the Judæo-Christian idea of history is obvious. His humanism retains the idea of history as salvation, but rejects its theological framework. This makes it incomparably more powerful than those humanisms that are liberal and individualistic.

The second reason for the power of marxism is its claimed practicality. Instead of leaving the worldly hope up in the air, it describes in concrete how it is to be brought about. It relates its achievement to the forces already around us in modern society. There is much that could be said about the superiority of marxism over other doctrines of progress, on account of its direct application to the world as it is, but I will single out one connection – the significance Marx gave to the natural scientists.

The fact to be explained is why many scientists in this century have been followers of Marx or have been deeply influenced by him. Because governments must concern themselves with treason, this fact has been surrounded with a miasma of anxiety in the last years. But the first problem is to give a serious explanation of why it has been so. The answer is surely this: marxism gave so satisfactory an account of science as essentially an ethical, indeed a redemptive activity, the means by which men were to be freed from the evils of pain and work.

Recently there was a syndicated American cartoon in our local paper. It was a drawing of a Russian commissar-for-foreign-aid speaking to a young student whom he wishes to send abroad on a technical mission. The commissar is saying: 'I don't care about your engineering degree, what do you know of Karl Marx?' Obviously this cartoon expresses the great need the Americans have these days to keep alive their sense of superiority over the Russians. What the cartoon says is this: we Americans are interested in helping under-developed countries quite honestly by giving them engineers; the Russians are not really interested in helping people through engineering but in dominating them through marxism.

This is to misrepresent entirely what marxism is and the hope that men see in it. The philosophy of marxism is regarded as the guide and control under which modern techniques can be brought to under-developed countries, and it claims that it alone can guarantee that these modern techniques will be the servant of the good of all and not of private profit. Marx's appeal was not to the scientist as an ethical man apart from his function, but primarily in his function itself. Scientists, like other men of intelligence, want to know what purpose their activity is serving. Marx gave them a systematic answer to this question. He showed (whether accurately or not) the role of the scientific function within an optimistic and worldly philosophy of history, which had place for the universal interests of humanity.

It may be said by way of digression that it was often a contradictory tendency in Marx that made his philosophy so powerful among certain scientists. Among modern scientists there have been two ways of looking at man that have been difficult to relate. On the one hand, assumptions from geological and biological studies have led certain scientists to judge man as but a product of nature. They have believed that history is but a part of nature. On the other hand, science as technology has been obviously the victory of human freedom over nature, which means that nature has been taken up into history. Many scientists have held both these views at the same time – as theoretical men they have often asserted that their science shows that man is but a product of nature; as practical men they have asserted that science is the domination of man over nature. It may be that some scientists have been adherents of Marx because his thought seemed to hold these positions together. His materialism seemed to make man simply a part of nature; his dialectic to make man firmly the master of nature. Thus the marxist could have the best of two worlds.

But leaving aside this digression, what is important is that marxism seemed to be tied to what was already in the world – the everyday world of technology and mass industry that surrounds us. He seemed to show men that through the present conditions of society the humanist Utopia could be achieved and progress brought to its consummation. His Utopia did not therefore seem an airy ideal, but something concrete, a possibility to be actualized in terms of what already existed. This is what has made marxism the most influential humanist religion the world has ever known. It is this that gives it its power over the East.

NOTES

1 The difficulty of studying Marx in his own writings must be emphasized. His master work, *Capital*, consciously imitates the structure of Hegel's *Logic*, with its scheme of being, essence, and idea. Also, some of Marx's profoundest thought is to be found in his early writings which are not easily available in English. For instance, his philosophy of history begins to take shape in a magazine article protesting a German law which penalized the collection of firewood by the poor. The reader is therefore advised to approach the study of Marx through such modern commentaries as A. Cornu's *K. Marx et F. Engels*, vol. 1 (Paris: Presses Universitaires de France 1955), vol 2 (Paris: Presses Universitaires de France 1958), and J. Hyppolite's *Études sur Marx et Hegel* (Paris: Rivière 1955).

2 It is difficult for English-speaking peoples to admit the spiritual greatness of the Germans. In our last two wars we have been taught to despise their civilization. Nevertheless, the fact remains that the highest European achievements in music and philosophy have come from the Germans. Indeed, the ambiguity of German history is that these people have been capable of the most appalling evil, but also of the highest reaches of the human spirit. In Western philosophy, for instance, two periods of thought stand out as the most brilliant: the fourth century B.C. in Greece, which we associate with Plato and Aristotle, and the late eighteenth century in Germany, whose masters were Kant and Hegel. There are no more remarkable books on human history than Hegel's *Philosophy of History* and his *Phenomenology of Mind*. Marx is the heir to this tradition of German philosophical genius. I write about Marx in these essays because his thought is the most influential way that German philosophy has gone out into the world, but under his thought at every point lies the much profounder genius of Hegel.

3 I need hardly stress what a different view this is of man and nature, and their relationship, compared with the Greek view of natural law.

SIMONE WEIL (1909–43)

Simone Weil was a French philosopher whom Grant admired more than any other contemporary thinker because she combined philosophic thought of the highest order with a life of saint-like denial and asceticism. Born into a secular Jewish family in Paris, she received an elite French education and worked for a while as a schoolteacher. However, after the German invasion of France, she was forced to flee, first to the south of France, then to New York, and finally to London, where she worked for the Free French. She published little during her lifetime, but the posthumous publication of her notebooks established her as one of the leading philosophical and religious thinkers of the twentieth century. Grant was deeply influenced by her from the 1950s and his last great work, 'Faith and the Multiversity,' shows how much he had learned from meditating on her writings for over thirty years. Grant did not consider the writings reprinted here to be anything more than an invitation to read Weil herself.

Let me say also that although my debt to Strauss is great as a teacher of what makes up modernity, Simone Weil is the being whose thought is to me the enrapturing. It is indeed true that I am scared of her because the unequivocal saints are scaring to somebody like myself who loves comfortable self-preservation, but nevertheless her thought is next to the Gospels the highest authority for me. Quite a different level of authority from Strauss. I can imagine being capable of writing something as perceptive & lucid as Strauss, but I cannot imagine loving God & being possessed by Christ as S.W. was. That is why I write of the same questions as Strauss and do not write of S.W. because she was divinely inspired and one can only approach that with fearful hesitation. She can be wrong about little scholarly details in a way that Strauss would not be, but on the greatest matters in the last years, she is writing out of the extraordinary event of being possessed by the second person (??) of the Trinity. If I can ever become quite a different person, I might be able to write something about her, other than just pointing to her writings.

– George Grant to Joan O'Donovan, 19 January 1981

Introduction to Simone Weil (1970)[*]

There must always be something unsatisfactory in writing or speaking about the productions of the great. For example, musicologists can write of Mozart's mastery of certain forms, his use of certain keys, his debt in the later part of his life to the Bachs, etc., etc.; but finally they must simply say – listen, be silent, pay attention, study – here one is in the presence of the highest. Indeed, much of the attitude of the expositor should be that of John the Baptist as depicted by Grünewald in the Isenheim altar.[†] As you will remember, he stands there pointing at the figure on the cross.

So it must be in speaking of the life and writings of Simone Weil. My muddy and confused words seem so tedious compared with the cutting clarity of her language.

Of course, to the young one must do a medium amount of talking so that they do not miss their encounters with the great – those sudden encounters which are the joy of education – and this talking has a particular use in a society in which the tawdry is all around them. There is, however, more reason to talk of a recent genius than an ancient one, because many people may not have read her works. Simone Weil died in 1943 and the twenty-seven years since then have been wordy and noisy ones, particularly here in North America. Ours is not an era in which the note of genius is heard through the avalanches of print, and this applies particularly to the genius of sanctity. There is, therefore, perhaps some purpose served in speaking of Simone Weil. But I must insist that my purpose is not to interpret her thought for you – that is, to put my own clumsy self between you and her, but rather to persuade you to read her works, and to pay attention to her genius. My paper is meant as an introduction to the reading of Simone Weil – to discover her life and her writings.

First, let me sketch the outward going of her existence. Simone Weil was born in Paris in 1909. Her parents were prosperous French who had come from the tradition of European Judaism. She had one older brother who is today a famous mathematician. She was brought up by her parents and brother in that civilized humanist agnosticism of the enlightenment, which so characterized middle-class European culture

---

[*] George Grant, a speech given to the Hamilton Association *c.* 1970, unpublished.
[†] Matthias Grünewald, active between 1500 and 1520, the last and one of the greatest painters of the German Gothic school.

before 1914. But it was that culture in its finest form. Whatever else she was to become, it must be remembered that she partook of two remarkable traditions; both her Frenchness and her secularized Jewishness gave her that intense love of learning and cultivation of the intellect, which may not of themselves be enough, but are the seedground from which even higher activities can proceed, and without which society and individuals are likely to become mediocre or even base. French education for the very clever is prodigiously difficult and highly competitive. Her achievement is therefore remarkable in taking her baccalaureate at the age of fifteen (the usual age being seventeen or eighteen) and in receiving the mark of nineteen out of twenty, when the usual youngster considers fifteen a high mark. She proceeded to the lycée and the College Henri IV and on to the École Normale Supérieure. Alain,[*] the famous teacher of philosophy, considered that she had philosophic genius of the first order. That is, in a country where the achievement of the elite was the best the West has produced, she was known as having shining intellectual eminence.

There is in her, however, from the beginning, something beyond the pattern of French brilliance, or for that matter beyond any intellectual brilliance. No sooner had she become a teacher of philosophy than she became part of a group of workers who produced a paper called *The Proletarian Revolution*, and soon after she took leave of philosophical teaching and became a worker in the Renault motor works. The best comment on that life is what she wrote later to her friend, Father Perrin; 'What I went through (in the factory) marked me in so lasting a manner that still today when any human being, whoever he may be and in whatever circumstances, speaks to me without brutality, I cannot help having the impression that there must be a mistake and that unfortunately the mistake will in all probability disappear. There I received for ever the mark of a slave, like the branding of the red-hot iron which the Romans put on the foreheads of their most despised slaves.'

In 1931 and 1932 she had been in Germany, and writing (at the age of twenty-one) in the proletarian magazine she made clear the reasons for the inevitable fact that the Nazis must win the struggle for power – as in fact they did a year later. In 1936 she went to Spain to work for the Republican army on the Catalonian front and experienced war in its

[*]Émile Auguste Chartier (1868–1951), French philosopher and one of the most important early influences on Weil's thought.

savagery. In 1937 her parents moved in and took her out of the public world, as by this time she was physically broken and was to suffer for the rest of her life from that hideous curse, migraine.

With the fall of Paris to the Germans in 1940 she moved to unoccupied France, working as a farm labourer for twelve hours a day and continuing her studies in Greek and Sanskrit. She was later involved in clandestine activities. In 1942 she was persuaded to move to New York by her parents, who as Jews obviously had to emigrate. But the six months in New York she considered a mistake, and immediately began to pester her friends who were high officials in General de Gaulle's entourage to send her on some mission to France. She was brought to London in December 1942 but her obviously Jewish physique and the brokenness of her health would not allow the officials to send her into France. She worked in London on reports about the kind of society which should be established in France after the war. One of her greatest writings, *The Theory of the Sacraments*, was a private letter to Maurice Schumann,[*] now Foreign Secretary. In the spring of 1943 she was in hospital, and dead in August 1943. Cause of death listed as 'suicide, not eating.'

This capsuled account of her life sounds singularly uninspiring, and my failure saddens me. I now must turn to that aspect of her life which is even harder to describe than outward events – what I would call the possession and distinction of her existence by God. This difficult subject cannot be avoided because it is in this fact that the greatness of her writings can only be understood. What gives her writings their startling force is that she writes of the divine (call it, if you will, reality) with an immediacy, certainty, and directness. Let me explain what I mean by this quality of her writings by making a comparison between two writers of our era. Both people like Masters[†] in his reports and D.H. Lawrence[‡] in his novels write of sexuality. Masters from his science knows a lot about the outlets and climaxes of American men and women. But he clearly knew almost nothing about human sexuality in itself. Can anybody imagine going to Masters to deepen their consciousness about the place of sexuality in their own life? The very idea is high comedy. Lawrence, on the other hand, knows what sexuality is

---

[*] Maurice Schumann (1911–), the chief official broadcaster on the BBC French service during the Second World War.

[†] W.J. Masters and his wife A.E. Johnson published a landmark study of sexuality, *Human Sexual Response* (1966).

[‡] D.H. Lawrence's (1885–1930) most famous novel, *Lady Chatterley's Lover* (1928), was banned in both Great Britain and the United States as pornographic.

because he has existed as a sexual being and knew others who have also so existed. My analogy is that Simone Weil writes about the divine like Lawrence, not like Masters.

It is therefore necessary for me to say something of those events between 1936 and 1943 whereby God's perfection became immediate to her. (And I use the word 'immediate' in the sense that we see each other right now.) But let me say that in doing so I have very great hesitation – and would like to cover my head with a cloth as Socrates did when he spoke with Phaedrus about most difficult matters. Let me begin by quoting her words which set the context of the problem:

> I may say that never at any moment in my life have I sought for God – I do not like this expression and it strikes me as false. As soon as I reached adolescence I saw the problem of God as a problem of which the data could not be obtained here below, and I decided that the only way of being sure not to reach a wrong solution, which seemed to me the greatest possible evil, was to leave it alone. So I left it alone. I neither affirmed nor denied anything. It seemed to me useless to solve the problem, for I thought that being in this world, our business was to adopt the best attitude with regard to the problems of this world.

Let me read you one extract about these events. In doing so one must remember it is part of an account written to an intimate friend which she never thought would pass beyond him.

> In 1937 I had two marvellous days at Assisi. There, alone in the little twelfth-century Romanesque chapel of Santa Maria degli Angeli, an incomparable marvel of purity where Saint Francis often used to pray, something stronger than I was compelled me for the first time in my life to go down on my knees.
>
> In 1938 I spent ten days at Solesmes, from Palm Sunday to Easter Tuesday, following all the liturgical services. I was suffering from splitting headaches; each sound hurt me like a blow; by an extreme effort of attention I was able to rise above this wretched flesh, and leave it to suffer by itself, heaped up in a corner, and to find a pure and perfect joy in the unimaginable beauty of the chanting and the words. This experience enabled me by analogy to get a better understanding of the possibility of loving divine love in the midst of affliction. It goes without saying that in the course of these services the thought of the Passion of Christ entered into my being once and for all.

There was a young English Catholic there from whom I gained my first idea of the supernatural power of the Sacraments because of the truly angelic radiance with which he seemed to be clothed after going to communion. Chance – for I always prefer saying chance rather than Providence – made of him a messenger to me. For he told me of the existence of those English poets of the seventeenth century who are named metaphysical. In reading them later on, I discovered the poem of which I read you what is unfortunately a very inadequate translation. It is called *Love*. I learnt it by heart. Often, at the culminating point of a violent headache, I make myself say it over, concentrating all my attention upon it and clinging with all my soul to the tenderness it enshrines. I used to think I was merely reciting it as a beautiful poem, but without my knowing it the recitation had the virtue of a prayer. It was during one of these recitations that, as I told you, Christ himself came down and took possession of me.

In my arguments about the insolubility of the problem of God I had never foreseen the possibility of that, of a real contact, person to person, here below, between a human being and God. I had vaguely heard tell of things of this kind, but I had never believed in them. In the *Fioretti* the accounts of apparitions rather put me off if anything, like the miracles in the Gospel. Moreover, in this sudden possession of me by Christ, neither my senses nor my imagination had any part; I only felt in the midst of my suffering the presence of a love, like that which one can read in the smile on a beloved face.

I had never read any mystical works because I had never felt any call to read them. In reading as in other things I have always striven to practise obedience. There is nothing more favourable to intellectual progress, for as far as possible I only read what I am hungry for, at the moment when I have the appetite for it, and then I do not read, I *eat*. God in his mercy had prevented me from reading the mystics, so that it should be evident to me that I had not invented this absolutely unexpected contact.

Yet I still half refused, not my love but my intelligence. For it seemed to me certain, and I still think so to-day, that one can never wrestle enough with God if one does so out of pure regard for the truth. Christ likes us to prefer truth to him because, before being Christ, he is truth. If one turns aside from him to go towards the truth, one will not go far before falling into his arms.

Such events cannot, of course, be spoken of simply. For instance, her involvement in the twentieth century through becoming a member of the industrial proletariat and through experience of war, shows that there was in her something beyond intellectual brilliance, namely what in the West is called attention of the will, or better, love and which has always been considered necessary to the highest knowledge. This already present attention was what led her to the afflictions of the century, even before she knew what she was doing, and in turn the afflictions are the condition of her amazing attention. Moreover, the afflictions of modern civilization taught her to question the philosophic principles on which modern civilization is based, and so enabled her to read and participate directly in what the Greeks and Indians have said about alternative principles, in a way that is quite impossible for most of us. Yet, in saying that her involvement in the afflictions of the world is central to the understanding of her sanctity, we must avoid being led to that anti-intellectual position which sees possession by deity as an happening which has little to do with intellectual life. (This I may say is a position very popular in many circles these days.) For it is perfectly clear from her own testimony that her reading of the Bhagavadgita, the Iliad, and above all Plato and the Gospels were the very means of her receptivity. What I am saying is, in its most general form, the following: in the tradition, and I can only speak of the Western, there has been much controversy about the respective places of the way of love and the way of knowledge, and indeed some followers of the way of love have been so presumptuous as to ridicule thought. This is not true of Simone Weil. In her the ways of love and of knowledge are inextricably bound together. It is particularly necessary to say this in our present society in which knowledge and love are so disastrously bifurcated that each falls into its own particular errors and perversions.

What is one to make of such a sentence as: 'It was during one of these recitations that, as I told you, Christ himself came down and took possession of me.' I, of course, believe that what happened is exactly what she says happened. And yet this seems to me highly surprising; for I do not like or trust the writings of most mystics and am full of suspicion of their claims. Also, as a twentieth-century person, I am inclined to a certain image of the relation of sexuality to religion and therefore such language as Christ taking possession of people is highly suspect – particularly from women. Yet I am sure it happened for the reason that what she knows and writes about elsewhere is, I am sure, true, and whatever her faults I cannot think they were those of self-delusion. This comment is of course in no sense a proof because I could not prove it unless someone would sit down and read in detail and discuss with me in detail what she has said about affliction and the beauty of the world in her notebooks. Let me also say that I think that official, institutional Christianity has been quite right in being so firmly suspicious of those claims to direct contact which we call mysticism, because of the obvious and manifold abuses to which they may lead. But when it happens, I am sure it happens, and I am convinced it happened here.

To turn from these absurd little comments of mine, I will now describe her published writings. First, I must mention several complications in sorting them out, which make it difficult to approach her thought at all or to understand it as a consistent whole. These stem from the fact that the most important of her writings were written in notebooks for her own purposes, not those of publication, and have only seen the light of published day since her death and under the editorial hands of other people. The comparison can be made between her writings and Pascal's *Pensées.* After 1945 her friends in the south of France, Monsieur Gustave Thibon and Father Perrin, published some of the manuscripts she had left in their hands. Thibon produced *Gravity and Grace,* a set of extracts from her notebooks; Perrin, *Waiting on God,* which are her letters to him and certain of her essays. These publications by her Catholic friends presented a particular difficulty. When they appeared in France they were met by the highest adulation. French writers of all kinds – whether believers or not – heralded them as the work of genius. In this fact Catholics were faced with an inevitable ambiguity. Here was a writer of clear genius and one who had entered the heights of the Christian life, and yet who had unequivocally and at great length stated that obedience did not call her to membership in the Catholic Church – indeed one who had written penetrating attacks on the form of the Church and some of its most authoritative teaching.

She remained, she has told us, at the intersection of Christianity and everything that is not Christianity: all the ancient wisdom of mankind of the Enlightenment that the Church had repudiated and excluded, the traditions banned as heretical, even the limited goods that resulted from what we hypostatize of the Renaissance. 'I remain beside them all the more,' she wrote to Father Perrin, 'because my own intelligence is numbered among them.' In her eyes the Church fails as a perfect incarnation of Christianity mainly because it is not truly Catholic. 'So many things are outside it – so many things that God loves – Christianity being Catholic by right but not in fact, I regard it as legitimate on my part to be a member of the Church by right but not in fact, not only for a time but for my whole life if need be.'

This may sound as if she were advocating a foolish syncretism or asserting the Church should embrace falsehood as well as truth. But, of course, politically she was in no sense a liberal (that is, an optimist about the results of falsehood) and so she recognizes the Church's duty to guard the truth and warn the public against error. But this guarding has been done in the wrong way by the use of force and anathema. This rejection of the Church meant that she excluded herself from the Eucharist which she knew to be a priceless treasure.

Now clearly it is difficult (I do not know whether it be possible) for a Roman Catholic to accept at its face value Simone Weil's position that it is Christ who demands for her the obedience of remaining outside the Church. It would be folly to say impossible considering the river of divine charity which in the last years has flowed from the Roman Catholic Church, which must make the rest of us humble. The alternative is to say that at the centre of her existence she has been in some way mistaken; she confused obedience with spiritual pride and Cardinal Daniélou has said that. It is quite honest to interpret her this way and in the last years there have been many books by Roman Catholic theologians explaining the sources of her errors. My point about her writings is it is quite evident that the extracts published by Thibon were affected by the contradiction on the one hand of his friendship and admiration for her, on the other the desire to play down her total thought. Obedience to their Church meant that M. Thibon and Father Perrin could not be expected to edit her manifold manuscripts properly. There were too many passages to which they were entirely unsympathetic. Nevertheless, the effect of their early editing on her public image still remains. Thibon's *Gravity and Grace* was the chief way her writings became known in English, and it is a very one-sided set of extracts. Father Perrin's book, *Waiting on God*, is fairer, and is indeed a good first volume to read (also cheaply available in English.) However, it must be noted that Father Perrin's introduction to that book has been withdrawn, and he has published elsewhere a more cautious and less enthusiastic account of her.

Now that her manuscripts are edited, not as extracts, but more in the way she left them, the central difficulty remains, however, of seeing her thought in unity, because her main writings were not intended for publication. This unification of her thought is further complicated by the fact that for a person who died at thirty-three, and spent most of her adult life as a labourer, her writings are voluminous. Since the end of the war this immense mass of material has been brought out by the French presses. Let me say that many of the theologians who have written books or articles about her have singled out certain aspects of her thought at the expense of others and therefore have interpreted her totality in a very limited way. Some of the descriptions of her in American journals could only have been written by people whose reading had been to say the least partial. There is such a desire on the part of scholars these days to get into print that they sometimes write about that of which they do not know enough.

For the sake of clarity I will divide her writings into two main classes: her political and social writings and her philosophical, scientific, and religious writings. Obviously this division is arbitrary because each depends on the other.

There are three main books about politics and society. First, *L'Enracinement (The Need for Roots)*. (In giving an English title, I am not implying any lack of French in my audience, but simply stating that there is an English translation of the work. Where there is no translation I will give only one title.) This is the only book that she wrote for a public purpose – indeed her only book which is not a collection of pieces. It was written as a report for the Free French government in London as to the principles on which French society should be based after the war. It is divided into three sections: (a) the needs of the soul in any society, (b) the cause of modern uprootedness, and (c) the possibility of enrootedness in advanced industrial society. By 'uprootedness' she means what Marx means by alienation, but uses it in a wider context because she has a fuller understanding than him of the demonic aspects of bureaucracy. This is the least absolute of her books because it was written as a report to practical men, who knew they would soon have responsibility for the reconstruction of a conquered society. Second, *Oppression et Liberté (Oppression and Liberty)*. This group of essays is in my opinion her most remarkable writing about politics, and is a good place to start the study of her thought. Albert Camus also thought it was one of the masterpieces of European political philosophy. At its centre is a long essay called 'Reflections on the causes of liberty and social oppression,' which is at base an understanding not only of the causes of social oppression in general, but of the particular forms of oppression which arise in societies which are oriented to the future, that is, which are progressive. This volume also contains her amazing critique of marxism. I must emphasize that this criticism of Marx is not of the order of those we have got used to in North America since 1945 – criticisms which miss the point because they distort Marx and therefore do not come to grips with his thought. Simone Weil has a profound understanding of Marx's greatness and therefore what she says is truly a critique, not the passing wind of propaganda. Third, *La Condition Ouvrière*. At the centre of this volume is her diary while she worked for the Renault factory. This is, however, no personal affair but comments about the relations between men and machines and men and bureaucracy. It also contains an essay on the conditions necessary if industrial work is not to be servile.

Besides these three mains works there are two volumes of miscellaneous essays on social and political subjects, ranging from several analyses of French colonial policy to essays on the Cathar religion and the civilization of Languedoc, that is, the Albigensians. Two of these essays I would particularly single out. A long essay called 'Reflections on the origins of Hitlerism' turns out to be a sustained and detailed criticism of the civilization of Rome. I single this out not only because it helps us escape some of the more comfortable platitudes about Roman history, but because in it is expressed her central theme about history in general – namely that the nobler and better does not necessarily survive, indeed because of the ultimate rule of force over the world, truth and beauty can only be tenuously held in the being of any society. She agrees with Plato that society is always and everywhere the Great Beast or the Cave. The other essay I would single out is 'The Person and the Sacred' in which she maintains that what is sacred in man is not what is individual or personal but what is impersonal. Seen negatively, this essay is an attack on so much popular modern writing, both inside and outside Christianity, which is based on a sentimentalizing of personality and mankind. These essays have been published in English by the Oxford Press under the editorship of Sir Richard Rees, who is the leading English exponent of her work.

The core of her philosophical and religious writing – indeed the core of all her work – is found in her notebooks. The first batch of these which cover her life in France have been published in English in two volumes under the title *Notebooks*. Her later notebooks written in the U.S.A. and England have been published in French under the title *La Connaissance Surnaturelle* (new translation in English under the title *First and Last Notebooks*. As to me the greatest modern European language is always French and she is a marvellous exponent of that language, try and read some of her in French.) This I think is the most remarkable but the most difficult of all her writings. What are all these notebooks about, taken as a whole? They are a sustained commentary on what she has been thinking, reading, and experiencing. She continually returns to such themes as the history of philosophy, the nature of ethics and religion, the Indian writings and Christian scriptures, northern and ancient mythology, French literature, the worship of the future, mathematics, physics, art, war, work, industrialism, and sexuality. Perhaps if one were to single out one subject that more than any other binds the whole together one could put it in her own words: 'I am ceaselessly and increasingly torn both in my intelligence and in the depth of my heart through my inability to conceive simultaneously and in truth, the affliction of men, the perfection of God and the link between the two.' Or, in other of her words: 'As Plato said, an infinite distance separates the good from necessity – the essential contradiction in human life is that man, with a straining after the good constituting his very being, is at the same time subject in his entire being, both in mind and in flesh, to a blind force, to a necessity completely indifferent to the good.' This contradiction above any other is for her the means by which the mind is led to truth. I quote again:

> There is a legitimate and an illegitimate use of contradiction. The illegitimate use lies in coupling together incompatible thoughts as if they were compatible. The legitimate use lies, first of all, when two incompatible thoughts present themselves to the mind, in exhausting all the powers of the intellect in an attempt to eliminate at least one of them. If this is impossible, if both must be accepted, the contradiction must then be recognized as a fact. It must then be used as a two-limbed tool, like a pair of pincers, so that through it direct contact may be made with the transcendent sphere of truth beyond the range of the human faculties. The contact is direct, though made through an intermediary, in the same way as the sense of touch is directly affected by the uneven surface of a table over which you pass, not your hand, but your pencil. The contact is real, though belonging to the number of things that by nature are impossible, for it is a case of a contact between the mind and that which is not thinkable. There is an equivalent, an image as it were, very frequent in mathematics, of this legitimate use of contradiction as a means of reaching the transcendent. It plays an essential role in Christian dogma, as one can perceive with reference to the Trinity.

Her *Notebooks* are indeed a sustained exercise in this legitimate use of contradiction, that is, in making as clear as can be the factual nature of the contradiction that human existence presents, and then in using those contradictions as pincers.

One point I must make in passing is about the word I have translated as 'affliction.' This word, which is central to her thought, is in the French 'malheur.' There is no word in English with the complete connotation of that French word. I use affliction, but if anyone can think of a better word I will be deeply grateful.

For any of you who may be interested in the history of philosophy, I single out her continuous commentary on the dialogues of Plato, which runs like a thread through all her notebooks. As well as her comments in her notebooks there is a group of essays on the same subject which has been published in English with the inapposite title of *Intimations of Christianity.* In these essays about Greece she writes not only on Plato, but on the *Iliad*, the *Electra*, the *Antigone*, Pythagoras, and Greek mathematicians. As I have more right to speak about Plato than the others, I would say that her comments on his writings go to the heart of the matter in a way that much modern scholarship does not. Most modern students of the philosopher start with the presupposition that since they come later than Plato in time they must be able to judge that thinker from a superior height. The result of such a standpoint is that instead of seeing what Plato thought, they say that he was really saying what he ought to have said if he were a modern intellectual. It is because the assumptions of modernity had been smashed in Simone Weil that her commentary on Plato is illuminating.

I must finally mention three books of hers that do not fit into my division. The first is *Sur la Science* (remember her brother). The second is *Lettre à un Religieux (Letter to a Priest).* This is a long letter she wrote to an American Roman Catholic priest, putting down in detail why she did not become a member of the Christian Church. The third volume is a play she worked at for many years but never finished called *Venise Sauvée.*

Let me now attempt to place Simone Weil within the tradition. In doing so, however, I in no way imply that such historical placing has anything to do with the question of whether what she says is true. I am not an historicist, and do not think that truth of the philosophical or religious order can be reached by historical analysis. To say that Simone Weil belongs to the extreme wing of Greek Christianity is not to imply that this tradition incorporates the truth more fully than

Western Christianity. The statement of historical fact simply leads forward to the fuller and more difficult question of truth. This evening my paper has been with a description of the life and writings of a person and I intend to leave aside for this occasion the incomparably more difficult question of the truth of what she says. The inference, however, must be made explicit that since I spend a great part of my life reading and thinking about this woman, it must be that I think I am there drinking at a fountain of the divine truth.

To place Simone Weil squarely within Greek Christianity is, however, to make one fact apparent. What she says will appear extremely alien and unlikely to Western Europeans or to North Americans because this form of Christianity has not played a significant role in our world for many centuries. To be a Western person is to think within Western Christianity – Catholic or Protestant – or within one of Christianity's secular offshoots – marxism or liberalism. Indeed, so powerful has been the West that it is possible almost to say that to be a man at all is to think in a Western way. But, of course, Christianity was more than western from the beginning, and Eastern or Greek Christianity included in itself things that have been lost in the West. But in saying that Simone Weil belongs to this Greek Christianity, I am not saying that she was near to the institutionalized form, namely the Greek Orthodox Church – because I am taking Greek Christianity to be something much wider than this – I include in it much that has disappeared from the world. Its last appearance in the Western world as more than an individual phenomenon was according to her in the civilization of Languedoc and the religion of the Cathars – the civilization which was extirpated by the Dominican order and the feudal knights of northern France, in what is known euphemistically as the Albigensian crusade. (History is indeed written by the victorious.) This Greek Christianity is nearest of any of the forms of our religion to Indian religion. While, of course, to take Hegel's dictum 'en pleine connaissance de cause'* that progress moves from East to West, North American Christianity is farthest from them. Indeed, she saw Europe in its Mediterranean form as a halfway house between America and India. It is not accidental then that Simone Weil should have written of the civilization of Languedoc as the highest that Europe has known; nor is it accidental that she should have learned Sanskrit and

---

*With full knowledge.

considered the Bhagavadgita as a work of revelation to be accepted at a level of authority only just lower than the Gospel according to St John.

Indeed, to state the matter in a trite historical way, Simone Weil's value as an object of study could be put thus: She was a person who as much as anyone I know experienced the twentieth century – knowing its wars and its intellectual assumptions, its hopes and its factories. In the full sense of the word she was incarnate in the twentieth century – that is, she knew it not only as an observer, but its afflictions became her flesh. It was because all that the twentieth century has been was immediately and mediately known, that she was able to transcend it and rediscover certain treasures which our world had lost for many centuries. Her pierced and piercing apprehension of our immediate world enabled her to overcome that loss in ourselves, so that the ancient religion can appear to us as more than an academic curiosity.

I end by singling out two aspects of her doctrine that clearly illustrate what I mean by placing her in the tradition of Greek Christianity. In stating her doctrine, I will compare what she says with the more usual western view on the same matter.

First, she stands unequivocally on the side of saying that the affirmation of the being of God is a matter of knowing and not of willing – that is, that belief or unbelief is never a matter of choice or commitment, but of intellect and attention. As the West has been without faith, faith has often been interpreted by men of faith who wished to get on with understanding as if it finally came down to an act of committal by the will. For instance, my experience of the clergy has often been that when one raises difficult intellectual questions, their answer is likely to be 'Have Faith,' and when one asks them why one should have faith they are likely to say 'Commit yourself to it,' as if truth were not a gift, but a free act. More and more, religion is talked about in the West as if it were some kind of choice or opting, despite or even against the evidence. In present-day Christianity, it is now leading to the pitiful grabbing at existentialist philosophy as a buttress to faith, as in Rahner[*] and Heidegger. For existentialism is after all the dead end of voluntarism in philosophy. Against this praise of commitment, Simone Weil makes clear that belief cannot ultimately be

---

[*] Karl Rahner (1904–84), German-born theologian who played a key role in the reforms of the Second Vatican Council. His thought was deeply influenced by Martin Heidegger.

based on choice. In her own words: 'The consent of the intellect is never owed to anything whatsoever. For it is never in the slightest degree a question of choice. Only attention is voluntary and thus is the only matter of obligation. If one wishes to provoke in oneself a voluntary consent of the intellect, what is produced is not consent to truth but auto-suggestion. Nothing more contributes to the degrading and enfeebling of faith and leads to the spread of unbelief than the conception that one ought to believe in anything.' In other words, one cannot force faith on oneself. The intellect should be entirely free to go where the necessity of the argument leads it. This approach to the divine is of course essentially Greek. Second and more difficult, she rejects the language of personality and individuality as the final truth about human beings. This language is of course basic to the way that Western people talk of the human condition. Today in our present world we see the consequences of such talking in the belief that religion is in essence warmth of feeling to other people. This worship of warmth, coated with the more comfortable parts of the Gospel or Judaism, takes a myriad of forms in the superstructure of talk which justifies our society, but its philosophical and religious basis is in Western philosophy and religion, which asserts that the individual qua individual is an ultimate irreducible in reality. So deep does this go in our culture that thinking outside personality language is very hard for us. Yet this is what we must do if we are to read Simone Weil. The concrete, the personal, the particular has some preliminary meaning in talking about human beings, but it is according to her not ultimate. In as much as we partake in the universal we partake in the divine. In this sense Plato is her master and she takes him seriously in a way that nobody can who makes the language of personality final.

Let me read you some words of hers which show clearly where the denial of personality language leads – words which could not be written by anyone who saw the Western tradition as sufficient.

God created; that is not to say that he produced something external to himself, but that he withdrew, allowing a part of being to be other than God. To this divine renunciation answers the renunciation of the created, namely, obedience. The whole universe is nothing but a compact mass of obedience studded with luminous points. Each of these points is the supernatural part of the soul of a rational creature who loves God and who consents to obey. The rest of the soul is part of the compact mass. The rational creatures who do not love God are only fragments of the compact and dense mass. They also are fully obedient, but only in the manner of a stone which is falling. Their souls are matter, psychic matter, subject to a mechanism as inexorable as gravity. Even their belief in their own free will, the illusions of their pride, their defiances, their rebellions, are, simply, phenomena as strictly determined as the refraction of light. Considered in this way, as inert matter, the worst criminals are part of the order of the world, and for that reason, part of the beauty of the world. Everything obeys God; everything is therefore, perfectly beautiful.

This universal love belongs only to the contemplative faculty of the soul. He who truly loves God leaves to each part of his soul its proper function. Below the faculty of supernatural contemplation is found the part of the soul that responds to obligation, and for which the opposition of good and evil must have as much meaning as possible. Below this, is the animal part of the soul, which must be carefully instructed by a skillful combination of whip-lashes and lumps of sugar.

Such a statement helps us to understand why, according to her, affliction is the lot of all human beings. It always includes in itself physical pain, but is more than this. It is the pounding in upon men that they are really nothing, by the blind force of necessity and of social and personal degradation. The final affliction to which all come is death. The only difference between people is whether they consent or do not consent to necessity. What most supports the possibility of this consent is our attention to the beauty of the world. For that beauty is our one image of the divine. And of its very nature it is not known as purposeful, but only lovable, in the sense that a great work of art has no purpose outside its own being. In her language, the beauty of the world is caused by the divine son because it is the mediator between blind obedience and God.

In terms of this very difficult language she would see the human condition in the following way: 'The portion of space around us, limited by the curve of the horizon, and the portion of time between birth and death, in which we live, second after second, and which is the tissue of out life, are together a fragment of that infinite distance crossed by divine love. The being and life of each of us are a small segment of that line whose ends are two persons but one God; and back and forth on this line moves love who is also the same God. Each of us is but a place through which the divine love of God for himself passes.'

Pétrement's *Simone Weil* (1977)[*]

Among the greatest teachers of the eternal, there is a small group of particular fascination: those who lay before us the most important truths out of very short lives. Simone Weil was dead at thirty-four, and yet her disparate writings are the supreme statement concerning eternity made in the West in this century. The account of her life by Simone Pétrement has now been well translated into English.

The lives of great thinkers are generally not of central interest; what is of interest is their writings. What matters to us about Kant is to understand *The Critique of Pure Reason*, not how he spent his quiet life in Königsberg. This is, of course, finally true of Simone Weil. What matters is to read such writings as her *Notebooks*, *Oppression and Liberty*, or *La Science et nous*.

Yet there are three reasons in her case why a biography is of particular interest. The first is the fact that she was not only a thinker but a saint, and the unity between justice and truth lies at the heart of her teaching. She taught that desire which has not passed through the flesh by means of appropriate action remains a sentimental phantom, and in saying that she affirms that our apprehension of the most important truths depends on the justice of our lives. One therefore wants to know what kind of a life produced a teaching so terrible in its demands.

Secondly, her writings are being attacked these days both by Freudians and marxists, who are saying that the truth she states is vitiated by her sexual or class position. The marxist attack is not surprising, when one considers that Camus called her criticism of Marx the most persuasive ever written. The Freudian attacks are similar to those launched against many women. Her writing is the product of penis envy, and this can be seen in her relation to her brother who is a famous mathematician. The extent of these attacks makes one want to understand the relation between her life and her writings.

Thirdly, she wrote in the midst of her intense involvement in the class struggle and wars of Europe between 1930 and 1943. Most of her work was not written for publication, and was published posthumously. It is, therefore, difficult to comprehend the teachings as a whole and to bring into unity writings which are mostly notebooks, letters, and

[*]George Grant, review of *Simone Weil* by Simone Pétrement, trans. Raymond Rosenthal (Random House 1977), *Globe and Mail*, 12 February 1977, 43.

articles. This is particularly hard for English speakers, because some of her greatest writings have not yet been translated. For these reasons an accurate biography is not only fascinating in its own right, but necessary to the understanding of her thought.

Simone Pétrement has succeeded in writing such a biography. Pétrement says in her introduction that she is going to put down everything she knows, leaving it to wiser minds to judge what is essential. In the first half of the book she brings before us the amazing family life which combined the clarity and intensity of both the French and the secularized Jewish traditions, the wonderful education received by the French elite in 'Les Grandes Écoles'; and then the ten years of Weil's life in the French class struggle of the 1930s in which she made industrial production part of her flesh. Her understanding of marxism might well be great, for during the decade of the 1930s she lived with Marxists in France, in Germany as it approached Hitlerism, and in the Spanish civil war. She was a friend of Trotsky. Indeed, this biography is not only an account of a particular life but of Western Europe as a whole, in that extraordinary decade leading up to 1939.

The second half of the book deals with more difficult events – the possession of her life by God, and the gradual movement from that point towards her death in 1943. It is extremely hard to write of such events with clarity, beauty, and restraint. Pétrement succeeds on all three counts. With great precision, she unfolds the steps which led Simone Weil to be able to receive the truths which were manifested to her. The details of her life are combined with lucid descriptions of the writings which poured forth in these last years. 'Poured forth' is the right metaphor when one considers the circumstances under which these limpid writings were composed. For example, her remarkable work *The Pythagorean Doctrine* was written while she lived in a crowded hall in North Africa with 700 refugees, while taking her father and mother (who were Jewish) away from Hitlerism to safety. The account that Pétrement gives of how she came to participate in the eternal never falls into the hot and romantic style sometimes used in such matters, but is always plain and clear and sane.

Pétrement was a close friend of Weil. Along with Camus she was chiefly responsible for the careful publication of Weil's work since 1945. It might be argued that a biography written from such closeness could not be 'objective' in the strange sense of the word used by modern scholars. It is well to remember that Boswell loved Johnson, and Bonaventure loved Francis, and these are two of the greatest lives in the Western tradition. Pétrement is not only writing as a friend but also as a leading French scholar and thinker. Her books about gnosticism stand in their own right. She brings to this biography not only friendship but high philosophic training, and that clarity of style which makes French such an instrument of the truth. In this sense the biography will continue to be central to any understanding of Simone Weil. It will replace other accounts which presented her life and thought in a more sensational and one-sided way. Raymond Rosenthal has done wisely in following the French literally and carefully in his translation. Something must be lost in English, particularly in the quotations from Weil herself. French was the instrument of her teaching and the writing is of that rare kind in which the words are transparent to the thought. The English translation has cut some of the philosophic passages from the original French edition. This is perhaps appropriate to its audience, but insulting.

In an age when oblivion of eternity has become the fate of Westerners (not least among its theologians and philosophers), it is difficult to read Simone Weil despite the clarity of her writing. Nevertheless, just because Western Christianity has realized its destiny of becoming secularized, it is essential to tear oneself free of the causes of that destiny, without removing oneself from the necessities of our present or from the reality of Christ. At the beginning of this biography, Pétrement puts down the saying of Christ: 'Happy are those who hunger and thirst for justice.' Such a statement must be incomprehensible and/or terrifying when we moderns try to think of it as true. Where does it lead one? Simone Weil's thought is a rigorous exposition of what is implied in the terms of that statement.

In Defence of Simone Weil (1988)[*]

The *Republic* is, at the least, a drama about how Socrates cures Plato's brother of righteous anger. I need to remember the benefits of that cure in reviewing this book. Dr Coles has written a book about Simone Weil in the Radcliffe Biography series. He is a professor of psychiatry at the Harvard Medical School. His book is in a biography series but is in

[*] George Grant, 'In Defence of Simone Weil,' *The Idler*, no. 15 (January – February 1988), 36–40, in response to Robert Coles, *Simone Weil: A Modern Pilgrimage* (Reading, Mass.: Addison-Wesley 1987).

fact a commentary on her personality and life, accompanied throughout by an *obbligato* of quotations from his conversations about her with
Dr Anna Freud, the daughter of the founder of psychoanalysis. I have
the temptation to anger because the two writers patronize a great saint
and thinker. By 'saint,' I mean those rare people who give themselves
away. By 'great thinker,' I mean somebody who is remarkably open to
the whole. Simone Weil wrote with genius about the two most important Western matters, Christ and Plato. It is hard to avoid anger when
one's chief modern teacher is patronized in the sweetie-pie accents of
Cambridge, Mass., and Hampstead, U.K.

Coles's and Freud's commentary reminds me of the following:
'Shakespeare was really quite a good poet. Some of his verses are to be
commended. He obviously did not have our advantages, but he wrote
pretty well. His writing shows how neurotic he was, but he can't be
blamed for that. He did not do too badly, considering that he did not
have the benefit of our help.'

To take two examples where Coles's words lead away from what
Simone Weil was:

1. Coles writes: 'She had no sexual life.' Simone Weil's closest friend
told me in the Gare du Nord in Paris: 'I can tell you that Simone Weil
knew human love in its most complete form.' Clearly the friend
thought I was some kind of American and would therefore judge sexual life as the decisive matter in the discussion of another human
being. She cared that I write properly of Simone Weil, and knew that
as a North American intellectual I was unlikely to understand the Mediterranean tradition of chastity. But she certainly would not have told
me this if it were not the case. Simone Weil wrote: 'The desire to love
another human being as the expression of the beauty of the world is
the desire for the Incarnation.' Does that sentence suggest that 'she
had no sexual life'?

As Coles and Freud are doing the psychoanalytical bit on Weil, it is
well to mention the account written for herself[1] just as she is preparing
to go to work in the Renault factory, at the age of twenty-five. In this
account she writes of what she must overcome in herself if she is to be
what she wants to be. It is extremely detailed about the particularities
of her body and soul. Because it is written for herself it is very intimate,
and therefore I have some hesitation in writing of it. But Mlle Pétrement is certainly a wiser human being than I am, and has published it.
It is probably true that concerning the saints all evidence must be
made public. It is not written in terms of the 'id' psychology that Freud

got from Nietzsche. It is, rather, a fine example of Socrates's 'Know thyself.'

2. It is now necessary to discuss the much more serious question of Coles's account of Simone Weil's relation to the Judaism of her ancestors. Obviously this must be written about with the greatest care because of the terrible events in Europe and the Middle East in this century. I think Coles does badly here for a reason of decency. He wants to open her thought to the students at Harvard, and knows that he must explain her refusal of Judaism if he is to succeed. But in this process he makes bad errors about her and her family, and about what can best be called the history of religions. It is therefore necessary to pursue this second subject in some detail.

Coles rightly calls Weil a Christian, but then makes the error of identifying that Christianity with modern Western Christianity. To put it religiously, one might say that Christianity on one side has turned towards Judaism and on the other towards the Vedanta. To put it philosophically, one might say that Christianity in its meeting with philosophy for the purposes of self-understanding has had Aristotelian and Platonic wings. Weil is clearly with the Platonists. Weil's writings therefore contain a clear and sustained rejection of Roman Catholicism – that is, a refusal of the most important tradition of the West. She criticized it more often than Judaism, though often on the same grounds.

The impression that Coles has gathered of Weil's flirting with Catholicism has some justification, but in essence misses the point. Weil did clearly long to take part in the sacrament of the Eucharist, because that sacrament concerns the suffering of God. She was a Christian in that she accepted the suffering of God. We should remember that some of the classical philosophers, such as Proclus, rejected Christianity because they did not believe that God could suffer. Although Weil accepted the suffering of God, nevertheless she could not fulfil her hunger for the bread of eternal life because she could not accept Roman Catholicism on other grounds.

Categorizing great thinkers is always a dangerous task. It may, however, be possible to cautiously call Weil a gnostic. Yet there must be immediate qualifications. As a follower of Plato, Weil holds within her thought that measured blending of 'gnosticism' and 'agnosticism' that characterizes her intellectual master. Moreover, 'gnosticism,' as a recurring historical fact, has had within it excesses and follies, as have all forms of Christianity. (It would be impertinent to speak of other

great religions.) In our time, as good a thinker about politics as Voege-
lin has wrongly used 'gnosticism' as a term of abuse in his fine book,
The New Science of Politics. Therefore, it is with hesitation that I catego-
rize Weil as a 'gnostic,' in order to make clear that it was more than
accident that held her from becoming a Catholic.

Nevertheless, it is not without significance that Simone Pétrement,
who has written the definitive biography of Simone Weil, is also a leading scholar of gnosticism. (Her biography is so clear and so complete
that it must be ranked among the great biographies.) Coles recognizes
in a short paragraph Weil's closeness to Marcion. What he does not
seem to recognize is that gnosticism has returned again and again
within Christianity, and Weil's writings are filled with references to
these recurrences. To take one example: she wrote frequently of the
gnosticism of medieval France, which produced the civilization of
Languedoc. The sympathetic have described this movement as the religion of the Cathars (from the Greek word for 'pure'); its members are
also known by the geographic name of Albigeois. Their civilization was
extirpated by northern knights under Simon de Montfort, encouraged
by the papacy. This extirpation goes by the title of the 'Albigensian
crusade.' The Inquisition was first founded for the purposes of that
crusade, and its ecclesiastical leadership was in the hands of the
Dominican order. As Stalin said, history is written by the winners, and
therefore we have few authentic records of this movement. Most of
what we have is the testimony of its adherents under torture. In this
century in France there has been a partially successful effort to find
out what Catharism was. Two of Weil's noblest writings are about the
Cathars.

The reason it is important to mention these historical matters in the
present connection is that Coles's lack of interest or knowledge of
them is, I think, determinative of the worst chapter of his book, 'Her
Jewishness.' Weil was essentially a gnostic saint, and her criticisms of
Judaism are similar to those which have appeared through the centuries in gnostic writings: namely, her rejection of the Hebrew Bible and
its account of God. Catholics quickly recognized this after her death.
Cardinal Daniélou edited a book of essays in which she is indicted for
her rejection of the Old Testament. Indeed, this book goes much farther than Coles's and Freud's patronizing psychoanalysis. It directly
accuses her of 'penis envy,' and her 'misinterpretation' of the Hebrew
Bible is laid at that door. Unlike Coles, the Catholics have had no
doubt that her Christianity was not at one with Western Christianity,

but rather with what had been continually rejected by official Western Christianity.

Apart from these comments about the history of religions, it is necessary to touch upon the particular details of 'her Jewishness.' I am hesitant to do so, because the details of the lives of thinkers are unimportant compared to the universal truths in which they participate. But sanctity is not the same thing as philosophy, and in describing sanctity, details matter. Coles writes of these details in such a way as to impugn that sanctity. Also, the relation between Weil and her parents is one of the tender parts of her greatness, and it is discussed by Coles with a singular lack of feeling. He writes of the hurt to her family when she left Judaism. I talked to Mme Weil at length about this matter. I cannot speak about Dr Weil because I did not meet him, but Mme Weil had obviously been very attached to her husband, and therefore had some right to speak of his opinions. Mme Weil came from a family which had moved west from Russia under the influence of the Enlightenment. Paris was after all the centre of that movement, and of the revolution that had attempted to realize its ends politically. She belonged to the France that believed that human freedom required putting away the superstitions of religion, whether those of Christianity or of Judaism. She early recognized that she had produced two remarkable children. (Her son, André Weil, is considered in many quarters to be the greatest mathematician of this century.) She loved the greatness in her daughter, and devoted herself to protecting Simone from its consequences. It was not always easy. When Simone Weil had Trotsky to stay with her family, her mother accepted this because her daughter's 'left-wing' opinions seemed only an extension of her particular brand of modern French nationalism. Like many of her generation, Mme Weil had learned to loathe war between 1914 and 1918, particularly from her connection with the wounded patients of her husband, who served the French army as a doctor during the first great massacre. Being a decent rationalist, she had thought of herself as French without any religion.

It was almost inconceivable to her to find suddenly that the racism of the gutter had come to power in Germany in 1933. This was a common experience of many progressive Western Europeans. Gershom Scholem has described it well in his autobiography.[*] Something had come to be in their midst, which they did not identify with a Western country

---

[*]Gershom Scholem, *From Berlin to Jerusalem*, trans. Harry Zohn (New York: Scholem Books 1980).

such as Germany, but with the superstitions of a pre-progressive age. Never having thought herself as in essence Jewish, she now had to realize that she was being forced to consider herself a Jew, because of this modern craziness.

At the end of Simone Weil's life, she indeed used a greeting from Krishna in her letters to her parents. Her parents knew little of her movement to Christianity, and at this difficult time of her dying far away from them, she knew that they might be disturbed or surprised by what had happened to her. But after all, the Bhagavadgita is an inspired text, and for Simone Weil Krishna and Christ were perhaps the same being.

After her daughter's death, Mme Weil spent her life holding together Simone's manuscripts, before Camus and Pétrement saw that they were placed in the Bibliothèque Nationale. When I talked to her, she had pondered every line of these manuscripts and thought they were of high truth. Once when I was leaving her flat, she stopped me and repeated Herbert's* great poem 'Love,' which had been central in her daughter's life:

> Love bade me welcome: yet my soul drew back,
>   Guiltie of dust and sinne.
> But quick-ey'd Love, observing me grow slack
>   From my first entrance in,
> Drew nearer to me, sweetly questioning,
>   If I lack'd any thing.
> A guest, I answer'd, worthy to be here:
>   Love said, You shall be he.
> I the unkinde, ungratefull? Ah my deare,
>   I cannot look on thee.
> Love took my hand, and smiling did reply,
>   Who made the eyes but I?
>
> Truth Lord, but I have marr'd them: let my shame
>   Go where it doth deserve.
> And know you not, sayes Love, who bore the blame?
>   My deare, then I will serve.
> You must sit down, sayes Love, and taste my meat:
>   So I did sit and eat.

*George Herbert (1593–1633), British metaphysical poet.

That was not the act of somebody who had been wounded by her daughter's acceptance of Christ. I have before me Mme Weil's account, in her own handwriting, of when and where her daughter wrote the 'Prologue,' in which she describes how Christ came to her. Mme Weil wrote it out for me, because there had been some historical confusion as to when the event had occurred. It cuts across what Coles has written about Simone Weil having wounded her parents. It is a document of lucidity and joy. Any confusion she may have experienced by having brought into the world this eagle was utterly subordinated to her acceptance that her daughter had been visited in the flesh directly by Christ.

The silliest thing in Coles's book is what he writes about her letter to Xavier Vallat,[2] who had the appalling title of Commissioner of Jewish Affairs in the Vichy government. Weil wrote that she could not get a teaching job in Vichy because she was considered Jewish. She says that it is irrational to consider her as Jewish because her intellectual traditions are entirely classical and French. Coles maintains that this was a weaseling letter of a coward denying her Judaism at a time when Jews were being persecuted. It is a long letter of ironic contempt from a well-known Frenchwoman to a powerful man in a position that Weil knew should not exist in any constitutional government. Of course, such an extreme difference of interpretation could only be decided by a long 'explication du texte,' which is not possible in a short review. Two things can be said. 1. Could Weil possibly have expected to get a job after writing such a letter? 2. Does Coles imply that Judaism is a given that one cannot leave?

Pétrement describes accurately the content of this letter: 'If in this letter Simone boldly affirms that she doesn't consider herself a Jew, it is not in order to disassociate herself in practice from the Jews – she would not disassociate herself from anyone, above all not from people being persecuted, and in Marseilles she did much to help Jews – nor in any way to deny her origins; nor is it to affirm a religious conviction that would have no interest for the Commissioner of Jewish Affairs. Instead, she did this in order to emphasize again the difficulty of defining the word 'Jew,' and to show quite clearly that she does not understand its significance and considers the statute concerning the Jews absurd and incomprehensible.'

Of course, the high style of irony is hardly the forte of Americans. The public spirits of the United States are capitalism, imperialism, and a certain form of democracy. Irony is too high a style to be consonant with any of these spirits. The mordant wit that suggests contradiction requires too great an attention for that swift-moving society. American-popularized Freudianism has not added to the capacity for irony. This book is indeed a warning to those who write about any 'kalos kagathos'* from the position of superiority. One is apt to expose oneself.

Of course, Coles has the right and perhaps the duty to defend Judaism. (I use 'perhaps' because I do not know whether he is a Jew. If he is, he obviously has the duty to defend Judaism.) Catholics have the right and the duty to defend Western Christianity against Weil's criticism of it. But the combination of the defence of Judaism with the patronizing tones of the Harvard Medical School is repellent. I am sure that the theologians of Judaism (for example, the Roth brothers in England) have a lot to say about where Judaism is correct and Simone Weil is wrong. Theological debate does not sit well with psychiatric imputation as to motive. Beyond matters of debate, it is absurd to impugn the courage of this undaunted woman.

Enough about this book. As Simone Weil's writings are largely in the form of notebooks and essays, it is hard to find one's way into them. Therefore I hope it will not seem impertinent to mention means of doing so. Simone Pétrement's biography is much the best. Before sanctity one can either be silent or matter-of-fact. Pétrement's life is astringent French scholarship at its best. Theoretical comprehension is of course easier than writing about sanctity. For such comprehension, M. Veto's La Métaphysique Religieuse de Simone Weil is the most careful among many good books. As Professor Veto is now at Yale, it is to be hoped that his book will be translated into English.[†]

The centre of what Simone Weil writes is something that human beings must learn for themselves in the terror of thought and prayer. To read her sentence 'matter is our infallible judge' is to understand what Christ meant when he said, 'I come not with peace but with a sword.' At a more theoretical and exoteric level, at a less immediate and therefore more palatable level, she is saying something about what is happening in the Western world. She returns continually to Plato's statement: 'How great is the real difference between necessity and the good' (Republic, 493c).

*Noble and good (Greek).
[†]M Vetö, La Métaphysique religieuse de Simone Weil (Paris: J. Urin 1971). As Grant hoped, the book was published in English: The Religious Metaphysics of Simone Weil (Albany, N.Y.: State University of New York Press 1994).

What is given in that sentence cannot but touch what is given in Christian teaching. Weil wrote that she was ceaselessly torn by the contradiction between the perfection of God and the affliction of human beings. How is it possible that human beings are given over to the afflictions of necessity? What is it to contemplate Goodness itself in the light of the afflictions of necessity? She waited upon that contradiction with ceaseless attention. In that waiting she restated the idea of creation, not in a new way in terms of what is given in the Gospels, but in a new way in the sense that her idea has not been primary in modern Western Christianity. The idea of creation is obviously an abyss in which our minds are swallowed up. Despite the absurd contemporary use of the word 'creativity,' we cannot think of something coming to be out of nothing. Nevertheless, quite rightly, people have tried to find analogies which can lead us to see as in a glass darkly.

For Western Christians – let us say, loosely, since Hildebrand – creation came to be thought of as an act of self-expansion. For Weil, creation is a withdrawal, an act of love, involved with all the suffering, renunciation, and willingness to let the other be, that are given in the idea of love. For her the passion of God is at one with the creation. In this sense it is one with the teaching about the Trinity.

It is not possible here to work out how this is so consummately developed in her writings. (To repeat, outside her own writings this has best been done by Veto.) Nor is it possible to discuss what is thought in the idea of God as love in relation to what is thought in the idea of God as power. It can be said, however, that the two leading forms of Western Christianity are in intellectual chaos. Can one imagine that large elements of Roman Catholicism took and take Teilhard de Chardin[*] seriously as a Christian theologian? It is clear that civilizational identity depends on primal religious affirmations, in this case the post-Augustinian self-understanding of Christianity. It is clear that the descent of Western civilizational identity into wild technological scrambling goes with the self-confusions of organized Western Christianity. Moreover, Nietzsche's formulation that Christianity produced its own gravediggers in the modern technological rationalists has some historical sense to it, but perhaps in a different way than Nietzsche's positive affirma-

---

[*]Pierre Teilhard de Chardin (1881–1955), French religious philosopher and paleontologist.

tions would suggest. One must remember that modern technological rationalism was itself more penetrated by Western Christianity than Nietzsche would allow. The self-expansion of the modern technologists attacked certain aspects of Christianity, but took from that which it was attacking the self-expanding power that came forth from the 'Rex tremendae majestatis,'* in which creation is utterly defined as power. At a time such as this when on the one hand the Gospels stand in their indubitable perfection, while on the other hand the civilization of the West has become mainly technology, it is well to read carefully a thinker of consummate intelligence and love who understood that Christianity becomes meaningless if the creating of God is detached from the passion of God. Simone Weil often speaks of 'the lamb that was slain from the beginning of the world.'

When in admiration and love I look for a description of Simone Weil, some lines from Crashaw's invocation to Saint Theresa of Avila come to mind:

> O thou undaunted daughter of desires!
> By all thy dow'r of *Lights* and *Fires*;
> By all the eagle in thee, all the dove;
> By all thy lives and deaths of love,
> By thy large draughts of intellectual day,
> And by thy thirsts of love more large than they –

NOTES

1 *'The account written for herself.'* – This is published in Simone Pétrement's *La Vie de Simone Weil (Simone Weil: A Life)*; in the French, vol. 2: 11–14; in the American translation, 219–22. It must be said that the American translation is often poor. In this passage, *'jouissance'* is translated as 'pleasure.' If possible, it is well to read it in French, especially when it comes to Weil's own words. She wrote the most luminous of Western languages with a clarity that is breathtaking. Nothing seems to stand between the words and what they are about.

2 'Her letter to Xavier Vallat.' – For the letter in full, see Pétrement's *Life*; in the French, vol. 2: 377–9; in the English translation, 443–4.

* King of fearful majesty (Latin), from the 'Dies Irae,' a thirteenth-century hymn used in masses for the dead.

LEO STRAUSS (1899–1973) AND
ALEXANDRE KOJÈVE (1902–68)

Grant was deeply influenced by a debate between the German-American political philosopher Leo Strauss and the Russo-French philosopher Alexandre Kojève on the question of whether ancient or modern political science could best explain the phenomenon of tyranny. Both writers had an impact on his thought. From Kojève he learned that the modern world was moving, inevitably, as Kojève had argued in his Introduction to the Reading of Hegel, *towards a universal and homogeneous state, in which there would be no war and no class struggle. Strauss's reply persuaded him that such an outcome would represent the worst, not the best, condition for human beings. Grant later read many of Strauss's books and returned to his writings for pleasure even in the 1980s after he had rejected many of Strauss's main conclusions.*

I have read and re-read *The City and Man.* I wonder if sometime you were free I could come to Chicago and take a very short bit of your time to ask you two questions. It would not be in the immediate future, as the questions about Socrates and the Christian tradition I have not yet properly formulated. The other question is concerning Aristotle and Plato's dialogues. I must express to you again my enormous sense of gratitude for every word you have written.

– George Grant to Leo Strauss, 21 January 1965

In reissuing an old book of mine I tried to pay you a compliment in a new introduction. I am enclosing my words on another page because my sense of debt is so great.

– George Grant to Leo Strauss, 25 April 1966

It was through Straus that I came upon Kojève. Let me say that I think Doull knows more about Strauss than Kojève (not having written much, Doull is only known to his friends.) It was to escape Hegel I found Strauss & through Strauss I found Kojève.

Let me say also that although my debt to Strauss is great as a teacher of what makes up modernity; Simone Weil is the being whose thought is to me the enrapturing ... I can imagine being capable of writing something as perceptive & lucid as Strauss, but I cannot imagine loving God & being possessed by Christ as S.W. was.

– George Grant to Joan O'Donovan, 25 January 1981

I have for quite awhile believed that one of the deepest strands in Strauss's writing about Plato has been to criticize the long hold of Xian Platonism in the western and eastern interpretation of Plato. He has done this wisely & with *no* foolishly polemical spirit. I have wanted to write about this, but have been held back because I see no good purpose served (as he did not) in emphasizing these days the difference between Jews & Xians. As he saw clearly it stems from the deep difference concerning the nature (I mean more than the content) of divine revelation. He was deeper & wiser about this than some of his epigones. I may write about this someday, but fairly indirectly.

– George Grant to Ed Andrew, 27 December 1983

Tyranny and Wisdom (1964)[*]

Professor Leo Strauss's book *On Tyranny* was published in 1948. In 1954 a French translation was published with an accompanying essay by Monsieur Alexandre Kojève, entitled *Tyrannie et Sagesse*, and a reply to Kojève by Strauss. In 1959 Strauss included his reply to Kojève in English in *What Is Political Philosophy?*[1]

My purpose in writing is not to give a summary of the controversy between Strauss and Kojève. Both men know better than I do what words are necessary to make clear what they mean. Modern academic writing is strewn with impertinent *précis* written by those who think they can say in fewer words what wiser men than they have said in more. In this paper many of Strauss's and Kojève's arguments will not be mentioned. Rather, I intend to comment on certain propositions and arguments in that controversy which interest me because they appear to be fundamental to political theory. Nevertheless, it is inevitable that I start by stating what the controversy in its most general form would seem to be about.[2]

Strauss affirms that 'tyranny is a danger coeval with political life.'[3] He maintains that modern social science has not been able to comprehend modern tyranny. He recognizes that there are differences between antique and modern tyranny. 'Present day tyranny, in contradistinction to classical tyranny, is based on the unlimited progress in the "conquest of nature" which is made possible by modern science, as well as on the popularization or diffusion of philosophic or scientific

---

[*] 'Tyranny and Wisdom,' in *Technology and Empire* (Toronto: House of Anansi 1964), 82–96. Used with permission.

knowledge.'[4] Nevertheless, to understand modern tyranny it is first necessary to understand 'the elementary and in a sense natural form of tyranny which is pre-modern tyranny.'[5] *Hiero* is 'the only writing of the classical period which is explicitly devoted to the discussion of tyranny and its implications, and to nothing else.'[6] Strauss's primary purpose is therefore to write a proper commentary on that work. By proper I mean that he is concerned with explicating what Xenophon wrote, not with his own thoughts about it. But it is clear that in doing this he affirms by implication that classical social science can understand tyranny in a way that modern social science cannot. It is this assumption in Strauss's commentary which Kojève makes explicit in his essay. Strauss in his reply to Kojève confirms that this is his contention.

Kojève never argues with Strauss about his interpretation of Xenophon. He continually uses the term Xenophon-Strauss in a way which makes clear that Strauss has correctly interpreted Xenophon's doctrine. He also agrees with Strauss that contemporary social science does not understand tyranny and in particular the relation between tyranny and philosophy. Kojève nevertheless rejects the classical solution to the definition of tyranny; indeed, he rejects classical political science in general. In its place he affirms the truth of Hegel's political theory as being able to describe tyranny correctly and indeed all the major questions of political theory. Strauss does not question that Kojève has interpreted Hegel correctly. I will therefore use the phrase Hegel-Kojève in this essay. The centre of the controversy is, then, whether classical political science or modern political science (as perfected in Hegel) can the better understand the relation between the tyrant and the wise man or indeed any of the basic political questions.

In stating that the issue of the controversy is between classical and Hegelian political science, one must avoid a possible misunderstanding which if entertained would prevent one from taking Strauss seriously. Strauss affirms both that present-day tyranny is different from ancient tyranny and that classical social science understood tyranny in a way that no modern social science can. From such statements the obvious question arises: how could the ancients understand something which did not exist in their day? (Such a question will be particularly pressing for those social scientists whose intellectual outlook may be briefly described as 'historicism.' Indeed, historicism may prevent such scholars from even reading Strauss's arguments.) The apparent inconsistency is resolved in this way: Strauss says that what distinguishes modern tyranny from ancient tyranny is the presence in the modern world of a science that issues in the conquest of nature and the belief in the possibility of the popularization of philosophy and science. Both these possibilities were known to the ancient philosophers. 'But the classics rejected them as "unnatural." *i.e.*, as destructive of humanity. They did not dream of present day tyranny because they regarded its basic presuppositions as so preposterous that they turned their imaginations in entirely different directions.'[7] In terms of this historical assertion, both Strauss's affirmations can be made. Classical political science was not familiar with modern tyranny, but it was familiar with the assumptions which distinguish it from antique tyranny. Strauss is obviously asserting the classical view that tyranny is a form of government common to all ages and that the political philosopher can have knowledge of what is common to these governments of disparate ages so that he can correctly call each of them tyrannies. The contemporary social scientist may criticize such a position, but his disagreement is a philosophical one. It does not arise from an obvious mistake about the facts on Strauss's part.

It is difficult to know where to plunge into the controversy. Such uncertainty is inevitable once the incipient political philosopher has recognized that his study cannot avoid being metaphysical and that therefore he must try to learn from those who can think more widely and consistently than himself. For whatever else may be said about the philosophers who related their doctrine on political matters to their desire to have knowledge of the whole, among the best of them there has been a monumental consistency which related their doctrine on one issue to what they taught on all others. Both Strauss and Kojève have studied the masters with great care and therefore know in detail the political teachings of the metaphysicians. They are both aware of the wide extent to which the difference between classical and Hegelian political teaching involves a difference of doctrine on nearly every major issue of political theory. Indeed to state the obvious, the controversy implies throughout a difference of opinion about the object and method of philosophy, in the more than political sense of that word. I do not want simply to check off these differences in detail, yet on the other hand I do not feel competent to define the central principles which divide classical from Hegelian metaphysics. For these reasons I take the plunge into the controversy at the point of a concrete political teaching.

Kojève affirms that the universal and homogeneous state is the best social order and that mankind advances to the establishment of such an order. The proof of this is, according to Kojève, found in Hegel's *Phenomenology of Spirit*, and Kojève sketches the argument of that book in a few pages of his essay. From that sketch his account of the proper relation between tyranny and wisdom emerges. Alexander, pupil of a philosopher, was the first ruler who met with success in realizing a universal state, that is, an empire of which men could become citizens not simply because of their common ethnic or geographic background, but because they shared a common 'essence.' And that essence was, in the last analysis, their sharing of what modern men call 'civilization' – the culture of the Greeks which was for Alexander the culture of reason itself. But according to Hegel-Kojève, Alexander, as a Greek philosopher, could not overcome the distinction between masters and slaves. Thus, his universal state could not be homogeneous – a society without classes. The distinction between master and slave was only overcome as a consequence of the Semitic religions (Judaism, Christianity, and Islam.) For the West this culminated in Saint Paul. To quote:

It is the idea of the *fundamental equality* of all those who believe in a single God. This transcendental conception of social equality differs radically from the Socratic-Platonic conception of the identity of beings having the same *immanent* 'essence.' For Alexander, a disciple of the Greek philosophers, the Hellene and the Barbarian have the same title to political citizenship in the Empire, to the extent that they have the same human (moreover, rational, logical, discursive) 'nature' (=essence, idea, form etc.) or are 'essentially' *identified* with each other as the result of a direct (='immediate') 'mixture' of their innate qualities (realized by mean of biological union.) For St Paul there is no 'essential' (irreducible) difference between the Greek and the Jew because they both can become Christians, and this is not by 'mixing' their Greek and Jewish 'qualities,' but by *negating* them both and 'synthesizing' them in and by this very negation into a homogeneous unity not innate or given, but (freely) *created* by 'conversion.' Because of the *negating* character of the Christian 'synthesis,' there are no longer any incompatible 'qualities,' or 'contradictory' (=mutually exclusive) 'qualities.' For Alexander, a Greek philosopher, there was no possible mixture of Masters and Slaves, for they were 'opposites.' Thus his *universal* State, which did away with *race*, could not be *homogeneous* in the sense that it would equally do away with 'class.' For St Paul on the contrary, the negation (*active* to the extent that 'faith' is an *act*, being 'dead' without 'acts') of the opposition between the pagan Mastery and Servitude could engender an 'essentially' *new* Christian unity (which is, moreover, active or acting, or 'emotional,' and not purely rational or discursive, that is, 'logical') which could serve as the basis not only for political *universality*, but also for the social *homogeneity* of the State.[8]

The union of the political ideas of universality and homogeneity could not, however, result in the universal and homogeneous state becoming a realizable political end when it came into the West as part of Christian theism. That religion did not suppose such a state to be fully realizable in the world, but only in the beyond, in the kingdom of heaven. Homogeneity based on faith in a transcendent God could only lead to the conception of the universal and homogeneous church, not to a universal and homogeneous state. For the universal and homogeneous state to be a realizable political end, Christian theism had first to be negated. This negation was the accomplishment of modern philosophy – an accomplishment of such men as Hobbes and Spinoza which was completed by Hegel. Modern philosophy was able to secularize (that is, to rationalize or transform into coherent discourse) the religious idea of the equality of all men. Thus, the idea of the classless society is a derivative of the Christian religion because modern philosophy in negating the Christian religion was aware of the truth present in that which it negated. The universal and homogeneous state became a realizable political order (because of modern philosophy) and has been, is, and will be made actual by rulers.

Whatever else should be said of Kojève's sketch of Western political history, it is surely accurate to affirm that the universal and homogeneous state has been the dominant ideal in recent modern political thought, not only among those who have recognized their debt to Hegel but among many who would scorn Hegel's philosophy. Indeed, the drive to the universal and homogeneous state remains the dominant ethical 'ideal' to which our contemporary society appeals for meaning in its activity. In its terms our society legitimizes itself to itself. Therefore, any contemporary man must try to think the truth of this core of political liberalism, if he is to know what it is to live in this world. The need to think the truth of this ideal remains even as its content empties into little more than the pursuit of technical expansion. It is Kojève's contention that Hegel's comprehension of the implications of asserting that the universal and homogeneous state is the best political ideal was complete in a way not present in any other political philosopher.

This sketch indicates the proper relation between politicians and philosophers, according to Hegel-Kojève. Only by discursive, philosophic reflection can a person become completely aware of the given historical situation at any moment. But the philosopher who is completely aware of the given historical situation must distinguish between that situation and the ideal. This distinction between the actual and the ideal leads to the negation of the given historical situation by struggle and work. Such practical negating has always been accomplished by political tyrants. There would thus be no historical progress if philosophers did not instruct politicians in the meaning of actual historical situations.

Equally there would be no philosophical progress if practising politicians did not realize the teaching of the philosophers in the world through work and struggle. This doctrine is, of course, of central significance in approaching the Hegelian dialectic. Philosophy is always the account of actuality as it has become in any particular epoch, including the contradictions of that epoch. Therefore, philosophy cannot hope to reach any conclusions which transcend the social situation of its age. Progress in philosophy, then, depends on the contradictions of a particular epoch being overcome by struggle and work, and this is always centred in the work of particular tyrants. Any other view of philosophy pre-supposes that philosophy is concerned with timeless concepts or, in other words, with an ahistorical eternal order. The belief that philosophy is concerned with the eternal order is based on the fundamental error of classical logic that being is eternally identical with itself. Kojève's motto could be the famous tag of Hegel's: '*Was die Zeit betrifft, so ist sie der daseiende Begriff selbst.*'[*] The fundamental assumption of Hegelian logic (that being creates itself throughout the course of history and that eternity is the totality of all historical epochs) is only taken seriously at the level of politics in the recognition of the dependence of philosophers on the activity of tyrants. Kojève returns again and again in his writings to the point that Hegel alone has recognized fully the relation between the modern negation of theism and man's freedom to make the world (history). Only in the radical negation of theism is it possible to assert that there is progress – that is, that there is any sense or over-all direction to history. This progressive and atheist interpretation of Hegel illustrates and in turn is

---

[*]What concerns time is the concept of the presence of Being itself.

illustrated by the doctrine that progress in philosophy and the successful practice of wise tyrants depend upon each other.

One related facet of this interdependence between wisdom and tyranny is Kojève's assertion that the realization of the universal and homogeneous state will involve the end of philosophy. The love of wisdom will disappear because human beings will be able to achieve wisdom. For Kojève, this realization of wisdom has been first achieved in the writings of Hegel. But this appearance of the Sage had to be preceded by the action of that tyrant (Napoleon) who established the basis of the universal and homogeneous state. According to Kojève, Hegel has produced the book (Bible) of wisdom which has definitely replaced the one with that title which we have had for two thousand years. This implies that for Kojève the events of 1830–1945 and after have been simply the completion in the world of that universal and homogeneous state which was initiated in one geographic area by Napoleon and which was completely understood by Hegel. Such an interpretation of Kojève would explain why he has used his philosophic talents simply to expound Hegel and why he has devoted most of his energies to the practical world.

Strauss's most general criticism of this account of Western history is that it is based on the assumption that the universal and homogeneous state is the best social order. That is, according to Strauss, the Hegelian philosophy of history is essentially an attempt to interpret Western history so that the two propositions 'the universal and homogeneous state is the best social order' and 'this social order will be built by man' will be shown to be true. Before proceeding to describe his arguments further, I must comment on what this general criticism by Strauss shows about the form of his argument as a whole. It is clear that in saying that Hegel's philosophy of history depends upon a universal proposition about all social orders, Strauss is speaking within the assumptions of classical philosophy; namely, that political philosophy stands or falls by its ability to transcend history, i.e., by its ability to make statements about the best social order the truth of which is independent of changing historical epochs and which therefore cannot be deduced from any philosophy of history which makes positive statements about the historical process. But this assumption about political philosophy is in turn dependent on the assumption that the Socratic account of philosophy as a whole is true. Strauss also knows that for Hegel-Kojève the truth about the best social order is not prior to an interpretation of history and could not be known except at a certain epoch. This truth is reached by an argument which appeals to an interpretation of the sum of historical epochs which in totality, for the Hegelian, constitutes eternity. For the Hegelian, political philosophy does not stand or fall by its ability to transcend history, but rather by its ability to comprehend all history. Strauss knows that the difference between Hegel and the classics about the place of 'history' in the whole depends upon and illustrates a profound difference between them about the object, method, and standpoint of the study of philosophy in a more than political sense.

The question may then be asked: Why does Strauss criticize Kojève from within an account of philosophy which Kojève does not accept? Why does he not argue about the fundamental difference as to the nature of philosophy rather than the implications which follow from this difference concerning the proper relation between tyranny and wisdom? The answer to this clarifies the limits of Strauss's intentions. His first concern is not to refute Hegelianism but to show that the classical account of the relation between tyranny and wisdom is required by the classical account of philosophy; that is, that there is consistency between what the classics say about the whole and about politics, and that therefore classical political philosophy is not to be judged as a first phase of the subject, which has been left behind as mankind has progressed. Should this seem a limited task, it is perhaps worth pointing out that it is a necessary preliminary to the more difficult matter of being able to say that the political teaching of the classics is true in a way that modern political teaching is not. Also, the need of this preliminary is particularly pressing for anyone who wishes to encourage the serious study of the classics in our era, when the doctrine of progress still influences the political beliefs of even the sophisticated. In such an era it is extremely difficult for men to contemplate the possibility that the political teachings of an ancient civilization could even be studied seriously, let alone in the light of the possibility that they are sounder than those of our day.[9]

Beyond this primary task, Strauss's secondary purpose is to show that the universal and homogeneous state, far from being the best social order, will be (if realized) a tyranny, and therefore within classical assumptions destructive of humanity. Modern political philosophy, which has substituted freedom for virtue, has as its chief ideal (and an ideal which it considers realizable) a social order which is destructive of humanity. The relation of Strauss's second purpose to his first is evident. If the assumptions of modern political philosophy can be shown to lead to the dehumanizing of people, there is reason for scholars to take a more careful look at classical political philosophy than has generally been the case in the age of progress.

Strauss first argues that the universal and homogeneous state will not provide reasonable satisfaction for men, even on Hegelian assumptions about the objects in which men find the highest satisfaction. Strauss points out that, according to Hegel-Kojève, men find the highest satisfaction in universal recognition:

> Men will have very good reasons for being dissatisfied with the universal and homogeneous state. To show this, I must have recourse to Kojève's more extensive exposition in his *Introduction à la lecture de Hegel.* There are degrees of satisfaction. The satisfaction of the humble citizen, whose human dignity is universally recognized and who enjoys all opportunities that correspond to his humble capacities and achievements, is not comparable to the satisfaction of the Chief of State. Only the Chief of State is 'really satisfied.' He alone is 'truly free' (146). Did Hegel not say something to the effect that the state in which one man is free is the Oriental despotic state? Is the universal and homogeneous state then merely a planetary Oriental despotism? However this may be, there is no guarantee that the incumbent Chief of State deserves his position to a higher degree than others. Those others then have a very good reason for dissatisfaction: a state which treats equal men unequally is not just. A change from the universal-homogeneous monarchy into a universal-homogeneous aristocracy would seem to be reasonable. But we cannot stop here. The universal and homogeneous state, being the synthesis of the Masters and the Slaves, is the state of the working warrior or of the war-waging worker. In fact, all its members are warrior workers (114, 116). But if the state is universal and homogeneous, 'wars and revolutions are henceforth impossible' (145, 561). Besides, work in the strict sense, namely the conquest or domestication of nature, is completed, for otherwise the universal and homogenous state could not be the basis for wisdom (301). Of course, work of a kind will still go on, but the citizens of the final state will work as little as possible, as Kojève notes with explicit reference to Marx (435). To borrow an expression which someone used recently in the House of Lords on a similar occasion, the citizens of the final state are only so-called workers, workers by courtesy, 'There is no longer fight nor work. History has come to its end. There is nothing more to *do*' (114, 385). This end of History would be most exhilarating but for the fact that, according to Kojève, it is the participation in bloody political struggles as

well as in real work or, generally expressed, the negating action, which raises man above the brutes (378n., 490–492, 560). The state through which man is said to become reasonably satisfied is, then, the state in which the basis of man's humanity withers away, or in which man loses his humanity.[10]

Strauss's criticism of Kojève then proceeds to a profounder level with the assumption of the classical philosophers that it is in thinking rather than in recognition that men find their fullest satisfaction. The highest good for man is wisdom. This being so, if there is to be satisfaction for all in the universal and homogeneous state, it must be that every human being is capable of systematic philosophical thought which alone, according to the classics, can lead to wisdom. Indeed, Strauss affirms that the classical realization that only the few are capable of pursuing wisdom is central to the classical account of politics and indeed of human history as a whole.

> The classics thought that, owing to the weakness or dependence of human nature, universal happiness is impossible, and therefore they did not dream of a fulfilment of History and hence not of a meaning of History. They saw with their mind's eye a society within which that happiness of which human nature is capable would be possible in the highest degree: that society is the best regime. But because they saw how limited man's power is, they held that the actualization of the best regime depends on chance. Modern man, dissatisfied with utopias and scorning them, has tried to find a guarantee for the actualization of the best social order. In order to succeed, or rather in order to be able to believe that he could succeed, he had to lower the goal of man. One form in which this was done was to replace moral virtue by universal recognition, or to replace happiness by the satisfaction deriving from universal recognition. The classical solution is utopian in the sense that its actualization is improbable. The modern solution is utopian in the sense that its actualization is impossible. The classic solution supplies a stable standard by which to judge of any actual order. The modern solution eventually destroys the very idea of a standard that is independent of actual situations.[11]

Here again one sees the combination of Strauss's two purposes. The showing forth of the classical position as consistent combines with the description of modern theory as including assumptions which are destructive of humanity. Here also can be seen the complex of inter-related questions which need to be thought through if one is to judge about the main issue of the controversy.

The classical assumptions about the dependence of man make it clear that if the universal and homogeneous state were to be realized, it would be a tyranny and indeed the most appalling tyranny in the story of the race. Strauss ends his essay with a description of that tyranny:

> It seems reasonable to assume that only a few, if any, citizens of the universal and homogeneous state will be wise. But neither the wise men nor the philosophers will desire to rule. For this reason alone, to say nothing of others, the Chief of the universal and homogeneous state, or the Universal and Final Tyrant, will be an unwise man, as Kojève seems to take for granted. To retain his power, he will be forced to suppress every activity which might lead people into doubt of the essential soundness of the universal and homogeneous state: he must suppress philosophy as an attempt to corrupt the young. In particular he must in the interest of the homogeneity of his universal state forbid every teaching, every suggestion, that there are politically relevant natural differences among men which cannot be abolished or neutralized by progressing scientific technology. He must command his biologists to prove that every human being has, or will acquire, the capacity of becoming a philosopher or a tyrant. The philosophers in their turn will be forced to defend themselves or the cause of philosophy. They will be obliged, therefore, to try to act on the Tyrant. Everything seems to be a re-enactment of the age-old drama. But this time, the cause of philosophy is lost from the start. For the Final Tyrant presents himself as a philosopher, as the highest philosophic authority, as the supreme exegete of the only true philosophy, as the executor and hangman authorized by the only true philosophy. He claims therefore that he persecutes not philosophy but false philosophers. The experience is not altogether new for philosophers. If philosophers were confronted with claims of this kind in former ages, philosophy went underground. It accommodated itself in its explicit or exoteric teaching to the unfounded commands of rulers who believed they knew things which they did not know. Yet its very exoteric teaching undermined the commands or dogmas of the rulers in such a way as to guide the potential philosophers toward the eternal and unsolved problems. And since there was no universal state in existence, the philosophers could escape to other countries if life became unbearable in the tyrant's

dominions. From the Universal Tyrant, however, there is no escape. Thanks to the conquest of nature and to the completely unabashed substitution of suspicion and terror for law, the Universal and Final Tyrant has at his disposal practically unlimited means for ferreting out, and for extinguishing, the most modest efforts in the direction of thought. Kojève would seem to be right although for the wrong reason: the coming of the universal and homogeneous state will be the end of philosophy on earth.[12]

NOTES

1 L. Strauss, *What Is Political Philosophy?* (Glencoe, Ill.: The Free Press 1959). In the English version of the essay, Strauss has cut out certain passages included in the earlier French version. These deletions do not radically change the English version. I regret them, however, because their inclusion in the French argument does bring out some of the implications in the controversy.

2 What an author has written at one place is inevitably illumined by what he has written at another. It is therefore impossible to write of Strauss or Kojève without having in mind their other writings. Nevertheless, in this paper I will stick as much as possible to their writing about *Hiero.* When their doctrine about a particular matter is taken from elsewhere, this will be made clear in the notes.

3 *On Tyranny,* 1.

4 *What Is Political Philosophy?* 96

5 *On Tyranny,* 2.

6 Ibid., 1.

7 *What Is Political Philosophy?* 96

8 Ibid., 273–4. The English translation of Kojève's essay has been made by Michael Gold. This translation has now been published with Strauss's writings on the matter. (L. Strauss, *On Tyranny,* revised and enlarged, Glencoe: The Free Press 1963).

9 That the first purpose of Strauss's argument is to stress the consistency between all aspects of classical philosophy might well have been made clearer. The difficulty of understanding his purpose is indeed increased for English readers by the fact that he does not include in the English edition of his work the last paragraph of the French edition, in which his purposes are beautifully described. Elsewhere in his writings Strauss has criticized historicism in its late-nineteenth-century form and shown the conse-

quences of such a doctrine for the scope of political science. At no point in his writings has he, however, argued at length with Hegel's claim to have included history within metaphysics, and with the resulting relation between concepts and time.

10 *What Is Political Philosophy?* 128–9
11 Ibid., 131–2.
12 Ibid., 132–3.

FRIEDRICH NIETZSCHE (1844–1900)

Before the 1950s Friedrich Nietzsche was little known in the English-speaking world. His writings had been celebrated by the Nazis and this taint delayed the reception of his thought into North American academic circles. Grant's Time as History *was broadcast originally as the CBC Massey Lectures for 1969. In them Grant praised Nietzsche's philosophy, assigning it a central place in the history of Western thought and declaring Nietzsche to be the thinker who had thought most profoundly about the character of modern civilization as technological. Publication of the lectures was delayed by a near-fatal car crash in which Grant was seriously injured. Consequently, Grant's work has not received the attention it deserved, though it has inspired several studies of Nietzsche, mainly by Canadian political scientists.*

Lately I have been reading Nietsche (?). To say that he is completely misunderstood by most people would be an absurd understatement. To say that he is the forerunner to such bestiality and cruelty as the Nazis is absurd. 'I love he whose soul is deep even for wounding and whom a slight matter may destroy.' 'Pity is the cross upon which he is nailed who loveth mankind.' That kind of thing is not like what he is supposed to be. He uses the theory of 'the blond animal'[*] in utter derision yet people say that that is the basis of Nazidom.
            – George Grant to Maude Grant, 14 November 1939

There is no doubt that for Plato the only rival to be taken seriously to philosophy is tragic and comic poetry, and the very heart of his writings is trying to show that philosophy takes you to the heart beyond tragic and comic poetry. In the modern era, it seems that the rival to philosophy becomes modern physics,

---

[*]Friedrich Nietzsche, *Genealogy of Morals* I, 11.

but it is the supreme genius of Nietzsche to see that in what he considers the death of philosophy, what arises in its place for the greatest men is a new kind of tragic and comic poetry.

– George Grant to Dennis Lee, 10 June 1974

My interests are in two related things: a) to understand 'technical reason' which I think has been done at its greatest philosophically by Nietzsche and his chief epigone Heidegger and which has been done also best by German scientists, e.g. Heisenberg. b) I am interested in explicating the truth of Christianity in relation to this height of modernity.

– George Grant to Patrick Atherton, 28 November 1974

Time as History (1969)[*]

I have brushed against the writings of Nietzsche because he has thought the conception of time as history more comprehensively than any other thinker. He lays bare the fate of technical man, not as an object held in front of us, but as that in which our very selves are involved in the proofs of the science that lays it bare. In thinking the modern project, he did not turn away from it. His critical wit about modern society might lead one to believe that he condemned its assumptions. Rather, he expressed the contradictions and difficulties in the thought and life of Western civilization, not for the sake of turning men away from that enterprise, but so that they could overcome its difficulties and fulfil its potential heights. In his work, the themes that must be thought in thinking time as history are raised to a beautiful explicitness: the mastery of human and non-human nature in experimental science and technique, the primacy of the will, man as the creator of his own values, the finality of becoming, the assertion that potentiality is higher than actuality, that motion is nobler than rest, that dynamism rather than peace is the height. The simpler things that Nietzsche says (for example, that men must now live without the comfort of horizons) seem so obvious to most people today that they are hardly worth emphasizing. Everybody uses the word 'values' to describe our making of the world: capitalists and socialists, atheists and avowed believers, scientists and politicians. The word comes to us so

[*]George Grant, *Time as History*, ed. William Christian (Toronto: University of Toronto Press 1995), 57–69. Used with permission.

platitudinously that we take it to belong to the way things are. It is for-gotten that before Nietzsche and his immediate predecessors, men did not think about their actions in that language. They did not think they made the world valuable, but that they participated in its goodness. What is comic about the present use of 'values,' and the distinction of them from 'facts,' is not that it is employed by modern men who know what is entailed in so doing; but that it is used also by 'religious' believers who are unaware that in its employment they are contradicting the very possibility of the reverence they believe they are espousing in its use. The reading of Nietzsche would make that clear to them. Indeed, even some of the deeper aspects of Nietzsche's thought increasingly become explicit in our world. If one listens carefully to the revolt of the noblest young against bourgeois America, one hears deeper notes in it than were ever sounded by Marx, and those are above all the notes of Nietzsche.

To repeat: the thought of great thinkers is not a matter for the chit-chat of television and cocktail parties; nor for providing jobs for aca-demics in the culture industry. In it the fate of our whole living is expressed. In this sense, the thought of Nietzsche is a fate for modern men. In partaking in it, we can come to make judgements about the modern project – that enormous enterprise that came out of Western Europe in the last centuries and has now become worldwide.

Nevertheless, as implied in the previous pages, the conception of time as history is not one in which I think life can be lived properly. It is not a conception we are fitted for. Therefore, I turn away from Nietzsche and in so turning express my suspicion of the assumptions of the modern project. Yet this immediately produces a difficulty. Before speaking against Nietzsche, one must affirm the language one shares with him, even as one negates his use of it. To illustrate: Nietzsche clearly uses the same language as the tradition in its eternal truth, when he says that the height for human beings is *amor fati*. Yet the love of fate, which he would call redemption, is not in any sense a call to the passivity that some moderns falsely identify with words such as 'fate' or 'destiny.' In him the love of fate is at one with his call to dynamic willing. The love of fate is the guarantee that dynamic willing shall be carried on by lovers of the earth, and not by those twisted by hatred and hysteria against existing (however buried that hysteria may be in the recesses of our instincts). Some marxists have taken his love of fate as if it were a call to passivity as the height, and as if, therefore, he were an essentially non-political writer. They have denied that love of fate (love of the injustices and alienations and exploitations of time) can be good. Is it not just a sufficiently deep and sustained hatred of these iniquities that brings men to fight and to overcome them? But Nietzsche's love of fate is not passive, but a call to dynamic political doing. He states explicitly that any philosophy must finally be judged in the light of its political recommendations. What he is saying beyond many marxists is that the building of the potential height in modern society can only be achieved by those who have overcome revenge, so that what they accomplish comes forth from a positive love of the earth, and not simply from hatred of what presently is. Dynamic willing that has not overcome revenge will always have the marks of hysteria and hatred within it. It can only produce the technical frenzy of the nihilists or the shallow goals of the last men. It cannot come to terms with the questions: 'what for, whither and what then?' However, against the complacency of any easy *amor fati*, Nietzsche makes clear that it must take into itself all the pain and anguish and ghastliness that has ever been, and also the loathing of that ghastliness and pain. Hatred against existence is, it would seem, limitless, and the more we are aware of the nervous systems of others, the more that hatred and hysteria must be actual or repressed for us. Only those of us who are not much open to others can readily claim that we think existing to be as we wanted it. *Amor fati* is, then, a height for men, not in the sense that it is easily achieved or perhaps ever achieved by any human being. The redemption that Nietzsche holds forth is not cheaply bought.

Yet having said this, I must state my simple incomprehension. How is it possible to assert the love of fate as the height and, at the same time, the finality of becoming? I do not understand how anybody could love fate, unless within the details of our fates there could appear, however rarely, intimations that they are illumined; intimations that is, of perfection (call it if you will God) in which our desires for good find their rest and their fulfilment. I do not say anything about the relation of that perfection to the necessities of existing, except that there must be some relation; nor do I state how or when the light of that perfection could break into the ambiguities and afflictions of any particular person. I simply state the argument for perfection (sometimes called the ontological argument): namely that human beings are not beyond good and evil, and that the desire for good is a broken hope without perfection, because only the desire to become perfect does in fact make us less imperfect. This means that the absurdities of time – its joys as well as its diremptions – are to be taken not simply as history, but as enfolded in an unchanging meaning, which is untouched by potentiality or change. So when Nietzsche affirms that *amor fati* comes forth from the contemplation of the eternity (not timelessness, but endless time) of the creating and destroying powers of man and the rest of nature, I do not understand how that could be a light that would free us from the spirit of revenge. It seems to me a vision that would drive men mad – not in the sense of a divine madness, but a madness destructive of good.

[That we must speak of two accounts of reason, the ancient and the modern, can be seen in the fact that for the ancients thought was at its height, not in action, but in what they called a passion. Whatever the differences in what came to us from Jerusalem and from Athens, on this central point there was a commonness. The height for man was a passion. In modern language we may weakly describe this by saying that thought was finally a receptivity. We can see that this is not true of modern thought because its very form is the making of hypotheses and the testing by experiment, something intimately connected with the acts of our wills, the controlling of the world, the making of history.

Indeed, the enormous difficulty of thinking outside the modern account of thought is seen in my using the very word passion. Words that once summoned up receptivity have disappeared or disintegrated into triviality. If I were to use the noblest Greek word for this receptivity, pathos, and say, as has been said, that philosophy arises from the pathos of astonishment, the suffering of astonishment, the word would bear no relation to our present use of it.]*

The preceding statements are not here proved or even argued. Indeed, it is questionable how much it would be possible to argue them in the modern world. For all those statements are made from out of an ancient way of thinking. And to repeat: the core of the intellectual history of the last centuries has been the criticism of that ancient account of thought. As that criticism has publicly succeeded, what comes to us from that ancient thought is generally received as unintelligible and simply arbitrary. All of us are increasingly enclosed by the modern account. For example, central to my affirmations in the previous paragraph are the propositions: the core of our lives is the desire for perfection, and only that desire can make us less imperfect. Yet clearly that account of 'morality' (to use a modern word) is quite dif-

---

*In this selection, the material in square brackets has been restored to the original published text from the broadcast typescript.

ferent from what has been affirmed about morality in the last centuries. The attempt to argue for my propositions would require a very close historical analysis of how the use of such words as 'desire' and 'reason' have changed over the last centuries. It would require, for example, what the ancients meant by 'passion.' Whatever the differences between what has come to us from Plato and from Christianity, on this central point there is commonness. The height for man could only come forth out of a 'passion.' Yet in using such a word, the enormous difficulty of thinking outside the modern account can be seen. When we use the word 'pathetic' we may be thinking of a defeated character in a movie [like Ratso in *Midnight Cowboy*], or the performance of the quarterback for the Hamilton Tiger Cats football team this season. [As for the word suffering, that means simply pain, which sensible men have always wished to avoid.] The word 'passion' has come to be limited for us to little more than an emotion of driving force, particularly intense sexual excitement. [The experiences of receptivity having dropped from our vocabulary, we think of art and thought and morality quite differently. We talk of what the artist does as creation, not as imitation, a begetting on the beautiful.] To say that philosophy arises from the suffering of astonishment would bear no relation to our present understanding of thought, because the archetype of thought is now that science that frames instrumental hypotheses and tests them in experiment, a kind of willing. How can we think of 'morality' as a desiring attention to perfection, when for the last centuries the greatest moral philosophers have written of it as self-legislation, the willing of our own values? Therefore, my affirmations in the previous paragraph use language in a way that can hardly be appropriated. [As an example of the poverty of modern language, let me say how partial it is to speak of Tolstoy as creating *War and Peace*, or Mozart his piano concertos. The disappearance of the words of receptivity, the words of passion, from the modern account of thought, shows what a wide separation there is between the ancient and the modern. It clarifies what it means to say that modern thinking is always a kind of willing. Because we are always surrounded in every conscious minute of our lives by the modern conception of thought, we cannot take what is given to us from the past as intelligible. If we take it at all, we take it more and more as sheerly arbitrary. Therefore, fewer and fewer people can appropriate it.]

Indeed, beyond this, there is a further turn of the screw for anybody who would assert that *amor fati* is the height, yet cannot understand how that height could be achievable outside the vision of our fate as enfolded in a timeless eternity. The destruction of the idea of such an eternity has been at the centre of the modern project in the very scientific and technical mastery of chance. As a great contemporary, Leo Strauss, has written in *What Is Political Philosophy*: 'Oblivion of eternity, or, in other words, estrangement from man's deepest desire and therewith from the primary issues, is the price that modern man had to pay, from the very beginning, for attempting to be absolutely sovereign, to become the master and owner of nature, to conquer chance.' And the turn of the screw is that to love fate must obviously include loving the fate that makes us part of the modern project; it must include loving that which has made us oblivious of eternity – that eternity without which I cannot understand how it would be possible to love fate.

To put the matter simply: any appeal to the past must not be made outside a full recognition of the present. Any use of the past that insulates us from living now is cowardly, trivializing, and at worst despairing. Antiquarianism can be used like most other drugs as mind contracting. If we live in the present we must know that we live in a civilization, the fate of which is to conceive time as history. Therefore, as living now, the task of thought among those held by something that cannot allow them to make the complete 'yes' to time as history, is not to inoculate themselves against their present, but first to enter what is thought in that present.

What has happened in the West since 1945 concerning the thought of Marx is an example of inoculation. Our chief rival empire has been ruled by men who used Marx's doctrine as their official language, while we used an earlier form of modernity, the liberalism of capitalist democracy. The thought of Marx, therefore, appeared as a threatening and subverting disease. The intellectual industry in our multiversities produced a spate of refutations of Marx. Most of these, however, were written with the purpose of inoculating others against any contagion, rather than with thinking the thoughts that Marx had thought. These books have not prevented the reviving influence of Marx's thought among many of the brightest young, anymore than the official marxism of the East has been able to stop the influence of existentialism among its young elites. [Why? Marx's thought abides because he thought some of what is happening in the modern world. His writings could therefore help other men to think about what was happening. What we were doing in Vietnam seemed to be explained by marxism.] Men may have to attempt this inoculation if they are concerned with the stability of a particular society, but it is well to know when one is doing it that it is not concerned directly with philosophy but with public stability. And you will not even be successful at inoculating those most important to inoculate, if you pretend you understand Marx when you do not. To apply the comparison: when I state that I do not understand how Nietzsche could assert *amor fati* to be the height, while at the same time asserting the finality of becoming, my purpose is not to inoculate against Nietzsche. [As I have said, Nietzsche thinks what it is to be a modern man more comprehensively, more deeply, than any other thinker, including Marx, including Freud, including the existentialists, including the positivists. Therefore, the first task of somebody trying to think time as history is not to inoculate, but to think his thoughts.] The task of inoculation is best left to those who write textbooks. [Yet if I am right that in the thought of Nietzsche we drink most deeply of the modern experiment, we cannot finally avoid making some judgments of that experiment, and so of that thought. We might start from our current experience, and argue that since Nietzsche's day more evidence is in. As one looks at the vulgar and chaotic results of our modern dynamism, it is possible to say that the modern project has led men away from excellence, and that this debasement is not accidental, but comes forth from the very assumptions of that project. Then one would say that these debasements are not to be overcome by a further extension of the modern assumptions, as Nietzsche would have it. If one denies the possibility of any returning to the past, and yet does not believe in the assumptions of the modern experiment, what then is the task of thought?]

What then could be the position of those who cannot live through time as if it were simply history, who cannot believe that love of fate could be achieved together with the assertion of the finality of becoming, and yet must live in the dynamism of our present society? In that position there is a call to remembering and to loving and to thinking.

What I mean by remembering was expressed for me by a friend who died recently. He knew that he was dying, not in the sense that we all know that this is going to happen sometime. He knew it because a short term had been put upon his life at an early age, long before what he was fitted for could be accomplished. Knowing that he lived in the close presence of his own death, he once said shortly: 'I do not accept Nietzsche.' Clearly such a remark was not intended to express a realized refutation of Nietzsche. Neither he nor I saw ourselves capable of that magisterial task. He had collected (at a time when such collecting must have been pressed upon him) what had been given him about the unfathomable goodness of the whole, from his good fortune in having partaken in a tradition of reverence. In the inadequate modern equivalent for reverence and tradition, his remark might be called 'religious.'

In an age when the primacy of the will, even in thinking, destroys the varied forms of reverence, they must come to us, when and if they come, from out of tradition. 'Tradition' means literally a handing over; or, as it once meant, a surrender. The man who was dying was in his remark surrendering to me his recollection of what had been surrendered to him, from the fortune that had been his, in having lived within a remembered reverence – in his case, Christianity. [He surrendered to me the affirmation that the whole is in some unfathomable sense good. The absurdities of time, indeed also its joys as well as its diremptions, are to be taken not simply as history but as enfolded in a meaning (call it if you will a transcendence) that is beyond potentiality, that is beyond change. I do not imply that what is handed over in tradition must be in conflict with reason or experience. The belief that reason and tradition are at loggerheads is only a product of modern thought. It comes from the doctrine of progress, that the race as a whole is becoming increasingly open to reason by shuffling off its irrational past. The traditions that came to us from Athens and Jerusalem claim to be, in the main, reasonable, but what was handed over in them is now accepted, if accepted at all, less and less as thought-filled because it is so assailed by the modern account of reason, and all of us are increasingly enclosed by that modern account. The core of the history of the last three hundred years has been the criticism of the ancient account of thought and the coming to be of the new account. As that criticism has publicly succeeded what comes to us from the past is received as unintelligible, as simply arbitrary.] In the presence of death, my friend had collected out of that remembrance an assertion for me that stated how he transcended conceiving time as history.

By distinguishing remembering from thinking, I do not imply that this collecting was unthoughtful, but that what this man had there collected could not have been entirely specified in propositions. For nearly everyone (except perhaps for the occasional great thinkers) there is no possibility of entirely escaping that which is given in the public realm, and this increasingly works against the discovery of any reverence. Therefore, those of us who at certain times look to grasp something beyond history must search for it as the remembering of a negated tradition and not as a direct thinking of our present. Perhaps reverence belongs to man *qua* man and is indeed the matrix of human nobility. But those several conceptions, being denied in our present public thought, can themselves only be asserted after they have been sought for through the remembrance of the thought of those who once thought them.

Remembering must obviously be a disciplined activity in a civilization where the institutions that should foster it do not. One form of it may be scholarship, the study of what the past has given us. But scholarship of itself need not be remembering. The scholar may so hold out from himself what is given from the past (that is, so objectify it) that he does not in fact remember it. There are scholars, for example, who have learnt much of the detailed historical and literary background of the Bible, and yet who remember less of what was essentially given in those books than Jews or Christians untutored in such scholarship. This is no argument against the necessity of disciplined scholarship. It is simply the statement that modern scholarship has to hold itself above the great gulf of progressive assumptions, if it is to be more than antiquarian technique and become remembering.

It may also be said that 'remembering' is a misleading word, because we should turn not only to our own origins in Athens and Jerusalem, but to those of the great civilizations of the East. Many young North Americans are learning from Asia, because of the barrenness of their own traditions. Indeed, many have only been able to look at their own past because they have first been grasped by something in Asia. It is hardly necessary for a member of a department of religion, such as myself, to assert that it can be a great good for Western people in their time of darkness to contemplate the sources of thought and life as they have been in the East. But that meeting will be only a kind of esoteric game, if it is undertaken to escape the deepest roots of Western fate. We can only come to any real encounter with Asia, if we come in some high recognition of what we inevitably are. I use the word 'remembering' because, wherever else we turn, we cannot turn away from our own fate, which came from our original openings to comedy and tragedy, to thought and charity, to anxiety and shame.

As remembering can only be carried on by means of what is handed over to us, and as what is handed over is a confusion of truth and falsity, remembering is clearly not self-sufficient. Any tradition, even if it be the vehicle by which perfection itself is brought to us, leaves us with the task of appropriating from it, by means of loving and thinking, that which it has carried to us. Individuals, even with the help of their presently faltering institutions, can grasp no more than very small segments of what is there. Nor (to repeat) should any dim apprehensions of what was meant by perfection before the age of progress be used simply as means to negate what may have been given us of truth and goodness in this age. The present darkness is a real darkness, in the sense that the enormous corpus of logistic and science of the last centuries is unco-ordinate as to any possible relation it may have to those images of perfection that are given us in the Bible and in philosophy. We must not forget that new potentialities of reasoning and making happen have been actualized (and not simply contemplated as mistrusted potentialities, as for example in Plato) and therefore must be thought as having been actualized, in relation to what is remembered. The conception of time as history is not to be discarded as if it had never been.

It may be that at any time or place, human beings can be opened to the whole in their loving and thinking, even as its complete intelligibility eludes them. If this be true of any time or place, then one is not, after all, trapped in historicism. But now the way to intelligibility is guarded by a more than usual number of ambiguities. Our present is like being lost in the wilderness, when every pine and rock and bay appears to us as both known and unknown, and therefore as uncertain pointers on the way back to human habitation. The sun is hidden by the cloud and the usefulness of our ancient compasses has been put in question. Even what is beautiful – which for most men has been the pulley to lift them out of despair – has been made equivocal for us both in detail and definition. [The very bringing into being of our civilization has put in question the older means of finding one's way, without discovering new means for doing so. Nevertheless, it is also clear that this very position of ambiguity in our civilization presents enormous hope for thought, if not for life. The questions whether the modern project opens out new heights for man, or whether at its heart it was a false turning for man, is so clearly before us. Questions that were settled, and therefore closed over the last centuries, are now open to us once again. Perhaps the essential question about the modern project is not that of Nietzsche – Who deserve to be the masters of the earth? – but the very question of mastery itself.]

Nevertheless, those who cannot live as if time were history are called, beyond remembering, to desiring and thinking. But this is to say very little. For myself, as probably for most others, remembering only occasionally can pass over into thinking and loving what is good. It is for the great thinkers and the saints to do more.

Nietzsche's View of Socrates (1977)[*]

The subject matter of this book is of central significance for those who study political philosophy. Socrates is the primal figure for that uniquely Western activity. More than any other modern thinker, Nietzsche placed Socrates at the centre of Western history as the creator of rationalism, and claimed in his own thought to have overcome that rationalism. Therefore, in Nietzsche's view of Socrates we are near the centre of thinking about the nature of political philosophy. For somebody from outside the U.S.A. (such as myself) it is a happiness to find that a professor of government at Cornell should devote his thought to so central a subject for our Western self-understanding.

I am even happier to say that Professor Dannhauser's book is very well done. He has read Nietzsche's writings carefully and comprehensively; he has also read the accounts of Socrates which are given us in Plato, Xenophon, and Aristophanes. Because of the political and economic conflicts between the English-speaking and German peoples in the last generations, English-speakers have not paid sufficient attention to modern German philosophers – the greatest of whom is Nietzsche. Now that Nietzsche is becoming powerful in our society (particularly among the young) his influence often comes to us in the form of a quick and one-sided apperception of his teachings. Indeed, Nietzsche's enchanting (if terrible) rhetoric encourages that one-sidedness. Therefore, Dannhauser's care must be highly praised. He has obviously read Nietzsche over many years and knows the extensive and complex corpus intimately. This is a scholarly book in the best sense of that term. The form of this book is to trace carefully Nietzsche's view of Socrates from the early writings, when Nietzsche was taken up with positivism and modern science, to the last writings where his final encounter with Socrates is put before us. Dannhauser wisely leaves to a separate chapter what Nietzsche says by implication about Socrates in *Thus Spoke Zarathustra*. He treats with proper caution the endless irony of the ambiguous speeches which largely make up that work.

[*]George Grant, review of Werner J. Dannhauser's *Nietzsche's View of Socrates* (Ithaca, N.Y.: Cornell University Press 1974), in *American Political Science Review*, vol. 71 (1977), 1127–9.

One great quality of Dannhauser's book is that it is unpretentious. By that I mean that his personality does not get in the way of laying before us clearly and carefully what Nietzsche is saying. The book is concerned with Socrates and Nietzsche, not with himself. This is a pleasure these days, when so many books about politics that pass beyond the simply 'objective' seem to be mostly an exposition of the author's personality and problems. If one wants to follow accurately the details of Nietzsche's changing view of Socrates, this book holds the subject together with accurate care. This is what the book is: a lucid exposition of a central (perhaps the central) issue of modern philosophy and therefore of political philosophy.

The present influence of Nietzsche in the U.S. owes much to Professor Walter Kaufmann of Princeton University, because of his extensive translations and his long book about Nietzsche's life and thought. This has been useful in the sense that Kaufmann has helped to free English-speakers from the picture of Nietzsche as a wild poet of nihilism, who politically was the precursor of the horrors of National Socialism. Kaufmann has destroyed amongst us, surely finally, the impression that Nietzsche somehow took part in the tradition of German anti-Semitism. He lays Nietzsche before us as the chief influence upon European existentialism and as a thinker who laid the foundations of what Freud was later to think. In that sense, the influence of Kaufmann's work has been salutary. On the other hand, Kaufmann has presented Nietzsche as if to make the latter's writings open and palatable to the social-democratic world of American academia. He has done this by presenting Nietzsche first and foremost as the expositor of what is assumed in modern society, rather than as the thinker who wants to overcome what stands against human nobility in the modern world. Kaufmann treats vaguely what Nietzsche took as his 'most abysmal' teaching, 'the eternal recurrence of the identical.' In short, Kaufmann does not take Nietzsche altogether seriously.

What makes Dannhauser's book welcome is that he takes Nietzsche's thought at the highest level of seriousness. For example, he confronts the fact that 'the eternal recurrence' is claimed by Nietzsche to be at the centre of what he teaches, and therefore cannot be put aside as some kind of ecstatic extra. This is to say that although Dannhauser is finally less persuaded by Nietzsche than is Kaufmann, he nevertheless treats Nietzsche as a greater thinker than does Kaufmann. It is indeed because Dannhauser (as he shows himself in his last pages) is a lover of Socrates, that he is able to treat Nietzsche deeply –

namely as the most lucid of all teachers of historicism. As Socrates is the supreme Western figure who taught that historicism can be transcended, Nietzsche's account of Socrates must be understood, if one is to look at the problems of historicism clearly. As historicism appears to be the fundamental presupposition of the dominant North American social science, Dannhauser's book is important in our present intellectual situation. I mean by 'historicism' the teaching that all thought is determined by belonging to a concrete dynamic context. If our contemporary academia is to face its main task, which is to try to understand the recent state of our intellectual tradition, this must include the understanding of Nietzsche's writing as it is, in all its greatness, as the work of a thinker who not only assailed Western rationalism, but claimed to have overcome it. Because Dannhauser's book deals with these central issues in Nietzsche's view of Socrates, it takes us to a more philosophic stage of Nietzschean scholarship in the U.S.A. His work is on the level of the best writing about Nietzsche in Germany and France since 1945.

When one admires a book, it is likely to sound ungrateful to mention extra things one wishes the book had done. Nevertheless there are three points I could wish had been developed further:

(a) Dannhauser does not seem to discuss sufficiently what Nietzsche says about Socrates and Platonism in *Beyond Good and Evil.* Dannhauser's chief acknowledgment is to the late Leo Strauss as a teacher. One of Strauss's last published writings was an article on how to read *Beyond Good and Evil.* Perhaps it is Dannhauser's respect for that writing which has made him decide to give *Beyond Good and Evil* a less central place than in my opinion it deserves.

(b) I wish Dannhauser had said more about Heidegger's work, *Nietzsche.* In my opinion this is the greatest book of commentary on a philosopher which has been produced in our age. Dannhauser's interpretation of Nietzsche refers to it several times, but does not deal with Heidegger's interpretation of Nietzsche at length. Perhaps this would have made his book too complex, and taken away from the fine clarity of his writing. It would have become a book not only on Socrates and Nietzsche, but on Heidegger, Socrates, and Nietzsche. Nevertheless, one is aware from this book that Dannhauser is capable of writing about Heidegger's interpretation, and one wishes that he had. After all, Heidegger's historicism is the supreme contemporary understanding of what is implied in the acceptance of that teaching.

(c) Most important. In the last pages of his book, where he makes clear that he is a follower of Socrates and not of Nietzsche, Dannhauser writes: Nietzsche's 'critique of dogmatisms and systems may hit Hegel, but it misses Socrates and Plato; and many of the attacks on reason, rationality, and rationalism may hit Descartes, but they miss Socrates and Plato' (p. 272). I wish Dannhauser had greatly expanded this passage, and said why this is so. However difficult such questions are, it is to be hoped that Dannhauser will turn to them in subsequent writings. In this book he presents us with plenty of evidence that he is capable of casting light on these extraordinarily complex issues.

Nietzsche and the Ancients (1979)[*]

Part II

There is no escape from reading Nietzsche if one would understand modernity. Some part of his whole meets us whenever we listen to what our contemporaries are saying when they speak as moderns. The words come forth from those who have never heard of him, and from those who could not concentrate sufficiently to read philosophy seriously. A hundred years ago Nietzsche first spoke what is now explicit in Western modernity. When we speak of morality as concerned with 'values,' of politics in the language of sheer 'decision,' of artists as 'creative,' of 'quality of life' as praise and excuse for the manifold forms of human engineering, we are using the language first systematically thought by Nietzsche. At the political level his thought appears appropriately among the atheists of the right; but equally (if less appropriately) it is on the lips of the atheists of the left. When we speak of our universities beyond the sphere of exact scientific technologies, what could better express the general ethos than Nietzsche's remark: 'Perhaps I have experience of nothing else but that art is worth more than truth.' And, of course, radical historicism is everywhere in our intellectual life. It even begins to penetrate the self-articulation of the mathematicized sciences.

In such circumstances there is need to read Nietzsche and perhaps to teach him. One must read him as the great clarion of the modern,

[*]George Grant, 'Nietzsche and the Ancients: Philosophy and Scholarship,' *Dionysius* 3 (December), 5–16 (reprinted in 1986).

conscious of itself. If the question of reading Nietzsche is inescapable, the question of whether and how and to whom he should be taught is a more complex matter. It is particularly difficult for somebody such as myself, who in political philosophy is above all a lover of Plato within Christianity. The following story is relevant. A man with philosophic eros[*] was recently asked the rather silly question: 'At what period of time would you best like to have lived?' He answered that he was lucky to have lived in the present period, because the most comprehensive and deepest account of the whole has been given us by Plato, and the most comprehensive criticism of that account has been given us by Nietzsche. In the light of that criticism, one can the better understand the depth of Platonic teaching. That is, one should teach Nietzsche as the great critic of Plato. The difficulty of reading Plato today is that one is likely to read him through the eyes of some school of modern philosophy, and this can blind one. For example, many moderns have in the last century and a half followed Kant's remark in the first Critique that he was combining an Epicurean science with a Platonic account of morality. With such spectacles how much of Plato must be excluded? The great advantage of Nietzsche is that such strange combinations are not present. His criticism of Plato is root and branch. In the light of it the modern student may break through to what the Platonic teaching is in itself.

Nevertheless, the teacher who is within the philosophic and religious tradition, and who also takes upon himself the grave responsibility of teaching Nietzsche, must do so within an explicit understanding with those he teaches that he rejects Nietzsche's doctrine. If I were not afraid of being taken as an innocent dogmatist, I would have written that one should teach Nietzsche within the understanding that he is a teacher of evil. The justification of such a harsh position is difficult, particulary in universities such as ours in which liberalism has become little more than the pursuit of 'value-free' scholarship. This harsh position is clearly not 'value-free.' Moreover, such a position is ambiguous in the light of the fact that I do not find myself able to answer comprehensively the genius who was the greatest critic of Plato. But there is no need to excuse myself. Who has been able to give a refutation of radical historicism that is as able to convince our wisest scientific and scholarly friends?

Without such capability, what is it to say that one should teach within

[*] Leo Strauss.

the rejection of Nietzsche? Is not this the very denial of that openness to the whole which is the fundamental mark of the philosophic enterprise? Is it not to fall back into that dogmatic closedness which is one form of enmity to philosophy? I will attempt to answer that by discussing Nietzsche's teaching concerning justice. As a political philosopher within Christianity, my willingness to teach Nietzsche within an understanding of rejection, while at the same time I am not capable of the complete refutation of his historicism, turns around my inability to accept as true his account of justice. At least we need have no doubts as to what Nietzsche's conception of justice is, and the consequences of accepting it.

A caveat is necessary at this point in the argument. I am not making the mistake that is prevalent in much condemnation of Nietzsche – namely that there is no place for justice in his doctrine. His teaching about justice is at the very core of what he is saying. To understand it is as fundamental as to understand the teaching concerning 'the eternal recurrence of the identical.' It is said unequivocally in a fragment written in 1885, towards the end of his life as writer: 'It happened late that I came upon what up to that time had been totally missing, namely justice. What is justice and is it possible? If it should not be possible, how would life be supportable? This is what I increasingly asked myself. Above all it filled me with anguish to find, when I delved into myself, only violent passions, only private perspectives, only lack of reflection about this matter. What I found in myself lacked the very primary conditions for justice.'[1]

This quotation does not give content to Nietzsche's conception of justice. Its nature appears in two quotations from the unpublished fragments of 1884. 'Justice as function of a power with all encircling vision, which sees beyond the little perspectives of good and evil, and so has a wider advantage, having the aim of maintaining something which is more than this or that person.' Or again: 'Justice as the building, rejecting, annihilating way of thought which proceeds from the appraisement of value: highest representative of life itself.'

What is the account of justice therein given? What is it to see 'beyond the little perspectives of good and evil'; to maintain 'something which is more than this or that person?' What is 'the building, rejecting, annihilating way of thought?' What is being said here about the nature of justice would require above all an exposition of why the superman, when he is able to think the eternal recurrence of the identical, will be the only noble ruler for a technological age, and what he must be ready to do to 'the last men' who will have to be ruled. That exposition cannot be given in the space of an article. Suffice it to speak popularly: what is given in these quotations is an account of justice as the human creating of quality of life. And is it not clear by now what are the actions which follow from such an account? It was not accidental that Nietzsche should write of 'the merciless extinction' of large masses in the name of justice, or that he should have thought 'eugenical experimentation' necessary to the highest modern justice. And in thinking of these consequences, one should not concentrate alone on their occurrence during the worst German regime, which was luckily beaten in battle. One should relate them to what is happening in the present Western regimes. We all know that mass feticide is taking place in our societies. We all should know the details of the eugenical experimentation which is taking place in all the leading universities of the Western world. After all, many of us are colleagues in those universities. We should be clear that the language used to justify such activities is the language of the human creating of quality of life, beyond the little perspectives of good and evil.

One must pass beyond an appeal to immediate consequences in order to state what is being accepted with Nietzsche's historicist account of justice. What does a proper conception of justice demand from us in our dealings with others? Clearly there are differences here between the greatest ancient and modern philosophers. The tradition of political thought originating in Rousseau and finding different fulfilments in Kant and Hegel demands a more substantive equality than is asked in Plato or Aristotle. What Hegel said about the influence of Christianity towards that change is indubitably true. But the difference between the ancients and the moderns as to what is due to all human beings should not lead us to doubt that in the rationalist traditions, whether ancient or modern, something at least is due to all others, whether we define them as rational souls or rational subjects. Whatever may be given in Plato's attack on democracy in his *Republic*, it is certainly not that for some human beings nothing is due. Indeed, to understand Plato's account of justice, we must remember the relation in his thought between justice and the mathematical conception of equality.

In Nietzsche's conception of justice there are other human beings to whom nothing is due – other than extermination. The human creating of quality of life beyond the little perspectives of good and evil by a building, rejecting, annihilating way of thought is the statement that politics is the technology of making the human race greater than it has yet been. In that artistic accomplishment, those of our fellows who stand in the way of that quality can be exterminated or simply enslaved. There is nothing intrinsic in all others that puts any given limit on what we may do to them in the name of that great enterprise. Human beings are so unequal in quality that to some of them no due is owed. What gives meaning in the fact of historicism is that willed potentiality is higher than any actuality. Putting aside the petty perspectives of good and evil means that there is nothing belonging to all human beings which need limit the building of the future. Oblivion of eternity is here not a liberal-aesthetic stance, which still allows men to support regimes the principles of which came from those who had affirmed eternity; oblivion of eternity here realizes itself politically. One should not flirt with Nietzsche for the purposes of this or that area of science or scholarship, but teach him in the full recognition that his thought presages the conception of justice which more and more unveils itself in the technological West.

NOTE

1 Friedrich Nietzsche, *Nachgelassene Fragmente 1884.*

MARTIN HEIDEGGER (1889–1976)

Grant considered Martin Heidegger the greatest philosopher of the twentieth century. Heidegger's early masterpiece, Being and Time *(1927), was the most influential existentialist work. However, in the 1930s, Heidegger joined the Nazi Party and his refusal to repudiate his membership after the war or to comment on the Holocaust made him an extremely controversial figure. Grant first took an interest in Heidegger in the late 1950s, but his meditations on Heidegger became central to his thought after the translation into French of Heidegger's four-volume study on Nietzsche. Heidegger's writings on technology influenced much of Grant's thinking on technology in the 1970s, and Grant returned to these volumes when David Krell's English translation was published in the early 1980s. At the time of his death, Grant had begun work on a book to defend Plato against Heidegger's attack.*

I have found in Martin Heidegger, the most famous of the German existentialists – indeed, the founder of existentialism as a philosophic movement – an interpretation of Greek philosophy which is very similar to some of the remarks I have been making this year. Not in his early works – but in his later works which are only now becoming available. What he says at great length and great subtlety is that Western thought has floated out upon a great tide of nihilism, and the origin of that nihilism is what happened to philosophy somewhere between the time of Parmenides and Plato. For Parmenides, being and awareness were one, and according to Heidegger human existence was rooted in that oneness; man was deep in Being, drew his life from the appearance of Being, which was truly appearance, not illusion; for the being of Being was again at one with Being, not the mere flux which modern interpretations of Heraclitus have led us to think it was.

What he is saying is that all our traditional separations like subject/object, substance/accident, etc. – in fact all the words we use to talk about philosophical problems – are so many veils over Being, so many chasms between ourselves and Being. To understand the pre-Socratic insight we must penetrate far into the first roots of our own language, cutting out all the deceiving growth of the centuries. For the pre-Socratics, truth was what Heidegger calls the unhiddenness of Being.

– George Grant, notes for a lecture, Dalhousie 1958

The question of importance is whether Heidegger's teaching is true. But we must be careful in facing that question too unreservedly, for the reason that here undoubtedly one is faced with a thinker of the highest order – so that one must be hesitant of one's own ability to judge.

What I fear in much North American education is the tendency to put even the very great into neat pigeon holes, and therefore put them safely away. This is part of 'technological' training. The thinker in question is placed at our disposal, like standing reserve, and is made accessible to us.

Let me say why I think this is dangerous with Heidegger, for two reasons:
(a) There are parts in Heidegger which are not accessible to me – I might add, as yet. For example I am coming a bit to understand what he means by *Sein* (to be) – but certainly not entirely.
(b) Second, and more important: what he has said about modern science has been staggeringly illuminating and I know that the truth which he has there laid before me I would never have understood if he had not shown me. For example, his writing on Leibniz – *Der Satz vom Grund* – the principle of reason, where he shows that that principle is central to the modern, scientific technological enterprise, has just made me understand the technological society as no other writing.

Another example: his exposition of what Nietzsche is thinking in the eternal recurrence in the first volume of his *Nietzsche* (Krell) – till I read that exposition I do not think I had ever known what was really thought in what Nietzsche calls his 'most abysmal thought.'

– George Grant, notes for a lecture, McMaster University 1978

I have been reading parts of Heidegger – what a master. Above all (in my own way) I would like to write like that. He seems not to be writing about things, but to summon up directly the things themselves, as if he was not thinking about what others had thought about things, but about the things themselves.

– George Grant to William Christian, 1982

I spend a great deal of life reading Heidegger. He is certainly the greatest philosopher of the modern era. Perhaps with the collapse of Europe, because of the last wars, he is the last philosopher, as philosophy is so essentially a western phenomenon. He is, of course, an ultimately modern philosopher & if I can summon the courage I would like to write an account of why his criticism of Plato is not true. But I doubt that I will ever have the skill to do it. One thing that makes it so difficult is that he is such a remarkable commentator on the history of philosophy. Of all the great German philosophers he is the only one who was by origin Catholic. If you ever feel any desire to read him, I think the best way is either through his book on Leibniz *The Principle of Reason* or through 'The Question concerning Technique.' I don't think *Sein und Zeit* is the best because that is the classic account of existentialism & he spent the rest of his life writing where he thought that inadequate.

– George Grant to Peter Self, 1987

For myself it is only in the last two decades that I have been ready to bring Heidegger into my writings. He is, after all, a very consummate thinker and also *very* prolific writer. It took me years to find the time to read H. comprehensively. The Nietzsche book[*] is now the catalyst to write a longer piece directly about him. Let me say clearly that H. must be for me a writer who ridicules Christianity & therefore, to write about him is to say a great 'NO.' His criticism of Plato is related to his ridicule of Christianity, but that is not of the same centrality for me. His Nietzsche book has been a great catalyst for me as it has come out in English.

– George Grant to John Siebert, 29 June 1988

[*]Martin Heidegger, *Nietzsche*, ed. David Krell (San Francisco: Harper and Row 1979–87).

Interview on Martin Heidegger (1986)[*]

Cayley: Earlier in our interview you described Martin Heidegger as the consummate thinker of our age. Why?
Grant: In his first great book, *Being and Time* – and there you have historicism right in the title, don't you? – Heidegger describes man as a being towards death. He says that human beings, insofar as they are conscious, are the beings who at every moment of their lives know they are going to die. Death is a temporal event and he is saying, I think with enormous clarity, that the centre of the modern world is choice, anxiety about death, and extreme individualism. All thought arises from the concrete, dynamic situation of the individual. This is what he says in *Being and Time*, and what I have called historicism. Now, I would say – and this is just my judgment – that since his experience with National Socialism and his experience of the war and the smashing of Europe in the war, all of his later thought has been an attempt to escape from this historicism. When I talk about historicism I think of it as just an expression of existentialism. Existentialism is the least of it; and when you think of the philosophic movement called existentialism the rest are nowhere compared to Heidegger. In a certain sense, Sartre is just a plagiarist of Heidegger. They're all little people who've just borrowed bits from Heidegger.

For Germany, existentialism was intellectually what National Socialism was politically. I'm not saying that Heidegger was trying to free himself from guilt or anything – that's not Heidegger at all. He had other reasons for trying to say what the limits of existentialism are in his writing since 1945. Right after the war, when he was prevented from teaching in Germany by the Allied forces and the French were longing to see him, the first thing he wrote was a letter to a French friend, called 'A Letter on Humanism.' There he expresses most wonderfully his dissatisfaction with existentialism as a category and says he wants to try to go on thinking. He doesn't say that this great and wonderful book *Being and Time* is wrong but he says he wants to say more.

I'm trying to express this in a spirit of fairness to Heidegger because he's been so abused in the Western world. This was a very great genius – I have no doubt at all that he is *the* great philosopher of the modern era. For myself, for instance, nobody has spoken so wonderfully about

[*]David Cayley, *George Grant in Conversation* (Toronto: Anansi 1995).

what technology *is*, and seen it with prodigious attention. I mean modern in the sense that there wasn't anything like what we call technology in the ancient world. There was technique, and there were arts, but technology is essentially a modern phenomenon, and it is to me the overwhelming phenomenon. Heidegger expressed this in a marvelous way when people asked him about capitalism and communism, and he said that capitalism and communism are just predicates of the subject technology. I think that is true. They make a difference; they are predicates and they are very different predicates. One can speak very profoundly against communism and, indeed, speak very profoundly against capitalism and their different vices; but I think Heidegger has seen that the essential event of Western civilization at its end is modern technology, which is now becoming worldwide.

Cayley: Heidegger, in a very beautiful passage, says that we're 'too late for the gods and too early for being.' 'Being's poem, which is man,' he says, 'has just begun.' So 'we must be claimed by being, we must be willing to dwell in the nameless.' And this reminds me of your own insistence that we must be willing to really experience the darkness of our time, and listen for what you have called 'intimations of deprival.'

Grant: I have to say that, for me, this is like talking about Mozart: I am honoured when you say I share anything with Heidegger, but here one is in the presence of genius I could never be near, and I must say that. Heidegger does say that 'we're too late for the gods,' but he also said towards the end, 'Only a god will save us.' Now, in the Western world, if you use an article before God, you're not talking about the god of the Bible, who is just God. You're talking about gods, in the sense that Apollo was a great god; and I think Apollo *was* a great god, and not just, as we now say, a 'myth.' Now, I think it is indubitably true that Heidegger is in some sense reaching for polytheism again. When he says we are too late for the gods, he does agree that we are too late; but in a way he is hoping, because he thinks that polytheism, the return to the gods, would be a wonderful thing.

I can't really speak about this without coming back to technology because it seems to me he is speaking about passing outside the position where everything is an object and our relation to it is to summon it before us to give us its reasons. What he means by 'being here' is very close in a certain sense to the ancient tradition, expressed not just in Christianity but in India, and in a different way in China, and the Mediterranean world. He is speaking against a view of life in which we are totally summed up in technology, in which all our relations are relations to objects which we summon before us to give us their reasons. He's speaking against everything being controlled, and in favour of waiting upon what is. We must not stand before what is in the relation of subjects who want to control objects. We must be open to what is and wait upon it. This is not so much said in *Sein und Zeit*, where he just lays down existentialism with consummate, extraordinary brilliance, but in the later works where he turns to the very great German poet Hölderlin. The poets are those who listen to what is. This is the point of his quotations from Mozart. It's all the language of participation in the later Heidegger, in his attempt to say not that existentialism is not true but that one must pass beyond it. I think he was very appalled by the existentialist movement and its silliness.

Cayley: He quotes from Hölderlin the line, 'Where the danger is grows the saving power also.' He seems to feel that in our extremity a god will appear, because the nature of the extremity opens us to being. Is this a view that you share with him?

Grant: Yes, certainly, if one says that this polytheism is in some sense within Christianity, and all I mean by within Christianity is allowing the Gospels to be present and allowing philosophy to be present. So I share it with him, but I have to make the qualification that I think Heidegger has in a very deep way – though there are things that say the opposite – said no not only to the details of Western Christianity but to what seems to me always true of Christianity. And I don't want to say yes to this.

One of the interesting things about Heidegger, and something which I think is very central, is that all the previous great German philosophers had been in their origins Protestants. Many of them later forsook it, but they were in their *origins* Protestant. Heidegger is the first very great German philosopher who was in his origins a Catholic. He was going to be a Catholic priest, though he left it a very long time ago. His origins are in Aristotle, and he is, it seems to me, the greatest commentator on Aristotle who has ever lived. But my origins are not philosophically in Aristotle, they're in Plato, and I want to be careful that this separation between the eternal and time, which is so central to Platonism, is maintained, and I'm not sure it is maintained in Heidegger. That's why I'm being cautious.

Cayley: In what sense is this distinction not maintained in Heidegger?

Grant: Well, this is a queer language to use, but whatever Christianity may be, it cannot get away from the crucifixion. Whatever Christianity may be, one sees here the just man being most hideously put to death, and this means to me that in Christianity there is always not only the presence of God but also the absence of God. I would say that this is central to Christianity, and that all the talk about what it is and what it isn't has often been an argument between the presence and the absence of God. Now, my question is how much the absence of God is maintained in Heidegger, and how much the absence of God is maintained in polytheism. I want to be very careful because the very substance of what I have thought about anything would go if I couldn't believe in the absence of God. And I'm not sure that this is maintained in Heidegger. This takes us to Simone Weil, who understood the absence of God with consummate genius.

It may be slightly opportunistic, but what I have learned from Heidegger is the meaning of technology. Nobody has written about it comparably or in such wonderful detail. Beyond that, I haven't really gotten that far with Heidegger, but I am inclined to think that the absence of God is not present. That's immediately talking in a contradiction, but emphasis on the absence of God seems to me to be necessary for Christianity and for anything which attempts to be true.

Confronting Heidegger's *Nietzsche* (1988)[*]

It may seem strange that I pay tribute to a friend (to whom my debt is great) by making some comments about a commentary. But the very nature of that debt is expressed in these comments, Professor Doull has never reduced his study of the past to antiquarianism. Although a remarkable and careful student of the past, he has always known that philosophy is an activity practised now, and that its end is far higher than that of scholarship. The present commentary being discussed here is masterfully achieved at the level of scholarship, but is far more than that. It is a philosopher confronting another philosopher and in that confrontation bringing to explicitness what he considers to be the great tasks of thought in the present.

One task of thought today is to try to understand the claims of the moderns concerning the novelty of their experiments. To use Platonic language, it is necessary to think about the novelness of those novelties. A hundred years ago Nietzsche's writing made explicit (whatever

---

[*] George Grant, 'Confronting Heidegger's *Nietzsche*,' intended for a collection of essays in honour of James Doull. This is a preliminary draft, unfinished at the time of Grant's death.

his extravagances) what is and must be assumed if one is within modernity. He did this from his own 'withinness' and with epigrammatic contempt for the deepest traditions of the West. Because of the extremity and high style of his writing, the response to his understanding of modernity has often been shallow, particularly among English-speaking people. It has consisted either of patronizing Nietzsche's thought, or of admiring simply its surface. Heidegger's gift to us in this commentary is to unwrap it as both profound and careful. I know no other writing about Nietzsche which is comparatively useful for the understanding of his thought, and so for the understanding of the modern within its own consciousness of itself.

This is done not only at the level of the immediacies with which technological society presents us. Heidegger places Nietzsche within the history of Western thought. He places him within his own wonderful account of how Western life has been determined by that history. (To say 'wonderful' is not to say 'true.') Anyone who wishes to come nearer to philosophy at this time, must look at this account of its history *en pleine connaissance de cause*. This account of the history turns on Heidegger's confrontation (one might even say his sustained attack) with Plato. Nowhere, not even within Nietzsche's writing, has there been a more consummate account of the modern position that Plato led Western thought into its basic misunderstandings. Within that context these lectures may be taken as an important stage of Heidegger's thinking. They were given between 1936 and 1940, and are clearly at least Heidegger's second magnum opus – second that is to *Sein und Zeit.*[*] Derrida[†] seems to take them as the centre of Heidegger's thought, and as the originator of deconstruction he is certainly a remarkable student of Heidegger. It is proper to say here that my writing about this subject in this place is apposite, because the heart of my debt to Professor Doull lies in the fact that he taught me how to read the central books of the *Republic*.

It is important that this remarkable commentary be studied by English-speaking people interested in philosophy. Many of us are not capable of the German necessary for the original. After the war of 1939–45, the English retreated into a provincial account of philosophy. As a young man I heard such leaders of the analytical school as

[*]Martin Heidegger, *Being and Time* (1927).
[†]Jacques Derrida (1930–), French literary critic, creator of deconstructionism, influenced by Heidegger.

A.J. Ayer and G. Ryle* give a two-evening seminar on Heidegger's thought, in which they mostly ridiculed it as consisting essentially of obvious mistakes in the use of the verb 'to be.' The later English school of the philosophy of language made central to their work the writings of the Austrian Wittgenstein. But they used his work as coming forth from someone who had taken upon himself the essence of English secularism. At that time, of course, most English people assumed they had won a victory in the war, and therefore saw no need to study the thought of their defeated enemies. The popular form of English progressivism had become the union of empiricism in science with utilitarianism in public and private ethics. Such a combination was deemed sufficient to come to terms with the immense uncertainties which were consequent on the growing realization of technological society. That is, they attempted to deal with technological modernity without seeing any need to understand it. They had no reason to study Nietzsche, who a hundred years ago had thought that modernity from within itself. A fortiori they had no reason to look at Heidegger's enucleation of that account, or his emendation of it in the light of the events of the intervening decades. The Americans, who in fact had won the war, were in the happier position of having little philosophic tradition of their own, other than in politics. Despite the usefulness of behaviourist models for capitalist organization, there were still chinks in the monolith through which alternative models of thought could arise. Into these chinks filtered a greater interest in the history of philosophy than was possible in England. This study was fostered particularly by German Jewish scholars who had been driven from their country by National Socialism.

It is by Americans that this excellent translation has been produced. The German text was published in 1961. It was translated into French in 1971. The final volume of this English translation was published in 1982. High praise must be paid to Professor David Krell, who edited all the volumes with care and intelligence. He also translated the first two volumes and participated in the translation of the third. He provides an 'analysis' at the end of each volume and a glossary of English and German words. (I put the word 'analysis' in quotation marks because I am not sure that this is the correct word for the useful

---

*Sir A.J. Ayer and Gilbert Ryle were prominent Oxford philosophers of the analytical school, who discounted the importance of metaphysics.

addenda.) But this is quibbling. All friends of philosophy must feel a debt of gratitude to Professor Krell for his splendid planning and execution of this work.

... It is not primarily for the purpose of understanding Nietzsche that I write about these books; nor simply for that of understanding Heidegger; but because in these volumes Plato and Christianity are shown as profoundly mistaken. My task is to justify Plato in the face of what Heidegger says. This will necessarily entail understanding what Heidegger is saying about the history of Western philosophy. For him, Plato is the first metaphysician, Nietzsche the last. To elucidate Nietzsche's thought Heidegger must say what metaphysics has been, he must face its originator. Heidegger has written elsewhere about Nietzsche, for example in *What Is Called Thinking?* He has also written elsewhere about Plato, notably in *Plato's Doctrine of Truth* – a work contemporaneous with these lectures. But it is in these four volumes that he 'confronts' both Nietzsche and Plato.

Heidegger has said that the only real criticism of another thinker is a confrontation with that thinker. The German word he uses is '*aus-ein-ander-setzung*.' As a verb it is '*aus einander setzen*.' It has often been translated as 'to explain.' Generally it is difficult to transcribe German words properly into English ones of Latin root. Yet in this case the German words can be almost literally transcribed as 'confrontation' and 'to confront.' To confront is to place oneself face to face with another. In the sixteenth century the word was used to mean 'to present a bold front.' As it is arrogance indeed to confront a genius such as Heidegger, and an even greater arrogance to speak, as it were, for Plato, let me say that I am indeed presenting a bold front to both Heidegger and Plato. Megalomaniac or not, I do it out of my loyalty to Plato. Perhaps even more it is done out of loyalty to Christianity. In these volumes Heidegger only mentions Christianity occasionally and it is always with the accents of contempt.

It hardly needs saying that this also makes my comment apposite in a tribute to Professor Doull. He shares with me the refusal to exclude Christianity from philosophy, or philosophy from Christianity. He has never been one to think that philosophy is a pleasant extra for cultivated human beings, but rather something to illuminate our very existence in the here and now.

I am going to indicate briefly what will later need much careful explication, and point to where in each volume the main confrontations between Heidegger and Plato take place.

Volume I

The title of volume I, *The Will to Power as Art,* is the title of the fourth chapter of the third book of Nietzsche's posthumous work. Before proceeding to the direct discussion of art, Heidegger states the basic philosophical intention of his interpretation of Nietzsche.

> The inquiry goes in the direction of asking what the being is. This traditional 'chief question' of Western philosophy we call the guiding question. But it is only the *penultimate* question. The *ultimate,* i.e. the *first* question is: what is Being itself? This question, the one which above all is to be unfolded and grounded, we call the grounding question of philosophy, because in it philosophy first inquires into the ground of beings as *ground,* inquiring at the same time into its own ground and in that way grounding itself. Before the question is posed explicitly, philosophy must, if it wants to ground itself, get a firm foothold on the path of an epistemology or doctrine of consciousness; but in so doing it remains forever on a path that leads only to the anteroom of philosophy, as it were, and does not penetrate to the very centre of philosophy. The grounding question remains as foreign to Nietzsche as it does to the history of thought prior to him. (67)

As has been said many times, the central difficulty of translating Heidegger into English, as compared for example with translating him into French, is the form of the English infinitive. The structure of the English infinitive, accompanied by any sense of English style, inhibits the translation of the German '*das Sein*' into 'the to be.' Neologisms are not always unacceptable but this one surely is. I think the present translation has used the happiest solution to this problem. It uses 'being' for all particular beings, and 'Being' for the German infinitive, and the substantive derived from it. Nevertheless, in reading the work one must always bear in mind the infinitive form of the verb when the word 'Being' is used. Any forgetting will lead one away from the core of Heidegger's thought.

As Heidegger is saying that the grounding question remains foreign not only to Nietzsche but to all thought prior to Nietzsche, he obviously is including Plato. The extremity of Heidegger's claim about his own thought in this passage must not turn our minds away from trying to reach what Plato would have thought about such a claim.

As Heidegger turns to Nietzsche's account of art, an explication of

Plato's account becomes his means of bringing out the essence of Nietzsche's position. He states why this is so in the following words:

> According to Nietzsche's teaching concerning the artist, and seen in terms of the one who creates, art has its actuality in the rapture of embodying life. Artistic configuration and portrayal are grounded essentially in the realm of the sensuous. Art is affirmation of the sensuous. According to the doctrine of Platonism, however, the supersensuous is affirmed as genuine being. Platonism, and Plato, would therefore logically have to condemn art, the affirmation of the sensuous, as a form of non-being and as what ought not to be, as a form of ` ˘ .* In Platonism, for which truth is supersensuous, the relationship to art apparently becomes one of exclusion, opposition, and antithesis; hence one of discordance. If, however, Nietzsche's philosophy is the reversal of Platonism, and if the true is thereby affirmation of the sensuous, then truth is the same as what art affirms, i.e., the sensuous. For inverted Platonism, the relationship of truth and art can only be one of univocity and concord. If in any case a discordance should exist in Plato (which is something we must still ask about, since not every distancing can be conceived as discordance), then it would have to disappear in the reversal of Platonism, which is to say, in the cancellation of such philosophy.
>
> Nevertheless, Nietzsche says that the relationship is a discordance, indeed, one which arouses dread. He speaks of the discordance that arouses dread, not in the period *prior* to his own overturning of Platonism, but precisely during the period in which the inversion is decided for him. (162-3)

To compare the felicitous discordance between art and truth in Plato with the raging discordance between the two in Nietzsche, Heidegger first describes Plato's account of the matter, and then shows how Nietzsche inverts the Platonic philosophy, and how from that inversion the relation between art and truth is changed. To do this Heidegger first comments on Plato's discussion of art as imitation (*mimesis*) in the *Republic,* particularly the discussion of this in Book X. He then discusses *Phaedrus* (248a–250a5) which passage is a height in Socrates's speech on love in response to Phaedrus. Heidegger writes: 'Plato deals with the beautiful and with Eros primarily in the *Symposium.* The questions posed in the *Republic* and *Symposium* are conjoined

*Mēon (Greek), translated here as 'that which ought not to be.'

and brought to an original and basic position with a view to the fundamental questions of philosophy in the dialogue *Phaedrus.*' (167)

It hardly needs saying that the commentaries on these passages are
written from out of that closeness of attention which characterizes
Heidegger's writing about other philosophers. Yet it must also be said
that the exposition of what Plato is stating in these passages is inevitably
expressed by Heidegger from within (the very preposition seems presumptuous) what he thinks thinking to be. At this point it is hard to
clarify the implications of this sentence. Suffice it to say that on the one
hand I must avoid any implication that what Plato is saying can be laid
before others from out of some neutral stance of 'objectivity.' Nobody
is clearer than Heidegger that the account of one philosopher by
another cannot be simply a matter of 'objective' scholarship. Whatever
else may be true of philosophy, it transcends the stance of 'objectivity.'
On the other hand, to state this must not cloud the fact that what Plato
is saying in these passages is, in the very moment of its exposition by
Heidegger, placed within the Heideggerian universe of discourse. For
example, the Greek *aletheia*, which has been traditionally translated as
'truth,' is there used as that 'bringing out of concealment,' which is
Heidegger's translation of the word. Beyond such translations, these
commentaries assume throughout that Plato is philosophizing without
raising what is for Heidegger the ultimate question of philosophy:
'What is Being (to be)?'

This does not imply anything about Heidegger as trivial as that he begs
the question. Indeed, the fact that he so little begs any question is what
raises these accounts of Plato to the immediacy of confrontation. To put
it barely: the very clarity of Heidegger's incomparable *thinking* of historicism, from out of his assertion that human beings are only authentically
free when they recognize that they are thrown into a particular historical
existence, meets here the clarity of Plato's insistence that thought, at its
purest, can rise above the particularities of any historical context, that
indeed philosophy stands or falls by its ability to transcend the historical.
Describing this as the central theoretical division in all Western thought
is perhaps a mere expression of my struggling uncertainty as to who
misses what in this greatest of confrontations.

Volume II

Of the four volumes, *The Eternal Recurrence of the Same* is most concerned with the direct exposition of Nietzsche's teaching. By calling it

'direct exposition' I mean to distinguish it from the illumination of Nietzsche's teaching which places it within the history of philosophy. There is in this volume a lucid account of Nietzsche's doctrine through the course of his later writing, and a consummate exposition of what it is to think this doctrine as true. Because this is the content, Heidegger's confrontation with Plato is less immediate than in the other volumes. Of course, Plato is present in the negative sense that the very nature of the teaching precludes the possibility that Plato's position on existential matters could be true.

Section 25, towards the end of this volume, is called *The Essence of a Fundamental Metaphysical Position: The Possibility of Such Positions in the History of Western Philosophy.* This is a propaedeutic to the last chapter on *Nietzsche's Fundamental Metaphysical Position.* The general section (25) must be chosen out as one of the heights of Heidegger's writing anywhere. As the thinker who announced 'the end of metaphysics,' he here lays before us why metaphysics has been at the core of the greatness of Western human beings. Although not by name, Plato is present throughout this chapter as the first metaphysician. Indeed, in any confrontation with Heidegger concerning his account of Plato, the question of the possibility of metaphysics will be near the centre, and the last chapters of this volume must be seen as preparatory to what will be discussed in the next volume.

Volume III

It has been frequently said that in the lectures of 1939 and 1940, which constituted volumes III and IV, Heidegger is turning away from Nietzsche and is less concerned with laying him before us than in the first two lecture courses. Be that as it may, the lecture course of Volume III, *The Will to Power as Knowledge*, is a wonderful exposition of what is involved in Nietzsche's account of truth as a form of illusion. I can only stand by my own experience, which is that these lectures have made clear to me in a quite new way what it is to think of Nietzsche's account of truth as a kind of error. Heidegger states as 'the all-decisive question': 'What happens when the distinction between a true world and an apparent world falls away? What becomes of the metaphysical essence of truth?' (134).

The confrontation with Plato in this Volume III is only partially explicit, but is of course always present. These lectures are in this sense very close to Heidegger's work of 1947: *Plato's Teaching Concerning Truth.*

This account of what Heidegger meant by 'truth' may indeed have come to him from Nietzsche (here the relations are very uncertain.) However, in what he says in Volume III about truth he is led beyond [?] Nietzsche. [The manuscript ends here.]

JEAN-JACQUES ROUSSEAU (1712–78)

Throughout the 1970s Grant had been satisfied that Nietzsche's account of modern consciousness, time as history, was the deepest. However, in the later 1970s he began to study Rousseau's second discourse, On the Origins of Inequality among Men, *and concluded that Rousseau had influenced the formation of the modern consciousness even more profoundly than Nietzsche. As always, Grant's strategy was that of a negative theologian. He wanted first to expose the true basis of modernity and then to show the inadequacy of that basis. This talk was delivered to a meeting of the Canadian Political Science Association in Halifax at a session in honour of Jim Aitchison, a long-time Dalhousie political scientist and New Democratic Party activist in Nova Scotia. Grant undoubtedly considered a paper on Rousseau to be a fitting tribute to his social-democratic friend.*

... it is only this year that I discovered that Rousseau was a greater former of the modern than even Nietzsche. The result is that at the moment I am writing a long piece called 'History and Justice' which is an attempt to understand the atheism of the left better than previously. Rousseau takes my breath away with how clever he is in destroying the old tradition by saying that reason is acquired by human beings in a way that can be explained without teleology. To try to demolish Rousseau (and, therefore, marxism) seems to me essential these days to free people from that which can hold them from ever thinking that Christianity might be true.

– George Grant to Joan O'Donovan, 1982

Why Read Rousseau? (1981)

... To start with a fact: English-speaking teachers of philosophy have rarely paid serious attention to the two most comprehensive thinkers of the anti-theological tradition – namely Rousseau and Nietzsche. (If I were speaking simply politically I would have said atheist thinkers.) This is an interesting fact about us. Of course, such neglect has required justification. In this case the justification has been that neither Rousseau nor Nietzsche were philosophers in the serious sense of that term. As English-speaking teachers of philosophy have generally been secularized Protestants or Jews, lack of seriousness was therefore considered a serious accusation. Indeed, both Rousseau and Nietzsche had a high sense of the comic. Rousseau has been taken as an unsystematic poet – a man of intense, if misguided insights, quite incapable of the sustained and disciplined thought necessary to the true philosopher. Such an account is found in many places from Bentham to Popper. One can find it perhaps in its barest folly in Bertrand Russell's *History of Western Philosophy*. One might have expected that Russell would have turned his ire most vehemently against Christian philosophers such as Augustine and Aquinas. But no: it is in the chapter about Rousseau that his contempt and anger reaches its height. Rousseau should not be called a philosopher; he is a self-indulgent poet. His thought is filled with contradictions of such an obvious nature that they could be discovered by any high school student of average ability. His insights culminate politically in National Socialism, etc., etc. Moreover, in this long chapter, précis are given of Rousseau's chief writings. In these précis I cannot recognize the originals.

Why have such interpretations of Rousseau been so consistently sustained within our tradition? After all, modern English thought has also been anti-theological in its intent. My purpose in this paper will be to touch upon the causes of this lack of attention and to say why it has had a bad effect on our self-understanding.

It will not be possible to substantiate the major premiss of my argument in the course of a short paper. To show that Rousseau is a comprehensive metaphysical philosopher of a very high order would require a long book of commentary. That premiss will simply have to be granted hypothetically if one is to follow what proceeds.

The causes of the lack of attention to Rousseau in the English-speaking world are not difficult to determine. The long ascendency of the English-speaking peoples – in the case of England from Waterloo till about 1880, of the United States since 1914 – was achieved under the rule of various species of bourgeois. (The word 'bourgeois' is itself almost a Rousseauian invention.) Members of classes are liable to consider their shared conceptions of political right to be self-evident, when their rule is not seriously questioned at home, and when they are successfully extending their empires around the world. Constitutional liberalism went with technological progress and was justified by various permutations and combinations of Lockeian contractualism and utilitarianism. Older elements of our tradition from before the age of progress, such as Protestantism, continued, but till lately in weakened political influence. There were outbreaks of more modern political thought, such as marxism in the United States of the 1930s and 1960s. However, these were but bubbles on the surface of a Lockeian ocean. English-speaking writers on political philosophy have largely been concerned with emendations of the Lockeian account. That Locke should be taken as the master of this tradition is always clarified for me in the fact that an atheist wrote a book entitled *The Reasonableness of Christianity.*

Why, then, should we read Rousseau? By 'we' I mean people concerned with political philosophy. If I were addressing modern political theorists at this gathering, I would have written a different paper and employed the style of Céline's three little dots. The reason we should read Rousseau is the presence of the concept 'history' on the English-speaking stage. I mean by the word 'history' that temporal process in which beings are believed by some to have acquired their abilities. Because of the ambiguity of the word in English, I must insist that I am using it not to denote a form of study but a realm of being. At this point German is clearer with its distinction between the words 'Historie' and 'Geschichte.' I use it here as the Germans use it in a phrase such as 'Die Geschichte der Natur' – the history of nature. (In so using it I neither assert nor deny that Geschichte is horse-Geschichte.)

For English-speaking peoples, 'history' took its place upon the public stage inescapably with Darwin. The historical sense was, of course, present in English intellectual circles long before that. But with Darwin it became central for the English because it was at the heart of the most important activity of the age – natural science. To use a too common German word, it entered our Weltanschauung. It is often said by interpreters of Darwin that his essential discovery was not 'evolution' but how evolution took place – namely by natural selection. After all the word 'evolution' had been part of the intellectual baggage of Europe since Diderot. This is true. But listen to Darwin himself, writing to Gray in 1863: 'Personally, of course, I care much about Natural Selection; but that seems to me utterly unimportant, compared to the question of Creation or Modification.' (*Life and Letters*, vol. II, 371.)

Obviously he is right, modification is the central issue. And obviously also, modification in this sense is just a synonym for 'history.'

Once 'history' is part of our intellectual baggage, what happens to the political science of Locke? Lockeian contractualism is ahistorical. This difficulty of holding together history and ahistorical contractualism is above all what has made English-speaking political philosophy thinner and thinner to the point of the sheer formalism of the analytical tradition. On the other hand, the freedom of our thought from historicism has in practical affairs helped to save us from some of the crimes of communism and National Socialism. Nevertheless, my concern here is not with the practical world but with the inanition that this disregard of the idea of 'history' has caused in our thought. The attempt to maintain contractualism freed from any ontological statements simply fails because it requires that science be taken in phenomenalist and instrumentalist senses. It may be possible to attempt this about the small results of academic technological scientists; it is quite impossible to assume it about the results of a great synthetic scientist such as Darwin. He knew that he was talking about what is. When one is taught Darwinism at school one is not taught it alone as a useful hypothetical tool, only of interest for those who are going to be specialists in the life sciences. The present controversy in the U.S., between those who want Darwinism taught in the schools and those who want creationism, cuts across all the clever talk by the analytical philosophers. Both parties know that what is at issue is ontology. (Let me say in parenthesis that I think the dominant academic community on this continent has been unwise to patronize these people known as the moral majority. My involvement with such people in common Christian tasks has taught me to the contrary.)

What is at issue here as far as political philosophers are concerned is that you cannot hope to combine successfully an ahistorical political philosophy with a natural science which is at its heart historical.

With the idea of history – call it if you will modification – we are inescapably led back to Rousseau. For it was Rousseau who first stated that what we are is not given us by what in the ancient language was called nature but is the result of what human beings were forced to do to overcome chance or to change nature (in the modern sense of that term.) Human beings have become what they are and are becoming what they will be. We are the free, that is to say the undetermined animals, who can be understood by a science which is not teleological. We can be understood 'historically.' It is well to bear in mind that late in his life Rousseau said that the 2nd Discourse was his boldest writing. It was in it that he risked most to say openly what he meant.

Why we must read Rousseau is that when we look at the sciences today we see that they are everywhere historical. I have quoted before the title of von Weizsäcker's book *Die Geschichte der Natur.*[*] And when we seek the originating moment of that idea of history we come upon Rousseau. Indeed, to use for a moment the modern way of talking which distinguishes the words 'philosophy' and 'science,' it seems to me that always when there is a great outpouring of scientific activity – in my present example the nineteenth-century historicizing of nature – there lies behind that activity some philosopher who in his thought about the whole had made a breakthrough as against all previous thought. When I say 'breakthrough' please do not think I am speaking in terms of the progress of truth. To put it extremely simply, breakthroughs can be into error. To say whether Rousseau's idea of modification was true or false is not a question I am qualified to answer. But to bolster my amour propre: Who is? We must wait and perhaps see.

What I am able to say, however, is that Rousseau as the originator of that idea of history is an example of another strange fact. Often the originator of a great breakthrough in thought understands the thought he is thinking in its implications more comprehensively than those who follow him and live within that thought, modifying it and clarifying it. In its primal moment – or, to quote Heidegger, in its coming out into unconcealment – that thought appears in all its ambiguity. What makes Rousseau such a master is that he ponders the implications of the idea of history with such care. If one reads, for example, one of Rousseau's most influential epigones, Marx, one does not find that battling with the contradictions raised by the idea of history that one finds in Rousseau. It is indeed this battling with these contradictions which has often led English-speaking commentators to take Rousseau as a weak thinker whose inconsistencies can be pointed out in some desultory tutorial at Oxford or Harvard. The contradictions which professors of philosophy often find in Rousseau come forth from his refusal to avoid the ambiguities which he finds in what he is given to think.

To praise Rousseau is not to forget his critics; to remember his critics is to speak of Nietzsche. Nietzsche may have had greater targets

---

[*] Carl Friedrich von Weizsäcker, *The History of Nature*, trans. F.D. Wieck (Chicago: University of Chicago Press 1949, 1959).

such as Plato for his contempt-laden rhetoric, but in terms of his own era it is Rousseau whom he singles out as most responsible for the decadence of European thought. Rousseau is the thinker who attempted to Christianize secularism. He is the epitome of that secularized Christianity which Nietzsche despises more than authentic Christianity itself. Yet, and it is a great 'yet,' a 'yet' which shows one the very power of Rousseau, Nietzsche accepts from Rousseau belief in the fact that we are historical, that we acquire our abilities in the course of time in a way that can be explained without teleology. Nietzsche indeed thinks that he is the first human being who has understood 'the finality of becoming' in a historical way. I am always loath to think that as a teacher of philosophy I can in any way transcend my betters. Nevertheless, I often wonder whether it be the case that in his anger towards Rousseau, Nietzsche fails to recognize how much of what he is thinking in the finality of becoming has already been thought by Rousseau. After all, we have been taught in the greatest book of political philosophy that anger is an emotion that corrupts the ability to be open to the whole. Nietzsche's hatred of equality, democracy, socialism, etc., however brilliant, often seems to fall over into anger – indeed, perhaps finally into madness. Did that anger obscure for him his debt to Rousseau? Perhaps somebody here with greater learning than myself knows for certain whether Nietzsche had read the 2nd Discourse. We could, of course, never know whether this is not the case. But it would be interesting to know whether it is the case.

The understanding that human beings acquire their abilities through the course of time expresses itself contemporaneously in that doctrine we call 'historicism,' and historicism is the fate of all branches of knowledge in our era. It is only necessary to remember that the outstanding thinker of this era is an historicist from beginning to end, however much some of his thought appears to be a quarrel with that fate. Indeed, Heidegger has expressed the consequences of historicism for the history of thought with greater clarity and profundity than any other writer. The attempts to refute historicism from within the tradition of English-speaking liberalism (for example, Sir Karl Popper's *The Poverty of Historicism*) are well intentioned, but feeble. Even Wittgenstein's effort in this direction is one of the most inadequate moments in his thought. It is sufficient reason why we should read Rousseau carefully that all efforts to know what it behooves human beings to know are today touched with the deadening hand of historicism.

To end at the level of the particular: This charming scoundrel, this enchanting paranoid, this man who often had no place to lay his head and had to flee from country to country, yet at the same time was cosseted and beloved of the great ladies of the court, this man who expounded the meaning of child-centred education and who left his own five children at the foundling hospital, this man who was the great teacher of the institutor of the Terror and the great teacher of the delicious sweetness of dalliance, this great democrat who loved the salons and boudoirs of the powerful, this man who wrote a very sane proposal for the government of Poland and who believed the height of life was to drift in a boat with his hand trailing in the water – it is a source of high comedy that he was also a careful and comprehensive philosopher. It certainly raises again the old question about which Plato and Aristotle were in disagreement: What is the relation of the moral virtues to the philosophic life? Even a Platonist such as myself who considers that what we can know is closely tied to what we love, is moved by the case of Rousseau to look again at the Aristotelian position. Whatever the truth of this difficulty, it certainly appears to me that Rousseau's influence over Europe should make us hesitant in affirming the scrutability of Providence. Perhaps it might lead us to apply analogically the attribute of comedian to Deity.

Part 4

George Grant on ... :

Reviews and Essays

FRANCIS BACON (1561–1626)

One of Grant's first publications after he accepted a teaching position at Dalhousie University in 1947 was a review of an historical study of Francis Bacon by Fulton Anderson, head of the philosophy department at the University of Toronto. Anderson was much annoyed by what he considered Grant's impertinent review, and his anger increased with the publication of Grant's 'Philosophy' article, reprinted in Part 2 of this volume. The importance of the short review of Anderson's piece on Bacon is that it shows that Grant's concern about the threat of technological was present from the beginning of his life as a philosopher. Indeed, it predated it, since the danger of technological civilization had begun to present itself to Grant while he was serving as an air raid precautions warden in London during the early stages of the Second World War.

The Philosophy of Francis Bacon (1948)[*]

Today we are faced with the paradoxical situation where the mob accepts as its priesthood those men we call scientists, when at the same time this very priesthood leads the mob shouting to the cliff. It is therefore extremely provoking to read a study of the thought of Francis Bacon, who, as much as any other, stimulated men to that study of nature, which on the one hand has given us ether and penicillin, and on the other hand mass production and scientific war. One may be allowed to say in the present journal, that it is especially interesting to read such a study by a distinguished graduate of Dalhousie.

Professor Anderson's study is not a popular essay for those who want to garner a few vague generalizations about Bacon. It is a careful and exact examination of all Bacon's writings. In the last chapter Prof. Anderson describes Bacon's contribution to thought under three headings which are worth quoting. '(1) freeing science from learning and

[*]George Grant's review of F.H. Anderson's *The Philosophy of Francis Bacon* (Chicago: Chicago University Press 1949), *Dalhousie Review,* vol. 28 (1948–9). Used with permission.

the privileges of the learned (2) separating completely truth which is humanly discoverable from the dogmas of revealed theology and (3) propounding a philosophy which is to be achieved by (a) a new sort of scientific organon (b) a "modern" interpretation of nature and (c) the identification of metaphysics with a generalized natural science based on natural history.'

Where one may criticize Professor Anderson is in his failure to judge the limitations of Bacon. The scholar is always called upon for a judgment of worth and surely in the light of what we know today, the enslavement of Bacon to the optimism of the scientific Renaissance is worth considering more deeply than Professor Anderson attempts. For instance, under point (2) quoted above, what meaning is there in Bacon's attempt to cut off truth humanly discoverable from the revealed dogmas of religion? Its only implication is that the truths of religion are not rational but arbitrary. Therefore, it leads to an exaltation of the truths of natural science, and such an exaltation, coupled with man's original sin, leads straight to the grinning mask of scientific humanism at Hiroshima. An even greater criticism of Bacon could be made at the ridiculousness of attempting an identification of metaphysics with natural science, however generalized. This book is a useful study of an earlier philosopher of natural science. It could have been an important one if Professor Anderson had judged how that philosophy had helped to bring us to the barrenness of today.

BERTRAND RUSSELL (1872–1970)

Although Lord Russell was one of the leading philosophers of the early twentieth century, especially celebrated for his contributions to mathematical theory, Grant was not particularly interested in his thought. In this essay Grant uses Russell as an eminent stalking-horse for a type of philosophy, common in Canada, which Grant thought banal and confused. He also uses his attack on Russell to disguise his assault on the Canadian philosophers, especially those in Ontario, who had criticized his essay 'Philosophy' for the Massey royal commission. Russell claimed that reason and philosophy could say nothing about questions of conduct yet wrote constantly about such questions.

Pursuit of an Illusion (1952)[*]

When Bertrand Russell has attempted to formulate the principles upon which the study of mathematics rests or when he has analyzed the nature of scientific propositions, he has made certain principles clearer than they were previously. Such activities are part of the philosopher's job and therefore it is possible to call Russell a philosopher. On the other hand, when Russell turns from discussing man as scientist to man as moral agent or as artist, he forgoes the philosopher's function. That is, in writing about conduct or art he makes no attempt to discover the principles underlying these activities. He freely admits this, of course, and says that it is simply a necessity of the human condition. Over and over again he repeats that reason has nothing positive to say about the fundamental questions of conduct.[1]

Yet having said that reason cannot tell us anything fundamental about conduct, Russell has spent most of his life writing at great length on this very subject. Since 1914 more and more of his work has dealt with such aspects of man's conduct as politics, education, religion, and sex. Why has he done this?

This would seem less contradictory if Russell simply admitted that what he has to say about human conduct is just his prejudices; admitting, in other words, that he is making no attempt to show others what are the principles of right conduct. But in his popular writings he never makes clear this distinction necessary to his own scepticism. He never states clearly when he is speaking as a philosopher and when he is gossiping about his own prejudices. From looking at Russell's writings, I am led to the conclusion that at one and the same time he has desired to assert moral scepticism (that is, the impotence of reason in the fundamentals of conduct) and has also desired to teach men about conduct, using his position of authority as a philosopher.

Of course, Russell cannot have it both ways. He cannot be sceptical about the positive role of the philosopher in discovering ethical principles and also expect us to take with any seriousness his statements about how we ought to live. His principle must apply to himself. If reason is basically impotent in practical matters, then he either ought to

[*]George Grant, 'Pursuit of an Illusion: A Commentary on Bertrand Russell,' *Dalhousie Review* (1952). Used with permission.

be silent about these questions or else openly admit that what he writes about them has no rational content. And, of course, if he admits the latter, then there is no reason why any man should take what he writes about conduct seriously. We do not listen attentively when the brilliant mathematician is talking baby talk to his children.

It is this contradiction that makes difficult any systematic analysis of Russell's recent broadcast talks, *Living in an Atomic Age*. Does he claim for them any of the persuasive power of reason, or are they just intended as so much rhetoric that will stir us emotionally? As to Russell's intention, it is hard to answer this question one way or the other. Indeed, the strange division in Russell's soul is particularly evident throughout these talks. I would say he must be a man with the worldly wit and cultivated style of the aristocrat, combined with a preacher's hatred of man's sin and desire to improve men; but that these excellent qualities were marred by continual contradictions and a failure to reduce any question to principles. Indeed, I would say that the author was a good man and a clever man, but not a philosopher. This is the dilemma in which Russell is inevitably entangled by the contradiction between the moral scepticism which he holds in principle and the moral fervour which he adopts in practice. Because of his moral fervour he wants to speak out and convince men to be good; because of his moral scepticism he cannot speak in principles and therefore cannot speak clearly.

Let me illustrate what I mean from Russell's writings on the problem of conduct. First an example from these broadcasts. Russell is describing the present state of the world and discusses what should happen in the future. One of his chief points is that modern industry is 'a kind of rape,' and that men are using up the natural resources of our planet frivolously. He condemns this state of affairs and demands that men 'should' think of posterity. Now, of course, I am not here arguing with Russell as to the facts. I quite agree with him as to what men are doing and that we should carefully husband our resources for the sake of future generations. I am not arguing with him as an economist, but as a philosopher. Within his own philosophical position, what does Russell mean by the word 'should?' The word 'should' presumably means men ought to do this or that. It is one of the fundamental words that Western men have used about their conduct. But if Russell is right and reason cannot speak about the fundamentals of conduct, then he is using the word 'should' with no rational significance. What, then, does he mean when he says that men 'should' think about posterity?

From what Russell has written on this matter elsewhere, I would infer either that he means that he likes men to take posterity into account, or else that he commands them to do so. That is, he would say that fundamental ethical terminology such as 'should' is not meant rationally, but either emotively (that is, imply like or dislike) or imperatively (that is, as implying command). Accordingly, there is nothing rational in saying that men should take thought of posterity. But again I ask, if these words of Russell are, on his own showing, no more than expressions of like and dislike or of command, why should anyone listen to them? When Russell writes of mathematical principles we do not accept their validity because he likes these principles rather than others, or because he commands us to them, but because he has convinced our reason. If in writing of conduct he can show us no reason for acting one way rather than another, why should we agree? And what is more important, how can he convince anybody who disagrees with him? There are obviously men in the world who do not care to take thought for posterity. Russell can present them with no reason for caring. He simply holds up his passion for posterity against other men's passion for immediate satisfaction.

I wish I could be sure that Russell always makes clear that he does not use such words as 'should' or 'ought' with rational content. Certainly in his writings for philosophers he has made his scepticism clear. He had done his utmost to be consistent. But the same cannot be said for these broadcasts. He uses, for instance, such sentences as the following: 'I have been concerned in these lectures to set forth certain facts, and certain hopes which these facts render rational.' The phrase 'rational hopes' is plainly inconsistent with an assertion about the impotence of reason in ethics. For admitting the facts as he sees them (e.g., the rape of our natural resources), there is still no reason on his view of conduct why anything follows rationally as a hope about man's behaviour either as it should be or as it may be predicted. Why, then, does he use such phrases as 'rational hopes'?

Russell implies one set of principles for philosophers and a quite contradictory set for the public. And he cannot here use the doctrine of economy as an excuse. For the man who applies this doctrine may rightly avoid the subtlety of principle in popular lectures, but he certainly cannot enunciate principles in his profound and popular writings.

There seem to me two possible explanations as to why Russell falls
into this contradiction. Perhaps he doesn't recognize he is falling into
it. If this is so then we may have less respect for him as a philosopher,
for it is the job of philosophers to ferret out contradictions. The other
possible explanation is that he wishes to convince his popular audience
that what he is saying about conduct has rational content, so that they
will accept his opinions. That is, he wishes to convince his audience of
the truth of a principle which he himself rejects as false. The idea that
reason does play a central role is so deeply embedded in the tradition
of the West that Russell perhaps thinks it is useful to foster the illusion
for his own purposes. But surely, if there is anything that all philosophers may agree on, it is that fostering illusions for whatever purpose is
not their function. Russell should have made clear in his writings that
his repeated use of the word 'should' has no rational content. I, on the
other hand, am quite ready to use the word 'should' about Russell, for
as I will attempt to show later it is a word that has in truth the deepest
rational content.

Another illustration from Russell's popular writings: in a recent
article on *Gladstone and Lenin,* he discusses the eminent men he has
known. He ends the article with the statement that 'what I have found
most unforgettable is a certain kind of moral quality, a quality of self-
forgetfulness, whether in private life, in public affairs, or in the pursuit
of truth.' He takes as an example of this quality E.D. Morel, the man
who was chiefly responsible for exposing the abuses of the Belgian government in the Congo, and who later was a pacifist in the war of 1914.
Of course I agree with Russell about the glory of the qualities he mentions. The self-forgetting man is surely the highest vision of God vouchsafed to us in this world. 'Though I speak with the tongues of men and
of angels.' E.D. Morel is equally one of my heroes. But I take issue with
Russell again at this point because his moral scepticism prevents him
from saying clearly why Morel was such a high type of human being and
therefore presumably the kind of man we should all attempt to
become. Russell can say nothing to those who would reply that Morel
was a bad type of man. And the last years leave us with no doubt that
there are men all over the world who would consider Morel misguided
or wicked. Any consistent totalitarian would say that Morel was vicious
because he considered there were principles demanding his loyalty
more than the principle of loyalty to the state. The hedonist would say
that Morel was misguided because he exalted self-forgetfulness above
his personal pleasure. Certain modern psychologists might say that

Morel's hungering and thirsting after righteousness was a sign of 'moral diabetes.' And because of Russell's scepticism, he can present no principles which will be valid against the totalitarian and which will show him why loyalty to the state cannot be a first principle of conduct. And, of course, the inference must be that if reason has nothing to say against the totalitarian, the non-totalitarian is as much confined by the prejudice and force and tradition. For either reason can speak about conduct, or else prejudice, force, and tradition are the deciding factors.

In fact, Russell, having been brought up in a certain section of nineteenth-century English society, happens to like the tradition of charity inherited from the broad line of Christian principles, the tradition of private judgment inherited from Puritanism, and the traditions of humane conduct that comes to the west from the Greeks. As he likes these, he admires Morel who partook of all of them so beautifully. But Russell's defence of these qualities can only lie in a completely irrational acceptance of one tradition as against another.

Russell, who has spent so much of his life making fun of tradition, finally must rest his case as to the central issue of human life – standards for action – on a traditionalism which reason is completely impotent to criticize or improve. The churches he so castigated for irrationalism and traditionalism were never so irrationalist or traditionalist as that. No Protestant or Catholic would go so far as Russell.

II

The question, then, which Russell's philosophy raises is whether reason can be practical. I believe this is the most important issue of all philosophy, for if we say with Russell that our action cannot be finally regulated by principles, we are saying that in the most important aspect of our nature reason is impotent.

In discussing this issue, it is first necessary to state Russell's position more fully. As I understand Russell, the place of reason in our life is to help us to find the means to achieve what our passions lead us to desire. Means belong to reason; ends to passion. If we desire riches more than anything else, the place of reason is to show us how to get rich. If our chief end is the conquest of women, reason will help us to become expert seducers. Reason can also show us the probable consequences of pursuing one course of action as against another. What reason cannot do is tell us whether those consequences are good or bad. It cannot tell us what is the proper end of all conduct. We must rely on our emotions for that central direction. According to Russell, the role of reason is confined to logical and empirical concepts, and does not extend to the regulation of our wills by principles.

In criticizing this view, up to this point, I have simply tried to make clear some of its consequences. The consequences for society are clearly that, when disagreement arises over ultimate principles of conduct, the issue must be decided by force or passion. If one American likes to lynch Negroes and another American says it is wrong, the issue can only finally be decided by force. The American who hates lynching can indeed say with reason that such and such are certain consequences of lynch law. If, however, the other American is ready to accept these consequences and still likes lynching, there is nothing further that reason can say. In personal life there is no point in using our intelligence to judge what persons we should accept as examples. There is no meaning in saying that Copernicus or Socrates or Milton chose worthier ends than Himmler[*] or Napoleon or Mickey Spillane.[†]

Any argument from consequences is, of course, only of limited value. It must be supplemented by some positive grounds for thinking otherwise. Clarity about consequences is, however, necessary, for down the ages it has led men desperately to inquire whether there is not some intellectually respectable position other than moral emotionalism. In the Platonic dialogues, Socrates returns again and again to the consequences of scepticism, so that he can persuade the young men to see how in fact reason does operate in their lives.

It is necessary now to turn to the positive reasons why philosophers have believed that our practical life can be regulated by reason. In stating these grounds I would point out to those readers who are not philosophers by profession (it will be obvious to those who are) that nothing I say has any originality. It has all been said, once and for all, in that most brilliant of philosophic works, Plato's *Republic*. In modern philosophy much the same argument has been put by Kant. Also, it will be clear that what I say on this matter is not meant as a complete statement of the case for ethical rationalism. That could only be done in greater compass than this article allows. It is simply an outline of the rationalist position, given to make clearer the difference between it and Russell's irrationalism. Anyone who wants a systematic account of ethi-

---

[*]Heinrich Himmler (1900–45), German Nazi leader, head of the SS.
[†]Mickey Spillane (1918–), American detective writer, creator of Mike Hammer.

cal rationalism can of course find it in Plato's *Republic*, Kant's *Critique of Practical Reason*, or the nineteenth book of Augustine's *City of God.*

Men act in the world to achieve purposes. We are moved to action by desire. We act because we think it will be good to achieve this or that object of our desire. The question, then, at issue is the relationship of desire to reason in our consciousness. To repeat, Russell's position is that reason helps us to find means to achieve what our passions lead us to desire. The position I maintain is that reason and desire are far more intimately bound in consciousness. The vast range of our particular desires does not appear simply as a chaos, because reason presents us with the idea of universality as an end, in which that very unity which we call the self, and not mere separate desires, will be satisfied. It is this idea of the highest good which allows the struggle between unity and diversity in our selves to seek reconciliation. Because of it all particular desires do not appear to us completely uncoordinated, but can be brought into some intelligible hierarchy, under the regulation of this principle of spirit. The union of reason and desire is even more intimate than this, because not only does reason give us this idea of a highest good, it also desires to realize itself therein. This is what is meant when we say our wills are rational. We are moved by the desire for rationality itself. I would say that we see this not only in personal conduct, but also in the striving of the scientist for universality, in the desire of the lawyer for a just law.

To put the same point in slightly different language, I would say that this is what we mean when we use words such as 'should' or 'ought' or 'duty.' When we say that it is the duty of man to do this or that we mean that he should follow a course of conduct not motivated by the particularities of his pleasure at any given moment, but by some principle that is universal and therefore is law for him, irrespective of the passing whims of his consciousness. What seems to us the conflict between duty and desire is just the conflict between the desire for the highest good and the desire for some less whole good which arises from the particularity of our natures. To use Russell's example of E.D. Morel, how did Morel transcend the particularities of his passing desires to hold to with sufficiently abiding desire the interests of the Africans in the Congo, unless his reason gave him this idea of a universal good, which by his formulation of it called him to the service of their proper interests? When Russell says that we 'should' take thought of posterity rather than our immediate greeds, surely such ethical foresight is only possible if reason does give us an idea of a highest good in the knowledge of which we can transcend the pressing particularity of our desires?

There are, however, two points I wish to make, because they always seem to arise in a discussion of the practical reason. The first concerns the appeal to the so-called facts of life. Is it not a fact, so this appeal runs, that men's conduct is dominated by force and passion? Is it not simply romantic to say that men act from principles? Just go into a big city during a heat wave and you will see that men are not ruled by reason. Just look at the African natives, the waitresses, the stockbrokers. Of course, the primary answer to this so-called appeal to experience is to make clear that the idea of a practical reason does not affirm what men accomplish in this world, but rather what they should accomplish. It is a matter of definition and therefore cannot be settled by the appeal to any particular experience. I am, however, quite willing to go farther and meet this appeal to experience by a contrary one. I have never met a human being who does not hold some conception of the highest good, however imperfectly formulated and imperfectly followed. That is, I have never met a human being who was not capable of giving some faint semblance of order to his desires.

To go even further, to deny that reason operates in the conduct of all men is to deny that most men have any chance of leading the rational life. For most men in this world have not the opportunity to develop their reasons in the practice of some art or science. The means for rationality is given to most persons only through their conduct. The slum mother has no chance for the life of science or art, but only achieves rationality by exalting her family's general good above her own. To deny that reason operates in action is, then, to deny that most people even enter into the glory of existence which is rationality. To appeal again to consequences, can we dare to be so presumptuous about other men?

To the contrary, I would say that it is the chief wonder of human life that at the profoundest level all men are equal. All men are given in conduct this idea of spirit, which, however imperfectly framed because of historical circumstances, is at least sufficiently clear for them to choose whether their wills be ruled by it or not. At the same time, no man is given this idea with such perfect clarity as would eliminate for him the possibility of choice. Only on such a conception of reason as I have outlined can equality, and therefore democracy, rest. To transpose into a different language, the conception of reason presenting to all men the idea of a highest good is just the Christian belief of the image of God in all men. The denial of this by Russell and others is the denial of the only possible theoretical grounds for democracy.

The second point I wish to make is that the formulation of the principles of morality is in some ways similar and in some ways different from the formulation of the principles of logic. It is necessary to make this point, because sceptics such as Russell always emphasize the greater public agreement about logical principles, and infer therefore the invalidity of moral principle. Looking both at the differences among logicians and at the broad acceptance of the idea of the highest good in Western philosophy, I am not impressed by any idea of total divergence. Nevertheless, it is true that the formulation of moral principles is more difficult than is those of logic. It is therefore necessary to discuss in what ways I consider them similar and in what ways different.

They are similar in the following sense. We can think scientifically before we have formulated the principles of scientific thought; we can act morally before we have formulated moral principles. Yet, in both cases, the highest principle of the theoretical reason and the highest principle of practical reason, when they are formulated, are seen to be necessary to the proper functioning of thought and of conduct. So the idea of the highest good is a necessary idea. Yet, having stated that firmly, I would also state that their formulation varies in difficulty. In the formulation of the principles of conduct our wills and our desires are more deeply involved than in the formulation of theoretic principles. When we formulate mathematical principles we can use those principles in physiology or physics (in one part of our lives), while we do not use them in our relations with our wives or neighbours or the world in general. Having formulated, on the other hand, the principles of the practical reason, we are committed to a total way of life. We are committed to the effort to apply those principles universally. So, in the practical reason, what we have to surrender for the sake of clarity is the whole body of our habits. The commitment is not partial but complete. It is, therefore, only by the profoundest effort of our wills, the greatest discipline of our habits, that we can sufficiently face the problem to come to the recognition of the highest good. It is just the understanding of this difficulty that led philosophers such as Plato and Augustine humbly to insist that their ability to isolate the principles of conduct was not finally due to their own efforts, but was a gift, or in other words, grace.

If seeking the psychological and historical causes of other men's lives were not generally just mud-slinging masquerading as science, I might be tempted to speculate why the principles of the practical reason have been unclear to Russell.

III

The following are two passages from Russell's writing. The first is from an essay he wrote in 1902 called *A Free Man's Worship*. The basic argument is summed up in the final passage. I quote:

> Brief and powerless is Man's life; on him and all his race the slow, sure doom falls pitiless and dark. Blind to good and evil, reckless of destruction, omnipotent matter rolls on its relentless way; for Man, condemned to-day to lose his dearest, to-morrow himself to pass through the gate of darkness, it remains only to cherish, ere yet the blow falls, the lofty thoughts that ennoble his little day; disdaining the coward terrors to the slave of Fate, to worship at the shrine that his own hands have built; undismayed by the empire of chance, to preserve a mind free from the wanton tyranny that rules his outward life; proudly defiant of the irresistible forces that tolerate, for a moment, his knowledge and his condemnation, to sustain alone, a weary but unyielding Atlas, the world that his own ideas have fashioned despite the trampling march of unconscious power.

The second passage is the final words of *Living in an Atomic Age,* spoken in 1951:

> Man now needs for his salvation only one thing: to open his heart to joy, and leave fear to gibber through the glimmering darkness of a forgotten past. He must lift up his eyes and say: 'No, I am not a miserable sinner; I am a being who, by a long and arduous road has discovered how to make intelligence master natural objects, how to live in freedom and joy, at peace with myself, and, therefore, with all mankind.' This will happen if men will choose joy rather than sorrow. If not, eternal death will bury Man in deserved oblivion.

I have not quoted these two passages because there may seem on the surface a contradiction between Russell's appeal to doom and to joy. In my opinion, when one threads one's way through the rhetoric one finds much that is true and much that is false in both passages. Even if upon analysis these passages could in no way be reconciled, a man has a right to change his mind at least every fifty years. I quote them rather because they are both about the fundamentals of human existence – what is man's final destiny, what are the motives which any knowledge about it should inspire in our conduct? I quote them because in neither case does Russell make any attempt to appeal to reason, but simply lays down propositions as dogmatically given. And in no place in his vast writings have I been able to find any attempt to argue this basic problem.

Even if the existentialists are right when they assert that the issue between doom and joy can only be settled irrationally (and here my rationalism would of course disagree with them), still it is the philosopher's job to show clearly how that decision between joy and doom should consistently affect our conduct. Russell never attempts this consistency. Indeed, in *A Free Man's Worship* he asserts the strange position that we must pursue the rational life, even though final reality is blind chance or matter. Fifty years later he is less paradoxical, but more dogmatic. He asserts the need for men to be joyful without giving any reasons why they should be. This appeal to contradiction, dogma, and rhetoric to settle the fundamental issue of life is a final illustration of how large is the irrationalism.

Naturally, I have not written the foregoing to convince Russell. He has presumably read Plato and Kant (though his *History of Western Philosophy* might leave one in some doubt as to this). I have written it rather because I so often hear Russell talked about as a great advocate of human reason as against the obscurantism and mysticism of the older philosophy and theology. The fact remains, however, that at the centre of the old philosophy and theology there lies the proposition that man is a rational animal. This proposition meant that man can only achieve his proper end by the perfection of his reason. At the heart of Russell's thought lies the denial of this. My argument is not with those people who admire Russell and recognize this central irrationalism. It is with those who admire Russell and think in so doing they are affirming the rationality of man.

This is, indeed, the contradiction that lies at the heart of much of the modern thought that took its impetus from our scientific achievements. Men such as Freud and Marx, starting from the claim that human reason can establish truth, end up with the conclusion that man's nature is ultimately irrational. This is, of course, patently obvious in crude and hesitant thinkers such as Marx and Freud. It is less obvious but equally true of subtler men such as John Dewey and Bertrand Russell.

What final value is there in any clarity about logical principles or any appreciation of wit (both debts we owe to Russell), if men are persuaded by his philosophy that they are not rational animals, but clever beasts with a facility for mathematics? For though men are not simply clever beasts, the fact is that when they are persuaded over a length of time that they are such, they more and more act as if they were. Surely the last years are an illustration that the ground of civilized life is the assertion of our essential rationality.

Of course, to a philosopher the denial that man's rationality is his essence is particularly distressing, for it denies the use or indeed the possibility of his study. Philosophy means simply the love of wisdom, and wisdom means knowledge of the true end of life. If men are not rational they cannot reach such knowledge and therefore the attempt is the pursuit of an illusion. This is why Russell is such a confused thinker. Calling himself a philosopher, he has tried to convince men that philosophy is a waste of time.

NOTE

1 If anyone doubts that I have stated Russell's position correctly, I would refer
   him to *The Philosophy of Bertrand Russell* – in the Library of Living Philosophers – vol. 5, 531–5, 720–7. There he will find a plethora of quotations from
   Russell on this subject.

SIGMUND FREUD (1856–1939)

Sigmund Freud was the founder of psychoanalysis and one of the leading intellectual figures of the twentieth century, and his influence was ubiquitous especially in North America after the Second World War. Before Freud there had been few treatments available for mental illness and little understanding of its origins. Although many of Freud's theories have been discredited, for a while in the 1950s, 1960s, and 1970s they appeared to offer a theoretical basis upon which to develop cures for individuals and to forge a better society. Freud's ideas, such as his theory of the Oedipus complex, passed into general intellectual currency, and Grant had lingering suspicions that perhaps they explained somehow his close relationship to his own mother. However, he completely rejected Freudian-based theories of social change as the way in which social-work professionals should approach their clients.

You would leaf over the articles, the technical psychiatric details, muttering 'God – God,' then shaking yourself, having worked yourself up into a state, your hair by this time falling again over your forehead, your eyes gleaming, you would rise from the couch, swaying, braced and clenched, throwing the book down, throwing one trench-clad arm out saying 'What they need is Love!'
                                – Alice Boissonneau, 'In My Room,' unpublished, *c.* 1945.

Conceptions of Health (1962)[*]

... To start from a traditional platitude: Health and disease are generally described in relation to each other, and therapy is defined with emphasis on one or the other. Thus, in the Oxford Dictionary one finds under 'therapy' phrases such as 'the art of healing' and 'the curative treatment of disease.' The verbs 'to heal' and 'to cure' are both defined as 'to restore to health.' To restore is to give back, and so curing implies the loss of something that is normally present and that now through therapy is given back. We are inclined, however, to look at the matter the other way around when we are being practical. We think of our breathing only when it is obstructed. Health is thought of as the absence of disease. Indeed, in the disease-therapy-health progression, therapy inevitably looks both ways, and in the various moments of its activity fastens its gaze now this way, now that. This is true of all the influential systems of therapy, both in the past and in the present. From the Western tradition I single out the two most influential – the Platonic progression, 'ignorance-conversion to dialectic-illumination,' and the Christian progression of 'sin-repentance through grace-salvation.' These two have often been united; they have often been thought of as one. Without discussing this subtle matter, I will for the present purposes distinguish them. From the modern world I single out the medical pattern, 'neurosis-psychotherapy-normality.'

In these systems, therapy has its positive and its negative moments. The philosopher must be continually aware of his ignorance if he would persevere in the pursuit of wisdom. If the Christian is to be in

[*] George Grant, 'Conceptions of Health,' in *Psychiatry and Responsibility*, Helmut Schoeck and James W. Wiggins, ed. (Princeton, N.J.: D. Van Nostrand 1962), 117–34.

true repentance before the Cross, he must face some of his past acts as sins. The patient must admit the unconscious source of some of his acts if the analysis is to be a success. On the other hand, philosophy will be frustrated by misologism if its dialectical struggles are not known as leading to the Good. The Christian's repentance will leave him a Stoic or a Pharisee if it is not seen as preparation for the divine love. The modern patient must give some meaning to the idea of normality. Indeed, one aspect of the art of the therapist is to find a rhythm between these positive and negative moments suitable to the individual case.

As modern psychotherapists have made their art central to North American society and established an institutional framework appropriate to their social power, two phenomena about their theory and practice become increasingly evident – the certainty of their conceptions of disease, the vagueness of their conceptions of health. To account for this would require a book of social history and is not my purpose here. Some generalizations about it can, however, be made.

1.) In the work of the master himself, therapeutic pessimism is continually present. This seems to me to arise above all from Freud's ambiguous relationship to modern science and the modern assumptions about man and civilization which are the framework of that science. He writes of himself as one of the dedicated priesthood of science who have put aside the ancient religious and metaphysical superstitions and who can, therefore, distinguish provable knowledge from mythology. Basic to this positivism is the identification of knowledge with human power to change the world. At the same time, one result of his science was an account of the structure of the mind in which reason is viewed both phylogenetically and ontogenetically, as arising from the suppression of the instinctual in man. That suppression of the instinctual is seen as the very cause of personal and social disease. The gaining of power over nature, central to modern science, is the very cause of disease when applied by man to himself.

This ambiguous relation toward science is illustrated in the very history of Freud's work and in his account of that work. In his writings before 1919, he is firm in stating the methodological principle that his conceptions are not final, but are hypotheses to be changed readily in the light of observation and practice. Yet even these earlier techniques and conceptions are themselves based on something extrascientific – his own self-analysis of the 1890s. To see that this self-analysis is extrascientific in psychoanalytical terms, it is only necessary to state that since

Freud's day all professional analysts must themselves be analyzed by somebody else. The very term 'self-analysis' is one of ridicule to the orthodox. Yet for psychoanalysis to come to be, there had to be an original self-analysis. It is for this reason that Freud's most loyal disciples, while praising him as the great scientist of the psyche, still write of this self-analysis in language that believers would use about the redemption of the world by the passion of Jesus Christ. According to Edward Glover,[*] there have been two moments in history of crucial significance – the first repression buried deep in primitive times and Freud's recognition of the causes of repression in his self-analysis. That language of uniqueness and victory is best found in Ernest Jones's life of Freud[†] on the first page of the chapter on the self-analysis. 'Once done, it is done forever,' writes Jones as a latter-day St Paul. This is not said to cast ridicule on this great act of Freud by comparing it with the act of acts, but simply to point out that the basis of modern psychotherapy is not a scientific discovery in the proper sense and that there is an ambiguity in the Freudians resulting from their insistence both that they are scientists and yet that they must pay homage to this act.

Indeed, in Freud's later writings (*Civilization and Its Discontents* most particularly), he passes completely beyond the scientific into the metaphysical. Eros and Thanatos,[‡] which are the final rulers of human existence, are not written about as scientific hypotheses, but as postulated realities from which he deduces a metaphysic of history in terms of which his therapeutic and social pessimism, implicit in his earlier practical works, is lifted to a new level of intelligibility. Civilization is a product of the ego and the superego, which arose as the individual was forced to come to terms with 'reality' – that is, to live by the reality principle rather than by the pleasure principle. Freud works out this tragic history, not only in terms of the life of the individual, but of the race as a whole. Sexuality is the basic manifestation of the life instinct, Eros. Civilization is produced by sublimated Eros. But sublimated Eros is desexualized Eros. Thus, though civilization is built by Eros, constant desexualization is necessary as civilization broadens its sway. Hence, Eros is weakened, and the death instinct is released, with all its potentialities for destruction. In fact, civilization moves to its destruc-

[*] Edward Glover, *Techniques of Psychoanalysis* (New York: International Universities Press 1958).

[†] Ernest Jones (1879–1956) *Life and Work of Sigmund Freud*, 3 vols. (London: Hogarth Press 1956–8).

[‡] Love and death (Greek).

tion as it moves to its fulfilment. Here is no optimistic 'gnosticism' of progress, but a statement of certain necessary limits to human existence. The earlier insistence by Freud that psychoanalysis is part of the liberating tradition of modern science here openly meets the fact that Western civilization's modern mark has been science, that the mark of that science has been the pursuit of power, and that, therefore, modern science is a result of the successful repression that Western man has imposed on the free play of his instincts, and this in turn causes the releasing of the death instinct.

Freud's therapeutic pessimism is thus understandable, and it is no wonder that health for man is a very limited state. Therapy does not result in a return of the repressed instincts to full play, but to a sublimation through recognition of what has been repressed – a sublimation which holds in check the death instinct, but which has inevitable stoical undertones. It is not too much to say that health becomes for Freud the making the best of a bad job. His metaphysical and tragic sense of life leads him to assumptions about human existence very different from the optimism so characteristic of the science of his day. Such a position could not include any clear or positive account of what constitutes health for human beings.

2.) As the psychotherapeutic movement changed from its origins as a minority of secularized Jews living in the alien atmosphere of the Hapsburg Empire to the wielders of social power that they are now in North America, it is not surprising that their conceptions of health should have been modified. Their enormously rapid rise to a position of ascendance was partly made possible by the fact that they remained within the medical profession. In early-twentieth-century America the medical profession had unequalled prestige because it combined the power of modern science with the practical 'do-goodery' of liberal Protestantism. And the medical profession itself – particularly its more advanced members, who were held by the religion of science – had a clear interest in accepting psychotherapy. The very arrogance of the modern medical profession saw in the new successes of psychotherapy – assumedly carried out entirely within naturalist assumptions – the chance for themselves to be the arbiters not only of the body but of the mind. American scientists and doctors were much more practical and immediate than the Europeans from whom psychoanalysis had sprung. Freud may have thought that he had freed his mind from finalist conceptions in the name of positivism, but this for him was mere theory compared to the unphilosophical practicality which was the very fabric of the American Protestant scientist. In accepting psychotherapy, therefore, American medicine was not only influenced by it, but also put its arrogant practical stamp upon it.

Further, as psychotherapy took over the leadership in providing mental health in a mass society, it was inevitably caught even deeper in the dilemmas of responsible success. So psychotherapy was influenced not only by American medicine but by the whole fabric of American culture. Professions do not gain power in any society unless in large measure they do what powerful influences in that society want. Psychotherapists adjusted themselves to the needs, desires, and interests of the industrialized, democratic, capitalist society. Finally, as responsibility for the mass society grows, the very immediacies of practicality push the profession farther and farther away from clarity about its ends. When a physician attends a child with earache, obviously something needs to be done. When the child is better, the doctor has a waiting room full of patients and has little time to define health other than to say that the child can now do what children generally do in our society. Most parents and doctors will settle for such a pragmatic account of health. So equally the office of the psychotherapist is crowded, and beyond is the spectre of the mental hospitals. The patient may still be neurotic, but she can now function as a wife and mother and need not come to the office or, worse, go on to the mental hospital.

In this paper I am criticizing the emptiness of modern psychotherapy in terms of ultimate truth. But let me state unequivocally that 'getting on with the job' is a necessary moral maxim for all men. What the world tends toward without it is seen in quietist societies, and against this we may thank God for our activist tradition. Any theorist who neglects the circumstances that make the maxim necessary neglects an essential aspect of truth in the name of theoretical pride. This is so even in North America, where the maxim is so often an excuse for idolatry. At the same time, however, it is permissible for the theorist to point out the ambiguity in men who arrogate to themselves more and more social power *and then* justify their confusion by how much work they have to do. The absence of any definition of health in modern psychotherapy is certainly in part a function of this latter process.

* * *

In contrast to the growing vagueness about health among psycho-therapists, there is one group of Freudians who give a definite and positive content to their concept of health and justify that account within a philosophy of nature and history. They are those who have attempted to unite the thought of Freud and Marx. For the rest of this paper I intend to describe and comment on these thinkers. I do so because in them the assumptions of modern humanism about man and society are enunciated in a most explicit way and also because in them much that is unsystematically assumed in official therapy is openly asserted.

To put the matter historically: Since 1914 it has surely become obvious that the truth of the assumptions of modernity cannot be taken with quite the uncritical certitude that they were previously. (I use 'the assumptions of modernity' in the broad sense to distinguish them from those of the antique world and from those of Christianity.) Yet modern psychotherapy is essentially a product of that modernity. And in these thinkers this modernity is given its widest scope. Therefore, in them the assumptions of modern psychotherapy are most openly explicit. I am also quite confident that the view of existence of these thinkers is becoming and will become increasingly a popular faith in our society.

.   .   .

The concept of health in these thinkers is reached by combining the progressivist view of history (as found in its most sophisticated expositor, Marx) with Freud's assumption that the alienation of man from his job is caused by the alienation of man from his instincts. In describing that position, I take the marxist account of history as given. These men believe, however, that Freud's recognition of the alienation of man from his instincts leads him to a therapeutic pessimism (as described above) because it is interpreted within a simple nineteenth-century naturalism. He expresses the relationship of man to nature biologically instead of historically. Scarcity for Freud is, therefore, seen as an ever-present condition, imposing the need for dominance and therefore repression in any possible society. He does not understand man's relation to nature as an historical process (to be understood dialectically) in which the domination of nature by man overcomes the very conditions that it arose to meet. He cannot conceive a society in which scarcity has been overcome and in which man can turn his full attention to liberating his instincts from repression by the very methods that he himself has discovered. Thus, he is forced to see the struggle between Eros and Thanatos as everlasting (I scorn the use of the word eternal in

this debased sense) and one in which there can be no final overcoming
of evil.

• • •

According to Hegel, history comes to an end with the dawn of the
age of reason (first realized in his thought, which is no longer *philo-
sophia*, but *sophia* itself). So with these marxists, true humanity will
come to be in this world of realized sexuality, in which the orders of
freedom and necessity are at last made one. The ecstatic longing for a
free society that has lain as an illicit dream in the history of mankind
now arises as a concrete possibility before us. ('How're they going to
keep him down on the farm, now that he's seen Paree?') In the full tide
of gnostic prophecy, Marcuse asserts that in such a society man will be
able to conquer his old enemies – time and death. In the world of the
instincts, measured time, the very mark of repression, ceases to exist.
Reconciled at last in the union of freedom and happiness, persons will
choose to go down to the grave when they so desire. Across this blissful
world will fall one shadow – the memory of those in the past who died
in alienation. The Kingdom of Man will thus be darkened, but even this
darkness will be alleviated by the knowledge that evil was not in vain.

• • •

There is only space for two comments on this orgasmic gnosticism,
though many more are required.
a) It brings out unequivocally that virtue and vice are not part of the
Freudian account of man. This is often slurred over in North America
because of the very brilliance of Freud's account of the history of the
instincts and the liberating effect the acceptance of that account can
have for us personally. Our debt is so great because Freud shows us in
detail how the very conditions of our early existence twist and chain us
and how we may overcome these distortions of our instincts. Moreover,
to speak theologically, Freud's discoveries give content to the doctrines
of Providence, Fall, and Redemption by showing how we do not move
simply and directly to our end, but must move to it by overcoming the
ambiguities and tragedies that are not accidental, but of the very necessity of our existence. He is closer to the Biblical doctrines of the Fall
and Providence than to the oversimplified Aristotelian teleology that
skirts the question of evil by saying that nature achieves its purpose in

the main. To admit this greatness on the part of Freud, however, must not allow us to forget that his account of man denies the essential practical truth about us – namely, that we are beings who must choose between virtue and vice. Nor must we minimize or sentimentalize this theoretical denial, because society has and will continue to pay a steep price for it. That this denial is made by Freud is most easily seen in his account of the structure of the mind as id, ego, and superego. The id is the determinative aspect of us all. The ego and the superego arise from it through historical circumstances. Thus, for Freud, thought is somehow artificial to man, something forced on him by necessity. In his own words it is 'a detour from the memory of gratification.' But even within this assumption, he does not think of thought in a way that would make possible virtue and vice. Thought for him is simply technical reason as conceived by nineteenth-century scientism. For where the ego is made the seat of reason, the superego is made the seat of morality. Thus, it is not reasonable to be moral, and morality belongs less truly to man than his ability to calculate. If reason is simply a calculating instrument and cannot teach us to choose between virtuous and vicious acts, then there is no objective morality in the public or personal sphere.

The orgastic gnostics bring out this theoretical implication with the greatest clarity, for they openly deny the platitudes of the old rational morality. The traditional morality presented itself in day-to-day practice as two simple statements that were taken as self-evident: (i) men should care not only for themselves but for others; (ii) they should sometimes control their instinctual appetites in the name of some greater good. These great platitudes were the court to which the doctrine of virtue and vice publicly appealed. Of course, the denial of virtue and vice is part of the whole tradition of modernity. One sees its beginnings in the arrogant immanentism of Spinoza (i.e., in his attack on the act of repentance as unworthy of a rational man). But it has never been made more clearly than in these orgastic gnostics. We may thank them for this lack of equivocation, for it brings out (what is elsewhere often slurred over) that the assumptions of modernity cannot consistently include a doctrine of right and wrong.

Of course, these gnostics have an answer to this criticism that is traditional among all gnostics. When people achieve genital primacy or orgastic potency, there will be no need for the idea of virtue, because the activities that the tradition called vicious will just disappear. Just as the marxists, true to their dogma that the cause of evil lies in property relations, believe, therefore, that evil will largely disappear when that cause has been eliminated, so these gnostics unite as the cause of evil bad property relations and sexual repression and believe that the overcoming of both will lead to the good society. Here indeed we come close to the very centre of modern man's image of himself. Evil is not in the free will, but arises from the realm of necessity. The most obvious implication of this is that it cannot be called sin.

b) Although this account of health must be condemned as having no moral doctrine, it has great religious advantages compared to the other types of humanism (educated and uneducated) that characterize our society. The chief of these is that it is a doctrine of hope, and Christians must believe that true hope is a virtue even when it has an inadequate object, just as true charity in an atheist is supernatural. There is no doubt that the young who read Mailer[*] or Miller[†] are attracted to this worship of the orgasm because it seems a true affirmation compared to what they have heard elsewhere. The young are, after all, reared in a society avid in its concentration on the mortal and the immanent. Yet in these days of tightened organization and the possibility of technological nightmare, an immanentism of despair is all too easy. Such an immanentism is the most influential philosophic basis for therapy in Europe today (*Daseinsanalyse*).[‡] Moreover, in the tightened society, sexuality is often the only form of creativity left open to persons and is certainly a more universal foundation of hope than the aestheticism of the culture addict or the worldly-wise empiricism of the social engineer. This is true even if we take this orgastic gnosticism at the point where it is more horrifying to the believer: Reich's[§] techniques of overtly sexual therapy (horrifying particularly when applied to children). Is there not more hope even here than in the widespread and indeed indiscriminate use of insulin and electric shock treatment carried out by order of the social engineers in the name of short-term adjustment?

Moreover, sexuality is for many the road not only to gratification but to ecstasy. 'With my body I thee worship.' The object of worship among the orgastic may be limited to the immanent and may therefore be justly characterized as idolatry. Nevertheless, in their very worshipping

[*]Norman Mailer (1923–), American novelist.
[†]Henry Miller (1891–1980), American novelist, best known for *Tropic of Cancer* (1934), which was banned as obscene until 1964.
[‡]Existential analysis (German).
[§]Wilhelm Reich (1897–1957), Austrian psychiatrist who trained under Freud, author of *The Function of the Orgasm* (1957).

they seem to discover something of the sacred in nature that has been lost by those held by the philosophy of human power and self-confidence. The rediscovery of that sacredness may be a condition for the rediscovery of a worship that is more than natural. For all its dangers, idolatry may be the only road back to worship. To carry this train of thought further, it would be necessary not only to criticize the modern view of nature but also to consider why our North American Christianity was so influenced by that view of nature that it failed to have any adequate theology of human love.

Having praised this concept of health for its hope, I must end by insisting that it fails religiously by placing its hope in life alone. The truism need hardly be supported here that suffering and death are as much facts as life and gratification. Yet this gnosticism cannot include these facts within itself despite all its efforts. The concept of health given us by Him who says, 'Take up your gallows tree and follow me' is complete in a way that no modern conception is, because it includes suffering and death in health, recognizing them not simply as the negation of happiness, but as the voluntary shedding of the mortal necessary to the putting on of immortality. Christianity may too often have forgotten a proper affirmation of life and gratification (and modern therapy has done well to remind it of this forgetting); but its incomparable truth has been never to forget that suffering and death must be included in health as much as life and gratification. Nowhere has modern psychotherapy more mirrored and influenced our society of progress than in the way it disregards death or looks at it with stoicism.

CARL GUSTAV JUNG (1875–1961)

A Swiss psychoanalyst and a rival of Freud, Jung drew widely on myth and developed the concept of the collective unconscious. His thought was often seen as religious, in contrast to Freud's aggressive atheism. This essay was the third broadcast Grant delivered for CBC radio's 'Architects of Modern Thought' *series. The earlier were on Sartre and Dostoevsky.*

... I am deep in Tolstoy and Jung and am finding all sorts of things about myself that I should have known years ago. In the business of the last years my intellect

had got detached from my roots and it is wonderful to begin to feel more whole
and less driven by neurotic tension of one kind and another.
— George Grant to John Graham, 12 December 1967

Carl Gustav Jung (1962)[*]

In modern psychology two men have been dominant: first the towering
figure of Sigmund Freud and close behind in influence Carl Jung. The
chief mark of our modern civilization has been what we call science. By
this word we mean a particular set of procedures by which men come to
understand the world and so have mastery over it. The application of
these procedures to the study of mind came late in the history of modern science. They were first used for the study of the physical world and
of the living world. It is only in the last hundred years that they have
been applied to the study of mind. But psychology is a product not only
of science, but also of the art of medicine — the art which is concerned
with the cure of disease — to use a beautiful Greek word, the therapeutic
art. Because medicine these days is so intimately connected with science, we often think of the two as if they were the same. But, of course,
they are not, because clearly one can understand something without
wanting to cure it of all its ills. The expert advertising man or the communist brain-washer may have consummate understanding of the
mind, but rather than want to cure he may wish to add to its ills that of
enslavement, so that the enslaver may add to his bankroll or power.
The psychologies of Freud and Jung were as much a product of the
therapeutic art as of scientific understanding. As Jung himself has written, 'Our psychology is — practical science. We do research not for the
sake of research but because of our immediate aim of helping. We
could just as well say that science was a by-product of our psychology,
not its main goal, which constitutes a great difference between it and
what is understood by 'academic science.' Neither Freud nor Jung,
therefore, ever divide their account of what the mind is like from what
they think its condition should be — its health, its integration — use what
terms you will. They are not pure scientists and it is indeed a good question whether psychology can ever be a pure science — that is, if the truth

[*]George Grant, 'Carl Gustav Jung,' in *Architects of Modern Thought*, 5th and 6th series,
twelve talks by various scholars for CBC Radio (Toronto: Canadian Broadcasting Corporation 1962), 63–74.

about mind can ever be understood if detached from the desire of the therapist to move minds to their health.

As is true of all intellectuals, the outward events of Jung's life are not what is important, but rather what he thought and wrote. He was born in 1875 in Switzerland – the son of a Protestant pastor. In 1900 he graduated in medicine and immediately took up the psychiatric branch of the art in Switzerland. In 1907 came his first meeting with Freud; he recognized that Freud's psychoanalytical techniques and theory had discovered facts which were becoming more and more central for his own understanding of mental disease. During the next years he worked closely with Freud in the development of psychoanalysis. In 1913 the break with Freud came. Jung had criticized some of Freud's theories of the unconscious in his famous book *The Psychology of the Unconscious*. Freud and his disciples were a closed group and intolerant of any disagreement about the central doctrines. They were quite unwilling to continue co-operation with therapeutic techniques which stemmed from different dogma. Jung, therefore, had to withdraw from the psychoanalytical movement and from then on he called his psychology 'analytical psychology' to distinguish it from dogmatic Freudian psychoanalysis. From that day on, Vienna and Zurich became rival Romes of the psychological church in Europe.

Jung did not die till about a year ago at the age of eighty-six and he continued as a productive scientist right up till his death. From 1914 to 1960 he carried on his investigations of the unconscious. His output of work was simply staggering. I think it is fair to say that the output of few scientists of our era can compare in range and quantity to that of Jung's. Not only did he continue as a practising therapist, but he constantly lectured on fundamental theory at the great universities of both East and West. Because he came to believe that the mind was an incomparably more complex entity than Freud or the Freudians had thought it to be, his researches took him into areas far from what is generally considered psychology. He became, for instance, the greatest interpreter of Asian religion to the West, because he saw in Asian religion remarkable techniques whereby the mind freed itself from ills. Anybody today who wishes to understand Asian religion would seem to me to have no alternative but to read Jung. He became an expert on primitive peoples and travelled widely among them because he saw a close relation between the contents of the unconscious of his Western patients and the manifestations of the primitive mind in myth and legend. He studied the medieval alchemists because he believed their doctrines were concerned with a scientific approach to human liberation. According to Jung, their doctrines were really descriptions of the unconscious and its processes, projected into externalized images. Indeed, in many ways Jung's chief influence has been outside psychology and immediate therapy; rather among those scholars who in our century have been trying to reach new insights into the civilizations and religions of the past. Around him in Switzerland there gathered a group of the learned from a wide variety of disciplines, who were concerned with this question from many angles. Anybody who wants to follow these researches should read the *Eranos Yearbooks* which are the proceedings of their yearly meetings.

It was not surprising in the Europe of the twentieth century that this desire to understand the past should be so actively pursued. Jung's writings are full of the sense that in our era Western civilization had entered a time of terrible cataclysm. This manifested itself not only in the outward events of the two world wars through which he lived and the potential holocaust now possible through the inventions of modern physics, but even more in the sense of meaninglessness and purposelessness which Jung considered so much the mark of his patients. He has said that in nearly all the therapeutic analyses he has undertaken the most deeprooted problem was always the religious one – that is, the need for the patient to see some meaning and purpose in his life. It was his desire to meet this need which led Jung back to the study of Asian religion and culture and to the study of primitive cultures.

Indeed, whatever else needs to be said about Jung's psychology as a whole, there is one point where it cannot fail to appeal to the educated person. He does not treat the past with contempt. One of the most alarming qualities in many modern scientists has been their discarding of ancient wisdom, both European and Asian. Their present triumphs and their faith in the doctrine of progress has made them contemptuous of pre-scientific civilizations and what those civilizations knew about the proper purposes of human existence. The present state of our civilization makes that contempt seem pretty juvenile. And it is to Jung's immense merit that among modern psychologists he is pre-eminent in studying the past not as a home of error and superstition but as something from which we must learn.

The range and profundity of Jung's writing make it impossible to encapsulate his teachings about the mind in a few neat sentences. I am therefore going to speak about what seems central in his thought and that which most clearly distinguishes his teaching from that of Freud.

This is his assertion of the existence of the 'collective unconscious.' It is important on this continent to emphasize those aspects where he differs from Freud, because it is here in North America more than anywhere else that the Freudian teachings have been most influential among practising therapists. Indeed, in North America Jung's influence among psychiatrists and psychologists has been minimal.

What Jung means by the 'collective unconscious' can best be described by stating his agreement with the Freudian doctrine of the unconscious and also where he differs from it. It was Freud who brought back into Western thought the conception of the unconscious: that is, the idea that the mind is made up of two spheres – first, those events of which we are conscious and, secondly, another sphere of psychic life of which we are *not* conscious. The metaphor which has been continually used to illuminate this is the iceberg. The conscious is the eleventh part of the iceberg which is visible above the ocean; the unconscious is the ten-elevenths which lies hidden in the deep. Freud made clear to modern men that their mental ills were often caused by conflicts in the unconscious and conflicts between the conscious and unconscious. He also saw that the unconscious manifests itself in our dreams so that the therapist by analyzing the dreams of his patients can help them to understand their conflicts by lifting them into consciousness and so to begin to overcome them. In such conceptions as the 'Oedipus complex,' Freud stated the causes of repression and gave some content to the unconscious. The scientific and rationalist West, which had cut itself off from any knowledge of the depths of the mind, owes an immense debt to Freud for his rediscovery of the ten-elevenths of the iceberg.

Jung took from Freud the conception of the mind as made up of both a conscious and an unconscious sphere. But he says that the unconscious itself must be divided into two spheres – the realm for the 'personal unconscious' and the realm of the 'collective unconscious.' The 'collective unconscious' is not made up of material which belongs to any individual history, but, to use Jung's own words, comes 'from the inherited possibility of psychical functioning in general; namely, from the inherited brain structure.' Or again in his own words, 'the collective unconscious is the mighty spiritual inheritance of human development, reborn in every individual.' It is this collective realm of the unconscious which is most deeply buried and which presents the most difficult problem to the therapist. The very words 'reborn in every individual,' which Jung uses to describe it, shows immediately his debt to

Buddhism with its central doctrine of the cycle of rebirths which are necessary to the law of *karma* and from which the enlightened alone escape. How different is his way of speaking from 'the once and for all' event language of Christianity.

The ordering content of the 'collective unconscious' Jung calls the 'archetypes.' The Oxford dictionary defines the word 'archetype' as 'original model.' Jung means by it 'self-portrait of the instincts.' But by instincts he does not mean anything individual but rather universal – the very patterns of behaviour which have been with man always. As the language of the unconscious in dreams is that of imaginative symbol, they appear in dreams as universal figures. Thus, for instance, the archetype 'mother' or 'great mother' appears in dreams in many forms. But what makes it an archetype is that 'mother' pre-exists in our unconscious every worldly manifestation of the motherly, and has existed in the unconscious of man so long as man has been man. We must not turn these archetypes into concepts and make out that the archetype of 'mother' is the universal concept of 'motherliness.' Rather, the archetypes are universal psychic forces which we can only begin to touch in experience.

When we experience these archetypes at all consciously, we are touching in our individual lives the whole task of humanity at all times and so are in a sense outside time. Jung indeed says that when we re-activate the contents of the collective unconscious by opening ourselves to the archetypes we have experience of the eternal. The word eternal is here used in no transcendent sense. It is timeless but in the world. What I think he means is that in re-activating the collective unconscious we cease to be simply individual human beings and partake of 'human beingness' in general. And the more archetypes we re-activate through analysis, the more we have entered into the fullness of being men. The neglect of them is the final cause of all neurotic and psychotic disorders.

Such an account of the collective unconscious clearly distinguishes Jung from Freud both in their science and in their therapy. It can not just be added on to the personal unconscious, as if Freud and Jung agreed about the conscious and the personal unconscious and then on top (or better at the bottom) Jung added the collective unconscious. On the contrary, it leads to clear distinction between their two accounts of the human condition – healthy or unhealthy. Freud is clearly here a Western man, moulded by the tradition of Semitic religion, and therefore thinks that what is ultimately real is the individual and his instincts.

This is not so for Jung. A man becomes a man as he re-activates the eternal archetypes, as he partakes in them. In this sense the individual person is not an ultimate any more than he is an ultimate in the great religions of the East. This very profound difference is apparent in what a Freudian and Jungian would mean by a successful analysis – or to put it simply, what is the goal of psychoanalysis?

To a Freudian the goal is to come to terms with one's own instincts. In Freudian language the 'ego' and the 'super-ego' and 'id' can through analysis come to live together. But such a living together can only be a compromise because the pleasure seeking of the id has to be limited by the reality principle so that people can go on living in the world. This is why there are such stoical and ironical undertones in Freud – to be successfully analyzed is to make the best of a bad job – to reach some compromise between reality and pleasure seeking. The goal of a successful analysis with Jung, on the other hand, is integration, that is, the combination of all the mental forces into a whole. And this immensely optimistic goal is possible because of his postulated eternal experience of touching the universal archetypes. Just compare Freud's *Civilization and Its Discontents* with Jung's *Modern Man in Search of a Soul* and one sees how incomparably more optimistic Jung is about the goal of analysis – and please let me make it quite clear that I do not use optimistic as a word of praise or blame. To say that a person's account of the human condition is more optimistic than another's is to say nothing about its truth.

From the foregoing it is easy to see why Jung has devoted so much time to the study of myth. He came to realize that the same material manifested itself in the mythic religion of primitive peoples as it did in the unconscious. The 'great mothers,' the 'trees of the world,' the 'wise old men,' which he had discovered in the unconscious, are of course the very stuff of the primitive peoples. Also, archaic religions have always been immensely aware of the need to integrate the soul and have been full of differing ways of achieving such integration. Jung studied such phenomena as a means of improving his techniques of therapy, and also to learn more of the very content of the unconscious.

Indeed, Jung believes that it is just because Western man has cut himself off from the depths of the unconscious that he has become irreligious and so lives in confusion. Our world is emptied inwardly as we think of religion as either nothing or else concerned with non-dynamic intellectual convictions; it is rationalized outwardly in a society dominated by its technical apparatus. So, cut off by such rationalism from the eternal archetypes, man in the West must become ever more prone to outward violence and inward meaninglessness. At this point Jung is particularly condemnatory of Western Protestantism which cut itself off from the whole world of symbol and myth and ritual and so condemned itself to be out of touch with the wholeness of archetypes. Jung is more friendly towards Catholicism because it has never attempted so to rationalize itself. When in the 1950s the Pope promulgated the doctrine of the Assumption of the Blessed Virgin, Jung hailed it as one of the crucial acts of our era because in it the feminine was taken back into the Godhead.

But – and this is a very large but – in thinking about Jung's interest in religion or in myth one must be clear that it is a very particular kind of interest. He always views religion or myth (and I do not use the words synonymously) as they serve the mental health of human beings. I think this is important because many clerics and theologians have maintained that Jung is a truly religious psychologist while Freud is essentially irreligious. I am *not* sure that the people who make these statements are really looking for their allies in the right place. These statements are made because it seems at first sight clear that Jung gives a more creative role to myth and religion than Freud does. To Freud all religion was mythical and the mythical arose as a response to a diseased psychological condition. The domination of the patriarchal father led to a belief in the existence of the first person of the Trinity. Such superstitions will drop away if we have had a successful analysis. Religion is a corporate neurosis of mankind which falls away from the wiser members of society in the age of scientific enlightenment. Compared to this negative approach to religion, Jung's insistence on the wisdom of religious cultures is refreshing to the believer and it is because of this that Protestant and more often Catholic clerics have seen him as an ally.

I think those who talk this way often seem to forget that Jung is not concerned with the truth or falsity of any particular religion; nor, as far as myth is concerned, with what transcendent reality is manifested in it. It is surely clear that the men of the ancient religious cultures when they apprehended myth thought they were apprehending the real and knew that the real so apprehended always led them to particular forms of conduct. They thought they were being opened to an absolute and universal reality. Now it is clear that Jung does not think this. When men come upon the archetypes of the collective unconscious they are concerned with the integration of their own psyches, not with being lifted to another realm of reality, the realm of the spirit. In other words,

Jung is concerned with myth in quite a different way from those who live in myth. They are concerned with being opened to reality; he is concerned with it as a psychological aid.

And this distinction becomes even more important when we pass beyond the limited subject of Jung's relation to myth and look at his relation to the living religions of the Western world. He is concerned with them insofar as the practice of them is an aid to the mental health of the practitioner. But he is not concerned with whether the affirmations these religions make about reality are true or false. Indeed, although he is cagey about this point in his voluminous writings, I think it can be fairly deduced that he thinks that the affirmations of Western religion about reality are nonsense. Now it does not seem to me that any serious adult practitioner of a religion can simply disregard whether what his religion says about ultimate reality is true or false. Can he just practise it for the good of his mental health if he think what it says is nonsense? It is surely particularly difficult to take this attitude to the Semitic religions of the West – Judaism and Christianity – both of which clearly involve making statements about reality. In other words, I don't think we can get away from the fact that Jung's relation to Western religion is one of patronizing. Is one more a friend of Western religion if one directly assails it like Freud or if one covertly patronizes it like Jung?

I have emphasized Jung's doctrine of the collective unconscious and his interest in myth and religion because it is relevant to the chief way in which Jung is an architect of modern thought. He is the leading exponent of Asian religion in the West. I don't see how anyone can take at its face value Jung's claim to be an empirical scientist – in any clearly defined sense of the word empirical – any more than one can take Freud's claim to be chiefly a scientist and not essentially a metaphysician and a prophet. Nevertheless, Jung must be regarded with the utmost seriousness because more than any other man of this century he has made Asian religion a *living* force in the West. And surely one of the key developments of our age is the spreading of the thought of the Orient through the Occident. The Western invasion of the world in the last centuries is such an obvious fact that we are inclined to forget how much influence has been reciprocal. And this process has been going on for some time. As early as 1625 there was a Chair of Oriental Studies at the University of Utrecht. Since that time, Asia has been a growing influence in the lives of European intellectuals. In our era it has become a flood touching not only the intellectual *élite* but all parts of our society. We are influenced not so much by such open missionaries as Dr Suzuki* but rather by Western people who consciously or unconsciously believe Asian religion (most often Buddhism, but sometimes Hinduism) to be true. A conscious example at a brilliant popular level are the Buddhist novels of J.D. Salinger.† The historian Arnold Toynbee‡ is another example – although it is difficult to know how conscious Toynbee is about his beliefs. But by far the most influential and effective exponent of Asian religion has been Jung. When I say Asian religion there are clearly Hindu influences in Jung's account of the psyche – but more obviously present are the influences of Buddhism.

The evidence for this is not found primarily in Jung's direct writings on Eastern religion – for instance, his interpretation of the *mandalas* (or magic circles) which are unifying symbols for the personality, or his interest in the quadernity (the fourfold) in distinction to the trinity. It lies rather in the fact that his psychology and Asian religion are concerned with the same questions – have the same centre. They both deal with the liberation of the soul as it discovers itself as immortal. They are both concerned with the means whereby the individual can experience immortality – and let me emphasize that experience is here the key word – the realization of timeless being in oneself. For Jung this is achieved when the opposing aspects of the soul, male and female, good and evil, are experienced not as opposites but as one.

To put the matter negatively, I think one can see how little Jung's religion has to do with traditional Western religion if one recognizes what is implied in this doctrine of the union of contraries. To Jung, God is an experience in the soul which can only be realized when we have overcome the opposition between good and evil. Integration – call it if you will enlightenment – is beyond good and evil. But such a doctrine unequivocally breaks with the main stream of Western religion. Moreover, it totally undermines the Western view of existence as essentially moral. It is surely no accident that Jung grew up in that Germanic generation which was so deeply shaped by Nietzsche. For

---

*D.T. Suzuki, author of *Studies in Zen Budhism* and in Grant's words, 'The chief missionary of Buddhism in the United States.' See George Grant, 'Philosophy and Religion,' in *The Great Ideas Today, 1961* (Chicago: Encyclopedia Britannica, 1961), 362.

†J.D. Salinger (1916–), American novelist and short story writer, author of *Catcher in the Rye* (1951). 'Zen artists paint Zen pictures and Zen poets compose Zen poems. The voice of Zen is heard in the novels of J.D. Salinger and Jack Kerouac.' Grant, 'Philosophy and Religion,' 362.

‡A.J. Toynbee (1889–1975), influential British historian, author of *A Study of History*, 12 vols. (1934–61). Grant met Toynbee at Oxford early in the Second World War.

Nietzsche's attack on Semitic religion went more to the heart than any other of the many attacks which have characterized the last centuries; and it was made exactly at this point – man should pass beyond good and evil. The only time that Jung ever spoke unequivocally and at length about his antipathy to Biblical religion was in his brilliant and witty commentary on the book of Job.

Those clerics and theologians who say that Jung is an essentially religious psychologist are then right – but it depends on what religion they are talking about. For the common liberal platitude that all religions are the same is an obvious fallacy. Now it may be that the Catholic theologians in France are right and that in our era the greatest task of Christianity is not to take marxism into itself or to come to terms with the Prometheanism of science but to include Buddhism within the universal faith. It is not easy to speak quickly about such matters because they raise subtle matters of principle and anything one says may sound on the one side like ignorant imperialism or on the other like vague eclecticism. One thing can, however, be said with certainty. As one looks at the history of the race, two figures tower above the rest – Jesus the Christ and Siddharta Gotauma, the Sammasambuddha, that is, the fully self-enlightened one. Presumably also, if a religion is catholic, all may and can be included within it. But certainly this is not what is present in Jung's mind. It is implied in every line he writes that what is true in Western religion can be included in the much richer religions of the East. In this sense he is an incomparably greater radical than Freud; for he is attacking the roots of Western civilization. Freud, after all, only attacks Semitic religion from within its own assumptions. But Jung, for all his surface conservatism and appeal to the past, attacks these very assumptions – the concrete historical person in the face of the transcendent. Those who do not see this radial centre of Jung's thought have chiefly been prevented from seeing it because they have accepted, in most cases unconsciously, Hegel's and Marx's accounts of Asian history.

HAROLD ADAMS INNIS (1894–1952)

Harold Innis was the first Canadian-born social scientist to achieve an international reputation. He was a distinguished economic historian, and in his later work he tried to understand the reasons for the decay and collapse of civilizations by studying their modes of communication. Although Grant was initially sympathetic to Innis, as his comments in the 'Philosophy' article included in Part Two of this book show, he later concluded that Innis's work was brilliant but limited. Innis was too much the social scientist to plunge into the mystery of existence.

The Idea File of Harold Adams Innis (1980)[*]

H.A. Innis was a Canadian who was outstanding at what he did, by any standards anywhere in the world. He became a famous historian of the fur, fish, and lumber trades early in his life. But he did not stick with his specialism. By the end of his life he was writing books which looked deeply at the question: What is human being? For example, his thoughts about the different means of communication (speech, books, radio, TV) and what can be communicated by each particular means was the influence from which the writings of Marshall McLuhan[†] have come forth.

But beyond such particulars, anybody who has read his last books will know that they cannot look at human history quite the same way again. He became a famous man in the Western intellectual world and was offered big jobs in the powerful American academia and the cultivated British version. He stayed in Canada because it was his own and he ambiguously loved it. His admirers were grateful to the University of Toronto when it gave his name to one of its colleges after his death in 1952.

• • •

We have in front of us a readable and fascinating book. The sheer range of Innis's interests must have made editing difficult. In a couple of pages he can move from comments on American and Canadian politics to the influence of India on Christian ideas, to the dependence of modern journalism on cable rates, to the worship of Isis, to the significance of the elevator for business. To present such far-seeing curiosity in readable form was difficult, and Christian has succeeded. Wisely, he

---

[*]George Grant, review of *The Idea File of Harold Adams Innis*, ed. William Christian (Toronto: University of Toronto Press 1980), *Globe and Mail*, 13 May 1980, E12.
[†]Marshall McLuhan (1911–81), Canadian social critic and communications theorist who was deeply indebted to Innis's communication studies for his own insights.

edited the material in chronological order, so that we can see Innis's thought unfold in the last pregnant years of his life.

When I say it is a good read, I mean that in a particular way. One cannot read it like John Le Carré's stories[*] – a breathless suspense-filled pursuit into the middle of the night. One cannot read it like [Charles Dickens's] *Bleak House* – an engrossment in a unified work of art with all its magic and wonder. This book is made up of small entries (six or seven a page) ranging over the reaches of human time and space. One simply gets indigestion if one reads too much of it at a sitting. I found the best way to read it was to put it next to my bed, read five pages a night, pay attention to what interested me and then put out the light. In the best sense of the phrase, it is a book that puts one to sleep. One takes into one's dreams the strange thoughts circling through time and space.

What was Innis? A philosopher? A social scientist? A historian? Little category boxes may seem Procrustean. Nevertheless, it is necessary to ask the question, because in trying to answer it, one makes explicit what one is learning from his writing. Certainly he was not a social scientist in the dominant sense of that activity. He did not see knowledge as something that gave us control, but as to be pursued for the sake of sheer curiosity alone. At the practical level, he wrote with brutal clarity about what would happen to universities which became servants of the institutions which dished out the research grants. He saw the proper university as the institution in society which served the pure desire to know, even if that meant that it remained small and poor and uninfluential. His account of social science is then very far from that in the great modern apparatuses of science.

On the other hand, Innis cannot be called a philosopher. He was a scientist in the sense that what he asked about anything, past or present, was how it worked. He did not ask those questions which belong traditionally to philosophy: What for? Whither? And what then? He was too much the secularised sceptic not to believe that those questions really had little point. His explanations were all in terms of the modern account of explanation: How did this social organization work? To put it mildly, the eternal was not his dish.

Innis never seems to have come to terms with this division in his work: he took methods from the moderns, but his motives for doing sci-

[*]John Le Carre (David Cornwell) (1931–), probably the greatest writer of Cold War spy stories and one of Grant's favourite novelists.

ence came from the ancients. He was at one and the same time both toughly cynical about modern social science, and sadly doubtful about the claims of the older science. The result is a kind of sadness in his work – even if it is a sadness well penetrated by wit and anger. Perhaps it is this ambiguity which has prevented Innis from having the continuing influence appropriate to a person of his high style. Nevertheless, it would be a shame if Innis did not continue to be read, particularly in the light of how tedious modern social science often is. His writing continually lights up whole areas of human history. And we need this light.

NORTHROP FRYE (1912–91)

Northrop Frye was the foremost Canadian literary critic of his generation and his work was renowned around the world. However, Grant did not admire Frye's style of criticism. He had praised Frye's work in his 1951 'Philosophy' article, but he later became more critical. He thought that Frye's literary treatment of the Bible was a form of secularized Christianity that debased the spiritual greatness of the Gospels.

I hope I did not attack Protestantism in my review of Frye, but only *secularized* Protestantism – quite another matter. I disliked the book because he was superior about the Gospels, which in my opinion are *perfect*.
                                                    – George Grant to Jonathan Mills, 19 March 1982

The Great Code (1982)[*]

This book about the Bible is written by a distinguished Canadian professor of English literature. I do not use the adjective 'Canadian' to qualify 'distinguished,' but rather because it is pleasant to associate distinction with one's country. The title of the book comes from William Blake's[†] remark: 'The Old and New Testaments are the Great Code of

---

[*] George Grant, review of Northrop Frye's *The Great Code: The Bible as Literature, Globe and Mail,* 27 February 1982, E17.
[†] William Blake (1757–1827), British poet, artist, and visionary. Frye's *Fearful Symmetry* was the classic study of Blake.

Art.' The second half of Frye's title is slightly ambiguous because it might imply that he is primarily discussing how the Bible has influenced the literature of the West, and English literature in particular. This is not the case. Rather, he is concentrating on the Bible itself, and using his powers as a careful student of literature to explicate what is present in it.

Reviews of books often have the perfectly proper function of making a synopsis of a book so that others can be saved the trouble of reading it, either because of a lack of interest in the material or because they already know it. I think this would be inevitably Procrustean in this case, and therefore I am not going to do it. The Bible is a large collection of very disparate books. Fry has read these books. He writes at length about them not only as a professor of literature, but as a person ready to make assertions coming from many fields of study – particularly theological and anthropological. Those who wish to know what is in Frye's book have no alternative to reading it.

Rather, I wish to say what kind of book this is, and where such a kind fits into the history and present state of studies. Art, in the sense of fine art, often is a kind of religion in our age, because it appears as a means of transcending society at a time when other means of such transcendence are no longer available for many people, particularly the educated. This deepest desire of human beings finds itself frustrated, and seeks its satisfaction in the arts, both past and present. At the same time, our era is concentrated on the science which issues in the conquest of human and non-human nature. The search for this knowledge has been institutionalized in our multiversities. When these two tendencies come together, the arts are brought into the universities to be classified.

But, of course, literature is not an object at our disposal, as the atom may be. Its organization does not result in bombs. The scientizing of literature is carried out by methods comparable with the work of Linnaeus. He catalogued and categorized the plants and animals so that they would lie before us in an intelligible arrangement.

Frye has been the leader of this form of the study of literature. In modern language, he has brought system to the given which lies before us. (The ancients thought that system was something appropriate to things such as armies, not to studies.) In this present book, the Bible is laid before us by the categories of language, myth, metaphor, and typology. Frye has read this literature with thoroughness. So many of us academics are lazy and Frye is free of that vice.

Indeed, Frye's interest in these writings both aids and stands in the way of his science as objective. It stands in the way because what often seems to lie before him is not those writings as they were in their originating moment, but rather as the Protestant Bible, which has come down to us from five centuries of English-speaking Calvinist reading. This may seem to be contradicted by the amount of time that Frye gives to arguing with contemporary fundamentalists. But this is rather the impatience one feels toward relations who have not arrived socially. Be that as it may, Frye's passionate interest in the Protestant Bible gives a bite to his science. I think chapters six and seven are the best in the book because here the Bible itself is most present.

To repeat, there is much in the book beyond the science of literature. There are many general theological pronouncements. (By 'theological pronouncements' I do not mean statements about theological pronouncements, but direct theological statements.) Some of these hit the nail right on the head with that fine shrewdness which is so much a part of Frye's writing. But in a way which is again very Protestant, he makes these statements (for instance, his remarks on prophecy) as though they were factual rather than his interpretation. That is, he writes theology as though it were not dependent on philosophy.

When these theological *obiter dicta* are directly philosophical, the confusion in his method and material is compounded. For example, Frye uses the words 'the master-slave dialectic on which the whole of human history turns.' Presumably, he knows that in making this statement, he has affirmed that modern political philosophy is superior to ancient political philosophy. After all, it is this affirmation more than any other which distinguishes modern from ancient political philosophy. In saying this, Frye shows he is judging the Bible through the eyes of modern philosophy. Why, then, does he then not say so? It would make things easier.

This comes out clearly in Frye's relation to the seventeenth-century Italian philosopher, Vico. He uses Vico's account of three stages in the history of language. With a philosopher of the order of Vico, one cannot accept such a part of his thought without being in closeness to his thought as a whole. Frye understands this because, later in his book, he expresses agreement with Vico's *verum factum* (we only know what we make). But in such agreement, he has committed himself to look at the Bible in a certain way – that is, through modern spectacles. To put the same point in another way: one has chosen to look at the Bible not as its writers looked at it.

For example, it is inconceivable that any of the writers of the Gospels could have thought the *verum factum* a true account of truth. It is of course quite proper for Frye to look at the Bible as a modern. But, to repeat, this should have been made much more explicit. It would then be clearer to the reader that what we get about the Bible in this book are not only conclusions from the science of criticism, but also what a well-educated secularized Protestant gets from a careful reading of these books.

Such a reading cannot but be deeply unsympathetic to what was believed to be known about the Bible from that long co-operation between philosophy and Biblical scholarship which was at the heart of centuries of the tradition. The great Islamic theologian El Farabi wrote that Plato's *Republic*[*] was the most important writing about prophecy. Whatever other differences there were between Islam, Christianity, and Judaism over the centuries, the leading theologians would have been in near agreement about such a statement. For example, there were no equivalents in the Bible for ideas such as 'nature' or 'history,' and therefore thinkers knew that they had to look elsewhere for such necessary means of interpretation.

This was not to lower the status of scripture, but to exalt it as prophecy. Frye does not seem nearly as aware as the older scholars of the need to find the best means for understanding the Bible. His interpretation in terms of modern philosophy is not laid before us *en pleine connaissance de cause.*

The part of Frye's book with which he seems to come nearest to unthoughtful prejudice contains his remarks about polytheism. He assumes that polytheism as a believable option only existed at a more primitive time in the history of the race and that educated human beings could only look at it as archaic. By 'believable option' I mean that educated men could think that there are gods. It is a fact, nevertheless, that the greatest thinker of our era, Heidegger, was a polytheist. When the founder of modern existentialism thought through the consequences of existentialism, he stated that there are gods. Heidegger does not make mistakes in logic or grammar, and he has said, 'Only a god can save us.' He is not confused about the difference between 'a god' and God. A saint of our era, Simone Weil, has written of the terrible consequences of the destruction of idolatry within

---

[*] Grant perhaps meant Plato's *Laws.*

Christianity. The patronizing eye that Frye casts upon polytheism[*] seems again to arise from the limitations of his scientism in its Protestant form.

Philosophy is always and everywhere the enemy of the opinions of any society, however much philosophers may have to conceal that enmity. The reason that Frye does not make his assumptions explicit may be because he is such a good friend of modern society. His account of what is present in the Bible as seen through the categories of metaphor, language, myth, and typology is full of interesting understandings. It is the product of hard work and of a zetetic intelligence. But it is a modernized Protestant intelligence. And such intelligence has been the most formative basis of our North American society.

DENNIS LEE (1939–)

Dennis Lee is one of Canada's leading contemporary poets – Grant especially admired his Civil Elegies *and* The Death of Harold Ladoo *– and one of the country's finest editors. He was largely responsible for the shape of Grant's first collection of essays in 1969, and he also assisted Grant greatly with his last collection in 1986. In return, Grant helped Lee to understand his visions into the unfolding of the modern world. This essay is one of Grant's rare forays into literary criticism.*

Dennis Lee – Poetry and Philosophy (1982)[†]

It is surprising for modern readers to find that a fifth of Aristotle's great book on ethics is devoted to friendship. I intend to write of Den-

---

[*] In a passage that seems to refer to this criticism, Frye wrote: 'There seems little interest in reviving gods or nature spirits: in contemporary academic journals references to Nietzsche and Heidegger are all over the place, but nobody seems to want to buy Nietzsche's Antichrist Dionysus or Heidegger's murky and maudlin polytheism.' Northrop Frye, 'The Expanding World of Metaphor' (1984), in *Myth and Metaphor: Selected Essays 1974–1988*, ed. R.D. Denham (Charlottesville: University of Virginia Press 1990), 121.

[†] George Grant, 'Dennis Lee – Poetry and Philosophy,' in *Tasks of Passion: Dennis Lee at Mid-Career*, ed. Karen Mulhallen, et al. (Toronto: Descant Editions 1982), 229–35.

nis Lee as a friend because friendship is a form of love and love illuminates the intellect. In that illumination we come to know things about
other people. The Platonic affirmation that our intelligences are illuminated by love has been darkened in our era both because our chief
paradigm of knowledge concerns objects, that is, things held away from
us so that we can master them, and also because the preeminence we
give to sexuality leads us to interpret all forms of love as too simply
dependent on instinct. For example, Laurel and Hardy have been
interpreted as completely understandable as homosexual lovers. Such
a Procrustean statement prevents us from understanding the many
forms of love. I mean by friendship a relation between equals interested
in certain common purposes which transcend either partner of the
friendship. Such a relation allows one of the parties to see things about
the other party. When one of the parties is a poet such things are of
more than personal interest.

Yet I am very hesitant to write of Lee just because he is a poet. The
accidents of my life have left me with a deeply neurotic fear of poetry.
Apart from the uninteresting personal reasons for this, it is clear that
the rejection of poetry in its completeness is widespread in modern
society, and is closely related to the rejection of philosophy as more
than analysis and ideology. The central reason for those rejections is
that the control which is necessary to human beings who would be masters of the earth is the enemy of receptivity, without which there cannot
be poetry or philosophy. By receptivity I do not chiefly mean that which
is necessary in listening to poetry, but that which is necessary to writing
it. Plato was indeed exalting poetry when he said that it was imitation;
moderns denigrate poetry (indeed make it impossible) when they say
that it is creation. To talk of 'the creative artist' is a contradiction in
terms. For the poet is the being who must be immediately open to all
that is, and who proclaims to others the immediate truth of what is.
That openness, that receptivity, that imitation, is an ability difficult to
sustain in a world where control for mastery is the paragon of human
endeavour. Of course, poetry is so fundamental a stance, belonging to
the deepest level of what it is to be human, that it cannot be destroyed
amongst us; but it is liable to appear in our society as entertainment, as
a turfing of the grave. As such its proclamations can neither be easily
proclaimed nor heard.

Indeed, at the heart of the tradition there has been a debate (of central importance in understanding politics) about the relation between
the proclamations of poetry and those of philosophy. Is Heidegger

right in saying that poetry and philosophy live at the top of two separate mountains? Or is Plato right that politics demands that poetry be ministerial to the truths of philosophy? But this debate can only be private and even secret in this era where only with the greatest difficulty can we participate in philosophy or poetry, as they are in themselves. When people have to hang on to what little they can make of these saving graces in the midst of the drive to change the world, it is hardly necessary to debate their relation. What is needed is to experience their healing balm.

My hesitation in writing about Lee's poems is, then, because the modern drive to control has vitiated my listening to what poetry proclaims. Therefore, I must proceed to thinking about them through the memory of meeting him when he was a young man. Memories can, I trust, throw light on his poetry.

It was in the baleful glare which the Vietnam War threw on the United States and Canada that I first had the good fortune to become a friend of Lee's. In a fast-changing technological society, memory is put in question. It is difficult even to remember how many people were illumined by the sinister light of that war, whatever little public consequence that illumination has had. What struck me about Lee at that time was that of all the academics who were rightly moved by the searchlight of that war, he was the one who saw that at the heart of those events was an affirmation about 'being.' That affirmation (call it, if you will, a statement about the nature of the whole) shaped what came forth in the actions of our dominant classes. Along with many others he saw that Canada was part of an empire which was trying to impose its will by ferocious means right around the other side of the globe. He saw with many others that Canada was complicit in the acts of that empire and that that complicity was expressed in the politics of Lester Pearson. He saw with some others that the technological multiversity was not outside that complicity but central to it. This was true not only in the obviously technological parts of the university, but had taken hold in the very way that the liberal arts were practised.

It is more difficult to express what Lee so evidently saw beyond this. As words fail, let me try. He understood that at the heart of our civilization lay an affirmation about 'being' which was that civilization's necessity. The rampaging decadence of imperial war was not to be explained (within liberalism) as an aberration of our good system; it was not to be explained (within marxism) as something understood in terms of the dynamics of capitalism. In the very roots of Western civilization lay a particular apprehension of 'being.' From that apprehension arose not only imperial war, not only the greedy structure of our society, but also the nature of the multiversity and of poetry, the culture of the cosmopolis and the forms of our sexuality. When Lee left Victoria College he was not only saying with Chomsky[*] that through research and consultation these institutions had become part of the war machine, but that their very understanding of knowledge, and in particular the understanding of poetry, came forth from an affirmation of 'being,' the essence of which made poetry part of a museum culture. In that sense it determined what could be 'poiesis.'

Lee saw that the turn of the screw in that situation was that this affirmation of 'being,' which was so necessary to articulate if we were to be free of it, was almost impossible to articulate because the very language which we could use for that articulation arose from the affirmation itself. It was therefore almost impossible to transcend it by knowing it. Lee expressed so clearly the baffling search to find language to speak what we are, when what is determining what we are has taken hold of language to fashion it into an instrument of its controlling power. The attempt to articulate our 'being' was therefore to enter the sad walks of impotence. What had happened to language was not only in the absurdities of advertising, the literature of entertainment, and the pretensions of journalism, but in the very studies of language in which Lee had been trained so well. Language described as the house of being is likely to hide the extent to which we are squeezed in that vice. It is perhaps Heidegger's continuing pride in his Europeanness (despite all that has been) which makes this description slightly more cosy than Lee as a North American would allow.

Lee has not rested in this impotence, or he would not be a poet. Instead he has turned the experience itself into poetry. The last verse of *The Gods* achieves a magnificent stance, while acknowledging the price he must pay – a limitation on his speaking, a limitation of his knowing. Naturally, his own words describe it best.

> for to secular men there is not given the glory of tongues, yet it is
>   better to speak in silence than squeak in the gab of the age
>   and if I cannot tell your terrifying
>   praise, how Hallmark gabble and chintz nor least of all

---

[*]Noam Chomsky (1928–), American linguist and conspiracy theorist; a fierce critic of the Vietnam War.

what time and dimensions your naked incursions
announced, you scurrilous powers yet
still I stand against this bitch of a shrunken time
in semi-faithfulness
and whether you are godhead or zilch of daily ones like before
you strike our measure still and still you
endure as my murderous fate, though I
do not know you.

It is Lee's openness to the whole which enables him to face the position from which as poet he must struggle to be. The question of the whole is present for him in all the parts including the parts which are his own living. What is meant by openness to the whole has been dimmed because the modern era has become a self-fulfilled prophecy. Modern scientists like the modern thinkers in Swift's *Battle of the Books* explain nature, human and non-human, without the idea of soul, and not surprisingly they have produced a world where it is difficult to think what it is to be open to the whole. Ancient thinkers are compared to the bee which goes around collecting honey from the flowers; modern thinkers are compared to the spider which spins webs out of itself and then catches its food in that web. If the search for honey is not the source of poetry, what is?

Indeed, Lee has described that openness beautifully when he described his vocation as listening to a cadence ('Cadence, Country, Silence,' *Open Letter,* Fall 1973, Toronto). The importance of the idea of cadence for understanding what poetry and music are can be seen in the fact that the most appropriate comment on it are the words about his own art by a genius of the supreme order.

The question is how my art proceeds in writing and working our great and important matters. I can say no more than this, for I know no more and can come upon nothing further. When I am well and have good surroundings, travelling in a carriage, or after a good meal or a walk or at night when I cannot sleep, then ideas come to me best and in torrents. Where they come from and how they come I just do not know. I keep in my head those that please me and hum them aloud as others have told me. When I have all that carefully in my head, the rest comes quickly, one thing after another; I see where such fragments could be used to make a composition of them all, by employing the rules of counterpoint and the sound of different instruments etc. My soul is then on fire as long as I am not disturbed; the idea expands, I develop it, all becoming clearer and clearer. The piece becomes almost complete in my head, even it if it a long one, so that afterwards I see it in my spirit all in one look, as one sees a beautiful picture or a beautiful human being. I am saying that in imagination I do not understand the parts one after another, in the order that they ought to follow in the music; I understand them altogether at one moment. Delicious moments. When the ideas are discovered and put into a work, all occurs in me as in a beautiful dream which is quite lucid. But the most beautiful is to understand it all at one moment. What has happened I do not easily forget and this is the best gift which our God has given me. When it afterwards comes to writing, I take out of the bag of my mind what had previously gathered into it. Then it gets pretty quickly put down on paper, being strictly, as was said, already perfect, and generally in much the same way as it was in my head before. (*Mozarts Briefe*, ed. L. Nohl, 2nd edition, pp. 443–44.)

These words are perhaps not a perfect fit for what Lee is saying about cadence. Yet I always hold both statements together because in both of them the difficult question of the relation between hearing and seeing – the sense so related to time, the sense so related to space – is understood as this relation is illuminated in poetry and music. (I never reached Lee's poems so well as when I heard him read them.) Both these accounts cut through the ghastly language about 'creative artists' found now on the pens of journalists and professors of English, of university officials and Canada Council executives. Obviously artists make things (not create them) but if anything great is to be made they do so by paying attention – by listening and seeing. (This is the trouble with Irving Layton's poetry.) To repeat: creation is a dangerous word, because it denies the primacy for art of what is listened to or seen.

The expression of Lee's openness is evident not only in his writings, but practically in his work as editor. That wonderful English word 'generosity' (for which there is no German equivalent) penetrated his work in setting up the Anansi Press and his editing a vast variety of writings. Whether for good or ill, a tiresome old manic-depressive such as myself would never have put the writings he cared about into a book if it were not for Lee's sane encouragement. And he dealt with equally queer types among the young and the middle-aged, always with that generosity which in human dealings is the mark of openness.

With hesitation I must now turn to Lee's long poems – the hesitation of my impotence before the proclamations of poetry. What I will say is at a lower level than the essential. There is a great change from *Civil Elegies* to *The Gods* and *The Death of Harold Ladoo*. To compare the rhythm and form of *Civil Elegies* with that of *The Death of Harold Ladoo* is to know that much more immediately happens in the second poem than in the first. My comment upon this must be made in the accents of philosophy (*ich kann nicht anders*).[*] To put the matter perhaps too simply: existentialism is the teaching that all thought about serious matters belongs to the suffering of a particular dynamic context; while traditional philosophy taught that thought was capable of lifting that suffering into the universal. Both teachings require openness, but traditional philosophy taught that thought was capable of lifting that suffering into the universal. Both teachings require openness, but traditional philosophy believed that the truth present in existentialism was only a preparation for its transcending. It would appear to me that *Civil Elegies* is written out of the struggle which makes human beings existentialists, while the two later poems have somehow raised up the sufferings of the particular dynamic context. *The Death of Harold Ladoo* moves back and forth with the fluidity of music, from 'the dynamic context' of a particular friend's particular death to the statements of self and other-ness, love and hate, living and dying. Never does the particular dissolve into the merely general, nor does the universal flatten out into abstractions. Because the later poems are more universal, they are more immediate. Cadence is more upon the page. This is not meant paradoxically in any sense. Immediacy and universality require each other. Even at the end when Mozart writes that 'the ice is around my soul' he is still able to receive and imitate that which includes even that ice. It is dangerous and indeed pompous to try to state what is universal in the *Iliad*, *Las Meninas*, the clarinet concerto, or *King Lear*,[†] but to say that there is nothing such present in them is just the modern denial of the proclamation which is the work of art. Certainly the truth of existentialism is included in them all, but it is also transcended in them all. The beautiful is the image of the Good, and this includes the truth of existentialism because the perfectly beautiful has been crucified.

It is easier to write of *Savage Fields* for the simple reason that Lee has written about it so lucidly himself. ('Reading *Savage Fields*' *Canadian Journal of Social and Political Theory*, Spring 1979.) Lee spells out there as

---

[*] I can do no other (Luther).

[†] Homer's *Iliad*, Velasquez's *Las Meninas*, Mozart's clarinet concerto, and Shakespeare's *King Lear* were Grant's favourite poem, painting, piece of music, and play respectively.

in a finely honed legal document what he was doing in the book. It is therefore unnecessary to speak of its surface ambiguities when this has been done so lucidly by its author. Anyway, when at the height of his own enunciation of *Beautiful Losers* Lee comes to the point where Cohen drops away from what he might have reached, it becomes quite clear why Lee calls his book 'an essay in literature and cosmology.' Nevertheless, let me end where I started with the relation of poetry and philosophy. At the end of *Savage Fields* Lee writes: 'Thinking proceeds by objectivity and mastering what is to be thought.' He asks: 'What form of thought can arise which does not re-embody the crisis it is analyzing?' The first statement is clearly true of our modern destiny. The second must drive anybody who asks it not only to what may be in the future but also to thinking of what was before the modern paradigm. The fact of this great change can be seen in Kant's statement that 'reason' is higher than 'understanding'; while Plato meant by 'the ideas' that 'understanding' is higher than 'reason.' I am not so foolish as to suggest that in the very midst of the modern fate we should try to avoid it by simply returning to ways of thought, the criticism of which was in the very substance of our fate. What I am saying is that as one looks at the height of modern philosophy in Heidegger or the height of art in the works of Céline, one must see the grandeur, the truth and suffering in both. To overcome those ravages (which are oneself) one must look for sustenance to times when poetry and philosophy had not been ravaged in this way. In God's name I do not will Lee to become a scholar of poetry or philosophy: but rather to live in the midst of these ravages, and to try to re-collect what those proclamations were. To do so is not to become simply a useful scholar or an amusing entertainer, but to take upon oneself the mystery of things. Lee, of course, has done much of this. He is a highly educated human being. But *Savage Fields* says to me that he must do more, because the milk of the joy of eternity must be more substantially present, if the ravages of fate are to be looked on, and one is not to be turned to stone. Perhaps it is not possible for the modern poet to reclaim poetry's power from the honey of the past. The ambiguity that makes Céline the poet of European modernity (in his last books about war) is that the light of eternity is not absent, even for him. On the other hand, who can rest in Céline's proclamations of the word? Céline and Heidegger both must be known as inadequate if there is to be any real proclamation. In the apogee of technological science the attention necessary for re-collecting and detrivializing can only be a fearful and consummate act. As an older friend watches Lee at the height of his powers, one cannot help wondering what we will owe to him in this re-collecting and detrivializing. Luckily it is nobody's business but his.

LOUIS-FERDINAND CÉLINE
(LOUIS-FERDINAND DESTOUCHES)
(1894–1961)

Céline, a French doctor and writer, wrote two important novels, Journey to the End of Night *and* Death on the Installment Plan, *in the 1930s. However, he also wrote a number of violently anti-Semitic diatribes. The French Left considered him a collaborator and, fearing execution after the defeat of the Nazis, Céline fled France. He was imprisoned after the war but later acquitted of collaboration. In the 1970s a friend had lent Grant his copies of Céline's war trilogy, and Grant was immediately and permanently enraptured by Céline's imagination. Although he took much pleasure from these books and did much to establish a following for the French writer among Canadian academics, he abhorred Céline's politics.*

Céline is a mystery, just to me in the same way that Heidegger is a mystery. Both so great & yet both tied to the criminality of National Socialism. When Céline says 'Europe died at Stalingrad,' well, I am quite willing for Europe to die if it is at Stalingrad under these auspices. But nevertheless they both see so much.
                                    – George Grant to William Christian, 7 January 1981

I have got engrossed in writing something about S. Weil, but I find it very slow, but my heart will be easier when I get back to that darling bastard Céline.
                                    –George Grant to William Christian, 8 January 1985

Céline: Art and Politics (1983)[*]

(O saisons, ô châteaux,
Quelle âme est sans défauts?)[†]

---

[*]George Grant, 'Céline: Art and Politics,' *Queen's Quarterly*, vol. 90, no. 3 (Autumn 1983): 801–13. Used with permission.
[†]O seasons! O castles! / What soul is without its faults? (Arthur Rimbaud, 1854–91, a pioneer of the symbolist movement in French literature).

English-speaking people may find it difficult to recognize that Martin
Heidegger, the leading philosopher of this Western era, and Louis Fer-
dinand Céline (1894–1961), its greatest literary artist, were both acquiescent (at the least) towards the National Socialist regime in Germany.
I do not make this claim for Céline because of his two famous novels of
the 1930s *Journey to the End of Night* and *Death on the Installment Plan*, but
because of his three books about his wanderings around Germany during its collapse in 1944–5, *Castle to Castle, North,* and *Rigadoon.* The first
purpose of this article is to state that this trilogy is one of the great masterpieces of Western art and the greatest literary masterpiece of this
era. It would be more prudent to flatter this age which worships 'individuality' and confine the claim to my 'personal' opinion. Aesthetics
would be a 'subjectivist' way of looking at the matter. But let's leave
these clever difficulties aside for the moment.

Such homage to Céline appears necessary since in the present literary scene in the English-speaking world his works have been shunted
aside because of his anti-Jewish pamphlets of the 1930s and his passive
acceptance of the German occupation of Paris in the 1940s. The contemporary way of writing about him is generally the following: here is a
writer whose two main novels in the 1930s were stylistically immensely
influential, and for these he will be remembered; but in the later 1930s
he degenerated into mad and vicious polemical writing and collabo-
rated with the Nazis. He will remain in the history of literature for those
two remarkable early novels, but his later writings are not worth our
attention. Some go much farther than this 'benign neglect,' and these
are not only the French polemicists of the Left, who continue their ven-
detta even when Céline is no longer alive to be shot. For example, in
March 1983 John Bayley, the Warton professor of English at Oxford
University, could write: 'When a worthless or odious self happens to
predominate (Céline, Montherlant,[*] William Burroughs[†]) it is the
defects themselves which skill must concentrate and carry to the limit
and beyond.'[1] As this is not a theological writing, I leave aside the firm
prohibition against saying about another human being that he or she is
worthless. It has been traditionally affirmed that it is proper to judge
the actions of others, but never themselves. If one did not know the
propensity of eager professors of literature to learn by writing and not

---

[*]Henri Montherlant (1896–1972), French playwright
[†]William Burroughs (1914–97), American novelist, author of the controversial *Naked
Lunch* (1959).

by reading, one might simply leave the answer to this statement as '*tolle, lege.*'[*] The answer to such attacks can only be in the reading and above all the reading of this last trilogy. To all the contempt that has surrounded Céline the central answer is just to say, 'Read.'

To say this, however, is not to deny that questions arise if one reads Céline with any knowledge of his life. In light of all the nonsense that has been written about him and in the light of his greatness, it is necessary to proceed carefully in the formulation of the question. At its most simple, the question might be: How can one be enraptured by the art of somebody who wrote anti-Jewish pamphlets in the thirties? But this is not the best formulation. Dostoevski's dislike of the Jews does not stand in the way of being enraptured by his novels. To go farther with the formulation: the present writing is not a life of Céline and therefore I cannot go into the details of the three pamphlets at issue. The one that appears to me the most distorting – *L'École des Cadavres* – is about the approach of the War of 1939. It is quite beyond the limits of discourse acceptable in a constitutional regime. Even if Céline's plea for peace at all costs between Germany and France was sensible, even if he was correct that the Jews were in favour of war between the two nations, even if he could not be expected to predict what crimes the National Socialists would come to before they were through, it is nevertheless wrong to publish such inflammatory writings against fellow citizens at any time. It is wrong because constitutional regimes require a certain moderation of discourse between the citizens of the society if they are to exist. Indeed, the French regime of the time understood this and banned the book. But lack of political moderation in an artist is not enough to condemn him to the extent Céline has been condemned. Dégas's painting has not been excluded from the canon because he was anti-Jewish. At a much lower level, the absurdities of Shaw's political and philosophical assertions do not prevent us from laughing at his plays. In an era such as ours, in which Western thought and tradition lie in ruins, it is not surprising that artists should be subject to the confusions of the age, and therefore should be more than usually excused.

The question can be best formulated in a slightly different way. Céline's judgments of the thirties make suspect for us the actuality we seem to be given in the trilogy about the fall of Germany. We are forced to ask as we drink from the chalice of his art whether its ingredients are not poisoned and therefore not to be commended to our own lips. If in

---

[*]Take, read (Latin)

the 1930s he can write as if the crisis of imperial technological Europe can be explained primarily in terms of the responsibility of the Jews, then is his art not marred at its core by simple failure of vision? To put the matter in the limited terms of my own experience: I am given in the trilogy the wonderful sense that this is the way things are; this is a monumental chronicle telling the truth about a great event in terms worthy of Homer. Then that apperception falls away as made suspect by the remembrance of the particularity and violence of his political judgments of the 1930s. I prefer this formulation of the question to those that are based on some supposed understanding of the worthlessness and odiousness of his character. I prefer it to those who say that he ought to have had better political judgments. It is best to say that the extremity of some of his earlier writing makes suspect the very substance of his later art.

In terms of that formulation, it is necessary to discuss (a) Céline's 'madness' and (b) his politics. These two questions are, of course, closely related. But I will discuss the first one simply in terms of the evidence for it in the trilogy. The second will be discussed in terms of a knowledge of the details of his life. It may seem tiresome antiquarianism to raise in detail the political questions of half a century ago. However, it seems important to do so, because of the claims I am making about Céline's genius. First it is necessary to say something about what the trilogy consists in as a story.

These three books describe how Céline and his wife Lili and his cat Bébert struggle through collapsing Germany in their effort to escape to Denmark. He had reason to want to escape. The French Left were baying for his blood. To put it violently but accurately: the plagiarizer of Heidegger[*] was calling for his execution. The journey takes place while the Russian armies get closer and closer, and while the American and British bombers flatten and reflatten the cities. Roosevelt's unconditional surrender is in full swing. Europe is being demolished by the two great continental empires with the help of the British. Céline's chronicle is of the collapse of that Europe and is laid before us with prodigality.

From that last sentence three points much be expanded. First, it is a chronicle – a chronicle 'of wasted time.' Céline keeps saying it is a chronicle, and one must take it that he knew best what he was doing. Second, it is a chronicle of great events. A great subject is necessary but not sufficient for a serious work of art, as the novels of Hemingway and

[*] J.-P. Sartre.

Mailer tell us negatively. I do not know whether Aristotle is correct in saying that war is coeval with humanity. But up to this point it has been. Therefore it has been a central subject of art. In our era war has been particularly prevalent because of technology, and has taken new forms because of technology. What distinguishes our civilization from all previous ones is the science which issues in the conquest of human and nonhuman nature. Nuclear science may scare us out of certain wars (who knows?) but in the meantime modern technological science has led both to a great increase in war and a great increase in its intensity. Céline chose for his last masterpiece technological war. (He died the day that *Rigadoon* was completed.) Third, it is a chronicle told with prodigality.

I must pause to say carefully what I mean by 'prodigality,' because its presence in Céline is central to this tribute. For us it must be a pregnant word, for it is used in the English translation of a parable in divine revelation. The shorter Oxford English Dictionary says that it means lavishness to the point of waste. Therefore, the word may not seem appropriate to great art. Who would dare say that there is waste in Shakespeare, Mozart, or Raphael? But what other word will do for this essential quality which seems common to the great artists? 'Profligacy' is the word for the vice, and the distinction therefore implies that prodigality is not of necessity vicious. 'Profuseness' means the ability to pour forth. But it sounds ridiculous to say that Shakespeare or Mozart was profuse. Indeed, the use of the word in the translation of Christ's parable points to its meaning in the present connection. The prodigality of the son is related to the particular joy in the father's welcome. An analogy may also be taken from nature. In nature there seems to be an extravagant waste that would not have been the case if a sensible human being had made it. It seems that all the very great artists share in this mysterious lavishness. This appears not only in the fact that a gatekeeper in Shakespeare is on the stage for a moment, and yet is utterly realized. It is shown also in the range of the great artists. Mozart can achieve the seemingly utterly separated worlds of Figaro and the G minor quintet. It is this prodigality which above all raises Céline's art to a different level from that of Proust or Joyce, James or Lawrence.[*] The

[*]Of the novelists Marcel Proust, James Joyce, Henry James, and D.H. Lawrence, Grant had a particular love for James, whose work he discovered while at Oxford after the war. 'What [Henry James] has done for me above anything else is that by his tremendous pessimism, he has shown one that to whatever depths one sinks one is not as he so often describes his characters as "a man without an alternative." One cannot in fact for what-

chronicle is spread out before us – ruined soldiers, refugees, collabora-
tionists, SS leaders, dying women, the animals, etc., etc., talking and
running, cheating and dying, loving and fearing, defecating everywhere from Pétain[*] on down. About the magic of the art in which the
dance of this prodigality is achieved – well, it is magic, and I cannot
speak of it here and perhaps not at all.

What about Céline's 'madness?' I do not mean by madness here that
divine frenzy which Plato tells us is necessary to the greatest poets. I am
the last person to say that Céline did not possess that 'mania.' But those
who write of Céline's madness do not mean that. They mean paranoia
as the OED defines it: 'chronic mental unsoundness characterized by
delusions and hallucinations.' When people speak of his madness they
mean some unsoundness which makes him distort reality in his art. Is
his art corrupted by such distortion, as indeed much art has been? In
such art reality is not laid before us so that we can take it to heart; what
is laid before us are the compulsive fantasies of the writer as if they were
the truth.

Two preliminary remarks are necessary before I proceed to the question. First, the old cliché: 'Just because you're paranoid doesn't mean
you aren't being persecuted.' To repeat, throughout the 1940s and 50s
the Left in France called for his blood. When he was writing these books
he had been allowed back into France, after 'solitary' in Denmark. He
had been cleared of any collaboration by a French military court. However, the Left continued its excoriations of contempt. His death was
kept quiet till after the funeral because it was feared his funeral would
be broken up. When he came back from the Soviet Union in the 30s he
had spoken of 'commissars with asses like archbishops,' and the Left
had not forgiven him. Secondly, hatred is present in all his books. He
had grown up in the lower reaches of the small bourgeoisie; in that class
which was trying not to be proletarianized, never having enough to eat
and always having to toady in order to stay out of destitution. He

---

ever reasons do what Milly Theale did in the *Wings of the Dove*, that is, turn one's face to
the wall. However much one may believe one is beyond the grace of the love of God,
that is a mere romantic conception and one can never escape from hope. Anyway read
him right away. Read the great novels *The Wings of the Dove, The Golden Bowl* and then
read the great short stories like the *Beast in the Jungle* and *The Altar of the Dead*. They are
of such greatness.' George Grant to Alice Boissonneau, Oxford, 1946, *Selected Letters*, ed.
William Christian (Toronto: University of Toronto Press 1996).

[*]Marshall Henri Philippe Pétain (1856–1951), head of France's Vichy government during the German occupation in the Second World War War.

describes it in the account of his youth in *Death on the Installment Plan*. 'If you haven't been through that you'll never know what obsessive hatred smells like ... the hatred that goes all through your guts all the way to your heart.' But are hatreds a mark of madness? Aren't all of us, other than the saints, full of hates of one kind or another? To deny that most human beings hate is to confuse the immediate facts with the highest end, and to deny that that end is supernatural.

To return to the centre of the question: Is reality distorted in the trilogy by Céline's madness? Those who think so fail to grasp what the book is. Céline is telling the story of himself and his wife and his cat wandering around a bomb-wrecked Germany. He is there as a storyteller, and he is there acting in the story. It is not some novel where the writer lives 'standpointless' outside the book. Céline's art may give the impression of madness because he is able to hold inwardness and outwardness together in a marvellous way. Céline is always present in the 1950s as well as in the 1940s. For example, the first hundred and twenty-five pages of the trilogy are about his enforced retirement in the suburbs in the 1950s. The old storyteller emerges as he goes on about the tricks of his publisher, the cold, the anguish of his patients, the nuts who come out to interview him, the memories of the hole in Denmark, the good sense of his wife, and always the animals. It culminates, when he has a return of malaria, in a vision of Charon taking people to the underworld. Then when the storyteller is there in all his concreteness the 1950s drop away and we come to Céline in the midst of Germany in its collapse. The old dying genius is there to tell us the story as we move into the chronicle itself. Or again, often he will drop away from some intense moment when Lili and he are nearly getting their throats cut, back into the France where he is now recollecting. The intensity of the chronicle overwhelms the storyteller and he comes back to the moment of telling. Near the very middle of the trilogy he once calls Lili by her full name, Lucette, as if her courage in the story brings back his love for her at the time of recollection. When at the height of the highest of the three books, *Rigadoon*, he is in the midst of the destruction of Hanover by the flying fortresses, we are present in his hallucinations when he is hit by a brick. But is this madness? How can one better tell what it is like to be in the midst of saturation bombing? When one says this, it is well to remember that English-speaking people have done most of the bombing in this era, not so much suffered it.

Céline's inwardness is not madness, but the art whereby he is present in the books both as storyteller and participant. Old men like to tell stories about the events of their lives. In comparison with the unity of the inward and outward in Céline's writing, Proust seems a Trollope of the Faubourgs and Joyce's Mollie Bloom a literary device. This is not somebody who would qualify as the idea of what psychiatric social workers want us to become. But it is worth remembering that the society which lives under this ideal is not one which seems to produce great works of art.

If I were to use a colloquial title for this writing, it would be *Up Yours, Matthew Arnold.** To see life steadily and see it whole is an admonition that is likely to be self-defeating for poets. Yet those who call Céline mad would have liked to have lived by it. To repeat: it is reported that the saints in prayer can at moments touch that love wherein 'the tears, the agony, the bloody sweat' can be loved. But for the rest of us, all too often the attempt to see it steadily is a method for not seeing it whole. Only a well-heeled bourgeois whose country and class were the most powerful in the world could have united the two, outside the supernatural love. Those who devote themselves to practice have to see life steadily to the extent that they have to get on with the job. It means, however, that they have to cut themselves off from trying to see life whole. This is why poets and philosophers know they are always in conflict with the workings of society, however much they must try to hide this fact. They must try to see life whole, but parts of that whole can hardly leave them steady. Céline was a dedicated doctor who at the height of his poetic art wrote of technological war with incredible tenderness. A steady story of what he had lived through would have been a distortion and corruption.

The definition of poetry as 'emotion recollected in tranquility' must be given greater respect than the 'steadiness' business, because it comes from a greater poet[†] than Arnold. After Céline had been cleared by the court, he had enough immediate tranquility to write his epic poem. Recollection certainly required tranquility at that basic level. But why should the storyteller in the suburbs pretend in his recollecting that he is some jolly old reconciled gent who has put on a mantle deemed appropriate by those who feed our academic fodder machines in cosy universities? Indeed, it appears to me that those who write of Céline's madness and how it vitiates his art are in fact trying to put aside

[*]Matthew Arnold (1822–88), British poet and social critic who rejected vulgarity in favour of culture and 'sweetness and light.'
[†]William Wordsworth (1770–1850), leading British romantic poet.

the truth he is telling us. They often seem to go further and wish for him to be mad so that what is told herein can be emasculated. This is of course closely related to the option that he must be mad, for how else could he have held such political opinions?

What then of Céline's politics? I must first state that it seems to me unimportant to take seriously the political judgments of most of us. They are caused mainly by necessity and chance – occasionally a little by good. They are better understood in terms of comedy than by behavioral science. And this still remains the case despite our extreme politicization in the technological age. It certainly applies to Céline's politics. They are only to be described because they have stood in the way of the proper recognition of his art – particularly in the English-speaking world. It is useful therefore to look at his politics – albeit they have no contemporary significance and are an historical curiosity.

Céline's first political principle was that war between France and Germany should be avoided at all costs. As a youngster he had been thrown into the carnage of the 1914 War, and had been badly wounded. He wanted the Europeans to stop killing each other before they were swallowed up by the alien empires which surrounded them. His account of the European situation was very close to Heidegger's statement of 1935: 'This Europe, in its ruinous blindness forever on the point of cutting its own throat, lies today in a great pincers, squeezed between Russia on the one side and America on the other. From a metaphysical point of view, Russia and America are the same; the same dreary technological frenzy.'[2] Céline wanted to save Europe (for him above all France) from tearing itself up, and from invasion by the two continental empires which wait in the east and west. It must be remembered that some English Conservatives shared this opinion. One of Chamberlain's reasons for the Munich pact was to keep both America and Russia out of Europe. Clearly by 1939 a majority of English followed Churchill's acceptance of Canning's principle of bringing in the new world to redress the balance of the old. This was not, however, possible in the same way for French traditionalists, because they did not speak the same language as the Americans. Bismarck had said, a century before, that the chief fact of European politics was that the United States spoke English. Céline was no lover of the church or of the army. But he was a French traditionalist, in that his loyalty was given to the small-bourgeois life of his country. As war approached, Céline thought that the Jews and the English were trying to push the French into war with the Germans, and that this should be avoided at all costs.

Added to this essentially European pacifism must be the fact that Céline was close to another dictum of Heidegger's, namely that capitalism and communism are both predicates of the subject technology. As a slum doctor he had come to hate capitalists who were the beneficiaries of slum misery. He had gone officially to the U.S.S.R. as the author of the early novels which had been taken by the communists as great documents of the proletariat. He came back to write an indictment of the system. He said of the regime in the early 30s that only three things worked: the police, propaganda, and the army. He had been at Ford in Detroit and had not admired that edition of technology. Although he did not discuss the meaning of industrialism in any systematic way, he clearly was not a utopian about its results for human beings, and thought it was not likely to be improved, whether it was organized by 'the Left' or by 'the Right.'

When the war came in 1939, Céline automatically tried to volunteer, and when turned down as unfit became a doctor on a ship which was torpedoed by the Germans. He saw no reason not to live in Paris under the Occupation. He did not have much to do with the Germans although they tried to court him as a great writer. In 1940 he already said the Germans were going to lose the war, and after the end of the Stalin-Hitler pact in 1941 with the invasion of Russia, he knew his life was more and more at risk as the Left became identified with the Resistance. With the invasion of Europe from the west in 1944 he knew he had to fly. In thinking of these French questions, English-speaking people do well to remember a remark of de Gaulle's in 1944. He had just had a tumultuous reception at Nantes where two months before Pétain had had an equally tumultuous reception. De Gaulle pointed out that the same people cheered at both. It is also well to remember that more French were murdered by the French after the Allied invasion than during the years of Pétain. The Left were ferocious in revenge during 1944–6.

Yet something more must be said about Céline's attitude to European politics. In the 1950s he often uses the phrase 'Europe ended at Stalingrad.' It may be true that the defeat of the German armies meant that Europe would be henceforth under the control of the eastern and western continental empires. It may be true that something essential to Europe would be lost when its civilization came to be shaped by the world of the U.S.A. and U.S.S.R. But it is clearly an implication of the statement 'Europe ended at Stalingrad' that the price of it not ending would have been a large German empire in Russia, and a slave empire at that. Whatever may be said against Soviet society, Russia as a German colony is surely as appalling as the Soviet conquest of Europe. It was of course a German argument that as the English and the French had world empires it was only fair that the Germans should not be excluded from empire. Moreover they maintained that the English and the French could only hold on to theirs if they let the Germans take part in the common European imperialism. At a wider level it was claimed that either in 1914 or 1939 the Americans and the English, the Germans and the French should have come together to set up an international system which would have been incomparably more secure than the present one. Something like this seems to lie behind Céline's opinion that this era marks the collapse of the 'white' races.

What seems so extraordinarily absent in this diagnosis is any recognition that in recent centuries the European races have been the dynamic imperialists. European civilization had brought forth that universalizing and homogenizing science which issues in the conquest of human and nonhuman nature. In Heidegger's dictum about Europe lying in the pincers of two continental empires dominated by technological frenzy, he forgets that Europe itself had brought into being that two-headed monster of technological science and dynamic imperialism. To speak of Germany alone, one simply has to remember its theoretical contributions to that frenzy – relativity and quantum mechanics. The U.S.A. obviously, and the U.S.S.R. through marxism, are but epigonal products of that Europe. After all, Marx said his thought was the union of English political economy, French revolutionary politics, and German philosophy. The chief influence on the American Constitution was the thought of Locke, which helped to loose technological frenzy. At the core of Céline's loyalties is a love of particularity – in part the particularity of the nation against the universalizing and homogenizing power of the cosmopolis. Yet the natural and moral sciences which would destroy particularity were themselves a creation of that Europe which he wished to save. Céline's politics is an abstraction from that science the consequences of which he describes so brilliantly in detail. But failure of understanding at this point hardly puts the greatness of his art in question.

A more pressing political question is the relation of Céline's art to his writings about the Jews in the 1930s. How seriously can one take the art of somebody who could put such emphasis on the Jews in explaining the crisis of imperial technological Europe? To speak of that question requires one to contemplate the mystery of the Jews. I use the word 'mystery' to distinguish it from 'problem.' It is out of the question ever to speak of the Jewish 'problem' because the answer to problems are solutions and we must have before us always in any such discussion the remembrance of that atrocious crime 'the final solution.' To mysteries there are no solutions; one simply lives in their presence with reverence and good judgment.

The mystery of the Jews is the continuation of this people through different civilizations in which the push to integration has been brought against them in vain. It is not necessary to speak here of the survival of the Jews in civilizations dominated by ancient paganism, by Christianity, or by Islam. We are here concerned with modern anti-Semitism. Indeed, my change of language from anti-Judaism to anti-Semitism illustrates the new situation. The traditional Christian anti-Judaism changed into an intellectual anti-Semitism, based on nationalism and later, worse, on race. This change happened at the same time that the Jews were pouring into Western Europe from the east. For obvious and seemingly sensible reasons, many Jews welcomed the political world of the Enlightenment and wanted to share in it. The politics of the Enlightenment expressed above all the belief that we were moving towards a universal society of free and equal human beings, in which differences about the eternal would be matters of opinion and therefore unimportant politically. Many Jews welcomed such beliefs as helpful to them, compared to those of the older Christian world. Indeed, many Jews became secularized, and believed the universal creed of that secularism – whether capitalist or communist progress. But insofar as many Jews remained Jews, that integration could not be absolute. Believing themselves a nation chosen of God, the Jews kept their distinctiveness and their interconnectedness across national boundaries. That is, they came into the universalist world of technology with strong exclusivist characteristics.

This new but partial integration of the Jews produced the new anti-Semitism in a secularized Europe. To many European intellectuals, the Jews appeared to want the benefits of the homogenized society while maintaining as final their loyalty to their particularist community. On these grounds there had been anti-Judaism from Voltaire, and his position was restated a century later by Marx. Worst, believing that religious belief was an illusion and yet wanting to attack the growing presence of the Jews, many intellectuals made the appalling step of basing their attack on race, and so claimed to be giving it a 'scientific' underpinning. The consequences of this secularism can be seen in the fact that the great logician Frege[*] wrote racialist pamphlets against the Jews. At the other end of the scale, many of those who remained Christians thought that the acceptance of the Enlightenment by intellectual Jews was just a method whereby they could attempt to weaken religious belief other than their own. It was believed that Jews wanted all faiths to be weak save their own.

Beyond intellectual anti-Semitism lay nationalist anti-Semitism. The Jews often appeared to take the side of internationalism and cosmopolitanism in the life of their own countries, and so to hurt the interests of those countries. They could be disliked at one and the same time as supporters of international revolution and as central to international capitalism. Both were cosmopolitan positions. This nationalist anti-Semitism led into the deeper and more sustained levels of populist anti-Semitism. This penetrated those classes particularly at risk under the new regimes. The very solidarity of the Jewish community helped them to be successful in the impersonal world of the new technological states. It allowed them to be tough in the economic world, because they were more freed from the straining loneliness which was consequent on the impersonal world of mass civilization. They could treat the public world without thinking of the consequences of destroying it, because they had a nation other than the nation which the public world manifested. They could retreat into their national and religious community in a way that Christians could not. The intellectual attack on Christianity was the more immediately devastating to simple people because Christianity was not a nationalist religion. People who were deprived of their particularism in technological society came to resent the Jews because their particularism had so obviously not been demolished. The economically weak in the mass cities saw their pasts taken away by finance capitalism. They came to see the Jews as the masters and creators of a world in which they could not function. Just read Hitler's account of his agony of loneliness in the gaudy decay of pre-World War I Vienna, and his identification of the Jews with that society, to understand an immediate cause of the immense calamity.

[*]F.L.G. Frege (1848–1925), influential German logician.

Céline's dislike of the Jews was of this populist variety. (It is hard, therefore, to know whether to call it anti-Semitism or anti-Judaism.) He was to say that the Stavisky* scandal in France and his work as a doctor for the League of Nations brought it to life in his writings. It was, however, essentially populist. What made it of such consequence for the future recognition of his art was that it came to the surface at a time when terrible events were brewing in Germany. Céline's intensity of desire that there should be no repeat of war between Germany and France led to his politicized writing, based on an inadequate premiss – namely, that the overriding cause of the European crisis in the 1930s was the Jews. He certainly must be credited with a major mistake in political judgment and a great lack of moderation in writing about it. Beyond this, he must certainly also be seen as somebody whose life and art is packed full of the modern ideas that had come to flower in the last centuries and which swept over Europe at the time of its collapse as a civilization. But this last has been a state common to all Western art and thought in this terrible era. Its consequences have, of course, been worse for philosophy than for art. Céline at the best of times was, both for good and for ill, a singularly unphilosophical being. He had all the contempt of the deprived for theories. This was good in that the immediacy of his art is not thinned by general ideas; it was for ill in that the absence of philosophy left him open to the 'spirits' of the age.

Céline often spoke of his 'disaster' – the period of his life from 1930 to 1950. He seems to have meant that period when he wrote of the public world, and the consequences he paid for it in persecution. Indubitably that long disaster is something to be regretted in the life of a great artist. In that disaster what is marred for us in Céline is his judgment, albeit at a time when such failure was widespread. By the time Céline is writing this trilogy in the 1950s he is all political passion spent. His hopes have been burnt out of him by prison and persecution, by poverty and by age. The splendour of his art lays before us Europe's collapse. Indeed, the very high splendour of his art is somehow related to the fact that his hopes have been burnt out. In this sense the question about this writing can be answered negatively. The greatness of his art is not corrupted by the follies of his 'disaster.' His trilogy is not a poisoned chalice. We drink from it the truth of the human condition.[3]

---

*A financial scandal in 1933–4 involving the French premier, Serge Stavisky, that led to his resignation.

NOTES

1 *Times Literary Supplement,* 18 March 1983, 255.
2 Martin Heidegger, *An Introduction to Metaphysics,* trans. Ralph Mannheim (New Haven: Yale University Press, 1959), 31.
3 W.L. Grant had much to do with starting the *Queen's Quarterly* ninety years ago. This article is, therefore, dedicated to my father, as memory.

Part 5

Technology and Modernity

THE GOOD OR VALUES?

Grant often discovered theoretical problems when faced with practical situations. He came to understand that the language of values was not just another way of talking about the Good; it was a way of talking that facilitated the progress of technology and increasingly foreclosed the possibility of understanding what had been meant by Good in the past. He delivered this talk to a meeting of social workers.

Value and Technology (1964)[*]

In turning to our society as it is, I do not want simply to run down the list of the most important social problems which arise at the present state of technological advance and proceed to discuss the problems of value created by these new technological conditions.

. . .

These are all questions about each of which important papers could be written. But you all know the facts of our society as well as I do, and you all know incomparably better than I what special questions these situations raise for your profession. It would be boring if I simply repeated the platitudinous descriptions of the new sociology; it would be impertinent if I told you how to do your work. In fact I do not want to talk about values but about value itself, because the crucial thing to see about our society is not simply that technology changes social values, but that it makes problematic the very idea of value itself.

. . .

What is it, then, about the age of progress which does not merely change values, but makes the very idea of value problematic to large numbers and particularly to those who are most explicitly part of the

---

[*]George Grant, 'Value and Technology,' in *Conference Proceedings: 'Welfare Services in a Changing Technology'* (Ottawa: Canadian Conference on Social Welfare 1964), 21–9.

age of progress. To give the most general answer to this question: the cause lies in the fact that there is an almost complete separation for many between their freedom and the myths. So to speak may seem to you highly general and rather pedantic, but this is the central condition of most modern human beings and therefore it is a fact with which your profession deals in its daily work. What then is myth? It is an account of existence in this totality which reveals to most men their own mode of being in the world. Myths are the way that systems of meaning are given to most human beings. And it is from systems of meaning that we make judgments about what is valuable. Why is meaning given to most human beings in myth? The greatest of all philosophers answered this in saying that myths exist 'to enchant the soul.' Why is it necessary for the soul to be enchanted?: so that it may be led to the true purposes of human existence. The myths are not, then, the truth about human life, they are the enchanting images by which most men are led to apprehend some purpose in their existence. They are the chief way that most of us apprehend the beauty of the world. Being what we are – neither gods nor beasts but human beings – we need to be enchanted into the good way. Let me make clear that in speaking about myths, I am not here discussing how we move through myth to truth. Truth is certainly more than myth. For example, in my opinion Christianity is more than myth, it is the truth. But it is certainly mythical in the sense that it has revealed to countless millions their own mode of being to the world. But insofar as I must be able to judge its relation to competing myths, for example in the modern world the myth of progress, I must be able to know it as myth, but more than myth. On the other hand, myths are not altogether other than truth, because they are more than particular tales. They carry with them the note of universality. The story of Oedipus tells us something universal in which we can live. Yet again it is not so universal as the story of the Bo tree[*] or beyond that of the cross, because they tell us of what is even more universal about human existence, about enlightenment and about dereliction.

By freedom is meant the modern account of self-consciousness: that is, of the self as absolute. This is, indeed, the very heart of what modern history has been and is – the belief that man's essence is his freedom.

---

[*]Tradition has it that the Buddha was sitting under the Bo tree when he achieved enlightenment.

The negative aspect of this authentic and absolute freedom must be that every meaning, every purpose, every value has to come before the court of that freedom and is under the judgment of that sovereignty. We conceive ourselves to be the source of ourselves, the source of our own order. But it is the very mark of any myth to speak of those things which transcend the individual, to speak of an order of which the individual is a part, but which does not originate in his freedom. The heart of any myth is to tell us of that which our freedom does not create but by which it is judged. This is, then, what I mean by that separation between freedom and myth. As modern people come to believe themselves to be the absolute source of themselves, all systems of order and meaning which appear to human beings as myth become other to them, and so in the very act of their sovereignty they experience the world as empty of meaning.

This affirmation that man's essence is his freedom is not something experienced by the few, but by more and more in our technological and mobile society. More and more find themselves separated from the myths in and through which most human beings found point and purpose. The last great myth which held masses in the modern world and still holds many was the myth of progress. It was the last by definition because it depended on the assertion of absolute human sovereignty. But once one has asserted that absolute freedom one has excluded oneself from myth. This process of alienation (to use the jargon) will affect great numbers of people in the universal and homogeneous state – from those at the pinnacles of authority in the bureaucracy down through the varying echelons of technical skill. The liberals who led in this definition of man as freedom acted in earlier generations as if those in the centres of power would be free, but that the ordering myths would continue among those in the sticks who were too foolish to see through them. But in our day and generation in North America we live in a world where emancipation from the myths touches every corner of our civilization and where imitation of the sophisticated is preached over the television and through the magazine in every home. We have achieved equality in our society at least at the point where we massively can liberate people from all sense of meaning. It takes a high degree of stubbornness in our society not to try and seem a sophisticate.

Now I have no doubt that this alienation of people's freedom from the myths and the ensuing sense of existence as arbitrary and contingent will be the chief phenomenon of our highly automated society. Therefore, an increasing number of these among whom you practise your profession will find themselves confronted with this situation. This separation will appear most clearly in new forms of what this generation called 'mental illness.' As Plato makes clear, mental illness must above all be defined socially, and therefore this new condition of separation will produce new forms of mental illness. It is very difficult to catalogue them because they are so new. But certainly that unclear and catch-all-term of modern psychiatry – schizophrenia – will be applied to them. As my experience is rather concentrated on bureaucrats of the second or third orders of power, let me speak of some of the phenomena I notice there.

. . .

But now our bureaucrats are increasingly of a new kind. For one reason or another, they have accepted the entirely modern and believe themselves to be the source of their own freedom. And the more sophisticated these people are, the less they see themselves as part of a common moral world and the more they see themselves as over against the world, dealing with it as otherness, as a series of objects which they move around as a means of proving to themselves that they are free. To put it crudely, many of the products of these new bureaucracies seem less and less able to imagine or to conceive that the objects with which they deal are in fact human beings who exist in the same way that they do. This atmosphere of solipsism will of course never be absolute, but insofar as it exists, political activity becomes an assertion of self and sexual activity a completion of one's own fantasies. This removal of the self from the shared world of moral striving, this vision of everything other as outside oneself, is in my Platonic book the source of many forms of madness. This is not to say that many of these bureaucrats of which I speak will be locked up; it is much more likely that they will do the locking up.

. . .

But what, however, could upset us is something more inner than these, this widespread separation from meaning (but as soon as we say that we must remember that the Roman Empire kept itself in being for centuries after any system of meaning had disappeared from its ruling classes).

. . .

There will be a hectic search for pseudo-myths in our society as also there will be profound attempts to live truly in ancient myths. Insofar as the modern craze for art is more than 'interior decoration,' it is obviously a search for myth, pseudo or otherwise.

One extraordinary aspect of this separation between myth and freedom is that where the political liturgy is full of appeals to the individual in his freedom to make society, the scientific analysis of society and individuals is centred in around the principle of a complete determinism. You all know the language of modern sociology and psychology so I do not have to describe it. Man is, then, conceived from the widest extreme. We assert 'scientifically' that human conduct can be absolutely predicted and therefore controlled; as individuals we believe ourselves to be free in the most absolute sense, as the makers of our own selves and our own values. And let me say about this extraordinary picture of man that the cause of meaninglessness lies more in the assertion of freedom than of determinism. It is sometimes asserted that modern social science is a danger to traditional morality and religion because it claims to be able to predict and control individual and collective behaviour. But it does not seem to me that this side of the modern picture of man has the highest danger. Rather, it is the other side, which asserts that man's essence is his freedom, that we are the cause of ourselves, which is much more the source of meaninglessness. It is certainly a slight misinterpretation to be told that one's conduct can be interpreted by analogies from the rats; but it does not destroy one like believing one is absolute, that is, that one is God. To put the point in another way, using the language of freedom we talk of people as 'selves' rather than 'souls.' But in changing the vocabulary we have changed how we consider ourselves. As Leo Strauss has said: 'The self is obviously a descendant of the soul; i.e., it is not the soul. The soul may be responsible for its being good or bad but it is not responsible for its being a soul; of the self on the other hand it is not certain whether it is not a self by virtue of its own effort.' And it is this absolute sovereignty of the self in its own effort which puts on people a burden which should not be put and which leads people to utter despair. To take a very simple illustration, Mrs Friedan's book *The Feminine Mystique.*[*] The book says a lot of true things about women in North America. But it is written as a sermon to encourage people to make their own lives and so puts a terrible burden of compulsion on women to be absolutely sovereign in their freedom.

Indeed, it can be said that this separation between freedom and myth expresses itself most profoundly in our very use of the word 'value.'

. . .

Any neophyte in social science can tell one these days that it is self-evident that we must distinguish between facts and values. What is meant by this distinction between facts and values? What is meant by this distinction is that there is a world of facts which we do not make but which we discover and about which we can make objective judgements. On the other hand, there are values which are made by human beings, which are not part of the objective world and about which our judgments are subjective, that is, relative to us. Man in his freedom makes values – they are what he does with the facts. To illustrate: those who make this distinction would say that when I state that Bessie Touzel[†] weighs 135 pounds. I am stating a fact; but when I state that she is a noble human being I am simply expressing my value preferences. But this use of the word values is a symptom of the very split between freedom and myth of which I have been speaking. Value is seen as something external to the facts; something which is created by man and not given in the world. This is to deny that the world apart from us is valuable, and to deny that the world is in itself good is the heart of blasphemy. In this sense the crisis of value in technology is nowhere better seen than in the social sciences which make the fact-value distinction. For in that very distinction is the denial that the world is in itself valuable. This is to leave the individual naked and alone in the dreadful pressure of time. No wonder ours is the most dynamic society on earth when we believe we have to make the meaning of our own lives. No

---

[*] Betty Friedan (1921–), American feminist, author of the landmark book *The Feminine Mystique* (1963).

[†] Bessie Touzel (1904–97), executive director of the Ontario Welfare Council, 1953–65, vice-president for North America of the International Federation of Social Workers (1956–8).

wonder the most explicitly modern men alternate between the rage to live and despair about their contingency.

• • •

To think that would be itself an example of the very separation that I am talking about. It would be to say that we could make the world meaningful, if we would only use our freedom to make it so. 'Just think right' or 'Be responsible' are not adequate mottos for social order. The worst of this nonsense is to be found in those psychiatric dramas with which the corporations flood the networks. All problems depend on some madness in our heads, and therefore we do not have to think about the nature of society. This is the cheapest form of idealism. No, what I am saying is that indeed the separation between myth and freedom originates in the way that modern men have thought of themselves for several centuries, but also that this way of looking at ourselves is made true for most of us by the immediate situations we encounter in the mass society. In the long run this view of man has created the situation; but in the short run it is the situations which give people this view of man. In our work and our play, in our dealings with people and with the environment, more and more of us find ourselves in more and more situations in which our freedom is the source of our existence.

• • •

A few years ago there was a kick on in which people talked about the dreadful results of conformity in our society.

• • •

This is indeed the chief cause of the ambiguity with which some look at the age of progress (and I use ambiguity here literally). On the one hand, one sees every day of one's life the convenience of that age – its production of commodities which ease this life and enable masses to live in the world with comfort and even affluence. On the other hand, one sees that at the heart of society there arises this meaninglessness – this sense of the atrophy of the soul. There are those who place the difficulties of our age in more external questions. Can we bring the underdeveloped nations to be like us quickly enough to prevent the population explosion? Can we stop some nutty government from using the Bomb?

etc., etc. If these external difficulties can be met then all will be well. But I think this is to miss the real ambiguity of our age: what is the quality of being in the age of progress? It is here above all in North America that that ambiguity most clearly arises, because we have first realized what in general everybody else is going to become. If you like to ride the crest of the wave of the future, you're on it in Chicago or Toronto.

THE CIVILIZATION OF TECHNIQUE

Jacques Ellul was a French Protestant sociologist whose work Grant encountered in the mid-1960s. Until that point, Grant thought that, because of Marx, Marcuse, and Kojève, he had made some progress in understanding the coming into being of modern technological society. However, Ellul's writings illuminated for Grant the character of the society that had come into being. For this, Grant gratefully acknowledged Ellul's works on the subject of technology, but he did not generally admire Ellul's later writings.

The Technological Society (1966)[*]

Two books by Jacques Ellul, *The Technological Society* and *Propaganda*, are the most important of all required reading for anybody who wants to understand what is occurring in the 'advanced' societies during our era. Modesty may require the words 'in my opinion' in the previous sentence, but I hesitate to qualify such praise of greatness by the subjective. Ellul is a professor of the history of law and of social theory at the University of Bordeaux. *The Technological Society* (called in French, *La Technique ou l'enjeu du siècle*) was published in France in 1954. It was translated very ably (by John Wilkinson) and published by Knopf in New York in 1964. *Propagandes* was published in France in 1962 and in the U.S.A. in 1965. *The Technological Society* lays down the broad lines within which Ellul understands modern society; *Propaganda* analyses one of the dominant forces shaping that society. For that reason this review will be concerned only with *The Technological Society,* although

---

[*]George Grant, review of Jacques Ellul's *The Technological Society* (New York: Knopf 1964), *Canadian Dimension*, vol. 3, nos. 3, 4 (March–April, May–June 1966), 59–60.

Propaganda is more closely written than the former book and greatly illumines it.

The thesis of great writing cannot be encapsuled into a few smooth phrases. *The New Statesman* or *The New York Review of Books* to the contrary, the purpose of reviewing is not to show that the reviewer is cleverer than the author. Ellul's book is of 450 pages and all of it needs to be read. The point of this review is to persuade others to read this wonderful book, not to summarize it.

Ellul defines technique as 'the totality of methods rationally arrived at and having absolute efficiency (for a given stage of development) in every field of human activity.'[1] Technique is not limited to particular examples, of which the most massively obvious is machines. Ellul includes within technique the sum of all rational methods used in any society, e.g., the police, propaganda, modern education, etc. He analyses (pp. 13–19) the leading definitions of technique found in modern sociological writing and shows that they are all too limited in that they do not take full account of the facts. He describes the character of technique in our society, how it has become both geographically and qualitatively universal, how it is self-augmenting and autonomous. To quote: 'Self augmentation can be formulated in two laws: (1) In a given civilization, technical progress is irreversible. (2) Technical progress tends to act, not according to an arithmetic, but according to a geometric progression' (p. 89). In my opinion, the most important part of the book is his account of how technique has become autonomous. What he means by autonomous is that technique is not limited by anything external to itself. It is not limited by any goals beyond itself. It is autonomous with respect to the areas of economics and politics – indeed, throughout society as a whole. It is the creator of its own morality. 'It was long claimed that technique was neutral. Today this is no longer a useful distinction. The power and autonomy of technique are so well secured that it, in its turn, has become the judge of what is moral, the creator of a new morality. Thus, it plays the role of creator of a new civilization as well. This morality, internal to technique, is assured of not having to suffer from technique. In any case, in respect to traditional morality, technique affirms itself as an independent power. Man alone is subject, it would seem, to moral judgment. We no longer live in that primitive epoch in which things were good or bad in themselves. Technique in itself is neither, and can therefore do what it will. It is truly autonomous' (p. 134). From other writings it is clear that Ellul is a Christian, and in some of the wittiest asides of the book he speaks of how the dominant religious institutions and thinkers of today have beautifully adapted themselves to be servants of the new authority. Nowhere is Ellul clearer than in dealing with the great liberal chestnut that technique in itself is never wrong but only the use men make of it (p. 96 et seq.).

The main bulk of the book is devoted to descriptions of how technique operates in the economic system, of its influence in the state and on the character of the state, and a long section on human techniques. One could wish that this last section was required reading for every behaviourial scientist and particularly for those psychologists whose work is dominated by the assumptions of B.F. Skinner at Harvard. His final section on 'Technical Anesthesia' and on 'Integration of the Instincts and of the Spiritual' are particularly masterful. He ends his book with the following clear paragraph: 'But what good is it to pose questions of motives? Of why? All that must be the work of some miserable intellectual who balks at technical progress. The attitude of the scientists, at any rate, is clear. Technique exists because it is technique. The golden age will be because it will be. Any other answer is superfluous.'

Ellul has been accused of pessimism and determinism, generally by liberals. They assert against him the following two dogmas of their faith: (a) that all will turn out well in the end and (b) that man's essence is his freedom, or in other words that man has the ability to make the world as he chooses. It is not my business here to point out the difficulty of asserting both these propositions at once. Ellul has evidently felt called upon to answer these charges which he does in his usually sparse way in the Foreword to the Revised American edition. 'The probable development I describe might be forestalled by the emergence of new phenomena. I give examples – widely different, and deliberately so – of possible disturbing phenomena':

  1. If a general war breaks out, and if there are any survivors, the destruction will be so enormous, and the conditions of survival so different, that a technological society will no longer exist.

  2. If an increasing number of people become fully aware of the threat the technological world poses to man's personal and spiritual life, and if they determine to assert their freedom by upsetting the course of this evolution, my forecast will be invalidated.

  3. If God decides to intervene, man's freedom may be saved by a change in the direction of history or in the nature of man.

But in sociological analysis these possibilities cannot be considered. The last two lie outside the field of sociology, and confront us with an upheaval so vast that its consequences cannot be assessed. Sociological analysis does not permit consideration of these possibilities. In addition, the first two possibilities offer no analyzable facts on which to base any attempt at projection. They have no place in an inquiry into facts; I cannot deny that they may occur, but I cannot rationally take them into account. I am in the position of a physician who must diagnose a disease and guess its probably course, but who recognizes that God may work a miracle, that the patient may have an unexpected constitutional reaction, or that the patient – suffering from tuberculosis – may die unexpectedly of a heart attack. The reader must always keep in mind the implicit presupposition that if man does not pull himself together and assert himself (or if some other unpredictable but decisive phenomenon does not intervene), then things will go the way I describe' (xxviii–xxix).

This answer incorporates in my opinion a valid methodology for any sociologist and has the added virtue of wit. Ellul's writing is informed by that quality which has belonged to the best writing about any subject, a quality for which the French have been notable in the West – a desire to see things as they are, founded on that belief which was most succinctly stated in the words 'the truth shall make you free.' He wants men to understand that 'the further the technological mechanism develops which allows us to escape natural necessity, the more we are subjected to artificial technical necessities. The artificial necessity of technique is not less harsh and implacable for being much less obviously menacing than natural necessity' (p. 429). He does not write of necessity to scare men, but to make them free. I certainly am freer for having read this book.

My main criticism of the book concerns the section on 'Historical Development.' He fails to answer satisfactorily the historical question which seems to me essential: Why did the civilization of technique first arise in Western Europe? In this section Ellul gives a useful analysis of the immediate factors present in Europe from the sixteenth century that were favourable to the origin of technological civilization. But these causes do not seem to me sufficient to explain the events. The civilization of modern Europe came out of Western Christianity. Modern secularism is secularized Christianity and particularly secularized Protestantism. (One has only to compare the presupposi-

tions of Lucretius with those of Bentham or Marx.) To understand
Western Europe, one surely has to understand the difference between
the Christianity that came to be there after the tenth century, with its
intense interest in reforming the world, and the older Mediterranean
Christianity. One indeed can see the origins of this difference in the
break between Augustine and the earlier Eastern fathers. What has
come into the tradition between classical philosophy and modern
philosophy is Biblical religion in its Christian form. Nobody has ever
seen this with greater clarity than Hegel in the *Phenomenology*. To
understand the origins of modern technique one must surely look
more closely than does Ellul at its intimate relation with Biblical
religion.

In no spirit of impudent psychologizing, but simply from his own
words, I would deduce that Ellul's lack of discussion at this point
comes from a highly conscious and noble turning away from philosophy toward a sociological realism. Indeed, his very turning away from
philosophy is surely in part responsible for the greatness of his sociological writing. The danger of attempting philosophy is that one can
be so taken up by the difficulties in knowledge of the whole that one
is overcome by a vertigo which demolishes one's ability to look at the
world with steadiness. This is perhaps the reason why so few human
beings have passed beyond that vertigo to the state where they are
'spectators of all time and all existence.' It must have taken immense
steadiness and courage to have maintained unflinchingly one's gaze
on modernity as Ellul has done. The price of this steadiness may be *en
pleine connaissance de cause* to limit one's gaze. But why quibble about
historical causes with the great? The answer to historical questions is
not practically important compared to certainty of analysis about the
immediacies of the present. Keats put perfectly my response to this
book: 'Then felt I like some watcher of the skies / When a new planet
swims into his ken.' Not to have read this book is to choose to
remain socially myopic when somebody offers you free the proper
spectacles.

NOTE

1 The page notes are taken from the English edition of the work (London:
Jonathan Cape 1965), xxxiii.

AMERICA: A NEW WORLD

George Grant has, as the author of Lament for a Nation, *a reputation as an anti-American, and from a political point of view the description is apt. Grant argued for the importance of minimizing, to the greatest extent possible, American cultural, economic, and political influence over Canadian life. However, from a philosophical point of view, he acknowledged that the United States was the spearhead of a dynamic technological modernity that was fated to encompass the globe. The phrase 'American exceptionalism' suggests that the United States is a unique society. Grant accepted this view and sought to explain how technological modernity had risen and was achieving fulfilment in North America.*

In Defence of North America (1969)[*]

To exist as a North American is an amazing and enthralling fate. As in every historical condition, some not only have to live their fate, but also to let it come to be thought. What we have built and become in so short a time calls forth amazement in the face of its novelty, an amazement which leads to that thinking. Yet the very dynamism of the novelty enthralls us to inhibit that thinking.

It is not necessary to take sides in the argument between the ancients and moderns as to what is novelty, to recognize that we live in novelty of some kind. Western technical achievement has shaped a different civilization from any previous and we North Americans are the most advanced in that achievement. This achievement is not something simply external to us, as so many people envision it. It is not merely an external environment which we make and choose to use as we want – a playground in which we are able to do more and more, an orchard where we can always pick variegated fruit. It moulds us in what we are, not only at the heart of our animality in the propagation and continuance of our species, but in our actions and thought and imaginings. Its pursuit has become our dominant activity and that dominance fashions both the public and private realms. Through that achievement we have become the heartland of the wealthiest and most powerful empire that

[*]George Grant, 'In Defence of North America,' in *Technology and Empire* (Toronto: Anansi 1969). Used with permission.

has yet been. We can exert our influence over a greater extent of the globe and take greater tribute of wealth than any previously. Despite our limitations and miscalculations, we have more compelling means than any previous for putting the brand of our civilization deeply into the flesh of others.

. . .

Yet those who know themselves to be North Americans know they are not Europeans. The platitude cannot be too often stated that the U.S.A. is the only society which has no history (truly its own) from before the age of progress. English-speaking Canadians, such as myself, have despised and feared the Americans for the account of freedom in which their independence was expressed, and have resented that other traditions of the English-speaking world should have collapsed before the victory of that spirit; but we are still enfolded with the Americans in the deep sharing of having crossed the ocean and conquered the new land. All of us who came made some break in that coming. The break was not only the giving up of the old and the settled, but the entering into the majestic continent which could not be ours in the way that the old had been. It could not be ours in the old way because the making of it ours did not go back before the beginning of conscious memory. The roots of some communities in eastern North America go back far in continuous love for their place, but none of us can be called autochthonous, because in all there is some consciousness of making the land our own. It could not be ours also because the very intractability, immensity, and extremes of the new land required that its meeting with mastering Europeans be a battle of subjugation. And after that battle we had no long history of living with the land before the arrival of the new forms of conquest which came with industrialism.

That conquering relation to place has left is mark within us. When we go into the Rockies we may have the sense that gods are there. But if so, they cannot manifest themselves to us as ours. They are the gods of another race, and we cannot know them because of what we are, and what we did. There can be nothing immemorial for us except the environment as object. Even our cities have been encampments on the road to economic mastery.

It may be that all men are at their core the homeless beings. Be that as it may, Nietzsche has shown that homelessness is the particular mark of modern nihilism. But we were homeless long before the mobility of our mobilized technology and the mass nihilism which has been its accompaniment. If the will to mastery is essential to the modern, our wills were burnished in that battle with the land. We were made ready to be leaders of the civilization which was incubating in Europe.

. . .

This connection between the English-speaking Protestants and the new physical and moral sciences is played down by those who point to the worldliness of thinkers such as Hobbes and Locke, as compared to the stern account of salvation found among the Calvinists. Such a contrast is indeed obvious but misses the nature of the connection. It was not that the new philosophers were held by the truth of Christianity. Protestantism was merely a presence in the public world they inhabited which was more compatible with their espousings than Catholicism. Rather, the connection was from the side of the Protestants who found something acceptable in the new ideas so that often they were the instruments for these ideas in the world, almost without knowing the results for their faith. At the least, Calvinist Christianity did not provide a public brake upon the dissemination of the new ideas as did Catholicism and even sometimes Anglicanism. For example, Locke, so important an influence on our North American destiny, may well be interpreted as contemptuous of Christian revelation and even of theism itself. The comfortable self-preservation to which he thought men directed is hardly compatible with what any Christianity could assert our highest end to be. Nevertheless, over the centuries it has been Protestants, both authentic and conventional, who have found his political and epistemological ideas so congenial. One of his great triumphs was surely that by the marvellous caution and indirectness of his rhetoric and by some changes of emphasis at the political level he could make Hobbes's view of nature acceptable to a still pious bourgeoisie. Most of us do not see how our opinions are gradually changed from what we think we believe, under the influence of ideas elucidated by others incomparably deeper and more consistent than ourselves. 'Worldly asceticism' was to become ever more worldly and less ascetic in the gradual dissolving of the central Protestant vision. The control of the passions in Protestantism became more and more concentrated on the sexual, and on others which might be conducive to sloth, while the passions of greed and mastery were emancipated from traditional Christian restraints. Weber was brilliantly right to place Franklin near the centre of his account of English-speaking Protestantism. Incomparably less philosophic than Locke, Franklin illustrates the influence back from Protestantism into the ideas of the New World modernity. He may have had contempt for revelation in his sensual utilitarianism, but the public virtues he advocates are unthinkable outside a Protestant ethos. The practical drive of his science beautifully illustrates what has been quoted from Troeltsch.[*] It takes one quite outside the traditionally contemplative roots of European science, into the world of Edison and research grants. In 1968 Billy Graham at the Republican Convention could in full confidence use Franklin in his thanksgiving for what the Christian God had done for America.

The fact that such men have so often been the shock troops of the English-speaking world's mastery of human and non-human nature lay not simply in the absence of a doctrine of nature into which vacuum came the Hobbesian account of nature (so that when revelation was gone all that was left was that account) but also in the positive content of their extraordinary form of Christianity. The absence of natural theology and liturgical comforts left the lonely soul face to face with the transcendent (and therefore elusive) will of God. This will had to be sought and served not through our contemplations but directly through our practice. From the solitude and uncertainty of that position came the responsibility which could find no rest. That unappeasable responsibility gave an extraordinary sense of the self as radical freedom so paradoxically experienced within the predestinarian theological context. The external world was unimportant and indeterminate stuff (even when it was our own bodies) as compared with the soul's ambiguous encounter with the transcendent. What did the body matter; it was an instrument to be brought into submission so that it could serve this restless righteousness. Where the ordinary Catholic might restrain the body within a comparatively ordained tradition of a liturgy rhythmic in its changes between control and release, the Protestant had solitary responsibility all the time to impose the restraint. When one contemplates the conquest of nature by technology one must remember that that conquest had to include our own bodies. Calvinism provided the determined and organized men and women who could rule the mastered world. The punishment they inflicted on non-human nature, they had first inflicted on themselves.

[*]Ernst Troeltsch (1865–1923), German historian who wrote on the history of Protestantism and the social teachings of the Christian churches.

Now, when from that primal has come forth what is present before us; when the victory over the land leaves most of us in *metropoleis* where widely spread consumption vies with confusion and squalor; when the emancipation of greed turns out from its victories on this continent to feed imperially on the resources of the world; when those resources cushion an immense majority who think they are free in pluralism, but in fact live in a monistic vulgarity in which nobility and wisdom have been exchanged for a pale belief in progress, alternating with boredom and weariness of spirit; when the disciplined among us drive to an unlimited technological future, in which technical reason has become so universal that it has closed down on openness and awe, questioning and listening; when Protestant subjectivity remains authentic only where it is least appropriate, in the moodiness of our art and sexuality, and where public religion has become an unimportant litany of objectified self-righteousness necessary for the more anal of our managers; one must remember the hope, the stringency, and nobility of that primal encounter. The land was almost indomitable. The intense seasons of the continental heartland needed a people who whatever else were not flaccid. And these people not only forced commodities from the land, but built public and private institutions of freedom and flexibility and endurance. Even when we fear General Motors or ridicule our immersion in the means of mobility, we must not forget that the gasoline engine was a need-filled fate for those who had to live in such winters and across such distances ...

When Calvinism and the pioneering moment have both gone, that primal still shapes us. It shapes us above all as the omnipresence of that practicality which trusts in technology to create the rationalized kingdom of man. Other men, communists and national socialists, have also seen that now is the moment when man is at last master of the planet, but our origins have left us with a driving practical optimism which fitted us to welcome an unlimited modernity. We have had a practical optimism which had discarded awe and was able to hold back anguish and so produce those crisp rationalized managers, who are the first necessity of the kingdom of man. Those uncontemplative, and unflinching wills, without which technological society cannot exist, were shaped from the crucible of pioneering Protestant liberalism. And still among many, secularized Christianity maintains itself in the rhetoric of good will and democratic possibilities and in the belief that universal technical education can be kind etcetera, etcetera. Santayana's remark that there is a difference between Catholic and Protestant athe-

ism applies equally to liberalism; ours is filled with the remnential ech-
oes of Calvinism. Our belief in progress may not be as religiously
defined as that of the marxist, but it has a freedom and flexibility about
it which puts nothing theoretical in the way of our drive towards it (or
in other words, as the clever now say, it is the end of ideology). In short,
our very primal allowed us to give open welcome to the core of the
twentieth century – the unlimited mastery of men by men ...

Indeed, the technological society is not for most North Americans, at
least at the level of consciousness, a 'terra incognita' into which we
must move with hesitation, moderation, and wonder, but a compre-
hended promised land which we have discovered by the use of calculating reason and which we can ever more completely inherit by the
continued use of calculation. Man has at last come of age in the evolu-
tionary process, has taken his fate into his own hands and is freeing
himself for happiness against the old necessities of hunger and disease
and overwork, and the consequent oppressions and repressions. The
conditions of nature – that 'otherness' – which so long enslaved us,
when they appeared as a series of unknown forces, are now at last
beginning to be understood in their workings so that they can serve our
freedom. The era of our planetary domination dawns; and beyond
that? That this is obviously good can be seen in the fact that we are able
to do what we never could and prevent what we have never before prevented. Existence is easier, freer, and more exciting. We have within
our grasp the conquest of the problem of work-energy; the ability to
keep ourselves functioning well through long spans of life, and above
all the overcoming of old prejudices and the discovery of new experiences, so that we will be able to run our societies with fewer oppressive
authorities and repressive taboos ...

That difficulty is present for us because of the following fact: when we
seek to elucidate the standards of human good (or in contemporary
language 'the values') by which particular techniques can be judged,
we do so within modern ways of thought and belief. But from the very
beginnings of modern thought, the new natural science and the new
moral science developed together in mutual interdependence so that
the fundamental assumptions of each were formulated in the light of
the other. Modern thought is in that sense unified fate for us. The
belief in the mastering knowledge of human and non-human beings
arose together with the very way we conceive our humanity as an
Archimedean freedom outside nature, so that we can creatively will to
shape the world to our values. The decent bureaucrats, the concerned

thinkers, and the thoughtful citizens as much conceive their task as creatively willing to shape their world to their values as do the corporate despots, the motivations experts, and the manipulative politicians. The moral discourse of 'values' and 'freedom' is not independent of the will to technology, but a language fashioned in the same forge together with the will to technology. To try to think them separately is to move more deeply into their common origin.

Moreover, when we use this language of 'freedom' and 'values' to ask seriously what substantive 'values' our freedom should create, it is clear that such values cannot be discovered in 'nature' because in the light of modern science nature is objectively conceived as indifferent to values. (Every sophomore who studies philosophy in the English-speaking world is able to disprove 'the naturalistic fallacy,' namely that statements about what ought to be cannot be inferred solely from statements about what is). Where, then, does our freedom to create values find its content? When that belief in freedom expresses itself seriously (that is, politically and not simply as a doctrine of individual fulfilment), the content of man's freedom becomes the actualizing of freedom for all men. The purpose of action becomes the building of the universal and homogeneous state – the society in which all men are free and equal and increasingly able to realize their concrete individuality. Indeed, this is the governing goal of ethical striving, as much in the modernizing East as in the West. Despite the continuing power in North America of the right of individuals to highly comfortable and dominating self-preservation through the control of property, and in the communist bloc the continuing exaltation of the general will against all individual and national rights, the rival empires agree in their public testimonies as to what is the goal of human striving.

Such a goal of moral striving is (it must be repeated) inextricably bound up with the pursuit of those sciences which issue in the mastery of human and non-human nature. The drive to the overcoming of chance which has been the motive force behind the developers of modern technique did not come to be accidentally, as a clever way of dealing with the external world, but as one part of a way of thought about the whole and what is worth doing in it. At the same time the goal of freedom was formulated within the light of this potential overcoming of chance. Today this unity between the overcoming and the goal is increasingly actualized in the situations of the contemporary world. As we push towards the goal we envisage, our need of technology for its realization becomes ever more pressing. If all men are to become free and equal within the enormous institutions necessary to technology, then the overcoming of chance must be more and more rigorously pursued and applied – particularly that overcoming of chance among human beings which we expect through the development of the modern social sciences.

The difficulty, then, of those who seek substantive values by which to judge particular techniques is that they must generally think of such values within the massive assumptions of modern thought. Indeed, even to think 'values' at all is to be within such assumptions. But the goal of modern moral striving – the building of free and equal human beings – leads inevitably back to a trust in the expansion of that very technology we are attempting to judge. The unfolding of modern society has not only required the criticism of all older standards of human excellence, but has also at its heart that trust in the overcoming of chance which leads us back to judge every human situation as being solvable in terms of technology. As moderns we have no standards by which to judge particular techniques, except standards welling up with our faith in technical expansion. To describe this situation as a difficulty implies that it is no inevitable historicist predicament. It is to say that its overcoming could only be achieved by living in the full light of its presence.

Indeed, the situation of liberalism, in which it is increasingly difficult for our freedom to have any content by which to judge techniques except in their own terms, is present in all advanced industrial countries. But it is particularly pressing for us because our tradition of liberalism was moulded from practicality. Because the encounter of the land with the Protestants was the primal for us, we never inherited much that was at the heart of Western Europe. This is not to express the foolish position that we are a species of Europeans-minus. It is clear that in our existing here we have become something which is more than European – something which by their lack of it Europeans find difficult to understand. Be that as it may, it is also clear that the very nature of the primal for us meant that we did not bring with us from Europe the tradition of contemplation. To say contemplation 'tout court' is to speak as if we lacked some activity which the Ford Foundation could make good by proper grants to the proper organizations. To say philosophy rather than contemplation might be to identify what is absent for us with an academic study which is pursued here under that name. Nevertheless, it may perhaps be said negatively that what has been absent for us is the affirmation of a possible apprehension of the world beyond that as a field of objects considered as pragmata – an apprehension present not only in its height as 'theory' but as the undergirding of our loves and friendships, of our arts and reverences, and indeed as the setting for our dealing with the objects of the human and non-human world. Perhaps we are lacking the recognition that our response to the whole should not most deeply be that of doing, nor even that of terror and anguish, but that of wondering or marvelling at what is, being amazed or astonished by it, or perhaps best, in a discarded English usage, admiring it; and that such a stance, as beyond all bargains and conveniences, is the only source from which purposes may be manifest to us for our necessary calculating ...

We live, then, in the most realized technological society which has yet been; one which is, moreover, the chief imperial centre from which technique is spread around the world. It might seem that because we are destined so to be, we might also be the people best able to comprehend what it is to be so. Because we are first and most fully there, the need might seem to press upon us to try to know where we are in this new found land which is so obviously a 'terra incognita.' Yet the very substance of our existing which has made us the leaders in technique stands as a barrier to any thinking which might be able to comprehend technique from beyond its own dynamism.

TECHNOLOGY AS WARNING

An invitation to speak to a body such as the Royal Society of Canada, of which Grant was a member, was an honour he took seriously. He chose to speak to this gathering of the most distinguished scientists in the country of the 'monster' over whose coming-into-being they were presiding. Heidegger's influence is apparent in the central distinction between knowing and making that Grant develops here.

Knowing and Making (1975)[*]

Different civilizations and different periods within the same civilization have different paradigms of knowledge. The principle of each of these

[*] George Grant, 'Knowing and Making,' *Transactions of the Royal Society of Canada*, Series IV, xii (1975): 59–67. Delivered to the Royal Society, June 1974.

paradigms has been the relation between an aspiration of human thought and the effective conditions for its realization. In our present civilization our paradigm is what we call 'natural science.' One does not have to be a physicist to know that physics has been the exemplary and the most remarkable intellectual achievement of our era. Therefore, it is appropriate in discussing 'the frontiers and limitations of knowledge' to start from a discussion of that paradigm. Indeed, at a meeting of the Royal Society such a discussion is particularly appropriate. Insofar as institutions are influential in such subtle matters as definitions of knowledge, our parent institution has for three centuries been closely associated with that paradigm.

Yet those of us who are not natural scientists face immediately an ambiguity concerning the propriety of our taking part in any such discussion. One side of that ambiguity arises because of the absurd pretension of speaking of what such scientific activity is, when one does not pursue that activity. When I read Heisenberg's[*] beautiful books about the works of physicists, I read them in the same way I read Mozart's beautiful letters about his art. The reading of either will not make me a physicist or a musician. Nor would such reading encourage me to make grandiose general statements concerning what a great physicist or great musician is about. Rather, they should teach one that there are realms of knowing and making which one does not enter but of which it is good to be aware, and which one might better understand were there but world enough and time for long years of preparatory study. One is now aware of them only in the sense of touching the fringes of their garments by means of parables from one's own thoughts as part of the same world. To put the matter crudely: if I had authority over university curricula, I would eliminate all courses on the philosophy of science taught by people who were not primarily engaged in a particular science. Still greater foolishness is to write as if one wished to reform or even replace such science. General discussions about the sciences can only be usefully carried on by those who have given long years to the serious and successful pursuit of some modern science.

On the other hand, the outsider is driven back to the discussion of the sciences because of the intimate relation of interdependence between the modern sciences and the arts. No special knowledge is

[*]Werner Heisenberg (1901–76), one of the leading theoretical physicists of the twentieth century and the formulator of a version of quantum theory known as matrix mechanics; awarded the Nobel Prize for Physics in 1932.

required to be aware of that fact. In seeking an illustration of this fact, it is misleading to take the example of modern science and the arts of war, because many men and women hope that the arts of war will one day cease to exist. Rather, one should take one's illustration from an art such as medicine, because that is an art which it is hard to see disappearing. In the case of medicine, the co-penetration of the arts and sciences in our era is obvious. We are moving on this continent to a society which is best described as the mental health state – that is, a regime in which massive coercion is above all exercised by the practioners of the art of medicine and its satellite arts. The ability of the medical profession to carry out this work of coercion will depend on its dependence on what we call 'the health sciences,' which themselves depend on more fundamental sciences.

This is the ambiguity concerning the propriety of non-scientists speaking about modern science. A true, if incomplete, definition of justice is minding one's own business. Clearly modern science is not my business. On the other hand, because of the intimate co-penetration of the sciences and the arts, it has become the business of all of us. We are going to be patients (and I use the word in its fullest sense) of the mental health state. And patients must try to maintain some ability to speak of their patienthood. It is therefore correct to say that those of us who are non-scientists are called to speak about science because of its evident co-penetration with the arts. But in doing so we must be continually conscious that we are not speaking out of the heart and greatness of modern science.

Therefore, I would say that the question of 'the frontiers and limitations of knowledge' presents itself to me more properly as the question 'the frontiers and limitations of making.' Not only is that formulation more practically pressing, but it does not hide the fact that our present paradigm of knowledge is one in which the traditional separation between science and making is increasingly overcome. To put the matter personally: people often say to me contemptuously, 'Why do you sound so fearful of modern science?' This always irritates me, because I am sure that the most comprehensive vision is not that of tragedy, and therefore I do not think that Oedipus was right to stab out his eyes. I am a rationalist. Insofar as science is concerned with telling us the truth about what is, how can it be anything but good? What makes one afraid is what can be made and unmade – the making of tyrannies, the making of monsters, the unmaking of species, etc.

The uniqueness of the present co-penetration of the arts and sciences can be seen by comparison with how they were once conceived in the West. Our word 'art' comes from the Latin 'ars' which the Romans took as their equivalent for the Greek word 'techne' One way of trying to figure out what the Greeks meant by 'technė is that it was a kind of 'poiesis' and 'poiesis' has generally been translated into English as 'making.' But this does not help much, because making is one of those elementary English words, which in its simplicity can hide from us what the Greeks meant by 'poiesis.' We get closer to 'technė when we translate 'poiesis' by the literal sense of the word production – a leading forth. 'Poeisis' was a leading forth, and 'technė one kind of leading forth. The fish hawk in the Atlantic storm would be for the Greeks a poiesis – a veritable production – as much as this desk has been led forth. The difference is that the chief cause of the osprey's production is not external to itself; while the chief cause of the desk's production is external to itself, in an artist, in this case a carpenter. 'Technė (call it if you will art) is the leading forth of something which requires the work of human beings. But led forth and from where? To where? To use this language about the present, we can make desks and microphones; so far we can only unmake the production of the osprey by our use of chemicals which unmake its reproduction. It remains to be seen whether we can remake ospreys when they cease to reproduce themselves.

Let me make two comments about the older way of speaking. First, there is in it none of that snobbish difference between the fine arts and the ordinary arts which has so debased bourgeois culture. For example, music just means the techne of the muses. In this language, then, Mozart is an inspired artist, but not an artist in a difference sense from a mechanic, a doctor, a politician, or a carpenter. Politics is the royal art, not only because it has to control all the other arts, but because its purpose is to lead into existence the highest thing here below – a good society.

For the Greeks, art was indeed one kind of knowledge. As Plato said, for something to qualify as an art the producer had to be able to give his reasons for what he was doing. The artist had to know how to lead things forth, not simply be an tinkerer. Nearly everybody in Canada knows the difference between the garage man who tinkers with one's car and the mechanic who can make it run. But although art was a kind of knowledge, it was strictly distinguished from theoretical knowledge – that 'theoretikeepistemė which through Latin was the origin of our word 'science.' They were above all distinguished because they were concerned with different entities. Art was concerned with what might or might not be – in that language, with entities that *were* accidentally. Science was concerned with what must be – in that language, with entities that *were* necessarily. Let me say that as a modern person I find it baffling to think exactly what was being thought in that distinction. Be that as it may, what is of concern at this point is that the distinction led to firm separation between the arts and the sciences.

Clearly what is given us in our era from that originating language has been quite transformed as regards science, art, and their relation. The words may be similar but what comes forth from those words is quite different. A great transformation which we sometimes call the scientific society or the industrial society or the technological society, and which has made Western ways world-wide, is nowhere more heralded than in the changed meaning of 'science' and 'art.' I can speak here, among learned people, of the osprey as poiesis, as production, but it is clearly a forgotten, an archaic, language. This is not how we now take production.

In this province the government has established colleges of applied arts and technology. The division which takes place here, so that the Latin 'ars' is made distinct from the Greek 'techne' mirrors what has occurred in our civilization. The arts have been divided into those which are co-penetrated with science (and called technologies) and those arts to which this has not happened. In the word 'technology' the two Greek words are put together, so that we have literally 'systematic speeches about the arts.' But in this fact we have something new in the world, those forms of making that are capable of being penetrated at their very heart by the discoveries of modern science.

In the Oxford dictionary, technology is defined as 'the scientific study of the practical arts.' In the seventeenth century, the word 'technology' was coined in English to describe the scientific study of the mechanical arts – assuming in that coining the long European division between the mechanical and the liberal. But still this definition will not do because of an ambiguity in the idea 'scientific study.' The word 'science' is used in two ways, to speak either about any systematic body of knowledge, or about the particular paradigm from which I started, particularly modern physics. The general usage is more often found in French or German than in English. For example, in my business the French speak of 'les sciences religieuses.' It tells us something of our place in modern history that this general use of science is rare in English. The statement that technology is the scientific study of the practical arts is, then, obscuring. It is obscuring because it hides the fact that something new has arisen in the world. It does not make clear that technologies arise not from a scientific study of the arts which leaves them systematized but essentially unchanged, but rather by the penetration of the arts by discoveries of science which changes those arts in their very essence.

What has changed is that the giving of reasons in the new way of making now comes from modern science. To take a negative example: Professor Northrop Frye has led the way in a new scientific study of literature. In the literal sense of the word, one could call his work technology. But clearly his art of criticism does not turn that art into what we now mean by technology. His science does not penetrate the art so as to transform it. His science is that of Linnaeus, rather than that of Newton or Planck.[*] The art of criticism is not transformed at its very heart as is the art of medicine by the science of chemistry. To illustrate that transformation again: during the sixties many of us were required, whether for good or ill, to hear a lot of rock music. Clearly science had touched that art through the application of amplifiers, etc. But such application had not transformed the very essence of the art of the muses, the leading forth of the beautiful into existence. Quantum physics has transformed the production of energy at its very heart. Technology comes to us as something new in the world, a production in which science and art are co-penetrated.

I used to think that the French and German distinction between the words 'technique' and 'technology' kept something that was lost in the English use of the single word 'technology.' It maintained the distinction between the particular means of making (technique) and the studies from which they came (technology). I have now changed my mind because the single word 'technology' brings out that the very horizons of making have been transformed by the discoveries of modern science. Technology may be a strange combination of Greek words, but it expresses what is occurring in the world. I repeat: that this word should have been achieved by the English-speakers also brings out the particular formative aspiration to making which has characterized our tradition of science. It is worth remarking that a man very enamoured of that English tradition – P.B. Medawar[†] – should call science 'The Art of

---

[*] Max Planck (1858–1947), German originator of quantum theory, received a Nobel Prize for physics in 1918.
[†] Sir Peter Medawar (1915–87), British zoologist and winner of the Nobel Prize for physiology or medicine, 1960.

the Soluble.'* Indeed, we can well say that in our world only those arts which can be turned into technologies can publicly be taken seriously. Fortunately it is not my job to say what this has done to the other arts. They have above all been turned into entertainment, decoration, and expressions of subjective fantasy.

I do not need to stress the more obvious side of the interdependence. The new inventions in these very arts make possible new discoveries in science.

These new arts inevitably call forth thought. Because they are new, this thought is above all questioning. Among the manifold questions, clearly the most important is: What is it in modern mathematical physics which brought into the world a new relation between making and knowing? What are we told about the whole, from the fact that the new algebraic equations have lent themselves so extraordinarily to giving us knowledge of a kind which has placed the race in a new relation of control towards the world of objects – including the race itself as an object. We often speak loosely of the distinction between theoretical and applied science. 'Applied' means originally 'folded toward.' But the question I am asking about modern physics is not asked as if the word 'applied' has to be added 'ab extra'† to the word physics. What is it in the very discoveries of physics that makes the world available to us in a new way, so that the very nature of the knowledge leads us to new technologies? That this new availability is a fact is just a platitude; what it is has never been completely fathomed. To put the matter in another way: in the first sentences I said that the principles of different paradigms of knowledge in different civilizations were to be found in the relation between an aspiration of human thought and the effective conditions for its realization. What is the central aspiration of modern physics and what are the effective conditions for the realization of that aspiration? What is it in the relation between that aspiration and those conditions which leads to these new arts? That is what I mean by this central question.

Let me repeat again as strongly as I can that it would be presumptuous folly for anyone not engaged in modern mathematical physics to believe that he could get very far with this question. It may very well be said: Why does such a broad question need to be thought about? Have not physicists and mathematicians enough to do for the progress of

---

* P.B. Medawar, *The Art of the Soluble* (London: Methuen 1967).
† From the outside (Latin).

their own study? Does not the modern world present us with enough tasks that need to be worked at, without a kind of thought which would necessarily involve a retreat from those tasks? Anyway, is it not already clear enough to any practising scientist what is given in such words as 'experiment,' mathematics,' 'reasoning,' 'objects,' 'research' (the art of the soluble), so that the relation between the sciences and the technologies is clear enough, and what matters is to work for the further progress of the sciences and technologies?

In answer one might say that from the very origins of modern physics and mathematics a certain new relation between knowing and making was already given. But what is given in any origin may become hidden from those to whom it is given, and may only become clear in the actualization of what was only potential in those origins. In the last decades we have started to live in the full noon of this actualization, so that what was given in our modern origins can now be thought more clearly.

There is, moreover, a great practical incentive to such thinking – namely the contemporary crisis concerning what should be made. The crisis arises because of the invention of a vast new power of making, and because of the absence of any clear knowledge of what it is good to make or unmake. Both the positive and negative sides of this situation are directly related to the achievements of modern scientists. As the scientists' discoveries have made possible the new arts, so also the paradigmatic authority of their account of nature has put in radical question the original Western teaching concerning the frontier and limitations of making. The story of what has happened concerning the negative side has been told so many times that I will not spell it out in detail again. Suffice it to say: for the ancients 'good' meant what something was fitted for. Our modern science does not understand nature in these teleological terms. Knowledge of good cannot be derived from knowledge of nature as objects. When the word 'good' was castrated by being cut off from our knowledge of nature, the word 'value' took its place, as something we added to nature. But now in our time the emptiness of that substitute becomes apparent. The only great achievement of the philosophical movement we call existentialism was to expose that emptiness by showing that the language of 'values' has nothing to do with knowledge.

The situation is often described by saying that morality has been put in question. Such a description may be true, but it is misleading unless it includes what men mean by morality. Morality was above all concerned with the frontiers and limitations of making. What was meant by traditional 'moral' philosophy or theology was the attempt to gain knowledge of the proper hierarchy among the arts. As a modern, I was for many years bewildered in reading Plato to find that the vast body of his writings, which seem to be speaking of what we call 'morality,' was taken up with detailed discussion of techne– the arts. For example, what is the relation of the art of medicine to the art of politics? How is the good life related to the arts of music, mathematics, mechanics, tragedy, etc, etc. What emerges from this greatest ancient authority is a careful account of the arts in which the frontiers and limitations of each art is claimed to be known in subordination or superordination to all the other arts. It is claimed that some people can come to a detailed knowledge of the frontiers and limitations of making.

The fact that that claim to knowledge has little surviving authority for the modern world can be seen with startling clarity in Mr Justice Blackmun's decision about abortion in the Supreme Court of the United States. He states as self-evident that the Hippocratic oath comes from a mythical and irrelevant past and therefore has no claim today on any doctor. The Hippocratic oath is a statement concerning the frontiers and limitations of one art. It is considered mythical and irrelevant by the Justice because he believes that the account of the universe on which it is based has been shown to be untrue and irrelevant by the discoveries of modern science. Even if one were to grant some substance to the Justice's shallow arguments, the question still remains: Where do we find any positive knowledge in the modern world that can give frontiers to the technological imperative – that imperative which was expressed so lucidly by Robert Oppenheimer when he said: 'If something is sweet, you have to go ahead with it.'

The new technologies are taking us into realms of making which occur as it were necessarily, that is, almost outside consideration of human good. The thrust of these arts is now turned to the making of our own species. Men cannot 'escape imitating nature as they understand nature.' This making of our species is thought of as subsumed under the ascent of man in evolution. But when making is directed towards our own species, it becomes clear that one man's making may be another man's unmaking. For example, what is one to think of the making in the programmes of behaviour modification now so usual in American prisons and asylums? Or again, I read recently the new medical euphemism for the unmaking of the undesired aged – 'suicide by proxy.' At my age one casts an interested eye on such phrases. Having solved the problem of the undesired members of the species at their beginnings, the medical profession turns to the problem of the undesired ones at the end. So that this problem can by solved within the language of freedom, the solution is to be called 'suicide by proxy.'

Fortunately, the monsters have proliferated in the last years. The word 'monster' originally came from 'monere,' a warning. In this sense, the evidence pointing to the possibility of the decay of the oceans is a monster. Indeed, the ancient doctrine was that these warnings were evidence of the beneficence of nature. It was beneficent in that it sent up warnings. But there are clearly profound differences among us as to what occurrences deserve the title 'monster.' I would make one distinction between types of monster. On the one hand, there are those warnings which nearly all of us would see as monstrous, and which we should be able to deal with technologically, if there be sufficient collective sanity – for example, the decay of the oceans. If we don't do something about them there will be visible disasters. But there are monsters of another kind. For example, we may soon be able to make a race of human slaves, whether by cloning or behaviour modification, who could be made to be content to be slaves and to live for the sake of their masters. If one called such making monstrous, one could not do so in the name of any visible disaster. Such a seemingly contented tyranny might go on ad infinitum. Nor if we say this is monstrous can we say it could be solved by technology. It would be monstrous to make such a race of happy slaves, it is something we must know in advance should not be done, whether we can do it technologically or not. What is the knowledge which allows us to judge that in advance? A modern account of the arts which could claim knowledge of their proper frontiers and limitation would require taking into account monsters not only of the first type, but of the second.

This is the chief reason why I am frightened by P.B. Medawar's account of research as 'the art of the soluble.' My central objection is to his use of the word 'soluble.' The archetypally monstrous event of this century was called by its perpetrators 'the final solution.' They thought they could solve what they called 'the Jewish question' because it seemed possible to dissolve the Jews. So we can solve the problem of the criminal by dissolving the imprisoned by behaviour modification. In North America we have recently decided to solve the population problem by the widespread dissolving of unborn members of our species. To speak of research as the 'art of the soluble' only seems harmless progressive rhetoric, if one assumes that the soluble is unambiguous concerning good and evil. But in our era it is just 'the soluble' which has become ambiguous in this respect and is therefore before us to be radically questioned.

It would be foolish to judge that thought has much immediate influence on events in any era, let alone in ours when a particular destiny of knowing and making moves to its climax. Our paradigm of knowledge is the very heart of this civilization's destiny, and such destinies have a way of working themselves out – that is, in bringing forth from their principle everything which is implied in that principle. Most scientists seem so engrossed within this paradigm (and at a lower level, so engrossed, like everybody else, with their own advancement within their community) that they seem unable to care to think beyond the unfolding of the paradigm, let alone to think about it as a particular aspiration of human thought and to relate it to the highest human aspiration – knowledge of good. Yet in the presence of the obvious disregard of thought in our era, the demand to think does not disappear. The very glory of the scientific community is that it produces some members who cannot avoid thinking beyond the dogmas of the scientific paradigm. The scientific community cannot become an engrossed irrationalism without committing suicide. It is therefore to be expected that some scientists (let us hope including physicists) will go on thinking about the frontiers and limitations of their paradigm at the moment of its most resplendent power, and in so doing help some of us outsiders to think more clearly about the frontier and limitations of making. The influence of such thought on the possible future of this civilization could not now be predicted.

TECHNOLOGY AS ONTOLOGY

The position taken by many writers is that technology is a tool like any other and can be used for good or ill. Grant rejected this position. He thought that technology had so penetrated the modern world that it had become a new mode of being. Modern human beings could not simply control technology, because technology arose from particular historical conditions and social circumstances. The computer, then, did impose on us how it should be used, because the pre-condition of its existence was a certain view of reason and nature, one that cut most human beings off from the divine and from transcendent justice. Grant delivered this paper in several different versions; its final version appeared as 'Thinking about Technology' in Technology and Justice.

The Computer Does Not Impose on Us
the Ways It Should Be Used (1976)[*]

'Beyond industrial growth' can be interpreted with the emphasis on any of the three words. Different issues will arise depending upon which word is emphasized. My task in this series is to emphasize 'beyond.' What will it be like to live on the further side of industrial growth? The other day when I had taken a foreign guest to Burlington she asked me on our return to Dundas: 'Where is Toronto?' I replied: 'Toronto is on the further side of Burlington.' (What it is to be beyond Burlington is of course quite beyond my imagination.)

The thinker who first caught the dilemmas of our contemporary society called his chief exoteric book *Jenseits von Gut und Böse,* which we translate as *Beyond Good and Evil.* Nietzsche claimed to say what it is for human beings to be on the further side of good and evil. Taking a spatial preposition, he applied it to the temporal unfolding of events. So equally 'beyond industrial growth' concerns temporality. It raises for us the uncertainty of what it will be like to live in a future society the chief end of which will no longer be able to be industrial growth.

How will it be best to live in a society on the further side of industrial growth? Those of us who have been conscious of living in North America have known what it is to live within industrial growth. To grasp the pure essence of what is given in that 'within' would be in Canadian terms to recollect fully the rule of C.D. Howe.[†] The uncertainty in 'beyond industrial growth' arises from having known what it is to live within it, while we do not know the passage of time to the future which will take us to live beyond it – if indeed we are intended ever to live on that further side.

The situation in which we find ourselves seems obvious: we are

---

[*] George Grant, 'The Computer Does Not Impose on Us the Ways It Should Be Used,' in *Beyond Industrial Growth,* ed. Abraham Rotstein (Toronto: University of Toronto Press 1976), 117–31 (one of six Massey College lectures presented at Massey College in 1974–5 and broadcast by CBC Radio).

[†] C.D. Howe, an American-born businessman, was a senior cabinet minister in the Liberal governments of Mackenzie King and Louis St Laurent. For Grant he symbolized the pro-American, pro-business policies that had imperilled Canadian sovereignty.

faced with calamities concerning population, resources, and pollution if we pursue those policies (here designated as industrial growth) which have increasingly dominated societies over the last centuries. The attempt to deal with these interlocking emergencies will require a vast array of skills and knowledge. Indeed, it will probably take a greater marshalling of technological mastery to meet these crises than it took to build the world of industrial growth from which the crises now arise. This mastery will now have to concentrate around the conquest of human nature rather than around the sciences concerned with non-human nature, as was the case in the past. As Heidegger has said, the governing and determining science is inevitably going to be cybernetics.

In North America the government of this science will be increasingly carried out by the dynamically proliferating power of the medical profession. Already this profession has been given control over mass feticide, and is more and more an instrument of social control through the mental health apparatus. North American capitalism increasingly attempts to establish itself as the mental health state, with the necessary array of dependent sciences and arts. Beyond the vast lists of new arts and sciences – which in their modern combination we call technologies – there will hopefully continue to be the political art. With its proper mixture of persuasion and force within and between nations, that political art is required if human beings are to deal sensibly with the immediate crises. The practical wisdom of politics was called by Plato the royal *techne*- that art which is higher than all particular arts because it is called to put the others in a proper order of subordination and superordination.

Clearly I am not presenting a paper in this series because of any expertise in the technologies. I have little knowledge of cybernetics. Certainly I have not the practical wisdom which should lie at the heart of politics. Being a practitioner neither of any particular technology nor of the royal *techne* what are my credentials for speaking about these crises? Presumably my business concerns the place of 'values' and 'ideals' in these crises.

In the difficult choices which will be necessary if we are to adapt to a new view of industrial growth, it is assumed to be essential that we hold before us 'values' which shall direct our creating of 'history.' If we are to deal with this future humanly, our acts of 'free' mastery in creating history must be decided in the light of certain 'ideals,' so that in coming to grips with this crisis we preserve certain human 'values,' and see

that 'quality of life' as well as quantity is safeguarded and extended in
our future. For example, clearly the problem of coming to terms with
industrial growth involves great possibilities of tyranny; we must therefore be careful that through our decisions for meeting this problem we
maintain the 'values' of free government. In the 'ascent of life' which is
our self-creation, we must see that we create a fuller humanity, a society
of 'persons.' Because of our secularized Christian tradition of liberalism, there is always someone to ice the cake of technological necessity
with some high-minded discussion of 'values' and 'ideals' in the midst
of more careful talk about difficult technological requirements. 'The
question is not simply to solve the problem of industrial growth,' it is
often stated, 'but to solve it in terms which will preserve and extend
human values.'

Yet – and it is a long yet – as soon as such an account is given, it forces
me to disclaim this kind of talk. Why? The way of putting the task – in
terms of such concepts as 'values,' 'ideals,' 'persons,' or 'our creating of
history' – obscures the fact that these very concepts have come forth
from within industrial growth, to give us our image of ourselves from
within that within. Therefore, to be asked to think 'beyond industrial
growth' is to be asked to think the virtue of these concepts. If we do not,
the significance of the phrase 'beyond industrial growth' fades away
into an unthought givenness.

To show that this is so is the purpose of this paper. This may seem a
negative job in the light of all the practical things that need doing. Yet
it is a necessary one. Nearly all our current moral discourse about technological society falls back to rest upon such unthought concepts as
'values' and 'ideals.' By so doing, it revolves within the hard-rimmed
circle of technological society and cannot issue in thought. The moral
exhortations of our politicians, our scholars, our psychiatrists, our
social scientists are caught in this circle, so that their words become a
tired celebration of technological society. Therefore this negative task
is a necessary preparation to anything positive which may lie beyond it.

I will carry it out by examining at length a statement by a man who
works at making and using computers. He said: 'The computer does
not impose on us the ways it should be used.' Similar statements are
heard about other technical fields and are often generalized into statements about all technologies.

Obviously the statement is made by someone who is aware that computers can be used for purposes of which he does not approve, for
example, the tyrannous control of human beings. This is given in the

word 'should.' He makes a statement in terms of his intimate knowledge of computers which transcends that intimacy in that it is more
than a description of any given computer or of what is technically common to all such machines. Because he wishes to state something about
the possible good or evil purposes for which computers can be used, he
expresses, albeit in negative form, what computers are, in a way which is
more than their technical description. They are instruments, made by
human skill for the purpose of achieving certain human goals. They are
neutral instruments in the sense that the morality of the goals for which
they are used is determined outside them. Many people who have never
seen a computer and almost certainly do not understand what they do,
feel they are being managed by them and have an undifferentiated fear
about the potential extent of this management. This man, who knows
about the making and using of these machines, states what they are, so
that the undifferentiated sense of danger is put into a perspective,
freed from the terrors of such fantasies as the myth of Dr Frankenstein.
The machines are obviously instruments because their capacities have
been built into them by men, and it is men who must set operating
those capacities for purposes they have determined. All instruments
can be used for wicked purposes and the more complex the capacity of
the instrument the more complex the possible evils. But if we apprehend these novelties for what they are, as neutral instruments, we are
better able to determine rationally their potential dangers. That is
clearly a first step in coping with these dangers. We can see that these
dangers are related to the potential decisions of human beings about
how to use computers, and not to the inherent capacities of the
machines. Here indeed is the view of the modern scene I have been
talking about and which is so strongly given to us that it seems to be
common sense itself. We are given an historical situation which
includes certain objective technological facts. It is up to human beings
in their freedom to meet that situation and shape it with their 'values'
and their 'ideals.'

Yet, despite the decency and seeming common sense of the statement 'The computer does *not* impose on us the ways it should be used,'
when we try to think what is being said in it, it becomes clear that computers are not being allowed to appear before us for what they are. To
show this, I start from an immediate distinction. The negation in 'the
computer does *not* impose' concerns the computer's capacities, not its
existence. Yet clearly computers are more than their capacities. They
have been put together from a variety of materials, consummately fash-

ioned by a vast apparatus of fashioners. Their existence has required generations of sustained effort by chemists, metallurgists, and workers in mines and factories. It has required a highly developed electronics industry and what lies behind that industry in the history of science and technique and their novel reciprocal relation. It has required that men wanted to understand nature, and thought the way to do so was by putting it to the question as object so that it would reveal itself. It has required the discovery of modern algebra and the development of complex institutions for developing and applying algebra. Nor should this be seen as a one-sided relation in which the institutions were necessary to the development of the machines, but were left unchanged by the discovery of algebra. To be awake in any part of our educational system is to know that the desire for these machines shapes those institutions at their heart in their curriculum, in what the young are encouraged to know and to do. The computer's existence has required that the clever of our society be trained within the massive assumptions about knowing and being and making which have made algebra actual. Learning within such assumptions is not directed towards a leading out but towards organizing within. This entails that the majority of those who rule any modern society will take the purposes of ruling increasingly to be congruent with this account of knowing. In short, the requirements for the existence of computers is but part of the total historical situation (the word 'destiny' is too ambiguous to be employed at this point) which is given us as modern human beings. And the conditions of that situation are never to be conceived as static determinants, but as a dynamic interrelation of tightening determinations.

Obviously computers are, within modern common sense, instruments, and instruments have always been things which are made to be at human disposal. However, when the capacities of these machines are abstracted from their historical existence, and when their capacities are morally neutralized in the negative 'do *not* impose,' we shut ourselves off from what 'instrumentality' has now come to mean. For example, computers are one kind of technology. But just look at what is given in this very recently arrived word. Two Greek words, *techne* and *logos*, are brought together in a combination which would have been unthinkable till recently. The new word 'technology' is able to stand because it brings forth to use the new situation: a quite novel dependence of science upon art and a quite novel dependence of art upon science – in fact, a quite novel reciprocal relation between knowing and making. This novel relationship stands at the heart of the modern era. The simple characterization of the computer as neutral instrument makes it sound as if instruments are now what instruments have always been, and so hides from us what is completely novel about modern instrumentality. It hides from us what we have to understand if we are to understand industrial growth. The force of the negative 'do *not* impose,' as applied to computers, leads us to represent them to ourselves as if the instrumentality of modern technologies could be morally neutral. At the same time the very force of the computer as neutral raises up in the statement, in opposition to that neutrality, an account of human freedom which is just as novel as our new instruments. Human freedom is conceived in the strong sense of human beings as autonomous – the makers of their own laws. This also is a quite new conception. It was spoken positively and systematically for the first time in the writings of Kant. It is indeed also a conception without which the coming to be of our civilization would not have been. But it is a conception the truth of which needs to be thought, because it was considered not true by the wise men of many civilizations before our own. In short, the statement 'the computer does not impose' holds before us a view of the world with neutral instruments on one side and human autonomy on the other. But it is just that view of the world that needs to be thought if we are concerned with 'beyond industrial growth.'

To go further: How widely are we being asked to take the word 'ways' in the assertion that 'the computer does not impose the *ways?*' Even if the purposes for which the computer's capabilities should be used are determined outside itself, are not these capabilities determinative of the ways it can be used? To continue the illustration from the structures of learning and training which are part of all advanced technological societies: in Ontario there are cards on which local school authorities can assess children as to their intellectual 'skills' and 'behaviour.' This information is retained by computers. It may be granted that such computer cards add little to the homogenizing vision of learning inculcated into the structure by such means as, for example, centrally controlled teacher training. It may also be granted that, as computers and their use are more sophisticatedly developed, the 'information' stored therein will increasingly take account of differences. Nevertheless, it is clear that the 'ways' that computers can be used for storing 'information' can only be ways that increase the tempo of the homogenizing process in society. Abstracting facts so that they may be stored as 'information' is achieved by classification, and it is the very nature of any classifying to homogenize what may be heterogeneous. Where classification rules, identities and differences can only appear in its terms. The capabilities of any computer do not allow it to be used neutrally towards the facts of heterogeneity. Moreover, classification by large institutions through investment-heavy machines is obviously not carried out because of the pure desire to know but because of convenience of organization.

It is not my purpose at this point to discuss the complex issues of good and evil involved in the modern movement towards homogeneity, or to discuss heterogeneity in its profoundest past form, autochthony. This would require a long discussion of Heidegger's thought. He, the greatest contemporary thinker of technique, seems to be claiming that beyond the homelessness of the present, human beings are now called to a new way of being at home which has passed through the most extreme homelessness. What is at issue here is simply that the statement about computers tends to hide the fact that their very capabilities entail that the ways they can be used are never neutral. They can only be used in homogenizing ways. And because this tends to be hidden in the statement, the question about the goodness of homogenization is excluded from the thinking of what it could be to be beyond industrial growth.

To illustrate the matter from another area of technical change: Canadians wanted the most efficient car for geographic circumstances almost similar to those in the county which had first developed a car usable by many. Our desire for and use of such cars has been a central cause of our political integration and social homogenization with the people of the imperial heartland. This was not only because of the vast imperial organization necessary for building and keeping in motion such cars, and the direct and indirect political influence of such organizations, but also because the society with such vehicles tends to become like every other society with the same. Fifty years ago men might have said 'the automobile does not impose on us the ways it should be used.' This would have been a deluding representation of the automobile. In fact, human beings may still be able to control the ways that cars are used by preventing, for example, their pollution of the atmosphere or their freeways from destroying the centre of our cities. Indeed, in Canada, we may be able to deal better with such questions, as the history of the Spadina expressway[*] may show, although the

---

[*] A proposed motorway through the centre of Toronto that would have destroyed many neighbourhoods. It was cancelled after protests from civic activists.

history of transportation in Montreal speaks in the other direction. Moreover, in the light of the huge crisis presented to Westerners by the awakening of the Arabs to modernity, we may even be forced to pass beyond the private automobile as the chief means of mobility. Be that as it may, this cannot allow us to represent the automobile to ourselves as a neutral instrument. In so doing we have abstracted the productive functions of General Motors or Standard Oil from their political and social functions, just as their public relations would want. Moreover, we would have abstracted the automobile from the relations between such corporations and the public and private corporations of other centres of empire. Can one speak about 'values' and 'ideals' as if unaware of what reliable economists tell us: If the present rate of growth of IBM is extrapolated, that corporation will in twenty-five years be a larger economic unit than the economy of any presently constituted state, including that of its homeland?

Because of the suffered injustices in both the eastern and western societies, many educated people see the cutting issue to be decided as centring around whether technical advance is to be directed under capitalist or socialist control. What matters is whether the computer is used in ways which are capitalist or socialist. Some of the best of the young in the West are held by marxism in revolt against our society, while it seems that some of the best in Eastern Europe are liberals in reaction against their society. Despite all the abuses committed in the name of marxism in eastern societies, this way of thought has remained a powerful minority influence in the West, just because it seems to point to a more equitable development of technical society than is possible under state capitalism. Also marxism, as a system of thought, is more successful than the liberal ideologies of the West in placing technique within a corporate framework of purpose beyond the individual. At any stage of capitalism the interest of all are contractually subordinated to the interest of some. Marxism has been the chief source of a continuing critique of the facts that our social purposes are determined by private interests and that science is often harnessed to those purposes by calling it 'value-free.' On the other side, the liberal ideologists have asserted that our structures lead to a profounder liberation than is possible under marxist socialism. This assertion is based not only on the negative criticism that communism is inevitably inhibited into a rancorous and cruel statism, but also on the positive judgement that capitalist freedom better opens the way to the development of technical science. The claims of the Western empire that their system better liberates technology are neither insincere nor unsubstantiated. The present desire of Russia for American computers surely illustrates that.

However, amidst the passionate ideologists, it is well to remember what marxism and American liberalism (two Western-produced beliefs) hold in common. They both believe that the good progress of the race is in the direction of the universal society of free and equal human beings, that is, towards the universal and homogeneous state. They both assert that the technology, which comes out of the same account of reason, is the necessary and good means to that end. In saying this I do not mean to encourage any of that nonsense about 'the end of ideology,' which was put about by a shallow America sociologist a decade ago. Those who think that the crucial question about technological societies is whether they develop under marxist or liberal 'ideals' are given in that thought a source of responsibility for our present situation. (Who cannot prefer such ardent people to the vast numbers of the detached who currently retreat into a banal privacy?) Nevertheless, because of their belief in these ideologies, they are likely to forget that both sides of the controversy share assumptions which are more fundamental than that which divides them. At the immediate and flaming surface is their common assumption concerning the dependence of the achievement of a better society in the future upon the mastery of the human and the non-human by technological science. And that assumption comes forth from a series of deeper assumptions concerning what is. For example, it is assumed there is something we call 'history' over against 'nature,' and that it is in that 'history' that human beings have acquired their 'rationality.' To put it in the pedantic language of scholarship about the history of Western thought: both marxism and liberalism are penetrated in their ultimate assumptions by the thoughts of Rousseau; and in his thought about the origins of human beings the concept of reason as historical makes its extraordinary public arrival.

What calls out for recognition here is that the same apprehension of what it is to be 'reasonable' leads men to build computers and to conceive the universal and homogeneous society as the highest political goal. The ways such machines can be used must be at one with certain conceptions of political purposes, because the same kind of 'reasoning' made the machines and formulated the purposes. To put the matter extremely simply: the modern 'physical' sciences and the modern 'political' sciences have developed in mutual interpenetration, and we can only begin to understand that interpenetration in terms of some

common source from which both forms of science found their sustenance. Indeed, to think 'reasonably' about the modern account of reason is of such difficulty because that account has structured our very
thinking in the last centuries. For this reason scholars are impotent in
the understanding of it because they are trying to understand that
which is the very form of how they understand. The very idea that 'reason' is that reason which allows us to conquer objective human and
non-human nature controls our thinking about everything.

It cannot be my purpose here to describe the laying of the foundations of that interpenetration of the physical and moral sciences which
is at the heart of Western 'history' and now of world destiny. Such a
mapping of those foundations would require detailed exposition of our
past: what was made and thought and done by the inventors, the scientists, the philosophers, the theologians, the artists, the reformers, the
politicians. Scholarship is very different from thought, although it
often pretends to be the same. But good scholarship can be a support
for thought, in the same way that good doctors can be a support for
health. Suffice it to say here that the root of modern history lies in a
particular experience of 'reason,' and the interpenetration of the
human and non-human sciences that grew from that root. It is an
occurrence which has not yet been understood. Nevertheless, it is an
event the significance of which for good or evil must now be attempted
to be thought. The statement, 'the computer does not impose on us *the
ways* it should be used,' hides that interpretation. To repeat, it simply
presents us with neutral instruments which we in our freedom can
shape to our 'values' and 'ideals.' But the very conceptions 'values' and
'ideals' come from the same form of reasoning which built the computers. 'Computers' and 'values' both come forth from that stance which
summoned the world before it to show its reasons and bestowed 'values' on the world. Those 'values' are supposed to be the creations of
human beings and have, linguistically, taken the place of the traditional 'good,' which was not created but recognized. In short, computers do not present us with neutral means for building any kind of
society. All their alternative ways lead us towards the universal and
homogeneous state. Our use of them is exercised within that mysterious modern participation in what we call 'reason.' Participation in that
particular conception of reason is the strangest of all our experiences,
and the most difficult to think in its origins.

To go further, because computers are produced from modern reasoning, the strongest ambiguity in the statement, 'the computer does

not impose on us the ways it *should* be used,' is that our novelty is presented to us as if human beings 'should' use these machines for certain purposes and not for others. But what does the word 'should' mean in advanced technological societies? Is it not of the essence of our novelty that 'shouldness,' as it was once affirmed, can no longer hold us in its claiming?

'Should' was originally the past tense of 'shall.' It is still sometimes used in a conditional sense to express greater uncertainty about the future than the use of 'shall'; ('I shall get a raise this year' is more certain than 'I should get a raise this year.' The same is in that wonderful colloquialism from the home of our language: 'I shouldn't wonder.') 'Should' has gradually taken over the sense of 'owing' from 'shall.' (In its origins 'owing' was given in the word 'shall' when used as a transitive verb.) In the sentence 'the computer does not impose on us the ways it *should* be used' we are speaking about human actions which express 'owing.' If the statement about computers were in positive form 'the computer *does* impose on us the way it should be used,' the debt would probably be understood as from human beings to machine. We can say of a good car that we owe it to the car to lubricate it properly or not to ride the clutch. We would mean it in the same sense that we owe it to ourselves to try to avoid contradicting ourselves, if we wish to think out some matter clearly. If we want the car to do what it is fitted for – which is, in the traditional usage, its good – then we must look after it. But the 'should' in the statement about the computer is clearly not being used about what is owed from men to the machine. What is, then, the nature of the debt spoken? To what or to whom do human beings owe it? Is that debt conditional? For example, if men 'should' use computers only in ways that are compatible with constitutional government and never as instruments of tyranny, to what or to whom is this required support of constitutional government owed? To ourselves? to other human beings? to evolution? to nature? to 'history?' to reasonableness? to God?

There have been many descriptions of our time as essentially characterized by a darkening or even disappearance of any conception of good. These have often been made by those who are dismayed by the uncertainty of our era and find solace from the suffering of that dismay in nostalgia for some other era. Indeed, as human beings have come to believe that their affirmations of goodness are not justified by reason or nature, history, or God, the effect upon many has been what some have called 'nihilism.' This belief has had wide political significance because it has become possible for many through mass literacy. Mass training has produced in North America that intensely vulgar phenomenon, popular wised-upness. I include within mass training the present university system. Nevertheless, it is incorrect to characterize the modern West as a society of nihilism, that is, as if people had no sense of what is good. If we used the word 'good' in its most general modern sense to stand for that which we approve, and 'bad' for that which we deplore, it is evident that the majority of modern people give their shared disapproval to certain forms of life. Can we not say that for most 'freedom' to do what they want in such realms as sexuality is an evident good? Most modern people consider good those political leaders who combine seeming resolution with evident charm. The very influence of ideologies in our era, whether marxism, American liberalism, or National Socialism, has surely not been a mark of nihilism, but rather a mark of how much human beings wanted the evident goods that were put before them evidently.

Therefore, it is deluding if we characterize our novel modern situation as nihilistic. But at the same time we have to be aware that some great change has taken place. To characterize that change, it is best to state that it has fallen to the lot of people who are truly modern to apprehend goodness in a different way from all previous societies. 'Goodness' is now apprehended in a way which excludes from it all 'owingness.' To generalize this as clearly as I am able: the traditional Western view of goodness is that which meets us with an excluding claim and persuades us that in obedience to that claim we will find what we are fitted for. The modern view of goodness is that which is advantageous to our creating richness of life (or, if you like, the popular modern propagandists' 'quality of life').

What is true of the modern conception of goodness (which appears in advanced technological societies and which distinguishes it from older conceptions of goodness) is that it does not include the assertion of an owed claim which is intrinsic to our desiring. Owing is always provisory upon what we desire to create. Obviously we come upon the claims of others and our creating may perforce be limited particularly by the state, because of what is currently permitted to be done to others. However, such claims, whether within states or internationally, are seen as contractual, that is, provisional. This exclusion of non-provisory owing from our interpretation of desire means that what is summoned up by the word 'should' is no longer what was summoned up among our ancestors. Its evocation always includes an 'if.' Moreover, the arrival in the world of this changed interpretation of goodness is inter-related to the arrival of technological civilization. The liberation of human desiring from any supposed excluding claim, so that it is believed that we freely create values, is a face of the same liberation in which men overcame chance by technology – the liberty to make happen what we want to make happen.

'The computer does not impose on us the ways it *should* be used' asserts the very essence of the modern view (human ability freely to determine what happens) and then puts that freedom in the service of the very 'should' which that same modern novelty has denied. The resolute mastery to which we are summoned in 'does not impose' is the very source of difficulty in apprehending goodness as 'should.' There-fore, the 'should' in the statement has only a masquerading resonance when it is asked to provide positive moral content to the actions we are summoned to concerning computers. It is a word carried over from the past to be used in a present which is only ours because the assumptions of that past were criticized out of public existence. The statement there-fore cushions us from the full impact of the novelties it asks us to con-sider. It pads us against wondering about the disappearance of 'should' in its ancient resonance, and what this disappearance may portend for the future.

Statements such as this are increasingly common in the liberal world because we feel the need to buttress the morality of our managers in their daily decisions. Indeed, the more it becomes possible to conceive that we might not be able to control the immensity of the apparatus and the constantly changing emergencies it presents us with, the more intense become the calls for moral 'values' and 'ideals.' Technological society is presented to us as a set of neutral means, something outside ourselves, and human beings are presented as in touch with some con-stant, from out of which constancy they are called upon to deal with the new external crises. But obviously all that is given us in the technologi-cal sciences denies that constancy, that eternality. What happens is that constancy is appealed to in practical life and denied in intellectual life. In such a situation the language of eternality is gradually removed from all serious public realms, because it is made completely unresonant by what dominates the public world. The residual and unresonant con-stant appealed to in the sentence about the computer is the word 'should.' But the intellectual life which allowed the coming to be of computers has also made 'should' almost unthinkable.

I have discussed this sentence at great length to show that when we

look at our present situation as if we in our freedom were called upon
to impose 'values' and 'ideals' on technological situations seen as
'objective' to us, we are not beyond industrial growth, but within that
which brought industrial growth to be. 'Values' and 'ideals,' 'persons'
and 'the creating of history' are at their very heart the technological
speaking. Let me concentrate my essential point in a criticism of a
recent writing by Professor C.B. Macpherson. In his *Democratic Theory*,
an early section is entitled 'The race between ontology and technology.' It is just such words that I am trying to show as deluding. Macpherson identifies ontologies with 'views of the essence of man,' and writes
of 'a fateful race between ontological change and technological
change.' One might ask: Is not technological change an aspect of what
is, and therefore not something other than ontological change? But
what is above all misleading in such words is that they obscure the fact
that every act of scientific discovery or application comes forth from an
ontology which so engrosses us that it can well be called our Western
destiny. Technology is not something over against ontology; it is the
ontology of the age. It is for us an almost inescapable destiny. The great
question is not then 'the race between technology and ontology,' but
what is the ontology which is declared in technology? What could it be
to be 'beyond' it, and would it be good to be 'beyond' it?

The foregoing has not been stated for the sake of increasing
the sense of human impotence. Aesthetic pessimism is a form of self-
indulgence to which protected academics are particularly prone. Insofar as one is aware that one is prone to such sick pessimism, it should
be dealt with in privacy and not presented publicly. It always matters
what we do. Moreover, at a much deeper level, authentic despair is a
human possibility and a very great evil. Therefore, it must be prepared
for. Our first obligation is to seek acquaintance with joy so that any
arrival of despair does not carry us into madness. The complete
absence of joy is madness. However, the stating of the facts in any given
situation has nothing to do with despair, but only with the possible
destruction of inadequate sources of hope – the destruction of which is
a necessary part of all our lives.

Rather, my purpose is to state the profundity with which technological civilization enfolds us as our destiny. Coming to meet us out of the
very substance of our past, that destiny has now become, not only our
own, but that of the species as a whole. Moreover, this destiny is not
alone concerned with such obvious externals that we can blow ourselves up or ameliorate diabetes or have widespread freedom from

labour or watch our distant wars on television. It is a destiny which presents us with what we think of the whole, with what we think is good, with what we think good is, with how we conceive sanity and madness, beauty and ugliness. It is a destiny which enfolds us in our most immediate experiences: what we perceive when we encounter a bird or a tree, a child, or a road. It equally enfolds us in less tangible apperceptions such as temporality. My cruder purpose is to make clear that that destiny is not a situation like picking and choosing in a supermarket; rather, it is like a package deal.

When we, as Western people, put to ourselves the question of what can lie 'beyond industrial growth,' we are liable to be asking it as a problem within the package which is that destiny. It is taken as a problem of the same order as that which we are currently meeting because of our dependence on oil and the Arab awakening. To say this is not to belittle such problems or to seem to stand in proud aloofness from them. They have to be met and will require great wisdom – indeed, greater wisdom than has characterized our English-speaking rulers since 1914.

However, even at the immediate level of the pragmatic, the questioning in 'beyond industrial growth' begins to reveal the universal which is spoken in technology. We move into the tightening circle in which more technological science is called for to meet the problems which technological science has produced. In that tightening circle, the overcoming of chance is less and less something outside us, but becomes more and more the overcoming of chance in our own species, in our very own selves. Every new appeal for a more exact cybernetics means, in fact, forceful new means of mastery over the most intimate aspects of the lives of masses of people. Particularly among some of those who are the patients of that mastery and among those who keep some hesitation about their part in enforcing it, questioning cannot be wholly repressed. For example, will it be possible to hide entirely what is being spoken universally about our own species in the massive programs of feticide which characterize modern societies? Will it be possible to hide what is being spoken universally in the advances in reproductive biology and behavioural psychology, as those advances become part of our everyday lives? Moreover, when what is spoken there universally is listened to, will it be able to be accepted as including in its universality the hunger and thirst for justice?

For thinkers, the universal in 'beyond industrial growth' must appear as the package deal becomes increasingly explicit. With that explicitness inevitably comes the central theoretical question of this era. Can our thinking be satisfied with the historicist universal? If the universal appearing as historicism can be known as only a masquerading of the universal, then it will be possible to ask the following question: In all that has been practised and thought and made by Western human beings in their dedication to the overcoming of chance, what has there been of good? What has perhaps been found? What has perhaps been lost? What have these possible losings and findings to do with what we can know of the transhistorical whole?

It looks very likely that amidst the pressing calls for cybernetic organization in our immediate future, there will be little social patience for those who think about these questions. Thinkers will be accused of vagueness and uncertainty, impracticality, and self-indulgence in times of crisis. For example, it is clear that the great intellectual achievement of modernity is its physics, and that the scientific community which ultimately feeds on that achievement is the most intellectually influential in our midst. Yet in its pride, that community is, with rare exceptions, contemptuous and impatient of any thought which is 'beyond' solutions. Historicist scholarship is tolerated because it is unlikely to pass over into thought. Therefore, I would predict that those who want to think will have to develop a more than usual irony to protect themselves from this impatience.

In the face of the complexity, immensity, and uncertainty of that which calls to be questioned, it may, indeed, seem that thinkers are impotent as aids to the inescapable immediacies of the public realm. The originating tradition concerning rationality in the West was that it had something to do with happiness and therefore something to do with throwing light upon the awful responsibilities of time. In the ambiguous heart of Plato's dialogues, philosophy included political philosophy. This relation to practice may seem to have been lost when thinkers are called to wander in the chasms which have been opened up by education for the overcoming of chance. It may seem that, when thought wanders in these chasms, it becomes useless to the public realm. Yet the darkness which envelops the Western world because of its long dedication to the overcoming of chance is just a fact. Thinkers who deny the fact of that darkness are no help in illuminating a finely tempered practice for the public realm. The job of thought at our time is to bring into the light that darkness as darkness. If thinkers are turned away from this by becoming tamed confederates in the solution of some particular problem, they have turned away from the occupation they are called to. The consequent division between thought and practice is therefore even greater than at most times and places. That division is a price that has to be paid by people given over primarily either to practice or to thought, because of the false unity between thought and practice which has dominated our civilization so long in its dedication to the overcoming of chance. That false unity presses on us in the two leading ideologies of our age – marxism and American liberalism – in both of which thought has been made almost to disappear as it was perverted into a kind of practice.

Those of us who are Christians have been told that there is something 'beyond' both thought and practice. Both are means or ways. In their current public division from each other, the memory of their joint insufficiency will be helpful to both. What is also necessary for both types of life is a continuing dissatisfaction with the fact that the darkness of our era leads to such a division between them. In this dissatisfaction lies the hope of taking a first step: to bring the darkness into light as darkness.

TECHNOLOGY AND FAITH

This important paper was delivered to an American audience and published in a large anthology that was not widely available. It deserves to be much better known than it is, since it contains some of Grant's most profound reflections on the origins of technology in Western Christianity. This version was corrected by Grant for future publication.

It seems to me the case that western Christianity is now going to go through a great purging of its authority because it was in the civilization where it was dominant that the worst form of secularity has arisen and is now likely to become worldwide. Both Roman Catholicism and Protestantism are going to pay terrible prices, both extrinsic and intrinsic, for the ultimate relation they maintained with that progressive materialism. This kind of historical remark has no relation at all to the truth of Christianity which is just given for me in the perfection of Christ, which to me can only be thought in terms of Trinitarianism (though through my own unclarity I never much understand what is meant by the third hypostasis). My particular function in the midst of what seems to me the evident fall of western Christianity is to try to understand just a small amount of what was at fault in this particular manifestation of Christianity, so that one plays a minute part in something that will take centuries – namely the rediscovery of authoritative Christianity. I have no doubt that that will, slowly and through very great suffering, occur – because Christianity tells the truth about the most important matter – namely the perfection of God and the affliction of human beings, and it has been given that truth in a way no other religion has.

– George Grant to Derek Bedson, 2 February 1978

Justice and Technology (1984)[*]

Christ said: Happy are those who are hungry and thirsty for justice (Matthew 5:6). Socrates said that it is better to suffer injustice than to inflict it (*Crito* 49b-e; *Gorgias* 474b ff). It is not my purpose here to discus the relation between these two statements. That would be to raise the question which in Jewish terms is the relation between Athens and Jerusalem, and in Christian terms the relation between Socrates and Christ. I will simply abstract from discussing whatever possible differences have been said to distinguish these two statements and take them as saying something common about justice. Nor is it my purpose to discuss the even more mysterious fact that one may be grasped by the truth of Christ's proposition, even when one's own hungering and thirsting is not much directed toward justice. It is never one's business to concern oneself with other people's ultimate hungers and thirsts; but I know something about my own, yet am still grasped by the truth of that proposition. Put generally, this question is: If the intellect is enlightened by love, and therefore access to the most important knowledge is dependent on love, how is it possible to assent to the truth of a proposition which is made from way beyond one's own capacities of love?

My intention is to discuss the relation between 'technology' and the statements of Christ and Socrates. I do not mean by 'technology' the sum of all modern techniques, but that unique co-penetration of knowing and making, of the arts and sciences which originated in Western Europe and has now become worldwide. Behind such descriptions lies

[*] George Grant, 'Justice and Technology,' in *Theology and Technology: Essays in Christian Analysis and Exegesis*, ed. Carl Mitcham and Jim Grote (Lanham, Md.: University Press of America 1984), 237–46.

the fact that 'technology' is an affirmation concerning what is; it remains unfathomed, but is very closely interwoven with that primal affirmation made by medieval Westerners as they accepted their Christianity in a new set of apperceptions. That affirmation had something to do with a new content given by Western people to the activity of 'willing.' 'Technology' is the closest, yet inadequate word for what that new affirmation has become as it is now worked out in us and around us. But to use that inadequate word is to grant the unfathomedness of the affirmation.

Leaving aside the crucial question of what it would be to live or think 'outside' or 'beyond' that apprehension, it is certainly true that all of us are in it in the sense that its manifestations, both outward and inward, make up most of our daily lives. For example, as university people the institutions we work for are in their heart and movement becoming more and more attuned to that apprehension in its modern moment. Moreover, it would be foolish to say that 'technology' dominates chemistry departments and not religion departments. Much scholarship in religion sounds the pure chord of the affirmation I have called 'technology.'

This paper is about an ambiguity in the relation between technology and justice (in its fullest sense.) Clearly technology has been an affirmation concerning justice. I need not press the obvious point that among its originators and its practitioners, it was thought that the progress of the arts and sciences would alleviate the human estate. Negatively it would eliminate many injustices which had characterized the past; positively it would open new apprehensions of justice by making a greater percentage of the population wise. Many of those in all parts of the globe who presently are most deeply engrossed in the progress of the arts and the sciences still see their engrossment in terms of the realization of justice. The ambiguity I wish to point to is not the practical one that from this technology have come forth powers that can be used for purposes that speak against justice. It is not my business here to describe behaviour modification, the organization of the mass destruction of the unborn, the corporate bureaucracies in which human beings are engulfed or, at a less immediate level, the destruction of such intermediate institutions as the family or the country. We could all make out lists of such issues which are now coming forth from technology in its most obvious sense, and which threaten justice in its most obvious sense. Indeed, many of the best people engrossed in that apprehension which I have called 'technology' are aware of these difficulties, and want to carry that apprehension to its limits in the hopes of making the world more congruent with justice. The enormous array of cybernetic techniques being used by the environmentalists is an example of what I mean. In so doing such people are denying that these present difficulties constitute a real ambiguity in 'technology.' (Of course, all of us as practical people living in our civilization must inevitably be concerned in the name of justice with trying to do something about one or other of these problems.)

The ambiguity with which I am here concerned is not that which arises from difficulties such as these. Rather, it has to do with the fact that the realization of technology has meant for all of us a very dimming of our ability to think justice lucidly. The ambiguity is that technology, which came into the world carrying in its heart a hope about justice, has in its realization dimmed the ability of those who live in it to think justice. Something has been lost. It is for this reason that I started with statements by Socrates and Christ.

At a common sense level it is clear what I mean by that dimming or that loss. 'Happy are those who are hungry and thirsty for justice.' What can the identity of the just and the fortunate mean to people who take their representation of reality from the terms given in technology? At all times and places, the unity between happiness and justice seems particularly incredible. (It is necessary to say in parenthesis why I have cut out the completion of the statement. 'Happy are those who are hungry and thirsty for justice because they will be satisfied.' I have done so to leave out any discussion of what that satisfaction will be. I take for granted that Christ did not mean any satisfaction or reward external to or other than justice itself. One could translate 'they will be satisfied' by 'they will have their fill of it.' Often when I am feeling vengeful, as Canadian Scots often are, for instance against the American oil corporations and their greed, I might say, 'I hope they have their fill of it.' So one can say of the saints, 'Happy are those who are hungry and thirsty for justice for they will have their fill of it.' Indeed, what makes one tremble when one thinks about the saints is that one knows how painful is going to be their journey to that joy.)

Most of our influential contemporaries would deny that anything essential has been lost in our ability to think justice during the realization of technology. At the centre of this denial would lie the pungent assertion about justice which was in the heart of 'technology' from its origins. Progress in the control of nature is essential for the improvement of justice in the world. And what is justice apart from its existence in the world? Progress in the control of nature has freed human beings from such obvious injustices as labour and disease. It has not only freed us from the bonds of necessity which held us in unjust situations, but also in that liberation has given us time to care about the realization of justice in a way that was not possible when we were bound to immediate tasks. Those who justify the modern with explicit ethical doctrines would assert, beyond the practical claim, that justice can now appear to thought with greater clarity than ever before, because it can now be understood as utterly the work of human beings. This assertion would be common to English-speaking liberals, to marxists, to Nietzscheans, or to those who hold some combination of all three. By saying that justice depends on a contract maintained in a formal democracy, or on the proletariat when it has become conscious of the needs of all human beings everywhere, or on the great persons who want to use our conquest of nature beautifully and nobly, we have allowed justice to appear 'authentically' by taking away from under it those safety nets which guaranteed it as being in the nature of things. As for hungering and thirsting for justice, that is more widely present than ever before. Democrats hunger and thirst when they work to see that the contract will become complete; marxists hunger and thirst when they strive for a society in which justice is not only formal but substantial; the noble and the beautiful hunger and thirst when they think beyond being masters of the earth and impose beauty and nobility upon that mastery. Where is, then, the loss? We have been freed negatively from those 'otherworldly' interests which diverted us from and allowed us to put up with the injustices of this world. We have been freed positively to take our lives into our own hands and to know that it depends on us alone to give them a just and noble content. What is, then, this talk of a loss concerning justice which has occurred with the coming to be of modernity?

I long to be able to express it with superb clarity, but am quite unable. The following, though inadequate, is as near as I can get: in affirming that justice is what we are fitted for, one is asserting that a knowledge of justice is intimated to us in the ordinary occurrences of space and time, and that through those occurrences one is reaching towards some knowledge of good which is not subject to change, and which rules us in a way more pressing than the rule of any particular goods. In the *Phaedrus* Plato writes of the beauty of the world, and Socrates states that that beauty is what leads to justice. Beauty is always seducing while justice often appears unattractive. If in this world we could see justice as it is in itself, it would engulf us in loveliness. But that is not our situation. Its demands make it often unattractive both to our conveniences and in our apprehension of the situations which call for our response. Because the harmony of beauty is in some sense immediately apprehended, it is the means whereby we are led to that more complete harmony which is justice itself. (The unseducing side of justice described by Plato always seems similar to Isaiah's statement that the redeemer will not be externally charming. This is well to remember in these days of charming political 'redeemers.') This affirmation about justice can be put negatively by saying that if we are realistic about our loves and realistic about any conceivable conditions of the world, and if we apprehend the unchangingness of justice, we must understand that justice is in some sense other to us, and has a cutting edge which often seems to be turned upon our very selves. I have tried to express elsewhere the unchangingness of justice as given us in the fact that we can know in advance actions which must never be done. What is meant by realistic about our loves is that justice is very often not what we want in any recognizable sense of 'want.' What is meant by realism about the conditions of the world is that I cannot imagine any conditions in which some lack of harmony in some human being would not be putting claims upon us – the meeting of which would often carry us whither we would not. But as soon as justice as otherness is expressed in that negation, we must hold with it the positive affirmation that we can know justice as our need in the sense that it is necessary to happiness, and we can have intimations of loving its harmony. The holding together in thought of our need and love of justice and its demanding otherness is expressed in ontological terms by Plato when he writes of justice as ιδεα.* To put the matter in a popular way: justice is an unchanging measure of all our times and places, and our love of it defines us. But our desiring need of an unchanging good which calls us to pay its price is theoretically incongruent with what is thought in 'technology.'

This has been stated unclearly not only for the reason that thinking about justice is not the same as loving it and therefore knowing it, but also because even within thought it is so difficult to balance carefully what is said positively with what is said negatively. It is inadequate either to affirm God in contrast to the world as a vale of tears, or to affirm God as subsidiary to process as in Whitehead. For example, one can easily

* A form (Greek).

describe realized human love these days as if it were the height for human beings; while some describe it as if it were not qualitatively different from our need for food. How difficult it is to see it neither as the height nor as simply an appetite, but as an intimation of that immediacy of justice which Plato has described as fire catching fire.

Let me say, in historical parenthesis, that this description tries to avoid both Aristotle's and Kant's accounts of the matter. This may seem like a remark of pride against such geniuses, and it would take too long here to express clearly why I want to reject Aristotle's criticism of Plato's account of *idea*, and Kant's assertion of the autonomy of the will. My failure of description is bound up with three difficulties concerning language. First, what is the point of speaking of this loss, in which we live minute by minute, with language which no longer has meaning for those minutes? When I said that Plato spoke ontologically about ιδεα, this used archaic language. Think what 'idea' means today. Any use of the word 'soul' falls into the same danger. Or again, the phrase 'oblivion of eternity' necessarily expresses the loss archaically. Secondly, one must, on the other hand, beware of using language about that loss which springs from the new forms of thought which have caused it. For example, the word 'transcendence' is now popular with many theologians. It seems to me a dangerous word because it generally comes forth from that account of freedom as autonomy, which is itself just part of the loss. 'Transcendence' has been so often used in an existentialist exaltation of human beings' inability ever to be at peace. Of course, there are more dangerous terms, used regularly by theologians, such as 'historical consciousness.' The modern world is full of language which arises inevitably and consistently from 'technology,' and which is better used by those who do not think the loss a loss. The main task of thought is the purging of such language. Rahner or Bultmann[*] would have been of more use if they had read and thought more, and written less.

Thirdly and more important, the question of language is difficult because it must never move away from what is pressed upon us concerning justice in our daily situations. This is the difficulty for all of us as thinkers. If we are to speak about the essence of justice we must always start from where it meets us in an immediate way every day. Put generally, this is to say that the language of ontology must proceed from the

[*]Rudolf Bultmann (1884–1976), controversial German theologian, author of *Jesus and Mythology* (1958).

nerve-racking situations of justice. It is often said these days that the task of thinkers is to reclaim the possibility of ontology, which has been lost in the realization of technology. This is why Heidegger is so popular with many continental theologians. But the difficulty of this position is that modern thought at its height does not deny ontology; rather it asserts an ontology which excludes what is essential about justice. It is not ontology per se which is the heart of our task as thinkers; rather, it is the search for an ontology which carries in itself the essence of justice. Even to begin this one must never turn away from the realities and immediacies of justice in the here and now. To take an absurd example of this from the English-speaking world, it has always seemed to me that Bertrand Russell, for all his crazy negations and confusions about ontology, is nearer to philosophy than his colleague Alfred N. Whitehead, despite the latter's appeals to ontology. Russell's thought is filled with the intensities of the modern world, however inadequate his response; Whitehead's writings taste of secularized Anglicanism seeking a Harvard substitute for prayer. To put this in all its terror: 'Human nature is so arranged that any desire of the soul which has not passed through the flesh by way of actions, movements and attitudes which correspond to it naturally, has no reality in the soul. It is only there as a phantom.'[1] Much modern theology seems to me such academic phantoms, because it gives the appearance of being abstracted from the immediacies of justice.

The failure to live in the world of 'technology' as it is can be found even in the writings of the best modern Anglican theologian, Austin Farrer. He wrote with beautiful accuracy about ontology as the foundation for any teaching of Christianity. Yet, in dispute with the analytical philosophers of his day in Oxford, he could write: 'The foundations of morality are platitudinous valuations; the subjects of moral discussion are contested priorities. People who discuss the platitudes are intolerable – why try, for example, to make an issue of the question, whether it is good that we should care for other men or for ourselves alone; or whether instinctive appetite should ever be controlled.'[2] I remember the shock of surprise in reading those words. Why, the man does not really know the world he inhabits! Here is an educated philosophic theologian deluding himself about what has come to be believed with 'technology.' If we attempt as thinkers (even in fear and trembling) the great task of ontology, the necessary cutting edge is only maintained by being in the world of 'technology' in as full a consciousness as we are able.

What has been lost is exposed even in the writings of Heidegger. This fact is itself a great ambiguity, because he is the writer who has expounded, as no other, what is given in the word 'technology.' This is not only done in the writing which has 'technique' in its title, but in all his later writings. I would single out *Der Satz vom Grund* (so inadequately translated as *The Principle of Reason*) as the writing where he most wonderfully brings it forth. His call to thought is to think beyond 'technology' in this night of the world. But – and what a 'but' it is – the ontology he is moving towards excludes the one thing needful – namely justice in its full and demanding purity. Let me refer quickly to two writings: (1) His discussion of *techne* and *dike* throughout his *Introduction to Metaphysics*, and much more important, (2) his 'Plato's Doctrine of Truth.' In the latter he is criticizing Plato's account of 'being' as 'idea,' because it is the foundation of the definition of truth as correctness and therefore is the foundation of the age of metaphysics. According to Heidegger, this is the originating affirmation from which Western technological rationalism comes forth. The work proceeds from a translation of 'the Cave' in the *Republic*, and a commentary on *aletheia* in that passage. It is a remarkable writing. However, what is so singularly absent is any discussion of the *politeia* or the virtues, in terms of which 'the Sun,' 'the Line,' and 'the Cave' were written. The extraordinarily powerful and painfilled language used by Plato concerning the breaking of the chains, the climb out of the cave into the light of the sun and the return to the cave, are all related to the virtue of justice and its dependence upon the sun. This is absent from Heidegger's commentary. From his translation and commentary one would not understand that in the Sun, the Line, and the Cave, the metaphor of sight is to be taken as love. That which we love and which is the source of our love is outside the cave, but it is the possibility of the fire in the cave and of the virtues which make possible the getting out of the cave. When Heidegger defines good as used by Plato simply formally, as what we are fitted for, he does not give content to that fitting as Socrates does when he says that it is better to suffer injustice than to inflict it. Heidegger describes Plato's doctrine of truth so that 'being' as 'idea' is abstracted from that love of justice in terms of which 'idea' can alone be understood as separate. Goodness itself is 'beyond being.' This is why I take even Heidegger's wonderful account of technology as having been written within that loss which has come with 'technology.' It is in this sense that Heidegger is an historicist, although the most consummate of the historicists.

Some theologians and scholars of the Bible take Heidegger's ontology as a means of bringing out of concealment the real truth of Christianity, because they think that his overcoming of metaphysics will allow Christianity to be expressed in a way that was not possible in the past. This is a worthy intention; but it is a practice of great peril if it can only be achieved by eliminating from Christianity that hunger and thirst for justice which is certainly absent from Heidegger's ontology. It is unwise of theologians to play around with ontologies without knowing their source. Many times Heidegger has quoted with approval Nietzsche's dictum 'Christianity is Platonism for the people.'[3] If the theologians who use Heidegger read his acceptance of that dictum, they may take it to be applied only to the Christianity which in the past clothed itself in Greek metaphysics. But in using the new ontology, will they be able to hold on to the happiness in hungering and thirsting for justice?

The trouble with talking about loss and perhaps even my constant references to Plato is that they may seem to imply a turning away from the present. In modern university circumstances such an implication can lead to the substitution of scholarship for thought, and it will be that historicist scholarship which has done so much to destroy for us the presence of the past. Certainly thought will not be achieved by turning away from 'technology.' Meeting 'technology' face to face means for the thinker neither acceptance nor rejection but trying to know it for what it is. (I must emphasize yet once again that justice may well require the rejection of particular techniques.)

The point of this writing has simply been to emphasize that knowing 'technology' for what it is requires the recognition of what has been lost politically and ethically. Equally important would be to understand what has been found in its coming to be. I must finally say that the thought which is the task of most of us, and is indeed important, always waits upon something of a different order – that thought which has been transfigured by hungering and thirsting for justice.

NOTES

1 Simone Weil, 'Théorie des sacraments,' in *Pensées sans ordre concernant l'amour de Dieu* (Paris: Gallimard 1962), 135. For the published English translation of this passage see Simone Weil, 'Theory of the Sacraments,' in *Gateway to God* (Glasgow: Williams Collins and Sons 1974), 65.

2 Austin Farrer, 'A Starting-Point for the Philosophical Examination of Theological Belief,' in Basil Mitchell, ed., *Faith and Logic: Oxford Essays in Philosophical Theology* (London: George Allen and Union 1958), 14.
3 See, e.g., *An Introduction to Metaphysics*, trans. Ralph Manheim (Garden City, N.Y.: Doubleday Anchor 1961), 90.

Part 6

The Beautiful and the Good

THE THEOLOGY OF THE CROSS

Grant was deeply moved by poetry and himself wrote poems from time to time. The following is the only one he published. It is significant that the topic is Good Friday, since Grant believed that Christ's sacrifice on the cross was the centre of the Christian faith. He rejected the idea that the resurrection was somehow a triumphant reversal of the defeat of the crucifixion.

Good Friday (1952)[*]

Oh dearest word, the very Word indeed,
Breathes on our striving, for the cross is done;
All fate forgotten, and from judgement freed,
Call Him then less – Who shows us this – Your Son?
Look it is here at death, not three days later,
The love that binds the granite into being,
Here the sea's blueness finds its true creator,
His glance on Golgotha our sun for seeing.
Nor say the choice is ours, what choice is left?
Forgiveness shows God's Will most fully done,
There on the cross the myth of hell is cleft
And the black garden blazes with the sun.
Hold close the crown of thorns, the scourge, the rod,
For in his sweat, full front, the face of God.

INTIMATIONS OF DEPRIVAL

This is one of Grant's most beautiful and profound essays. Written as a concluding piece for Technology and Empire, *it addresses what Grant calls 'intima-*

---

[*]George Grant, 'Good Friday,' *United Church Observer,* vol. 14, no. 3 (1 April 1952), 3.

tions of deprival,' the paradox that we are often most aware of justice and the good when they are absent from a thing or a person where we would expect them to be. The injustice of the death of a child, for example, often makes us aware of the existence of justice and its claims. If there were no justice, how could we feel that a child's death was unjust?

A Platitude (1969)[*]

We can hold in our minds the enormous benefits of technological society, but we cannot so easily hold the ways it may have deprived us, because technique is ourselves. All description or definitions of technique which place it outside ourselves hide from us what it is. This applies to the simplest accounts which describe technological advance as new machines and inventions as well as to the more sophisticated which include within their understanding the whole hierarchy of interdependent organizations and their methods. Technique comes forth from and is sustained in our vision of ourselves as creative freedom, making ourselves, and conquering the chances of an indifferent world.

It is difficult to think whether we are deprived of anything essential to our happiness, just because the coming to be of the technological society has stripped us above all of the very systems of meaning which disclosed the highest purposes of man, in terms of which, therefore, we could judge whether an absence of something was in fact a deprival. Our vision of ourselves as freedom in an indifferent world could only have arisen insofar as we had analysed to disintegration those systems of meaning, given in myth, philosophy, and revelation, which had held sway over our progenitors. For those systems of meaning all mitigated both our freedom and the indifference of the world, and in so doing put limits of one kind or another on our interference with chance and the possibilities of its conquest.

It may be said that to use the language of deprival is to prejudice the issue, because what has gone can more properly be described as illusions, horizons, superstitions, taboos which bound men from taking

---

[*] George Grant, 'A Platitude,' in *Technology and Empire* (Toronto: Anansi 1969), 137–43. Used with permission.

their fate into their own hands. This may be the case. What we lost may have been bad for men. But this does not change the fact that something has been lost. Call them what you will – superstitions or systems of meaning, taboos or sacred restraints – it is true that most Western men have been deprived of them.

It might also be said that the older systems of meanings have simply been replaced by a new one. The enchantment of our souls by myth, philosophy, or revelation has been replaced by a more immediate meaning – the building of the society of free and equal men by the overcoming of chance. For it is clear that the systematic interference with chance was not simply undertaken for its own sake but for the realization of freedom. Indeed, it was undertaken partly in the name of that charity which was held as the height in one of those ancient systems of meaning. The fulfilment that many find in the exploration of space is some evidence that the spirit of conquest may now be liberated from any purpose beyond itself, since such exploration bears no relation to the building of freedom and equality here on earth. What we are can be seen in the degree to which the celebration of the accomplishments in space is not so much directed to the value of what has actually been done, but rather to the way this serves as verification of the continuing meaning in the modern drive to the future, and the possibility of noble deeds within that drive. Be that as it may, the building of the universal and homogeneous state is not in itself a system of meaning in the sense that the older ones were. Even in its realization, people would still be left with a question, unanswerable in its own terms: how do we know what is worth doing with our freedom? In myth, philosophy, and revelation, orders were proclaimed in terms of which freedom was measured and defined. As freedom is the highest term in the modern language, it can no longer be so enfolded. There is therefore no possibility of answering the question: freedom for what purposes? Such may indeed be the true account of the human situation: an unlimited freedom to make the world as we want in a universe indifferent to what purposes we choose. But if our situation is such, then we do not have a system of meaning.

All coherent languages beyond these which serve the drive to unlimited freedom through technique have been broken up in the coming to be of what we are. Therefore, it is impossible to articulate publicly any suggestion of loss, and perhaps even more frightening, almost impossible to articulate it to ourselves. We have been left with no words which cleave together and summon out of uncertainty the good of which we may sense the dispossession. The drive to the planetary technical future is in any case inevitable; but those who would try to divert, to limit, or even simply to stand in fear before some of its applications find themselves defenceless, because of the disappearance of any speech by which the continual changes involved in that drive could ever be thought as deprivals. Every development of technique is an exercise of freedom by those who develop it, and as the exercise of freedom is the only meaning, the changes can only be publicly known as the unfolding of meaning.

I am not speaking of those temporary deficiencies which we could overcome by better calculations – e.g. cleverer urbanologists – failures of the system which may be corrected in its own terms. Nor do I mean those recognitions of deprivation from the dispossessed – either amongst us or in the southern hemisphere – who are conscious of what they have not got and believe their lack can be overcome by the humane extension of the modern system.

Also, in listening for the intimations of deprival either in ourselves or others we must strain to distinguish between differing notes: those accidental deprivals which tell us only of the distortions of our own psychic and social histories, and those which suggest the loss of some good which is necessary to man as man. As I have said elsewhere, thought is not the servant of psycho-analysis or sociology; but a straining for purification has the authority of the Delphic 'know thyself,' and of the fact that for Socrates the opposite of knowledge was madness. The darkness of the rational animal requires therapy, and now that 'philosophy' sees itself as analysis, men who desire to think must include in their thinking those modern therapies which arose outside any connection with what was once called philosophy. This inclusion of what may be health-giving in psychoanalysis and sociology will be necessary, even within the knowledge that these therapies are going to be used unbridledly as servants of the modern belief that socially useful patterns of behaviour should be inculcated by force. Anything concerning sexuality will serve as an example of the distortions I am trying to describe, because such matters touch every element of fantasy and the unconscious in ourselves, so that judgments about good are there most clouded by idiosyncracy. For example, if a man were to say that the present technical advances were so detaching sexuality from procreation as to deprive women of a maternity necessary to their fullest being, his statement might be suspect as coming from a hatred of women which could not bear to see them free. To take an example from myself, a sophisticated and lucid sociologist[*] has asserted that I was saddened at the disappearance of the Canadian nation into the American empire, not because of my written reasons from political philosophy but because of my biographically determined situation. I belonged to a class which had its place in the old Canada and could find no place for itself in the new imperial structure. Or again, I know that my thinking about modern liberalism is touched by a certain animus arising from tortured instincts, because of the gynarchy in which I came to know that liberalism. Thought may first arise from the ambiguities of personal history but if it is to stand fairly before the enormous ambiguities of the dynamo, it must attempt to transcend the recurring distortions of personal history. To listen for the intimations of deprival requires attempting a distinction between our individual history and any account which might be possible of what belongs to man as man.

Yet even as one says this, the words fade. The language of what belongs to man as man has long since been disintegrated. Have we not been told that to speak of what belongs to man as man is to forget that man creates himself in history? How can we speak of excellences which define the height for man, because what one epoch calls an excellence another does not, and we can transcend such historical perspectives only in the quantifiable? Aren't such excellences just a crude way of talking about values, pretending that they have some status in the nature of things beyond our choosing? We are back where we began: all languages of good except the language of the drive to freedom have disintegrated, so it is just to pass some antique wind to speak of goods that belong to man as man. Yet the answer is also the same: if we cannot so speak, then we can either only celebrate or stand in silence before that drive. Only in listening for the intimations of deprival can we live critically in the dynamo.

Whether there are intimations of essential deprivals which are beyond elimination by the calculations of the present spirit is just what must remain ambiguous for us, because the whole of our dominating system of thought denies that there could be such. When we sense their arising, at the same time we doubt that which we sense. But even among some of those who use the language of sheer freedom as protest, there

---

[*] Rod Crook, 'Loyalism, Technology and Canada's Fate,' *Journal of Canadian Studies*, vol. 5 (1970) 50–60.

seems to be heard something different than the words allow. Because they have been taught no language but the modern, they use it not only to insist that the promises of the modern be fulfilled, but also to express their anguish at its denials.

Any intimations of authentic deprival are precious, because they are the ways through which intimations of good, unthinkable in the public terms, may yet appear to us. The affirmation stands: How can we think deprivation unless the good which we lack is somehow remembered? To reverse the platitude, we are never more sure that air is good for animals than when we are gasping for breath. Some men who have thought deeply seem to deny this affirmation: but I have never found any who, in my understanding of them, have been able, through the length and breadth of their thought, to make the language of good secondary to freedom. It is for this reason that men find it difficult to take despair as the final stance in most circumstances. Deprivation can indeed become absolute for any of us under torture or pain or in certain madnesses. We can be so immersed in the deprival that we are nothing but deprivation. Be that as it may, if we make the affirmation that the language of good is inescapable under most circumstances, do we not have to think its content? The language of good is not then a dead language, but one that must, even in its present disintegration, be re-collected, even as we publicly let our freedom become ever more increasingly the pure will to will.

We know that this re-collection will take place in a world where only catastrophe can slow the unfolding of the potentialities of technique. We cannot know what those potentialities will be. I do not simply mean specific possibilities – for example, whether housework will be done by robots, how far we can get in space, how long we can extend the life span, how much we can eliminate socially undesirable passions, in what ways we can control the procreation of the race, etc., etc. Some of these possibilities we can predict quite clearly, others we cannot, or not yet. But what is more important, we cannot know what these particular possibilities tell us about the potential in the human and the non-human. We do not know how unlimited are the potentialities of our drive to create ourselves and the world as we want it. For example, how far will the race be able to carry the divided state which characterizes individuals in modernity: the plush patina of hectic subjectivity lived out in the iron maiden of an objectified world inhabited by increasingly objectifiable beings? When we are uncertain whether anything can mediate that division, how can we predict what men will do when the majority lives more fully in that division? Is there some force in man which will rage against such division: rage not only against a subjectivity which creates itself, but also against our own lives being so much at the disposal of the powerful objectifications of other freedoms? Neither can we know what this unfolding potentiality tells us of the non-human. As we cannot now know to what extent the non-human can in practice be made malleable to our will, therefore we also do not know what this undetermined degree of malleability will tell us of what the non-human is. Is the non-human simply stuff at our disposal, or will it begin to make its appearance to us as an order the purposes of which somehow resist our malleablizings? Are there already signs of revolts in nature?

Despite the noblest modern thought, which teaches always the exaltation of potentiality above all that is, has anyone been able to show us conclusively throughout a comprehensive account of both the human and non-human things, that we must discard the idea of a presence above which potentiality cannot be exalted? In such a situation of uncertainty, it would be lacking in courage to turn one's face to the wall, even if one can find no fulfilment in working for or celebrating the dynamo. Equally it would be immoderate and uncourageous and perhaps unwise to live in the midst of our present drive, merely working in it and celebrating it and not also listening or watching or simply waiting for intimations of deprival which might lead us to see the beautiful as the image, in the world, of the good.

DEATH AS ABSENCE

Jelte Kuipers was a graduate student who showed promise. The Grants attended in short succession his wedding and his funeral. This appreciation, written for the McMaster student newspaper, shows one of the reasons why Grant was respected as a great teacher: his profound respect for and understanding of his students.

Jelte Kuipers – An Appreciation (1970)[*]

Individual life is always the loser in nature. Because human beings are

[*]George Grant, 'Jelte Kuipers – An Appreciation,' *Silhouette*, 2 October 1970, 6.

self-conscious, the apprehension of this is a startling presence, even when the death concerned has been long expected and comes at the end of a natural span. But when death comes for the young – a child before his parents, a young man who has only begun the course – death appears unnatural and therefore more terrible. When the young death is that of a noble person (in origin the words noble and beautiful mean the same) then there is a deep revolt against the fact of death – against its waste and seeming uselessness.

Jelte Kuipers, who was a graduate student at McMaster, was killed this August in a motor accident at the age of twenty-five. Love is the way we glimpse the actual and potential beauty in other people. It is therefore good at the time of revolt against the waste of his death, to remember what it was about him that made those who knew him apprehend him as beautiful.

At an early age Kuipers had come into a manhood which knew there were good and evil purposes in human life, and knew also that our present society (Canada in particular and the Western world in general) has for a long time been promoting amongst us those destructive purposes which frustrate the fullness of humanity. In the last decade it has not been difficult for young North Americans to face the negations of our society, in the war we have been waging, in the banality of the society we are building from the fruits of imperialism, and now also in the destruction of the very nature of which we are a part. But many cannot pass to any vision of good underlying the destructive present. At a very early age Kuipers passed beyond this negative bind, so that he saw that any vision of the barrenness is only valuable when it is the occasion for searching through to the noble roots of human existing. Because he saw the emptiness of resting in negation even in a time of negation, one can say that he had come upon his manhood.

Yet he had looked at the negation unflinchingly so that the positive he asserted was not simply a set of banal platitudes. He had watched his North American society as it pressed its patterns on the individuals and institutions of which he was part. Knowing those patterns for what they were, he could resist their shaping of his own life and the lives of those who depended upon him. He had come to see the universities (including his own) as places where vast numbers of the young were kept off the labour market in kindergartens, and filled with trivia. Yet that vision did not turn him from hoping that the university might be the place where human beings would have time to think about the most important matters. In the last years he had turned from the immediate negations of our institutions to see the central issue of our society in the deep questioning of ecology. The greatest negation for him was the dynamism of our conquest of the planet – a conquest which has become so total that it threatens the very possibility of life for man in that environment of which he is a part. The recognition of this negation above all brought him from youth to an early maturity.

He was brought to maturity in the face of that terrible vision because he was able not to be swallowed up in that world of shifting personal relations and of drugs (that is, the world of 'democratic' existentialism) which has become the private retreat for so many of his generation. Nor on the other side was he content with the reaction of marxism because he saw clearly that much of the protest advocated was just part of the system, and that the call to revolution in marxism had at its heart a further extension of the modernity which has brought us where we are. Because he had watched carefully, he had seen early that the crisis of Western society was too total to be met by any 'ad hoc' solutions. It needed a repossession of the roots of heaven through a deep understanding of nature and what is beyond nature. It was because of this that he turned to the understanding and production of Greek drama, and to the study of what was great in the ancient near east. It was because of this that he could at the end of a short life become part of the Roman Catholic Church. *Qui verbum Dei contempserunt, etiam eis auferetur verbum hominis.*[*]

The desire to partake through thought in the roots of wisdom did not, however, turn him away from the practical world to a life of easy solitude. In his impatience with injustice and his involvement in the practical there could be seen his debt to the long line of Calvinist forbears in Holland. He knew clearly that the thought of those who have not the courage to deal with the world is bound to become sterile and even vacuous. He had learnt the lesson of the founder of philosophy (repeated by its practitioners from Socrates to Wittgenstein) that philosophy is not a value-free, analytical game, but a study which can only be grasped as its truths are lived out in the world. Just before his death, Kuipers had decided to put aside his studies in religion and to devote himself to working full-time with those groups of people in Canada who are determined to try to stop the pollution of nature. He would have brought to that activity all the sharp determined will which was part of

---

[*]They that have despised the Word of God, from them shall the word of man also be taken away (as translated by C.S. Lewis in *That Hideous Strength*, 224).

his manhood. He had made that decision because he believed that he had no right to proceed with his own studies at a time when the very possibility of natural life was so obviously threatened. In the year before that decision, he had spent most of his time at the McMaster Board of Publications, drawing and writing and editing a series of papers to arouse people against pollution. His death came just as he was to embark (with all the assistance his wife would have given him) into the public world to help in the mobilization of this country against the enormous continental forces dedicated to the destruction of nature. He was not leaving the studies which fascinated him because of any optimism that he was taking on a winning cause. He was not touched by the modern blasphemy about being on the side of history (that is, the side of worldly success). But he knew that for many men at many times, it is necessary to keep certain flags flying even when it is likely that that flag will finally go down before the superior public forces of unreason.

As those who knew him think now of his sudden accidental death, and contemplate what he might have done and been, a sense of unexplainable waste must be present. Why in the midst of so much folly and vacuity should a beautiful young man be taken away, as if it were by chance? Yet in that presence we must remember that we have also been told: 'The souls of the righteous are in the hands of God and no torment shall touch them.'

THE ABSENCE OF JUSTICE

Although it might seem strange to have an article on torture in a section entitled 'The Beautiful and the Good,' we include it here because it illustrates so clearly Grant's belief that it is sometimes much easier to feel the presence of the good as justice when it is absent, and there is no justice at all in torture, particularly in the torture of the innocent.

Torture (1977)[*]

Torture is obviously the central crime against justice. Justice is rendering others their due. The shattering of the moral will by the systematic

[*] George Grant, review of Amnesty International's *The First Torturer's Trial 1975*, *Globe and Mail*, 11 June 1977, 41.

infliction of pain is the most complete denial that anything is due to human beings. Indeed, justice is affirmed in the fact that all of us, when we suffer injustice, cry from the centre of our souls that this is not our due. And this cry must never ring more terribly than from those who endure sustained torture. When I have met people who have so endured there is always a grim distance in their eyes which is the recognition that they have suffered the inexcusable. Clearly torture is most unjust when it is employed by the state. Yet it is a useful means for any government. Therefore, as torture is at the same time both useful and a crime against justice, its control is a continuing problem. As its limitation must always be difficult of achievement, the proper means towards that limitation is one of the key questions of political philosophy.

The present volume is an account of the trial in 1975 of thirty-two Greek military police officers and soldiers on charges of acts of torture, carried out under the rule of Greece by the junta of colonels from 1967 to 1974. It is an appalling account. As torture is the temptation of all governments, it is well to read this record as to what takes place when a government overtly throws away limitations upon what it is permitted to do. The record of this trial is of particular significance, because it is rare in our era for regimes which have indulged in massive torture to have then been brought down, so that their record could be exposed to the light of day.

Most torture in the modern world takes place under regimes which are not likely to be brought down. In this case the regime fell because of its folly towards Archbishop Makarios,[*] and therefore its crimes have been exposed. Decent people owe Amnesty International a debt for presenting an English record of this trial about what happens when a regime finds it useful to put aside limitations upon torture. It is an exemplary document which should be read by students and teachers in our law faculties and police academies, as an example of what above all needs to be politically avoided, and as a preparation for thought as to how such avoidance is achieved.

Who were responsible? As torture should be forbidden against anybody, whether they be 'fascists' or 'communists' or whatever, this is a much more important question than who were the victims. At the top were the leaders of the junta who were faced by problems of the greatest political difficulty. They lived in a society on the edge of the East-West conflict; they were nationalists who envisaged their opponents as

---

[*]Makarios III (1913–77), archbishop of the Orthodox Church of Cyprus, elected president of Cyprus in 1959, 1968, and 1973.

betraying their country to a foreign empire. They believed that a high level of public order was necessary if they were to modernize their country quickly without it losing its national traditions. From this they were led into the belief, so prevalent in all the varying forms of modern thought, namely that if one's ends are good, one has the right to achieve them by any means.

Underneath the leaders were the officers who were actually responsible for these abominations. From this report one gets the sense that when 'political necessities' unleash torture, there is a natural tendency for those who get pleasure from the infliction of pain to gravitate to where these methods of investigation and prosecution are taking place. The attempt to limit this terrible tendency is therefore one of the key responsibilities of those who are the final guardians of law and order in any society.

At the lowest level were the soldiers who carried out orders from their officers; this was for me the greatest point of tragedy in the report. Young conscripts were trained to be torturers by having been themselves tortured, in their training. Always the plea in court was that those responsible were just carrying out orders, and indeed, blame is a quite inadequate response to such a report. Blame is generally the language of self-righteousness when it comes from people in our easier situation. The essential lesson of this report cannot be blame, but rather the necessity that those responsible for investigation and prosecution and punishment in any society should be educated as to what actions are impermissible, and why they are impermissible, and should be aware that they are open to prosecution when they pass beyond the limits of the permissible.

In Canada, which may be moving towards more stringent necessities, care about such education has become a priority. In highly advanced societies, public decency depends above all on the medical, legal, and police professions. Their religious education is the central core of the control of torture. One cannot be optimistic about that core, because of the weakness of such education in these professions. This education is the sustaining force behind formal constitutional guarantees.

In the twentieth century, discussion of torture has been too often carried on within the framework of ideology. People of the 'left' affirm that torture is a phenomenon of the 'right,' and will disappear as progressive regimes arise. People of the 'right' concentrate on the extremities of the communists, and gloss over their own extremities. In the 'democratic' world it is often implied that we have passed beyond torture, and that it is only a phenomenon of non-democratic regimes. Such ideological talk makes people forget that torture is a political problem at all times and places. In the modern era it is returning not only in its old form but in new forms. The quick changes and expansions consequent on technology make the maintenance of public order difficult, and torture is an invitingly useful instrument. At a subtler level, the central driving force of our society is the science which puts nature 'to the question,' and why should that 'putting to the question' stop with non-human nature, when it is useful or convenient to control human beings? Despite the advantages of our English-speaking constitutional systems, all kinds of new forms of social control are arising which verge on torture or are directly torture. The growth of deprogramming in North America is a simple example. Our torture of non-human species grows and is taken for granted.

Beyond the pressing needs of practice, thoughtful human beings are ceaselessly torn by the contradiction between the perfection of God and the misery of man. Torture is the height of that misery. The fact that the central symbol of Christianity is an instrument of torture has made that religion the supreme way of contemplating that contradiction. But one must think about it in the realities of injustice which are going on now. Amnesty International does a notable service in opposing torture in whatever regime it arises. One aspect of that opposition is bringing out books such as this which keep the reality before us.

BLISS

Of all his colleagues at McMaster, Grant felt closest to those who studied Hinduism. His understanding of the meaning of the Gospels was informed not just by Plato but also by what he had learned from Indian religion.

We can never touch in one's writings these moments of miraculous power and glory – reasonless and triumphant. They just come; it is as if one had seen a wonderful plumed bird. Katherine Mansfield[*] gets the idea best in that story 'Bliss,' but how could one ever describe the deep and real warmth of feeling

---

[*]Katherine Mansfield (1888–1923), New Zealand writer, author of *Bliss: And Other Stories* (1920).

one feels for Barc?[*] It is not just sentimental, but based on the thousand incidents of growing up. 'Oh love that interests itself in thoughtless heaven.'

– George Grant, Journal Entry, 1942

Foreword to *Neo-Vedanta and Modernity* (1983)[†]

To a Westerner such as myself, uneducated in the truth of the Vedanta but with knowledge of what has happened to Christianity in the face of the modern, Dr Mukerji's [book is] of the greatest interest. I am not qualified to speak with authority on Indian thought, but having read these chapters with close attention I can affirm that Dr Mukerji's argument is beautifully expounded. The thesis of that argument is that the impact of Westernization on Indian thought has resulted in obscuring what was meant by 'bliss' in the Vedanta, and therefore distorting that philosophy ...

Above all, what is particularly wonderful in Dr Mukerji's book is her enucleation of the ontology of *Ananda*. This is breathtaking for any Western listener. How right it is that the word *Ananda* be translated as bliss. The word 'joy' would be too subjective and miss the knowledge that what is spoken of here concerns Being. What has come to be in the dynamic civilization of North America – indeed, in all these societies which express in themselves the thoughts of Locke and Marx, Rousseau or Darwin or Hume – is the restless search for bliss, which escapes one because it cannot be known as being itself. Modern life has become the joyless pursuit of joy. One of the truly great stories of the English-speaking world is called *Bliss*. (It is also written by a woman, Katherine Mansfield.) The story recognizes beautifully the crying need that bliss be more than the subjectivity of feeling but rooted in the Being of beings. What is more pressing for us Westerners than the understanding that there is an ontology of bliss? That this should be unthinkable is perhaps the greatest price that we have paid for modernity. For those of us who are Christians, it is the elimination of the understanding of the Trinity as bliss, which leaves Christianity floundering in the midst of the modernity it so much made. What is sad in the Western world is the deep desire to participate in bliss, for instance through the detached pursuit of the orgasm, which because it is outside any ontological

---

[*] Sarah Barclay, the Grants' housekeeper.

[†] George Grant, 'Foreword,' in Bithika Mukerji, *Neo-Vedanta and Modernity* (Varanasi: Ashutosh Prakashan Sansthan 1983), iii–vi.

understanding of bliss results in the good of the pursuit often being blackly negated.

LOVE

Grant began work on this essay about 1977 and produced several versions of it before the final one appeared in Technology and Justice. *It is a difficult essay because it deals with the absence of love in modern technological society, a great subject in a small space.*

Faith and the Multiversity (1986)[*]

'Don't let me catch anyone talking about the Universe in my department!'
– Lord Rutherford

'Faith and the multiversity' is a subject which could be tackled from many angles, both practical and theoretical. The essence of the issues is, however, the relation between faith and modern science. It might be maintained that there has already been enough discussion of this over the last centuries. I do not agree. Thought has not yet reached the core of that relation. Many Christians turn away from the relation because they want there to be no conflict here. Nevertheless, it remains fate-filled with conflict.

It is important to be clear what is meant by the multiversity, particularly because it is an institution which has realized itself in Europe and North America only in the last half of this century – although its coming to be was a slow emergence over the last four centuries. I often meet people of my generation who went to university in the 1930s, and who speak as if the institutions their children or grandchildren are now attending are really the same as those they went to. But this is simply an illusion. The names are the same, but they are such different places that they should have different names. To say what they now are, it is necessary to describe the dominating paradigm of knowledge which rules them and determines what they are.

[*] George Grant, 'Faith and the Multiversity,' in *Technology and Justice* (Toronto: House of Anansi 1986), 35. Used with permission.

Different civilizations have different paradigms of knowledge, and such paradigms shape every part of the society. The principle of any paradigm in any civilization is always the relation between an aspiration of human thought and the effective conditions for its validation.

The question then becomes what is given in the modern use of the word 'science.' This is the paradigm which has slowly reached definition over the last centuries, and has since 1945 come to its apogee of determining power over our institutions. Of course, it would be folly to attempt to summarize in a paragraph the results of that brilliant progress of self-definition by philosophic scientists.

Suffice it simply to say that what is given in the modern paradigm is the project of reason to gain objective knowledge. What is meant by objective? Object means literally some thing that we have thrown over against ourselves. *Jacio* I throw, *ob* over against; therefore, 'the thrown against.' The German word for object is *Gegenstand* – that which stands against. Reason as project (that is, reason as thrown forth) is the summonsing of something before us and the putting of questions to it, so that it is forced to give its reasons for being the way it is as an object. Our paradigm is that we have knowledge when we represent anything to ourselves as object, and question it, so that it will give us its reasons. That summonsing and questioning requires well-defined procedures. These procedures are what we call in English 'experimental research,' although what is entailed in these is more clearly given in the German word *Forschung*. Often people in the university like to use about themselves the more traditional word 'scholar,' but that word means now those who carry on 'research.' Those procedures started with such experiments as balls running down an inclined plane, but now the project of reason applies them to everything: stones, plants, human and non-human animals. Thus in North America we have divided our institutions of higher learning into faculties of natural science, social science and humanities, depending on the object which is being researched. But the project of reason is largely the same, to summons different things to questioning.

In the case of the humanities the object is the past, and these procedures are applied to the relics of the past. For example, I have lived in a department of religion in which much work was done to summons the Bible before the researchers to give them its reasons. Each department of these institutions, indeed almost each individual researcher, carries on the project of reason by approaching different objects. The limitations of the human mind in synthesizing facts necessitates the growing division of research into differing departments and further subdivisions. This paradigm of knowledge makes it therefore appropriate to speak of the multiversity.

The achievements of the modern project are of course a source of wonder. The world as object has indeed given forth its reasons, as it has been summonsed to do over the last centuries. The necessities that we now can know about stones or societies surely produce in us astonishment. These achievements are not simply practical, but also have theoretical consequences. All of us in our everyday lives are so taken up with certain practical achievements, in medicine, in production, in the making of human beings and the making of war, that we are apt to forget the sheer theoretical interest of what has been revealed about necessity in modern physics or biology.

My purpose is to discuss the relation of this paradigm of knowledge to faith. 'Faith' is one of the central words of Western thought which has had many meanings. What I intend by it is Simone Weil's definition: 'Faith is the experience that the intelligence is enlightened by love.'[1] Such a sentence, of course, simply moves one from the uncertainty of 'faith' to the even greater complexity of the word 'love.' Obviously this word has been used to cover a multitude of disparate meanings. Heidegger has used the beautiful metaphor that language is the house of being. In our epigonal times that house has become a labyrinth. Nowhere are we more in that labyrinth than when we try to sort out the relation between such words as 'love,' 'desire,' 'appetite,' etc. I cannot attempt that sorting out here, but will simply express what I think is given in the word 'love' in the sentence about faith.

What is first intended is that love is consent to the fact that there is authentic otherness. We all start with needs, and with dependence on others to meet them. As we grow up, self-consciousness brings the tendency to make ourselves the centre, and with it the common sense understanding that the very needs of survival depend on our own efforts. These facts push us in the direction of egocentricity. When life becomes dominated by self-serving, the reality of otherness, in its own being, almost disappears for us. In sexual life, where most of us make some contact with otherness, there is yet a tendency to lose sight of it, so that we go on wanting things from others just as we fail to recognize their authentic otherness. In all the vast permutations and combinations of sexual desire the beauty of otherness is both present and absent. Indeed, the present tendency for sexual life and family to be held apart is frightening, because for most people children have been the means whereby they were presented with unequivocal otherness. In political terms, Plato places the tyrant as the worst human being because his self-serving has gone to the farthest point. He is saying that the tyrant is mad because otherness has ceased to exist for him. I can grasp with direct recognition the theological formulation of this: 'Hell is to be one's own.'[2]

The old teaching was that we love otherness, not because it is other, but because it is beautiful. The beauty of others was believed to be an experience open to everyone, though in extraordinarily different forms, and at differing steps towards perfection. It was obviously capable of being turned into strange channels because of the vicissitudes of our existence. The shoe fetishist, the farmer, and St John of the Cross were on the same journey, but at different stages. The beauty of otherness is the central assumption in the statement, 'Faith is the experience that the intelligence is enlightened by love.'

Nevertheless, any statement about the beauty of the world is so easily doubted in our era, because it appears meaningless within the dominant language of modern science. Our uses of 'beauty' have been radically subjectivist. 'Beauty is in the eye of the beholder.' (But what then is beholding?) At the simplest level it is said that the sentence, 'We love otherness because it is beautiful,' is tautologous, because beauty is already defined as what we love. Our loves are determined by the vast varieties of necessities and chances which have constituted our desire, and these could 'ideally' be explained by behaviourial psychotherapists and sociologists. The fact that I call 'beautiful' the curves and lights of rock and sea in a North Atlantic bay can be explained by my particular 'psyche,' with its particular ancestors. I remember taking the American explorer and scientist, Stefansson, to that bay and saying: 'A hard country, but beautiful.' His response was to say how misleading it was to use such subjective language about terrain, and he proceeded to give me a lecture on modern geology and the modern discovery of 'objectivity.' In all scientific explanations we are required to eliminate the assumption of the other as itself beautiful. The Platonic language which asserts that the world is beautiful and love is the appropriate response to it is believed to be based on a fundamental assumption of trust, because Plato was too early in the history of the race to have a proper scientific understanding of subjects and objects. That trust was shown to be a naive starting point by those who formulated doubt as the methodological prerequisite of an exact science.

Indeed, the language of 'subjects' and 'objects' is one of the ways through which the beauty of the world has been obscured for us. This language was of theoretical use in the coming to be of technological science; one of its prices, however, was to obscure beauty. To state the literal meaning of 'objects' yet once again: it speaks of anything which is held away from us for our questioning. Any beautiful thing can be made into an object by us and for us and we can analyze it so that it will give us its reasons as an object. But if we confine our attention to any thing as if it were simply an object, it cannot be loved as beautiful. This is well illustrated in the division between useful and non-useful criticism by professors of literature and music who explicate the texts of works of art. For example, many such explications of Shakespeare or Mozart add to our understanding of the works concerned. But one central way of dividing the useful from the non-useful among such criticisms is the recognition by the critic that his work is a means to an end, which is the further understanding of the beauty of what is being studied.

When such writing appears stultifying, it is that the critic has stood over the thing studied and therefore the thing has remained an object. Its objectivity has not been a passing means but an end. (It may be said in parenthesis that such failed works often seem to appear because the professors concerned want to share the prestige of objectivity with their colleagues from the mastering sciences.) Only as anything stands before us in some relation other than the objective can we learn of its beauty and from its beauty. To say this may seem no more than a linguistic trick upon the use of the word 'objective.' But this is not so. The language of 'subject' and 'object' can easily suffocate our recognition of the beauty of the world. In stating that the beauty of otherness is the central assumption in the aphorism 'Faith is the experience that the intelligence is enlightened by love,' it is necessary to bring into consciousness the sheer power of the contemporary language of 'subjects' and 'objects,' so that the statement is not killed by that language.

Indeed, the central difficulty of using the language of beauty and love, in the affirmation that one knows more about something in loving it, is that in that language beauty was known as an image of goodness itself. Yet through the modern paradigm of knowledge the conception of good has been emptied into uncertainty. The first stage of this emptying was when good came to be used simply in discourse about human ethical questions. In the last century the emptying has gone farther. 'Good' has largely been replaced in our ethical discourse by the word 'value.' The modern emptying of 'good' can indeed be seen in the emptiness of its replacement. Even its chief philosophic originator, Nietzsche, has not been able to tell us what a value is. This vagueness has resulted in the word generally being used now in the plural – our 'values.'

At a time when the word 'good' has been so emptied of content by the modern paradigm of knowledge, it is necessary to proceed hesitantly in trying to say what it meant in relation to our love of the beautiful. It must first be stated that what was given traditionally in the word 'good' was not confined to Christians. The majority in the classical Mediterranean tradition would have so used it – Epicureanism being then a minority. A similar conception is in the Vedanta. Christianity's particular call was not to this language, but to the fact that Christ declares the price of goodness in the face of evil.

In the old language 'good' means what any being is fitted for. It is a good of animals to breathe; we are not if we do not. The good of a being is what it is distinctively fitted for. Human beings are fitted to live well together in communities and to try to think openly about the nature of the whole. We are fitted for these activities because we are distinguished from the other animals in being capable of rational language. In living well together or being open to the whole in thought we are fulfilling the purpose which is given us in being human, not some other type of animal. Good is what is present in the fulfilment of our given purposes. To avoid the modern view of temporality as futurity I use a different example. A child is good, not only as a preparation, but insofar as it is at all. One loves children for what they are now. In this sense the Western word 'good' appears close to what the Vedanta means by the word 'ananda' (bliss) – not as a feeling, but as being itself.

At the heart of the Platonic language is the affirmation – so incredible to nearly everyone at one time or another – that the ultimate cause of being is beneficence. This affirmation was made by people who, as much as anybody, were aware of suffering, war, torture, disease, starvation, madness, and the cruel accidents of existing. But it was thought that these evils could only be recognized for what they were if they were seen as deprivations of good. (It must be remembered that in this account of good and evil the verb 'to be' is used differently from the way it is employed in most educated modern parlance.)

Clearly this language of the given goodness of what is must be a language founded upon trust. The archetypal expositor of this language, Socrates, knew that doubt was a necessary means to philosophy. But *The Republic* makes clear that such doubt is within the overreaching assumption of trust. We start with trust in our knowledge of those things we are presented with immediately, and doubt is the means of moving to an understanding of what makes possible that trust in an educated human being. The identity of doubt and systematic thought which lies in the origin of the modern experiment was not present in Socrates's enterprise. The modern assertion that what we are is best expressed as 'beings towards death' would certainly have been in Socrates's mind in what he said at the time of his execution. But it was not for him the final word about what we are. At the moment when his death was immediate he made clear that we are beings towards good. It was indeed for this reason that in the scene of his death, Socrates asserts that the absence of knowledge of good is not ignorance but madness.

The central cause of the modern emptying of the word 'good' is that the new technological scientist defined the scopes and method of their activity in terms of their criticism of the old Aristotelian science, which had described things through the conception of purpose. The modern understanding of things in terms of necessity and chance, through algebraic method, has led not only to our conquest of nature, but to an understanding of things outside the idea of purpose. The successes of this method are a source of wonder (use the synonym 'admiration' if you will) to any sane person.

The new science (however one may sometimes flinch at what it says) had some appeal to certain Christians, in the very fact that it had defined itself against the teleological science of medieval Aristotelianism. When this science was used unwisely by official Christianity, in the name of ecclesiastical power, to assert that purpose in nature pointed to an overriding purpose given for the universe as a whole, it is understandable why many turned away from a science so triumphally used. The more representable the purpose of the whole was said to be, the more this natural theology became a trivializing, a blasphemy against the cross. Some of the most depressing episodes in Christian history have been the spilling of much silly ink to show that the universe as a whole vouchsafed a representable purpose of design analogous to the way that the purpose of the automaker is given in the design of the automobile.

Nevertheless, it is obvious that faith cannot turn away from the idea of good. Faith affirms that all that is, proceeds from beneficence. If faith is said to be the experience that the intelligence is enlightened by love, and love is said to be the apprehension of otherness as beautiful, then the question must arise whether this definition is not the kind of blasphemy of which I have been writing. Is it not saying that the beauty of the world gives us a representable purpose for the whole? Is it not just the kind of distortion which turns us from the facts of the world so that we seem able to affirm what is contradicted by the evident experience of living? Through it are we not led to assert that evil is good and good is evil, and so lose what is essential to any love of truth – namely the continual recognition that the world is as it is?

In writing about love of beauty, it is therefore necessary to say something of how the language of good and purpose is used about the beauty of the world without trivializing suffering. It is best to start from works of art, for here there is obvious purposiveness in that they are made by human beings, in some sense comparable to the automobile, in some sense not. They are both purposive in that means are arranged in the light of a purposed end. We can speak both of a well-made car and a well-made concerto. But it is certainly harder to represent to ourselves the purpose of the work of art. Certain works of art can be partially understood in terms of their well-defined external purposes. Bach's Passions were written to help believers focus their attention and their prayers around the originating events of Christianity. But when we turn to Bach's concerto for two violins it is less clear that we can represent its purpose.

Nowadays much of our time is filled by works of art. Their purpose is to entertain. Entertainment is the agreeable occupation of our attention – in the sense of what we happen to like. What was spoken in the Greek *techne* became the Latin *ars*. Plows and plays were both made by human beings and the making was named by the same word. In our world the activities called technical and artistic have separated between the practically useful and the entertaining. In both cases means are carefully adjusted to ends to produce a good car or computer, play, or concerto. The skillful gathering together of means for the car is for the purpose for getting us around; in the play for the agreeable occupation of our attention. This account is everywhere in democratic capitalistic societies.

It is against this account of art that it is necessary to write. It stands between us and any proper apprehension of works of art and ruins our partaking in their beauty. The purpose of a car can be represented rightly as a means of getting us around; the purpose of a work of art is not properly represented as merely entertainment. Indeed, the greater the work of art the less can its purpose be represented at all. The staggered silence with which we can watch *King Lear* is evidence that something of great import is before us. Afterwards we can study it so that we can better understand the parts in relation to the whole. Whether watched or read, it clearly has a purpose. When we are enraptured we can say that it seems purposiveness itself. But can we ever represent that purpose to ourselves? Who has been able to tell us what is the purpose of *King Lear*? In a certain sense the purposiveness is nothing but the gathering together of the means employed by its author; in another sense its purpose is present but we cannot represent it. The beautiful at its heights gives us purposiveness but its good transcends us (oh dangerous word). It is not chiefly entertainment that we have consumed when we are consumed by great beauty.

This is well illustrated in the non-verbal and non-representational language of music – for example, in the last piano concertos of Mozart (let us say numbers 14 to 27.) It is clear that these are purposive in the sense that the techniques of Italian and German music are here supremely used. It is also clear that we partake in their purpose the more we are able to follow the intricacies of modulation and counterpoint, and understand the unity between the three movements of each work. We can be aware of the moods of majesty and gaiety and desolation which are expressed in the music. We can also know that Mozart needed to entertain the Austrian upper classes to make money. Entertainment is occupying our attention agreeably. But with what? To some cultures and to some people their attention is more agreeably occupied by *Rhapsody in Blue*[*] than by K.482.[†] This fact raises inevitably the question : are there some works that are more worth paying attention to than others? What is given in those that are most worthy of attention? What is it that enraptures us about them, so that even in the desolation of *King Lear* or K.491[‡] we are enraptured? Can we describe that enrapturing as the immediate engrossment in the beauty of the work, which points to good which is quite unrepresentable?

Here indeed one must pay attention not only to looking or reading or listening, but to the very making of such works. To do so would be a staggering impudence, had not the activity been described by Mozart himself.

The question is how my art proceeds in writing and working out great and important matters. I can say no more than this, for I know no more

[*] George Gershwin (1898–1937), piano concerto in F major, opus 2 (1924).
[†] Mozart's piano concerto in E flat.
[‡] Mozart's piano concerto in C minor.

and can come upon nothing further. When I am well and have good surroundings, travelling in a carriage, or after a good meal or a walk or at
night when I cannot sleep, then ideas come to me best and in torrents.
Where they come from and how they come I just do not know. I keep in
my head those that please me and hum them aloud as others have told
me. When I have that all carefully in my head, the rest comes quickly, one
thing after another; I see where such fragments could be used to make a
composition of them all, by employing the rules of counterpoint and the
sound of different instruments etc. My soul is then on fire as long as I am
not disturbed; the idea expands, I develop it, all becoming clearer and
clearer. The piece becomes almost complete in my head, even if it is a
long one, so that afterwards I see it in my spirit all in one look, as one sees
a beautiful picture or beautiful human being. I am saying that in imagination I do not understand the parts one after another, in the order that
they ought to follow in the music; I understand them altogether at one
moment. Delicious moments. When the ideas are discovered and put into
a work, all occurs in me as in a beautiful dream which is quite lucid. But
the most beautiful is to understand it all at one moment. What has happened I do not easily forget and this is the best gift which our God has
given me. When it afterwards comes to writing, I take out of the bag of my
mind what had previously gathered into it. Then it gets pretty quickly put
down on paper, being strictly, as was said, already perfect, and generally
in much the same way as it was in my head before.[3]

The combination expressed in these words between the free work of
the artist and his receptivity allows us dimly to perceive what that wonderful making must have been. Obviously his mastery of technique has
come from long training and attention. We know that the last piano
concertos were written after he had studied Bach, late in his short life.
His own hard work is united with his receiving of melodies and his hearing of the whole piece all at one moment. Fire has always been the word
to describe love, and it has been written that flame touches flame. The
making of a beautiful piece is an act of love, a love which illuminates
the lucidity in his making of it.

Two points may be made, not to add anything to these words, but
because the dominant language in modern education may cut us off
from listening to the words. First, it has been a central theme in modern philosophy that there is no such thing as 'intellectual intuition.'
This has gone with the teaching that the great mistake of the Platonic
tradition has been the affirmation of such. 'Intuition' comes from the

Latin *tueor,* to look. When Mozart says that after composing a piece of music he sees it 'all in one look' and when he says he understands it all at one moment, he is surely describing an act which can properly be named 'intellectual intuition.' Secondly, it is worth remembering when Mozart speaks of understanding (in German the very similar word *verstehen*) he did so at a time when Kant was exalting reason above understanding, in the name of his account of human being as 'autonomous.' This was to place on its head the teaching of Plato in which understanding is the height for human beings. Indeed, the English 'to understand' and the German *verstehen* were in their origins filled with that very sense of receptivity which Kant lessens in the name of our freedom.

Critics who write within the historicist assumptions of our time might choose to deconstruct this letter in one way or another. They say that Mozart's music is a different matter from his justifying explanation of his understanding of it. At another level it might be said in languages of modern physiology and psychology that the language of gift and the fire of love can now be better understood for what they are than in Mozart's 'naive' words. Indeed, with our new knowledge it may be said that we will be able to add to the Mozartian corpus by means of the computer. Mozart's assertion that he understood the whole of a piece in one look and heard it all at one moment can only be wiped away if we speak entirely within the languages of the new sciences. What has been lost as against what has been found in the self-definition of the modern paradigm here appears to me evident.

What can be meant by the beauty of the world becomes more ambiguous when we pay attention to those things which have not been made by human beings. At a common sense level, Vico's insistence that we understand what we have made in a way we cannot understand what we have not made seems correct. More importantly, it is difficult to partake in the beauty of the world because of the misery, the hardness, the sadness of so much of our lives, which is caused not only by the ugliness in ourselves, but by the very conditions of the non-human world. As has often been said, the very drive to technological science arose with the desire to overcome these vicissitudes. The key difficulty in receiving the beauty of the world these days is that such teaching is rooted in the act of looking at the world as it is, while the dominant science is rooted in the desire to change it.

I am not saying that the beauty of the world is vouchsafed above all when untouched by human making. It would be senseless to think of cultivated land as unbeautiful. Race horses are beautiful. Nevertheless, it was possible for Canadians to admire the chthonically beautiful places, where nature existed untouched by human making, and moreover to see these places as beautiful even in the awareness of how rigorous pioneering society had been – my ancestors, for example, were forced to eat the flesh of their dead companions to survive. In the Western world today, fewer and fewer people can ever find nature untouched by technological science. On His return, it may not be understandable for Christ to repeat what He said about the lilies of the field, because if there are any lilies they will have been improved by human skill. For most people, animal existence appears as cats and dogs, meat to be eaten, or wild animals protected in zoos or wilderness areas. The heavens, the oceans, and the mountains are as yet only partially conquered and the heavens may be at points untouchable. Indeed, the beauty of the world in its primal sense is rarely present for us, and that assertion need not depend on the ambiguous doctrine of 'the Fall.' It is indeed necessary to call modern science 'technological' because in the modern paradigm nature is conceived at one and the same time as algebraically understood necessity and as resource. Anything apprehended as resource cannot be apprehended as beautiful. At some stages of our capitalist development, certain rhetoricians used to say: 'Canada's greatest resource is its people.' That well-meaning sentence expresses what has been lost as well as found in modernity.

Of course, the beauty of the world manifests itself most intensely for us in the beauty of other people. The manifold forms of love, for example sexual and parental, friendship and admiration, take in each case many forms themselves. Who could in a lifetime write down the ways in which sexual love penetrates every moment of our consciousness and is never absent in any loving of the beautiful – present even when that love is universal?

Indeed, the manifold ways in which sexual instinct and love are held together and detached from each other make up much of our existing. On the one hand, sexual desire can be the recognition of others as beautiful; on the other hand, it can be the occasion for such calculated self-engrossment that other people are made instruments for producing sensations. Sexual desire can be the occasion when we see the truth of what others are, in the flame of its attention; or it can lock us in the madness of ourselves so that nothing is real but our imaginings. So intense are the pleasures of sexuality, so pressing its needs, so detached can the bodies of ourselves and others be from any humanity, that sexual desire can drive love out from its presence. It can become the rock of 'reality' on which the search for the beauty of the world founders.

In an age in which the paradigm of knowledge has no place for our partaking in eternity, it is understandable that orgasmic fulfilment has been made out to be the height of our existing – indeed, that which gives our existing some kind of immanent justification. The materialists have taken it as their heaven. But this modern union of individuality and materialism has meant a transposition of older beliefs about the relation of sex and love. In the older beliefs sexual desire was one means through which love between human beings could abound; in our era love seems sometimes to be thought of as a means for the abounding of sexual enjoyment.

Because sexuality is such a great power and because it is a means to love, societies in the past hedged it around with diverse and often strange systems of restraint. Such restraints were considered sacred, because their final justification (whatever other justifications were present) was the love of the beautiful, and that was considered sacred. Modern social scientists have changed the original meaning of 'taboo' into the socially and psychologically 'forbidden,' in the attempt to teach us that restraints are not sacred. This is of course useful to a capitalist society because everything must be made instrumental to the forwarding of 'production,' and the sacred restraints cannot be made instrumental. Social scientists follow their creator, because social science was created by capitalist society.

It is the reversal in the hierarchy of love and sex which has led in the modern world to the attempt to remove the relation between sexuality and the birth of children. The love of the beauty of the world in sexual life was believed to have some relation to the love of the beauty of the world found in progeny. (In using the word 'some' before 'relation,' I imply that I am not speaking against contraception.) But if orgasmic fulfilment is the height of all existing, it has no need of such extension. Obviously, love has to be protected by societies, because the human condition is such that the tenderness of the flesh leaves everybody at the terrible mercy of others. Yet at this time in 'advanced' societies, justice has been massively withdrawn from unborn children.

In the pre-progressive societies, however differently (and often perversely) love was brought within different orders, those loves were not considered entirely blind, because they were the way that human beings were moved out of self-engrossment to find joy in the world. Indeed, the words 'to love' and 'to know' were joined. For example, because of the intensity and intimacy of orgasmic love, it was said when people freely participated in it, they 'knew' each other. Love was not considered in its essence blind. It was for this reason that the family – in such varied forms as polyandry, polygamy, monogamy, etc., – was given enormous power (sometimes indeed too much) because it was believed that in the main the family was a guardian of the interests of its members.

Indeed, one of the growing beliefs of our era is the idea that love in its essence is blind. For people of my generation the great teacher in matters sexual and familial was Freud. He seemed a writer who gave sexual life its central place after the repression of the early industrial era. But for all his concentration on love, he (like his master Nietzsche) gave love poison to drink, because he so placed ambiguity at the centre of love as to say that in its heart love was blind. His influence may not be intellectually lasting. But he has been influential, particularly in North America, in placing sexual and familial life under the hands of the objectifiers. The 'helping' professions – psychiatrists, social workers, etc., – are an important means of bringing people under that objective control. This is largely done by the claim that they understand families better than the families understand themselves.

Luckily many people are not much interested in such assumptions and just go on loving or being indifferent or hating. But deep changes in ways of looking at things slowly permeate, particularly in societies whose democratic origins were bound up with the idea that philosophy could be open to nearly everyone. Thus when a popularizer of philosophy such as Sartre writes that 'hell is other people,' he makes starkly open the modern division between love and intelligence.

The results of the division of love and intelligence are evident when one speaks of knowledge of justice. In the older tradition, justice was defined as rendering to anything what was its due. Political justice was the attempt to render what was due among human beings. For ourselves, justice was rendering what was due to every aspect of our own being, body and soul, as we were then considered to be. In the non-human world it was rendering the proper due to cattle and bears, wheat and stones, to God or the gods. Justice was then not only arrangements to be realized in any given society, but also a state of the individual which was called a virtue. Of course, the question arose to thought, why is anything due to anything? Once any due had been granted, the question came to be what was properly due to any being. Socrates shows in his debate with Callicles in *Gorgias* that life demands the idea of due.

He then proceeds in *The Republic* to show how we come to know what is due to anything.

What Christianity added to the classical account of justice was not any change in its definition but an extension of what was due to others and an account of how to fulfil that due. Christ added to the two great commandments the words that the second is 'like unto' the first. At the height of the Gospels we are shown the moment when a tortured being says of his torturers that their due is to be forgiven. Despite all the horrors perpetrated by Christians, both in the West and more particularly outside the West, despite all the failures of Christians to understand the consequences of justice for the law, nevertheless the rendering to each being its due, in the light of the perfection of that rendering, could not be publicly denied among Christians. Indeed, Christianity calls human beings not only to the reasonable decencies of the particular purposes and goods of this or that situation, but to be perfect as God in heaven is perfect. There is no short cut to this perfection by a mysticism without price. As Simone Weil says, 'Matter is our infallible judge.' Perfection is not isolated from the immediate requirements of the world. We can only fulfil those requirements here below insofar as we partake to some degree in that perfection. Goods in the here and now are only good in that they participate in goodness itself. Our freedom is just our potential indifference to such a high end.

Indeed, among all the Western criticisms of Christianity the most substantial was that Christianity led to overextension of soul. It was said that too much is demanded of human beings and this has made steady political orders impossible where the Gospel was influential. The call to perfection made difficult the handling of the necessities of the world, and laid too grave a burden upon individuals. This criticism and the replies to it were both made by people who accepted that justice was rendering each being its due.

The call to perfection caused the persecution of the saints, not only in communities alien to Christianity (e.g., in the early Roman Empire or in modern secular empires) but in the heart of what was known as Christendom. The call to perfected justice seemed to question the elementary justice possible in the world. The harsh imprisonment suffered by St John of the Cross was administered at the hands of churchmen because of his desire to fulfil the original Franciscan perfection. The intelligence's enlightenment by love is a terrible teaching (in the literal sense of the word). Contemplate what happens to those who have been deeply illuminated by love! After the resurrection

Christ told Peter that he must expect to be carried 'whither he wouldst not.' In the traditional teaching about justice it was recognized that human nature is so constituted that any desire which has not passed through the flesh by way of actions and settled dispositions appropriate to it is not finally real in the soul. The saints are those in whom the desire for justice has so passed through the flesh that it has become transparent to justice.

The very call to perfection in Christianity has been above all that which has made so difficult the establishment of proper systems of government. The compromises between the world and perfection were particularly necessary in this area. 'Render unto Caesar the things that are Caesar's; and unto God the things that are God's' is a brilliant epigram, but hard to particularize. In any given society where Christianity has been influential only few hear the call to perfection and who those few may be is not easy to specify. Most of us make something of trying in a half-hearted way to render others their due. Some lose all sense of others having any due. For most of us it is easier to envisage the unrepresentable end for those near and dear. It is harder to envisage it even among those in the same neighbourhood, let alone farther away. Love of the good due to others can easily become little more than love of our own. Saddest is when love of our own becomes no more important than love of our own bodies and our own immediate needs.

It was recognized that the wicked were not alone the individual criminals, but those who wished to rule for their own self-assertion. Such people were more destructive of justice even than those who ruled simply in terms of the property interests of one class. They were worse than those who climbed the slippery pole of politics to get some place of influence. Because such tyrants were the most dangerous for any society, the chief political purpose anywhere was to see that those who ruled had at least some sense of justice which mitigated self-assertion.

For these reasons there were in the pre-progressive societies those complicated systems of education wherein the truth of justice was made central to education. Indeed, the pressing reason for this is given with startling clarity by Socrates in *Phaedrus*. For most of us justice must initially appear as unattractive. Justice is not easy to be loved because it is not, at first sight, beautiful. Socrates also says that the more we come to love it the more we come to find it beautiful. Indeed, it has been recounted by those advanced in the journey that justice which once appeared ugly or tiresomely distracting comes to appear as overwhelmingly beautiful.

As traditional societies were economically limited and therefore the possibilities of education were directed to the few, it was to those most likely to rule that this education was given. Among the young, the cultivation of habit was considered central. Justice was, in its origins, good habit. The early practice of fulfilling some small segment of justice was necessary to the overcoming of self-assertion among the young. For those likely to rule this was not sufficient. It was necessary to understand justice within the whole scheme of the cosmos. When one compares the education of Queen Elizabeth the First, or of Gladstone, with that given to nearly all modern rulers, one may come to understand why they were such masters of what Plato called the highest art. Is there anything greater in modern politics than Gladstone's attempt in his last years to turn England back from the absurdities of expansionist imperialism, which were leading directly to the disaster of 1914?

In our history this education in justice depended greatly on the careful division of function between church and state. The state was concerned 'ideally' with the immediate instituting of justice in the world; the church was 'ideally' concerned with holding high perfection in its cosmic significance, and with the education which proceeded therefrom. Obviously at nearly every moment each of these institutions abused their proper functions and trespassed on each others prerogatives. Indeed, whatever the difficulties in understanding the origins of technological society in the Christian West, one of the moments where its origin is evident lies in the activity of the pope whose popular name was Hildebrand. In this controversy with the empire, Hildebrand not only insisted on the spiritual rights of the church, but also on the control of the world, by the papacy's power over the naming of the emperor. By this vast extension of the church's power over the world, he turned the church from its traditional role of holding forth the mystery of perfection, to the role of control in worldly affairs. The apparatus of education in the church was turned to the world, including the activity of thinkers. We should not be surprised that Swift's *Battle of the Books* places Thomas Aquinas among the moderns, not the ancients.

The accounts of justice which have become dominant during the age of progress have not been based on its definition as rendering each being its due. This has happened largely because it has not been widely thought in our age that we can have knowledge of what is due to each being. An analogy has often been used to describe the central difference between pre-progressive and progressive theories of justice. In all theories of political justice it must be assumed that some limitation is placed on individual liberty. In the traditional theories this limitation was vertical, received by human beings in what they knew about the whole, which quite transcended any individuality. What was given in our knowledge of the whole was a knowledge of good which we did not measure and define, but by which we were measured and defined. The modern theories depended on a horizontal limitation, which arose from the fact that one human being's right to do what he wanted had to come to terms with the right of others to do what they wanted. The basis of society was the calculation of the social contract wherein sensible human beings calculated that all had to surrender some part of their unlimited desire for freedom in order to enjoy the benefits of settled society. This contractarian view of the state was as much part of communism through the dependence of Marx upon Rousseau, as it was part of American democratic capitalism through the founders' dependence on Locke's rights to 'life, liberty, and property.' In *Perpetual Peace* Kant put the matter lucidly. He wrote that it would be possible to have a just society composed of a nation of clever devils. If they were smart enough to negotiate the social contract, they could have a just society.

As it is my intention to state that something has been lost for us with the waning of the old account of justice, it is well to think about what has been gained in and through the modern accounts. Some examples: whatever the differences in theory or application between democratic capitalism and communism, clear statements about equality were present in both theories. And before one ever speaks against equality, it is well to remember what it was like for those at the bottom of the ladder when the principle of equality was modified by the principle of hierarchy. It is bad enough for those at the bottom of the ladder under our systems, but at our best this cannot be justified by theory. Or again: Locke was the chief philosophical progenitor of the American pursuit of 'life, liberty, and property' and he said what he said about government because he thought the end of life was comfortable self-preservation. It is well to remember how much comfortable self-preservation is a key end in life. The modern union of contractarianism and technological science has, despite all the terrors of modernity, added to many people's 'comfortable self-preservation.' Or again: the question can be formulated by saying that the pre-progressive thinkers said virtue was the core of a just political order, while the moderns have given freedom that position. It is well to remember how much all of us want to do what we want to do, and do not want to be interfered with by others, particularly when that interference is in the name of some virtue which seems completely alien to us.

Nevertheless, it seems necessary to state what has been lost theoretically in the modern definitions of justice. What has been lost is the belief that justice is something in which we participate as we come to understand the nature of things through love and knowledge. Modern theories of justice present it as something human beings make and impose for human convenience. This is done in a physical environment which is understood in terms of necessity and chance. Obviously the traditional belief, as much as the modern, included cognizance that human beings were responsible for doing things about justice. Human beings built cities, empires, etc., and some regimes were better than others. To use the favorite expression of the Enlightenment, human beings have in modernity taken their fate into their own hands. Their theories of justice teach them that our institutions are what we make in terms of our own convenience.

The central cause of this great change has been modern natural science. Brilliant scientists have laid before us an account of how things are, and in that account nothing can be said about justice. It is indeed not surprising, therefore, that in the coming to be of technological science the dependence of our objective science upon calculus has been matched by the dependence for knowledge of justice upon calculation. When the world is understood as necessity and chance, then justice has to be made by the 'authentic' freedom of human beings, so that conflicts between our pleasure seekings can be worked out. It is not surprising that those studies in our multiversities which depended on our intelligence being enlightened by love, and which were publicly sustained because they taught people to participate in justice, should now have faded into antiquarian research. After all it is not very difficult to know these days what justice is, what beauty is. The first is the result of interested calculation; the second is the means of entertainment.

• • •

The woman who wrote the definition of faith from which I have proceeded once also wrote: 'One can never wrestle enough with God if one does so out of pure regard for the truth. Christ likes us to prefer truth to him because, before being Christ, he is truth. If one turns aside for him to go towards truth, one will not go far before falling into his arms.' That is a great hope given us by a woman who had pure regard and who had gone far. But did she, in the sheer force of her intellect, know how much the rest of us can be diverted by the modern paradigm from that fearful wrestling – and indeed from the pure regard? How is it possible to think that the modern paradigm is sufficient to the needs of human beings? And yet how is it possible, in the midst of that paradigm and its stranger and wilder consequences, to reach into the truth that the world proceeds from goodness itself?

. . .

Of course, for both Christianity and Platonism, goodness itself is an ambiguous mystery. In Christianity, God's essence is unknowable. In *The Republic* it is said that goodness itself is beyond being. Both Christianity and Platonism have therefore often been ridiculed as final irrationality. If the purpose of thought is to have knowledge of the whole, how can we end in an affirmation which is a negation of knowing? It is, above all, these agnostic affirmations which bring Platonism and Christianity so close together. Without this agnosticism humans tend to move to the great lie that evil is good and good evil. In Christian language this great lie is to say that providence is scrutable.

. . .

Why not turn to the language of modern philosophers to present Christ in relation to all that is? The chief argument for so doing would be that the great event between ancient and modern philosophy was Christianity, and therefore most modern philosophy is impregnated with Christian language (even if only in the form of secularized memory). Would it not therefore be wise to use such modern language to explicate the relation of Christ to all that is?

My answer to this argument would be in one word – Heidegger. His writings make up the profoundest and most complete modern philosophy – certainly the deepest criticism of ancient thought which has ever been made in the name of modernity. Yet it is a philosophy which excludes something essential to Christianity. Heidegger writes that Nietzsche's dictum 'God is dead' means that the God of morality is dead. Now indeed Christianity is not morality; nor is it 'morality tinged with emotion.' Nevertheless, we have been told, 'Blessed are those who hunger and thirst after righteousness.' 'Morality' is indeed a boring word; but finally it is the same as 'righteousness.' If God who calls for righteousness is dead, then Christianity's God is dead. Do we think that we know better than Heidegger what he means, and thus use him to write about Christianity? But if not Heidegger, who? He speaks more comprehensively and more deeply than any modern philosopher.

It is not wise to criticize Christianity in public these days when so many journalists and intellectuals prove their status by such criticism. Nevertheless, it seems true that Western Christianity simplified the divine love by identifying it too closely with immanent power in the world. Both Protestants and Catholics became triumphalist by failing to recognize the distance between the order of good and the order of necessity. So they became exclusivist and imperialist, arrogant and dynamic. They now face the results of that failure.

Modern scientists, by placing before us their seamless web of necessity and chance, which excludes the lovable, may help to re-teach us the truth about the distance which separates the orders of good and necessity. One of Nietzsche's superb accounts of modern history was that Christianity had produced its own gravediggers. Christianity had prepared the soil of rationalism from which modern science came, and its discoveries showed that the Christian God was dead. That formula gets close to the truth of Western history, but it is nevertheless not true. The web of necessity which the modern paradigm of knowledge lays before us does not tell us that God is dead, but reminds us of what Western Christianity seemed to forget in its moment of pride: how powerful is the necessity which love must cross. Christianity did not produce its own gravediggers, but the means to its own purification.

NOTES

1 S. Weil, *La Pesanteur et La Grace* (Paris: Plon 1948). My translation. The greater the writer the more hesitant is the translator.

2 The tendency of human beings to become self-engrossed has been encouraged in our era, because the distinctiveness of modern political thought has been the discovery of 'individuality.' It is not my purpose here to discuss the good or evil of that 'discovery' but simply to state that one of its consequences has been to legitimize concentration on the self.

3 *Mozarts Briefe*, ed. L. Nohl, 2nd edition, 443–4. It is significant that in quoting this passage Heidegger stops before Mozart's words about the best gift of God. (See *Der Satz vom Grund*, Pfullingen 1957, chapter 9). Indeed, in his comments on this quotation Heidegger writes of Mozart as 'the lute of

God' – a metaphor he takes from a poem of Angelus Silesius. But is Mozart's account of his activity properly grasped in calling him 'the lute of God?' To put the matter directly, was there not some moment when Mozart could have exercised the liberty of indifference to what had been given him? On the one hand Kant's insistence on our own autonomy kills a proper partaking in beauty and in its extremity leads to the modern doctrine of art as human creativity (whatever that may mean) and so art is understood quite apart from the divine gift. But on the other hand the metaphor of 'the lute of God' about Mozart sweeps away the liberty of indifference which is what we properly mean by freedom, in this case the freedom of the artist. At the height of sanctity Angelus Silesius's metaphor might be appropriate. But Heidegger uses it here about an artist, albeit a supreme one. There has been some questioning of the authenticity of this passage from Mozart's letters, but in 1957 Heidegger says it is authentic.

Index